Andrew Greet

beating
unusual
chess defences:
1 e4

dealing with the Scandinavian,
Pirc, Modern, Alekhine
and other tricky lines

EVERYMAN CHESS

Gloucester Publishers plc   www.everymanchess.com

First published in 2011 by Gloucester Publishers plc (formerly Everyman Publishers plc), Northburgh House, 10 Northburgh Street, London EC1V 0AT

British Library Cataloguing-in-Publication Data
A catalogue record for this book is available from the British Library.

ISBN: 978 1 85744 621 0

Distributed in North America by The Globe Pequot Press, P.O Box 480, 246 Goose Lane, Guilford, CT 06437-0480.

All other sales enquiries should be directed to Everyman Chess, Northburgh House, 10 Northburgh Street, London EC1V 0AT
tel: 020 7253 7887 fax: 020 7490 3708
email: info@everymanchess.com; website: www.everymanchess.com

To Tori

Everyman Chess Series
Chief advisor: Byron Jacobs
Commissioning editor: John Emms
Assistant editor: Richard Palliser

Typeset and edited by First Rank Publishing, Brighton.
Cover design by Horatio Monteverde.
Printed and bound in Great Britain by Clays, Bungay, Suffolk.

Contents

Bibliography

Books

Alekhine Alert!, Timothy Taylor (Everyman Chess 2010)

Opening for White according to Anand (Volume 4), Alexander Khalifman (Chess Stars 2005)

Opening for White according to Anand (Volume 5), Alexander Khalifman (Chess Stars 2005)

Play 1...b6, Christian Bauer (Everyman Chess 2005)

Play 1...♘c6!, Christoph Wisnewski (Everyman Chess 2007)

Play the Alekhine, Valentin Bogdanov (Gambit 2009)

Play the Scandinavian, Christian Bauer (Quality Chess 2010)

San Luis 2005, Alik Gershon & Igor Nor (Quality Chess 2007)

Starting Out: The Alekhine, John Cox (Everyman Chess 2003)

Starting Out: The Scandinavian, Jovanka Houska (Everyman Chess 2009)

The Modern Philidor Defence, Vladimir Barsky (Chess Stars 2010)

The Philidor Files, Christian Bauer (Everyman Chess 2006)

The Pirc in Black and White, James Vigus (Everyman Chess 2007)

The Sniper, Charles Storey (Everyman Chess 2011)

Tiger's Modern, Tiger Hillarp Persson (Quality Chess 2005)

Electronic Resources

ChessPublishing.com

MegaBase 2011 (ChessBase)

The Fighting Philidor, Viktor Bologan (ChessBase 2010)

Preface

Greetings, dear reader! In this short introduction I will tell you a bit about the content of this book, although I imagine you will already have a fair idea after reading the catchy title.

Why this subject?

I always thought there was a gaping hole in chess literature for a book of this type. If you play 1 e4, then you have to be ready for a wide array of defences. The Sicilian, Caro-Kann, French, and 1...e5 are all huge topics, and you can find entire books (or in some cases, multiple volumes) dedicated to fighting against each one of them. But the 'big four' are not the only riddles with which the 1 e4 player finds himself confronted; there are numerous other less common but still highly respectable defences for which one must be prepared. The Alekhine, Modern, Pirc, Scandinavian, and others all require serious attention, but where can you find the information needed to meet each one effectively? There are individual books offering a complete repertoire after 1 e4, and while such works may have a lot to offer some players, it is hardly possible for the author to go into much detail, especially against these minor openings.

Another approach would be to purchase specialist works on each defence. This enables you to obtain more detailed information, but buying separate books on each opening will hit your wallet where it hurts. Not to mention that a book about a particular defence is more likely to be written from Black's standpoint, which is hardly ideal for those looking for a path to an advantage for White.

This book is intended to solve the said problem. In these pages I have laid out a comprehensive repertoire for White against each of the aforementioned openings, plus all other irregular defences after 1 e4 which fall outside of the 'big four'.

Repertoire choices

My approach has been to meet each of these openings in a principled manner, choosing well-established main lines for White. Generally we will be looking to

5

seize space in the centre and pursue the initiative in whichever way best meets the demands of the position. Speaking from my own experience, there was a time when I used to feel apprehensive about meeting these unusual defences, but once I studied them properly and learnt how to confront them head-on, I began to relish facing them. I hope that after reaching the end of each chapter, the reader will feel the same way about the defence in question.

Unlike my previous repertoire books on the Ruy Lopez and Queen's Indian, I decided to cover the material using complete illustrative games rather than a tree of variations. I would love to tell you that this was due to some profound piece of creative insight, but the truth is I just thought it would be fun to do something different. At the start of each chapter you will find a plan describing which variations can be found within each game.

Open theory is ever-expanding, and even casting aside the 'big four' defences, there was a lot of ground to cover in a single volume. I have endeavoured to cover the material pragmatically: you don't need 20 moves of hard analysis telling you how to refute a useless move that shows up on the database having once been tried by a 1400-rated player on the internet; however, you do have every right to demand detailed coverage of the most theoretically critical lines. This kind of sensible balance is what I have endeavoured to provide. In each chapter I have started by analysing the most critical main lines, before gradually working backwards through the various secondary set-ups and sidelines.

I hope you will enjoy reading this book, and wish you every success in beating the unusual defences after 1 e4.

Andrew Greet,
Glasgow,
September 2011

Chapter One
Scandinavian Defence

1 e4 d5 2 exd5

From this, the basic starting position of the Scandinavian Defence (I am disregarding White's various second-rate options on move 2), Black has two options: 2...♛xd5, the subject of the first two sections of this chapter, and 2...♞f6, which will be seen in the third and final section.

2...♛xd5

3 ♞f3!?

I decided to advocate this move, instead of the more traditional 3 ♞c3, for a few reasons. Firstly, it has received comparatively little attention in other theoretical manuals, which made it a more interesting topic of study. Secondly, it is a genuinely good move which poses an interesting set of problems for the opponent. I am generally not in favour of 'dodgy sidelines', but this move seemed to strike a sensible balance of avoiding the most theoretically-intensive variations while also being objectively strong enough to stand up to scrutiny.

Black can choose to react either aggressively or solidly, and I have organized the material accordingly.

Part 1 – Set-ups with long castling after 2...♛xd5

The first part of the chapter will deal with the most theoretically challenging lines in which Black castles on the queenside.

3...♝g4

This is the soundest move order. Black can also play 3...♞c6, but Game 7 makes a strong case against this move.

4 ♝e2 ♞c6 5 d4 0-0-0 6 ♝e3

This is where the theory begins to branch off.

6...e5

This is Black's most popular and challenging approach.

The most-common alternative is 6...♘f6 7 0-0. From here 7...♕f5 is Game 4, while 7...e6 and other moves will form the subject of Game 5.

Game 6 deals with Black's remaining options on move 6, with particular focus on 6...♘h6!?.

Returning to 6...e5, the main line continues as follows:

7 c4 ♕a5+ 8 ♗d2 ♗b4 9 d5 ♗xf3 10 ♗xf3 ♘d4

Game 3 will address 10...♗xd2+ along with a number of deviations

available to Black from move 7 onwards.

11 ♘c3

From here Black normally chooses either 11...♕c5 (Game 1) or 11...♕a6 (Game 2).

Part 2 – Set-ups with short castling after 2...♕xd5

Things are a lot simpler here! Game 8 will deal with the respectable 3...♘f6 and Game 9 with the dubious 3...e5?!.

Part 3 – 2...♘f6

Black can also aim to recapture on d5 with the knight, leading to a different type of fight.

3 ♘f3 ♘xd5

The soundest move. 3...♗g4?! is mentioned in the notes to Game 12.

4 d4

From here Black has three main moves:

4...g6 is the main line and will be considered in Game 10.

The two bishop moves, 4...♗g4 and 4...♗f5, will be dealt with in Games 11 and 12 respectively.

Part 1 – Set-ups with long castling after 2...♕xd5

> ### Game 1
> ### S.Movsesian-J.Tomczak
> Warsaw (rapid) 2009

We will jump straight in at the deep end, with a game featuring one of the most critical lines of the 3 ♘f3 system. It is fitting that we begin with a game by Sergei Movsesian, as the Slovakian Grandmaster is one of the most ardent supporters of White's opening system.

1 e4 d5 2 exd5 ♕xd5 3 ♘f3 ♗g4 4 ♗e2 ♘c6

This is the most challenging response to White's opening system. Black develops quickly, intending to castle and strike in the centre with ...e5 at an appropriate moment. Black can of course opt for a more solid handling of the opening by arranging short castling, for which see Game 8.

5 d4 0-0-0

6 ♗e3

The main alternative is 6 c4, which more or less commits White to a pawn sacrifice. The critical continuation is 6...♕f5 7 ♗e3 ♗xf3 8 ♗xf3 ♘xd4! 9 ♗xd4 ♕e6+ 10 ♗e2 ♕e4 (10...c5!? is also interesting), when Black regains his piece while keeping a pawn in the bank. White has some compensation and the resulting positions may well appeal to some players, but overall it seems to me that Black is holding his own in this variation.

6...e5

The immediate central strike has been Black's most popular choice, but he can also defer it for one or more moves. 6...♘f6 is the subject of Game 5 and Black's other options will be examined in Game 6.

7 c4

7 ♘c3 is less ambitious and after 7...♕a5 (7...♗b4 is also playable) 8 ♘xe5 ♗xe2 9 ♕xe2 ♘xe5 10 dxe5 ♕xe5 White has a minute edge at best.

7...♕a5+

Alternatives are clearly weaker – see the notes to Game 3 for details.

8 ♗d2 ♗b4 9 d5

A good rule of thumb for these positions is that White should almost always strive to meet ...e5 with the space-gaining d5 where possible. It is worth mentioning briefly that 9 ♘xe5?? is a blunder due to 9...♗xe2 10 ♘xc6 ♖e8!! when White suffers a fatal loss of material.

9...♗xf3 10 ♗xf3 ♘d4

10...♗xd2+ will be considered in Game 3, along with Black's other deviations between moves 7-9.

11 ♘c3

I consider this to be White's most promising continuation. The first player now has quite a serious positional threat of a3 followed by easy play on the queenside. The immediate 11 a3 is possible, but after 11...♗xd2+ 12 ♘xd2 f5 Black has enough counterplay.

11...♕c5

Black intends to transfer his queen to a more purposeful position while gaining a tempo by attacking the c4-pawn.

The most popular move has been 11...♕a6. This will be considered in the next game, along with a few rare 11th-move alternatives.

12 ♗e2

12 b3?! is inaccurate, as the queen on c5 makes an inviting target for a quick a3 and b4.

12...♘f6 13 0-0

The immediate 13 a3 can be met by 13...♗xc3 14 ♗xc3 ♘e4, but after castling White will be ready to begin his queenside attack. At this point Black must make an important decision.

I cannot help but point out that at the time of writing White has made a frankly ridiculous score of 100% from the present position. While there is no doubt that this flatters his position somewhat, it also serves as a strong hint that it is the second player who faces the tougher practical problems.

13...♖he8

Once again some other moves have been tried:

a) The illogical 13...♗xc3?! was played in M.Sanchez-D.Bescos Cortes, Aragon 1998 and now after the simple 14 ♗xc3 White stands better and in some lines he will be virtually a tempo up due to the absence of a3.

b) 13...c6 is a principled reply; Black risks exposing his king in order to open the d-file for his rook. After 14 ♗g5 (this seems like the most natural move, although 14 ♗e3!? is also interesting; after 14...cxd5 15 ♘xd5 ♘xd5 16 cxd5 ♕xd5 17 ♗xd4 exd4 18 ♗f3 White had reasonable compensation and went on to win in F.Hedke-J.Rudolph, Kiel 2009) Black has a few possible replies:

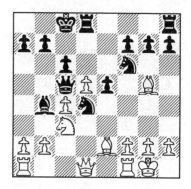

a) 14...♕a5 was Black's choice in S.Movsesian-I.Papaioannou, Bled Olympiad 2002, the only game to have reached this position thus far. In that encounter White chose to play 15 ♗g4+ and eventually won, but improvements have been suggested for Black and the overall evaluation is rather cloudy.

Instead it seems to me that the modest 15 ♖c1!? gives White the better prospects. Here is an illustrative line: 15...♔b8 16 ♗d3 ♗xc3 17 bxc3! (in some variations White may prefer to avoid compromising his pawn structure with ♖xc3, but in the present position White gains more by chasing the knight, especially as it can no longer exchange itself on e2) 17...♘e6 18 ♗xf6 gxf6 19 dxe6 e4 20 ♕g4 exd3 21 e7 ♖de8 22 ♖ce1 ♕xc3 23 ♕f4+ ♔a8 24 ♖e3 when Black's extra pawn is immaterial, but his problems are quite real due to the difference in quality between the respective passed pawns.

b) 14...♗xc3!? 15 bxc3 ♘e6 16 ♗e3 ♕a5 is a critical alternative. Now both 17 ♖b1 cxd5 18 ♕c2 ♖d7 19 ♖b5 ♕a3 20 ♖b3 ♕a5 21 c5 and 17 ♕b3 cxd5 18 cxd5 ♖xd5 19 c4 ♖d7 20 c5 ♖c7 21 ♖fc1 offer White promising compensation for the pawn, in view of his bishop pair and attacking chances.

Returning to 13...♖he8:

14 ♖c1

The immediate 14 a3 also looks promising: for instance, 14...♗xc3 15 ♗xc3 ♕d6 (15...c6 16 b4 ♕d6 17 ♗xd4 exd4 18 ♗f3 cxd5 19 ♕xd4 gives White some advantage, as pointed out by Karolyi), as in J.Koscielski-K.Krug, Recklinghausen 2003. At this point the most purposeful move looks to be 16 ♖e1 ♘xe2+ 17 ♕xe2 with a typical edge for White, based on his superior minor piece and more mobile pawn majority.

14...♚b8 15 a3 ♗xc3 16 ♗xc3 ♘xe2+ 17 ♕xe2

White has a pleasant position, again with the better minor piece and the more mobile pawn majority.

17...c6?!

This only makes Black's situation worse.

18 b4 ♕d6 19 dxc6 ♕xc6

19...bxc6 weakens Black's pawn structure and after 20 ♖fd1 he will still lose a pawn.

20 ♗xe5+ ♚a8 21 ♕b2

Black has absolutely no compensation for the missing pawn and the rest is not much more than a formality.

21...♘e4 22 ♗d4

22 ♗xg7!? would have been tactically viable, but there was no point in going for complications at this stage.

22...♖e6 23 b5

The precautionary 23 ♗e3 would also have been strong.

23...♕d7 24 ♗e3 f5 25 ♕c2 ♕c7 26 ♖fd1 ♖de8 27 ♗d4

27 b6 axb6 28 ♕a4+ ♚b8 29 ♖d7 was also good, but Movsesian prefers to keep everything under control.

27...f4 28 f3 ♘c5 29 ♗f2 ♖e2

29...g6 would have been more resilient, although there is no doubt that White should be winning with correct play.

30 ♕xh7

White deposits a second pawn in the bank.

30...♕b6

The threat of ...♖xf2 will be easily parried.

31 ♖c2

31 ♕h5 and 31 ♖e1 were also both good enough.

31...a5?

Allowing an instant kill, but Black's position was thoroughly lost anyway.

32 ♖xe2 ♖xe2 33 ♕g8+ ♚a7 34 ♖d8 1-0

Our next game is a recent affair which eventually ends up in Black's favour, but the opening battle was definitely won by White.

Game 2
I.Snape-I.Rausis
Gatwick 2011

1 e4 d5 2 exd5 ♕xd5 3 ♘f3 ♗g4 4 ♗e2 ♘c6 5 d4 0-0-0 6 ♗e3 e5 7 c4 ♕a5+ 8 ♗d2 ♗b4 9 d5 ♗xf3 10 ♗xf3 ♘d4 11 ♘c3

So far everything has been the same as in the previous game, but now Black tries a different queen move.

11...♕a6!

This has been Black's most popular choice and I believe it to be more promising than Tomczak's 11...♕c5. One advantage is that the queen is not a target for a quick a3 and b4. Also, the likely transfer of the queen to g6 can help to facilitate Black's kingside counterplay.

A few other moves have been played, but none of them are good enough to equalize:

a) 11...f5?! (this move has the potential to be useful, but at this stage of the game it should not be at the top of Black's list of priorities)

12 0-0 ♘f6 13 a3 ♗xc3 14 ♗xc3 ♕c5 15 ♗xd4 exd4 16 ♕d3 ♘e4 17 b4 ♕b6 was reached in D.Lardot-E.Marjusaari, Kokkola 2006, and now after 18 ♖fe1 White is set to win a pawn in the near future.

b) 11...♘xf3+ (Black should generally avoid making this exchange too early, unless there is a truly pressing reason for it) 12 ♕xf3 ♘f6 13 0-0 (White intends a3 followed by the usual queenside and central play) 13...♕c5 (13...♖he8 14 a3 ♗xc3 15 ♗xc3 ♕a4 16 ♖ac1 ♔b8 17 ♖fe1 is clearly better for White, as pointed out by Karolyi) 14 b3 ♕d4 was seen in V.Kuritsin-I.Shchedrin, Voronezh 2008, and now after 15 a3 ♗e7 16 ♗g5 White has an obvious advantage.

c) 11...♘f6 12 a3 ♗e7 13 0-0 (the immediate 13 b4 can be met by

13...♘xf3+ 14 ♕xf3 ♗xb4, but after castling it becomes a serious threat) 13...♕a6 14 ♗e2 (White avoids 14 b3 as the b-pawn might want to move two squares in certain positions) 14...c6 was M.Richter-F.Zipfel, German League 2007.

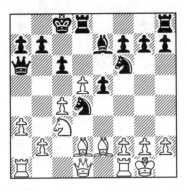

At this point I agree with Karolyi's suggestion of 15 ♗e3 (15 ♖e1!? also looks promising) 15...cxd5 (15...♘xe2+?! 16 ♕xe2 cxd5 17 ♘b5! d4 18 ♗xd4 is very good for White, as indicated too by Karolyi) 16 ♗xd4 exd4 17 cxd5 ♕b6 18 ♘a4 when White keeps the advantage.

Returning to 11...♕a6:

12 b3

12 ♗e2 is an important alternative which I also spent some time analysing. The critical continuation is 12...♘f6 13 a3 ♖he8! (13...♗xc3 14 ♗xc3 would be too compliant, as White is left with a pleasant edge with at least one dominant bishop) 14 axb4! (14 0-0?! runs into 14...♗xc3 15 ♗xc3 ♘xe2+ 16 ♕xe2 ♖xd5! when regaining his pawn to reach equality is about the full extent of White's ambitions) 14...♕xa1 15 ♕xa1 ♘c2+ 16 ♔f1 ♘xa1 17 ♗d1! c6! with a highly unclear endgame, S.Movsesian-M.Petr, Czech League 2010. White is the exchange down, but he has some compensation as the black knight is trapped on a1 with no easy escape route; on the other hand, White has no way to capture the knight at present. The position is fascinating, but overall it seems to me that it holds at least as many dangers for White as for Black.

12...♕g6

Black sensibly transfers his queen to a more promising post. A few other moves have also been tried:

a) 12...♘xf3+?! (Black can make this exchange at more or less any point over the next few moves and he has little to gain from committing to it so soon) 13 ♕xf3 ♕f6 occurred in J.Mittermeier-H.Kunze, German League 1998, and now White could have obtained a pleasant advantage by means of 14 ♕e3 ♔b8 15 a3 ♗xc3 16 ♗xc3 ♘h6 17 0-0 ♖he8 18 ♖ae1 when he has the better minor piece and pressure against the e5-pawn.

b) 12...♕a5!? 13 ♖c1 f5 14 0-0 ♘f6 was played in P.Leko-V.Ivanchuk, 6th matchgame, Mukachevo (rapid) 2009. From this position I like the look of 15 a3!? as suggested by Tibor Karolyi.

Black has a few possible replies:

b1) Declining the pawn does not equalize: for instance, 15...♗d6 16 ♘b5 (16 ♘a4!?) 16...♘xf3+ 17 gxf3 ♕a6 18 ♗e3 (Karolyi's suggestion of 18 ♕c2 g6 19 b4 also looks promising) 18...b6 19 a4 when White's queenside initiative is more significant than his doubled f-pawns.

b2) 15...♘xa3 16 ♖a1 ♕c5 17 ♗e3 a6 (if 17...♗b4?! 18 ♘b5 – Karolyi) 18 ♗xd4 ♕xd4 (or 18...exd4 19 ♘a4 ♕b4 20 ♕xd4) 19 ♕c2 ♗b4 20 ♕xf5+ ♔b8 21 ♘e2 and White's better pawn structure gives him a slight plus.

b3) 15...♘xa3 16 ♘b5 ♘xb5 17 ♖a1 ♕xa1 18 ♕xa1 ♗xd2 19 cxb5 e4 20 ♖d1 ♗b4 21 ♕xa7! exf3 22 ♕a8+ ♔d7 23 ♕xb7 when White keeps the better chances, as pointed out by Karolyi. In material terms Black has more than enough pieces for the queen, but his

pieces are uncoordinated and his king is less than secure.

13 0-0

13...♘f6

Once again there is no reason for Black to rush the exchange on f3: 13...♘xf3+?! 14 ♕xf3 f5 15 ♕e3 ♔b8 was K.Bailey-D.Calvert, Coulsdon 2007, and at this point White could have obtained a decisive attack with 16 ♘b5! ♗xd2 17 ♕xa7+ ♔c8 18 ♖ad1 ♗b4 19 ♕a8+ ♔d7 20 ♕xb7 ♕b6 21 d6!, as shown by Karolyi.

14 a3

Having completed his development White begins to drive his opponent backwards.

14...♗d6

14...♗xc3 is too cooperative and after 15 ♗xc3 White has a comfortable edge with easy play in the centre.

15 g3!?

A new and quite logical idea. White bolsters his kingside, anticipating the opening of the h2-b8 diagonal, and also prepares a retreat square on g2 for his bishop. This forces Black to consider the future of the knight on d4 rather carefully.

I checked a few alternatives, but found nothing special for White:

a) 15 ♖e1 ♕c2! 16 b4 (16 ♘b5!? could be worth a punt) 16...♘xf3+ 17 ♕xf3? (17 gxf3 was better, although White has no advantage here) 17...♕xd2 saw Black win a piece and eventually the game in J.Novkovic-F.Grafl, Austrian League 2009.

b) 15 ♗e2 e4 16 ♖c1 (I searched long and hard for a convincing improvement here, but found nothing; the computer likes 16 ♗e3!?, intending to meet 16...♘f5! with 17 ♗xa7, but after 17...h5! Black's kingside counterplay is very real) 16...♕f5 (16...h5!? looks promising here too), and White eventually prevailed in S.Movsesian-F.Grafl, German League 2006, but Black had no reason to be dissatisfied with the outcome of the opening.

15...♕c2

The same move worked well for Black against 15 ♖e1 (see note 'a' to White's previous move), but here it does not equalize, as we will soon see.

The present position only occurred for the first time a short while before this book was finished, so it remains to be seen how Scandinavian players may strive to improve Black's play. Here are a couple of speculative lines:

a) 15...h5 should be met by 16 h4: for instance,

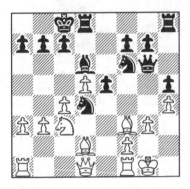

16...♘xf3+ (it looks prudent to exchange the bishop before it can retreat to g2) 17 ♕xf3 e4 18 ♕e3 ♔b8 19 ♘b5 b6 20 ♕g5! ♕xg5 21 hxg5!? (or 21 ♗xg5 ♗e5 22 ♖ad1) 21...♘g4 22 ♘xd6 ♖xd6 23 ♗f4 intending ♖ae1, with some initiative for White.

b) 15...♘xf3+ 16 ♕xf3 e4 (16...h5 17 h4 reaches the previous line) 17 ♕e3 ♔b8 18 ♘b5 b6 19 ♘xd6 (19 ♕g5 would be less effective, as Black can take back with the h-pawn) 19...♖xd6 20 ♖ae1 and White has the more comfortable game.

16 ♕xc2 ♘xc2 17 ♖a2 ♘d4

After the suicidal 17...♘xa3? 18 ♗c1 ♗b4 19 ♘e4 the knight on a3 is trapped.

18 ♗d1

White has the two bishops and a nice central pawn wedge. Given time he will improve his coordination, perhaps exchanging the strong knight on d4, and then put the two aforementioned assets to good use.

18...a6

Rather slow. More purposeful is 18...c6, although White keeps an edge after 19 ♗g5 cxd5 20 ♗xf6 gxf6 21 ♘xd5 f5 22 f4!.

19 ♔g2 h6

19...b5 can be met by 20 ♗g5 or 20 cxb5!? axb5 21 b4, with good prospects for White in both cases.

20 f3 ♔b8 21 ♘e2

I would prefer 21 ♘e4! with two main paths for Black:

a) 21...♘xe4 22 fxe4 f6 23 b4 c5 24 ♗h5! when White has the better prospects thanks to his bishop pair and superior pawn structure. Black has a lovely knight on d4, but White should be able to play around it.

b) 21...♗e7 22 ♗c3 (22 ♘f2!? intending ♘d3 is also promising) 22...c6

(Black cannot do without this move forever) 23 dxc6 ♘xc6 24 ♗c2 ♘d4 25 b4 and White maintains the better chances.

21...c5 22 dxc6 ♘xc6

23 ♗e3

23 b4! would have maintained an edge for White.

23...♖he8 24 ♗b6?!

Now the position starts to turn against White, who is wasting several tempi in order to make a positionally undesirable bishop exchange.

24 ♗c2 was better.

24...♗c7 25 ♗xc7+?

White could still have kept a reasonable position with 25 ♗c5 e4 26 ♘c3.

25...♔xc7

Now Black has a clear advantage. The rest of the game is a sad story for White, but the opening was a success for him and the relevant improvements have been pointed out.

26 b4

26 ♘c1 was more resilient.

26...♖d3 27 ♗a4 ♖ed8 28 ♗xc6 ♔xc6

29 ♖c1 g5 30 h3 e4 31 f4 g4 32 ♖cc2 h5 33 h4 ♔c7 34 a4 ♖f3

34...e3! would have won more quickly, but the text is also good enough.

35 ♖d2? ♖xd2 36 ♖xd2 e3 37 ♖c2 ♖f2+ 38 ♔g1 ♘e4 39 ♘d4 ♖d2 0-1

In the next game we will conclude our coverage of the critical 6...e5 variation by reviewing the less common alternatives available to Black on moves 7-10.

1 e4 d5 2 exd5 ♕xd5 3 ♘f3 ♗g4 4 ♗e2 ♘c6 5 d4 0-0-0 6 ♗e3 e5 7 c4

7...♕a5+

Other moves are asking for trouble:

a) 7...♕d7?! has only been played once: 8 d5 ♗xf3 (after 8...e4 9 dxc6 ♕xd1+ 10 ♗xd1 exf3 11 ♘d2 ♗b4 12 cxb7+ ♔xb7 13 ♗xf3+ ♗xf3 14 gxf3 the

doubled f-pawns can hardly make up for Black's one-pawn deficit) 9 ♗xf3 ♕e7 10 0-0 e4 11 ♕a4!? (Karolyi points out the much simpler 11 ♗e2 when White is clearly better) 11...exf3 12 dxc6 ♕e4 (or 12...a6 13 cxb7+ ♔xb7 14 g3) 13 cxb7+ ♕xb7 14 ♘c3 a6 15 ♖fd1 ♖xd1+ 16 ♖xd1 ♘f6 was L.Urbanec-D.Mlensky, Brno 2000, and now 17 ♘d5! would have been winning for White.

b) 7...♗b4+ 8 ♘bd2 when Black has tried two moves:

b1) 8...♕e4 9 d5 ♘d4 10 ♘xd4 exd4 11 ♗xg4+ f5 12 0-0 ♕xg4 13 f3 ♕h4 14 ♗f2 ♕h6 15 ♘b3 ♗d6 16 g3 and Black is about to lose a pawn for no compensation, S.Movsesian-A.Pakhomov, Pardubice 2010.

b2) 8...♕d7 9 d5 ♗xf3 10 ♗xf3 ♘a5 (10...♘d4 11 ♗xd4 exd4 12 0-0 ♘f6 13 ♘b3 is good for White – Karolyi) was seen in the game V.Plhacek-R.Dolezel, Czech League 2006, and here Karolyi points out the simple continuation 11 ♕c2 b6 12 a3 with a clear advantage to White.

8 ♗d2 ♗b4

This natural move has been by far the most popular choice, although two queen moves have also been tried. The first is simply bad, but the second is tricky and should not be underestimated:

a) 8...♕b6? 9 c5! ♗xc5 10 dxc5 ♕xb2 (or 10...♕xc5 11 0-0 and Black had no real compensation for the piece in N.Aliavdin-J.Jozwicki, Barlinek 2010). This was K.Skaperdas-A.Dounis, Athens 2008, and here White could have won a piece with 11 ♗c3! ♖xd1+ 12 ♔xd1 ♕xa1 13 ♗xa1 when the endgame should not present too many challenges for him.

b) 8...♕a6!? 9 c5! (this must be critical; instead 9 d5 ♗xf3 10 ♗xf3 ♘d4 has proven to be quite reliable for Black) 9...♗xf3 (Black should take the opportunity to damage White's pawn structure; in the event of 9...b5, as in M.Pap-Z.Bogut, Bosnjaci 2009, I suggest a similar course of action with 10 cxb6 ♕xb6 11 dxe5 – I doubt that Black can hope to benefit from omitting the

move ...♗xf3 at a time when White has to recapture with the g-pawn) 10 gxf3 (White must recapture this way in order to maintain the attack on the queen) 10...b5.

So far this position has only been reached in a single game, I.Dorfanis-A.Nikomanis, Greek Team Championship 2008. Although this variation is not necessarily bad for Black, it is hardly surprising that players have not been queuing up to take on a position where the black king's shelter has been compromised so severely. In any case, in the event that you encounter this position over the board, I recommend the following improvement: 11 cxb6!? (it looks logical to open the position for the white bishops; the game continuation of 11 d5 ♘d4 was extremely murky, but not unfavourable to Black) 11...♕xb6 12 dxe5 when the position is rather messy, but White's bishop pair is an important asset. Here are some illustrative lines: 12...♕xb2 (perhaps Black should try 12...♘xe5, although I still prefer White after 13 ♘c3 ♗c5 14

0-0) 13 ♘c3! (White is clearly doing well) 13...♖xd2?! (or 13...♗b4? 14 ♗a6+ ♔b8 15 ♖b1) 14 ♗a6+! ♔b8?! (14...♘d7 is the lesser evil, although after 15 ♕xd2+ ♕xd2+ 16 ♔xd2 White's extra exchange gives him a clear advantage in the endgame) 15 ♕xd2 and White is winning, as 15...♕xa1+? 16 ♔e2 ♕xh1 17 ♕d5! forces mate, although it is not too late for White spoil everything with 17 ♕d7? ♕xf3+! when Black survives.

Returning to 8...♗b4:

9 d5 ♗xf3

9...e4? is just bad and after 10 ♘g5! ♗xe2 11 ♕xe2 ♘d4 12 ♕d1 Black faces a depressing choice:

a) 12...e3 13 fxe3 ♘f5?! (13...♗xd2+ 14 ♘xd2 ♘f5 is the lesser evil, although Black is still struggling after 15 e4!? ♘e3 16 ♕b3! ♘xg2+ 17 ♔d1, threatening both ♘xf7 and ♕h3+ picking up the knight) 14 0-0 ♘gh6 and here in K.Kiik-H.Rasch, Gibraltar 2009, White could have increased his advantage with 15 ♘xf7!.

b) 12...♘h6 13 0-0 ♗xd2 14 ♘xd2 e3 was tried in T.Tuominen-M.Grabics,

Warsaw 2001, and now White should have played 15 fxe3 ♘df5 16 ♕e2 (16 ♘xf7!?) 16...♕b6 (or 16...♖he8 17 ♘xf7 ♖xe3 18 ♕f2) 17 ♖ae1!? (17 ♘de4 is also good) 17...♕xb2 18 ♘xf7 ♘xf7 19 ♖xf5 ♘d6 20 ♖f2 when Black has the option of restoring material equality by taking on a2, but in that case White's strong and mobile central pawns will become the dominant feature of the position.

10 ♗xf3

From this position the main line is 10...♘d4, which was examined in the previous two games. Apart from that, Black has one respectable alternative and one dubious one. In the present game Black chooses the former:

10...♗xd2+

Instead 10...e4?! is questionable. After 11 ♗g4+ Black has two options, neither of which enables him to equalize:

a) 11...♔b8!? is tricky but ultimately insufficient after 12 dxc6 ♘f6 13 ♘c3 when Black does not have enough for the piece: for instance, 13...♖d6 (if 13...♖d3 14 ♗e2) 14 a3! ♗xc3 15 bxc3

♖hd8 16 ♕b3! ♕b6 17 ♕xb6 axb6 18 ♗g5! and White keeps a material advantage, as pointed out by Karolyi.

b) 11...f5 12 ♗xf5+ ♔b8 13 0-0 ♘f6 14 ♘c3 ♖he8 15 a3 ♗xc3 16 ♗xc3 ♕c5 was C.Neethling-L.Fredericia, Bled Olympiad 2002, and now after 17 ♕e2 Black is a pawn down with a bad position.

11 ♘xd2 ♘d4 12 0-0

12 a3 reaches the note to White's 11th move in Game 1. It seems clear to me that White can achieve more by castling and mobilizing his pieces before attempting to advance his queenside pawns.

12...♕b4

This looks a little strange, but it has been Black's most popular choice. Black hopes to make a nuisance out of the queen before relocating her to a better square; we saw the same idea in both of the previous games.

Two other moves have been tried:

a) 12...♘xf3+ 13 ♘xf3 f6 14 a3 (14 ♕c2!? is another idea, removing the queen from the d-file before doing any-

thing else) 14...♘e7 15 b4 ♕a6 was V.Repina-Z.Iordanidou, Sibenik 2007, and now both 16 ♕c2 and 16 b5!? look promising for White, who is clearly ahead in the race to create threats against the enemy king.

b) 12...♘f6 13 ♘b3 ♘xf3+ 14 ♕xf3 ♕b4 15 ♖ac1 ♖he8 16 ♖fd1 ♕e7 17 a3 e4 18 ♕e3 ♔b8 (M.Heika-J.Dey, German League 2003), and here White could maintain a slight plus with Karolyi's suggestion of 19 h3!? followed by ♘d4.

13 ♖e1!

A few other moves have been seen, but to my mind this developing move is the clear favourite, especially as the b2-pawn is poisoned.

13...f6

Two other options have been tried:

a) Surprisingly when Almond reached the same position a year later, he chose to 'improve' with 13...♕xb2?! 14 ♖b1 ♕xa2.

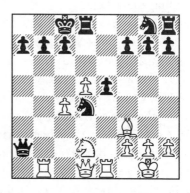

This was N.Rutter-R.Almond, Sunningdale 2008, and here White could have obtained a serious advantage by means of 15 d6! c6 16 ♖xe5. This was suggested by Christian Bauer, who convincingly demonstrated Black's troubles with the following variations:

a1) 16...♘xf3+ 17 ♕xf3 ♕xd2? 18 ♕f5+ ♔b8 19 ♕xf7 and Black can resign.

a2) 16...♕c2 17 ♕xc2 ♘xc2 18 ♖a5 ♖xd6 19 ♘e4 followed by ♖xa7 with decisive threats.

a3) 16...♘f6 17 ♗g4+ ♘e6 18 ♗xe6+ fxe6 19 c5 ♘d7 20 ♖g5! when White keeps his c5-pawn and with it an overwhelming advantage.

a4) 16...♖xd6 17 ♖e8+ ♔c7 18 c5 ♖e6 (after 18...♘xf3+ 19 ♕xf3 ♖xd2 20 ♕f4+ ♔d7 21 ♖be1 White wins) 19 ♖f8 ♕c2 20 ♕xc2 ♘xc2 21 ♗g4! ♘h6 22 ♖xh8 ♘xg4 23 ♖xh7 and Black has only minimal chances to save the endgame.

b) 13...♘f6!? has only been played once, but may be Black's soundest move. After 14 b3 (14 ♖xe5?! is well met by 14...♘xf3+ and Black is doing fine after 15 ♘xf3 ♕xc4 or 15 gxf3 ♕xb2) 14...♖he8 15 a3 if the queen retreats along the a3-f8 diagonal, White will play b4 with the makings of a

queenside initiative. Therefore the following invasion into enemy territory is critical, 15...♕c3!?.

We have been following the game B.Predojevic-D.Sermek, Portoroz 2005. At this point White's best looks to be 16 ♖a2! (16 ♖e3 can be met by 16...♕c2 or 16...♕b2) 16...♕d3 when Bauer evaluates the position as roughly equal, but I decided to analyse a little further: 17 ♗e2! (I checked a few other continuations, but it soon became clear that the text was the top choice) 17...♕g6 (after 17...♘xe2+ 18 ♖xe2 White can aim for pressure on the e-file, so I prefer his position ever so slightly).

Here it is worth mentioning a couple of ideas for White:

b1) 18 ♘f1 ♚b8 19 ♘e3 leaves the knight ideally placed. Given time, White could continue to improve his pieces with moves like ♖d2 and ♗f1. Therefore 19...c6! looks critical when White should reply 20 dxc6! ♘f3+ 21 ♗xf3 ♖xd1 22 ♖xd1 e4 23 ♗e2 bxc6 24 ♖ad2, giving him good compensation for the missing queen, with the safer king and better-coordinated pieces, although it is hard to say if it adds up to a real advantage.

b2) Another idea is 18 b4 e4 19 ♗f1 (not 19 ♘b3? ♘f3+ or 19 ♘f1? ♘f3+ 20 ♗xf3 exf3 21 g3 ♖xe1 22 ♕xe1 ♖e8) 19...♚b8 20 a4!? with the idea of activating the rook along the third rank.

Returning to 13...f6:

14 ♕c1

14 ♖c1 has been played too, but with the e5-pawn now defended Black can consider 14...♕xb2!?, the consequences of which are not at all clear.

14...♘h6 15 ♗d1!

Areshchenko reveals a second point behind his previous move. The d4-knight is Black's best piece, but in the game it soon becomes a target.

15...g5

Black embarks on kingside play, but it will take a long time for him to generate any real threats in that area.

16 ♕c3! ♕xc3?

Black cannot resist the temptation of doubling his opponent's pawns, but he will never get a chance to attack them. 16...♕d6 was better, although after 17 a4 ♘hf5 18 a5 (Karolyi) White keeps the better chances. The d4-knight is unquestionably a strong piece, but its colleague on f5 lacks a useful role, and White is also ahead in the attacking race.

17 bxc3 ♘df5 18 ♘e4 ♖hf8 19 ♗b3

White finds an ideal role for his bishop. By defending the d5-pawn he prepares c5 in the near future.

19...♘g8

Black has no immediate prospects for counterplay, so he decides to improve his knight.

20 c5 ♘ge7

21 ℤed1!

21 ℤad1 would also have maintained a clear advantage, but Areshchenko has correctly judged that the rook has a brighter future on the queenside.

21...♘g7 22 ♗c4 h6

Preparing ...f5, but White has just enough time to carry out a strong plan before his knight is driven away from the centre.

23 c6! b6

23...bxc6? would have been suicidal, in view of 24 dxc6 and with ♘c5 coming next, Black will either be mated or suffer fatal material losses.

24 ♗a6+

There was a strong alternative in 24 ♘c5!?, relying on the fact that 24...bxc5? 25 ♗a6+ ♚b8 26 ℤab1+ ♚a8 27 d6! is winning for White.

24...♚b8 25 c4

With this move White solidifies his pawn wedge and vacates the c3-square for his knight.

25...f5

Black might have offered more resistance with 25...♘gf5, based on the principle of 'pieces before pawns'. The best response looks to be 26 ℤdb1! ♘d4 27 ℤb2, preventing any irritating knight incursions and preparing a4-a5 or ♘c5. Black's position is so bad that the computer already recommends the rather desperate piece sacrifice 27...♘xd5 when Black succeeds in prolonging the game, although ultimately he must be losing.

26 ♘c3 ♘e8 27 a4! ♘d6 28 a5

Black has found a nice blockading square for his knight and if he could magically remove all four rooks from the board he would be doing just fine. Unfortunately for him, the cold hard reality is that he is about to be annihilated on the queenside.

28...e4 29 c5 ♘dc8

29...bxc5 30 ℤab1+ ♚a8 31 ♘a4! is crushing.

30 axb6 cxb6 31 ♘b5

Black could easily have resigned here, but he stumbles on for a few more agonizing moves.

31...ℤxd5 32 c7+ ♚a8 33 ℤxd5

White has multiple wins at every turn, 33 ♘d6 being one of the most effective.

33...♘xd5 34 c6 ♘xc7 35 ♘xc7+ ♚b8 36 ♘b5 f4 37 c7+ ♚a8 38 ♗xc8 1-0

That concludes our coverage of 6...e5. We have seen that this move leads to rich positions, full of resources for both sides. At present it seems to me that White's chances are slightly higher in most variations, although the theoretical debate will surely continue well into the future.

We will now turn out attention to Black's alternatives on the sixth move, beginning with a natural knight development.

Game 4
I.Aldokhin-D.Rodin
Voronezh 2009

---

1 e4 d5 2 exd5 ♕xd5 3 ♘f3 ♗g4 4 ♗e2 ♘c6 5 d4 0-0-0 6 ♗e3 ♘f6

While 6...e5 is arguably Black's most principled and challenging option, it is by no means his only playable one. Indeed, there is a certain logic behind developing another piece and keeping the pawn thrust in reserve.

7 0-0 ♕f5

The queen was vulnerable on d5, so she wisely sidesteps the attack that would have resulted from c4. I consider this Black's most challenging option, although numerous alternatives have

been tried and they will be examined in the next game.

By the way, the actual move order in the present game was 2...♘f6 3 d4 ♗g4 4 ♘f3 ♕xd5 5 ♗e2 ♘c6 6 c4 ♕f5 7 ♗e3 0-0-0 8 0-0, but I have shuffled it in order to remain consistent with the proposed repertoire.

8 c4

We are now officially back in Aldokhin-Rodin.

8...e5

Striking at the centre is Black's most active and thematic idea. The alternatives are less challenging:

a) 8...♗xf3 9 ♗xf3 ♘xd4? (9...e5 10 d5 reaches the note to Black's 9th move in the main game) 10 ♗xd4 e5? (funnily enough Black could have kept himself in the game with 10...c6 when White cannot escape the pin along the d-file, but still after 11 ♕a4! ♖xd4 12 ♕xa7 Black's vulnerable king gives him problems) occurred in R.Stepp-L.Kline, Stillwater 2010, and here White could have obtained a decisive advantage by means of 11 ♕b3! ♖xd4 12 ♕xb7+ ♔d8

13 ♘c3. Black is busted as his king is too exposed.

b) 8...e6 is playable but a bit passive after 9 ♘bd2 (I like the idea of reinforcing the knight on f3 while breaking the pin along the d-file; 9 ♘c3 is also possible, after which the critical line continues 9...♗c5 10 ♕b3 ♗xd4 11 ♘xd4 ♖xd4! 12 f3 ♕e5 when Black obtained reasonable compensation for the sacrificed exchange in J.Gonzalez Gambau-E.Palacios, Aragon 2005) 9...♗d6 (other moves have been tried, but the text seems like the most logical) 10 h3! when Black must make a difficult choice:

b1) 10...♗xh3? is refuted by 11 ♘h4!.

b2) 10...♗h5 is well met by 11 ♕b3! when Black has some problems, as a natural move such as 11...g5 runs into 12 ♗d3! ♕a5 13 a3!? when the black queen is running short of squares.

b3) 10...h5 11 ♕b3 e5 (once again ♗d3 was a troublesome threat, so Black feels compelled to take immediate action) 12 dxe5 (12 d5 ♘d4 13

♗xd4 exd4 should also be somewhat better for White) 12...♘xe5?! (12...♗xe5 was the lesser evil, although it is understandable that Black wished to preserve this important bishop) 13 ♘h4! ♕d7 14 hxg4 hxg4 15 g3 and Black did not have enough compensation for the sacrificed piece in V.Malakhov-E.Senoner, Bled 2001.

Returning to 8...e5:

9 d5 e4

The main line, but there is a significant alternative in 9...♗xf3 10 ♗xf3 e4 (after 10...♘d4? 11 ♗xd4 exd4 12 ♕xd4 Black was a pawn down for nothing in A.Axelrod-R.Goldin, Haifa 2009) 11 ♗e2 when Black has tried three moves:

a) 11...♕e5 12 ♘c3 ♔b8 (12...♗b4? 13 ♕a4 ♗d6 14 g3 ♘d4 was B.Junaidi-A.Keiper, correspondence 2001, and now after 15 ♕xa7 White is winning) 13 ♘b5! a6 14 ♕b3 (the computer likes 14 ♕c1!? axb5 15 dxc6, but the text move leads to a clear advantage in a stable position) 14...♘a5 15 ♕c3 ♕xc3 16 ♘xc3 ♗b4 17 ♖ac1 and in G.Melson-A.Chernyak, correspondence 2001,

White was clearly better thanks to his bishop pair and the misplaced knight on a5.

b) 11...♞e5 12 ♞c3 (12 ♗xa7!? is also possible) 12...a6 transposes to variation 'c'.

c) 11...a6 12 ♞c3 ♞e5 13 ♕c2 ♕g6 (13...♞eg4 14 ♗xg4 ♕xg4 was played in T.Tamasanu-C.Ionesi, Eforie Nord 2001, and now after 15 ♗d4 followed by ♖ae1 White looks to be winning the e4-pawn) 14 ♔h1 when Black has tried two moves:

c1) 14...♞ed7 15 b4!? ♗xb4 16 ♞a4!? (the simple 16 ♖ab1 also looks good) 16...♞g4? 17 ♗xg4 ♕xg4 18 ♕b3 ♗a5 19 ♖ab1 (19 c5 should also be enough to win) 19...b6 20 c5 b5 21 ♞b2 ♞e5 22 ♕a3 ♖xd5 23 ♕xa5 ♔b7 24 ♞a4 1-0, W.Pannekoek-M.Ibar, correspondence 2004.

c2) 14...h5 15 ♗d4 ♞eg4 was preferred in S.Teichmeister-P.Spitz, correspondence 1999. Now after the simple 16 ♖ae1 White is the better mobilized and the e4-pawn will soon come under fire.

10 ♞d4

10...♞xd4

After 10...♗xe2 11 ♞xe2 ♞e5 12 ♞g3 ♕g4 13 ♕d4! White was clearly better in I.Bajo Gutierrez-R.Lopez de Lerma, Gijon 1999.

11 ♗xd4 ♗d6

Instead 11...♗xe2 12 ♕xe2 ♗d6 13 ♖e1! (taking the sting out of any ...♞g4 ideas; 13 ♞c3 transposes to variation 'b' in the next note, which is not advantageous to White) 13...b6 (13...♞g4?! 14 h3 gets nowhere for Black, as the knight jump to h2 will not hit the rook) 14 ♞c3 c5 15 ♗xf6 gxf6 16 ♞xe4 left Black a pawn down for nothing in J.Kap-P.Warkentin, Bad Ems 2005.

12 ♞c3

The position is rather sharp. White has the makings of a positional advantage, as his d5-pawn is securely defended, whereas Black's e4-pawn does not enjoy the support of a fellow pawn. If White can complete his development and place at least one rook on the e-file, then the e-pawn may become a long-term weakness. Furthermore,

Black must constantly be on the look-out for a queenside pawn storm with c5-c6. On the other hand, Black enjoys fluid piece play on the kingside and White will have to be on guard against tactical ideas there, especially over the next few moves.

12...♖he8?!

This is natural and sensible, but it fails to put White under immediate pressure, unlike the following alternatives which should be studied carefully:

a) 12...♗h3!? has not been tested, but could easily cause problems for an unsuspecting player. The best response is 13 ♘b5! ♕g5 14 ♘xa7+ ♔b8 15 g3 ♗xf1 16 ♗xf1 when White has a pawn and great compensation for the exchange, as pointed out by Bauer.

b) 12...♗xe2! is the most challenging move, after which it seems to me that a new approach is in order for White, with 13 ♘xe2! (so far only 13 ♕xe2 has been played, but after 13...♘g4! Black is in no way worse), and here I checked the following replies:

b1) 13...♗xh2+? 14 ♔xh2 ♕h5+ 15 ♔g1 ♘g4 16 ♖e1 ♕h2+ 17 ♔f1 ♕h1+ 18 ♘g1 ♘h2+ 19 ♔e2 ♕xg2 20 ♔d2 and White is winning, as the king escapes easily.

b2) 13...♘g4?! 14 h3 ♘h2 15 ♖e1 gets nowhere for Black, whereas in the analogous position with the queen on e2 instead of the knight, Black could safely check on f3 with the knight.

b3) A waiting move such as 13...♔b8 should be met by 14 ♕c2 intending ♖ae1.

b4) 13...♖he8 14 h3!? (securing the kingside; if 14 ♕c2 ♕g6!?) 14...a6 (14...♔b8 is similar) 15 ♕c2 when White intends ♖ae1 and later ♕c3, with a slightly preferable position.

13 ♖e1!

The mutual rook moves appear to be of equal value, but in fact it is White who has benefited more, as his rook is no longer tactically vulnerable.

13...♗e5

In this position 13...♗xe2 can safely be met by 14 ♕xe2 or even 14 ♖xe2!?, as the ...♘g4-h2 idea will not come with gain of tempo.

14 ♗xe5

14 ♗xa7!? b6 15 a4 may also be good for White, but the text move maintains his advantage without allowing the game to become too complicated.

14...♗xe2 15 ♕xe2 ♕xe5 16 ♖ad1

This type of position is quite characteristic of the whole opening. White enjoys a slight but risk-free advantage, due to the vulnerability of the e4-pawn and the mobility of his queenside pawns.

16...♖e7 17 h3 a6 18 ♕e3 ♔b8 19 f4!?

19 ♖d4 and 19 b4 were good alternatives. Instead White decides to gain some space on the kingside, while also freeing the f2-square for his king, which might prove useful in an endgame.

19...♕f5 20 b4

20...h5?

Failing to appreciate the danger on the queenside. Black had to try something like 20...♖g8 when the threat of ...g5 at least creates some distraction.

21 b5!

Black has no good defence and his position quickly collapses.

21...a5 22 b6 ♔c8 23 ♕c5 ♖d6 24 ♘b5 ♕xf4 25 bxc7 1-0

Our next game will deal with Black's alternatives after 6...♘f6 7 0-0.

1 e4 d5 2 exd5 ♕xd5

Once again I have fiddled the move order. For readers who care about such things, the present game began with the sequence of 2...♘f6 3 d4 ♗g4 4 ♘f3 ♕xd5 5 ♗e2 e6 6 ♗e3 ♘c6 7 c4 ♕a5+ 8 ♘bd2 0-0-0 9 0-0 ♗b4.

3 ♘f3 ♗g4 4 ♗e2 ♘c6 5 d4 0-0-0 6 ♗e3 ♘f6 7 0-0

7...e6

This has actually been played more frequently than 7...♕f5, but both analysis and practical results indicate that it is less challenging to White. In addition to these two main moves, Black has three notable alternatives:

a) 7...♕d7 8 ♘bd2 ♘d5 (Black secures the advantage of the bishop pair, but it costs him valuable time) 9 c4 ♘xe3 10 fxe3 e6 11 a3 g6 (11...♗e7 is less accurate, as there is nothing to stop White from advancing with 12 b4 ♗f6, as in F.Rayner-S.Zeidler, Swansea 2002, and then 13 ♘b3 with some initiative) 12 ♕c2! (it is important to avoid 12 b4 ♗h6 13 ♕b3 ♘xd4!, as noted by Bauer) 12...♗h6 13 ♕c3 ♕e7 14 ♖ae1 ♗g7 15 b4 (only now, after first completing his development, does White begin his queenside advance) 15...♗xf3 16 ♘xf3 ♘b8 17 c5 e5 18 ♗c4 left White clearly better in S.Movsesian-I.Rogers, Enschede 2005.

b) Black would not usually exchange of f3 without provocation, but his idea with 7...♗xf3!? 8 ♗xf3 ♕b5 is to inhibit White's attempts to castle while also facilitating a quick attack along the d-file. White should react resolutely and 9 ♘c3! is the order of the day, after which Black has tried two moves:

b1) 9...♕c4 was seen in H.McAndrew-H.Mujica, correspondence 2003. At this point White could have obtained a nice edge with either 10 ♗e2 ♕e6 11 ♕d2 followed by ♖ad1, or 10 ♕e2 ♕xe2 11 ♘xe2. In both cases his bishop pair gives him the upper hand.

b2) 9...♕xb2 10 ♘e4 ♘xe4 11 ♗xe4 ♕c3 12 ♕f3 ♕c4 13 ♖ab1 gives White more than enough play for the sacrificed pawn and after the careless 13...g6? 14 ♖xb7! ♔xb7 15 ♗xc6+ ♔c8 16 ♗b7+ ♔d7 17 d5 he was already winning in B.De Schepper-V.Baci, correspondence 2000.

c) 7...♕h5?! has been played in a number of games, but is excessively risky. White should react with 8 h3 e5 9 ♘bd2! when Black has tried several moves, none of which promise him satisfactory play:

c1) 9...exd4? is weak in view of 10 hxg4 ♘xg4 11 ♗f4 when White is just winning, as noted by Bauer.

c2) 9...h6 10 ♖e1 (10 hxg4!? ♘xg4 11 ♘e4 should also be good for White) 10...♗d6? (10...♗xf3 was the lesser evil, although after 11 ♗xf3 it is obvious that Black's opening strategy has failed) 11 hxg4 ♘xg4 12 ♘e4 ♘xd4 13 ♗xd4 exd4 14 ♘xd6+ ♖xd6 15 ♘h4 f5 16 g3 and Black had no real compensation for the piece in Ji.Houska-T.Le Duin, Montreal 2008.

c3) 9...♔b8 10 ♖e1!? (10 hxg4 ♘xg4 11 ♘e4 is also promising according to Bauer) 10...♗d6 11 d5 ♘e7 12 c4 ♘f5 13 hxg4 ♘xg4 14 ♘e4 ♘fxe3 15 fxe3 ♕h6 16 ♗d3 and White soon won in O.Korneev-A.Fernandes, Elgoibar 1998.

c4) 9...♗xf3 10 ♗xf3 ♕f5 11 ♗xc6 exd4 was A.Magalotti-M.Van der Werf, Balatonkenese 1999, and now after 12 ♘b3! bxc6 (12...dxe3? 13 ♗xb7+) 13 ♘xd4 White is clearly better, as pointed out by Bauer.

c5) Finally, there is 9...♗d6

10 hxg4 (also after 10 d5!? ♘d4 11 ♗xd4 exd4 12 hxg4 ♘xg4 13 g3 Black does not have enough compensation) 10...♘xg4 11 ♘e4 ♘xd4 (11...exd4 12 ♘xd6+ ♖xd6 13 ♗f4 was winning for White in L.Vigil Alvarez-F.Menendez Rey, Asturias 1997) 12 ♗xd4 exd4 13

♘xd6+ ♖xd6 14 ♘h4 f5, as in F.Agter-D.Meijer, Hengelo 1997. At this point there was no need for White to rush to exchange on g4. Instead after the calm 15 g3! White should eventually be able to convert his extra piece.

Returning to 7...e6:

8 c4

The following alternative is also interesting: 8 ♘bd2 ♕h5 9 h3 ♗d6, as in S.Alonso-A.Cabanas Jimenez, Madrid 2000. Now 10 c4!? is recommended by Bauer, but matters are not so clear. I checked two replies for Black:

a) The French Grandmaster rightly points out that 10...♗xh3 can be met by 11 ♘e5!.

b) However, Black can do better with 10...g5! 11 c5 (or 11 ♖e1 ♗xh3! 12 gxh3 g4) 11...♗f4 12 ♗xf4 gxf4 13 hxg4 ♘xg4 intending ...♖hg8 with promising counterplay.

For this reason, I would urge the reader to stick with the move played in the game.

8...♕a5

Once again Black has tried a variety

of alternatives:

a) The most-common reaction has been 8...♕f5 when 9 ♘bd2 transposes to note 'b' to Black's 8th move in the previous game.

b) 8...♕d6 9 ♘bd2 h6 occurred in Y.Dembo-E.Titova Boric, Rijeka 2009. Here Dembo recommends the following strong improvement: 10 c5! ♕d7 (or 10...♕d5 11 ♕a4) 11 b4 when White is doing well, as 11...♘xb4? is refuted by 12 ♕b3 ♘c6 (12...♘fd5 loses to 13 ♘e5) 13 ♖ab1 b6 14 ♕a4 and White is winning.

c) Just like on the previous move, 8...♕h5 should be met by 9 h3! when Black has tried two moves:

c1) 9...♘xd4? is simply unsound: 10 ♘xd4 ♗xe2? (10...♖xd4 is better, although 11 hxg4 ♘xg4 12 ♗xg4 ♖xg4 13 ♘d2 should win easily enough for White) 11 ♕xe2 1-0, T.Ly-J.Davenport, Melbourne 2002.

c2) 9...♗d6 10 ♘c3 and once again White is doing well: for instance, 10...♗xh3?! 11 ♘e5! ♕f5 12 ♗d3 ♗g4 and now in E.Abou Jawdeh-T.Moud-

allal, Beirut 2004, the most convincing win would have been 13 f3!, leading to heavy material gains.

d) 8...♕d7 is more solid, although Black still falls short of equality: 9 ♘bd2 ♗b4 10 ♘b3! ♗e7 11 a3 (intending ♘bd2 and b4; 11 ♘e5!? looks like a sensible alternative, although after 11...♘xe5 12 dxe5 ♕xd1 13 ♗xd1 ♖xd1 14 ♖fxd1 ♗xd1 15 exf6 ♗xb3 16 fxg7 ♖g8 17 axb3 a6 White has only a minimal advantage) 11...h5 12 ♘bd2 g5 was reached in M.Schurade-H.Cording, German League 1992. From here White continued with 13 b4 and eventually won, although it is hard to say if his chosen move was the best. Instead 13 ♘xg5 ♘xd4! leads to rather murky complications, but I would be tempted to consider 13 ♕b3!? followed by ♖ad1, switching to central play, which seems like a logical reaction to Black's kingside pawn advance. I definitely prefer White's position here, although the game is likely to become rather sharp.

9 ♘bd2

Calmly developing another piece. White is now ready to start driving his opponent backwards with a3 and b4, perhaps flicking in a timely h3 on the kingside.

9...♗b4!?

Trying to develop the bishop actively, but now there is an obvious danger that a3 will come with gain of tempo. 9...♗xf3 has been played in a few games, but it is hardly surprising that this fails to solve Black's problems: for instance, 10 ♘xf3 h6 11 a3 ♕f5 12 b4 ♘g4 13 b5 ♘b8 was S.Zojer-M.Steinert, Austrian League 2010, and here I like the straightforward 14 h3! ♘xe3 15 fxe3 when Black is under pressure on both flanks.

10 h3!

Posing a difficult question.

10...♗xf3

10...♗h5 should be met by the resolute 11 g4! (11 ♘b3?! ♕f5 is unclear) 11...♘xg4 (both 11...♗g6 12 c5! and 11...♗xg4 12 hxg4 ♘xg4 13 c5! are noted as good for White by Bauer) 12 hxg4 ♗xg4

13 d5! exd5 14 ♘b3 ♕a4 15 cxd5 ♘e7 16 ♕d4 when White is clearly better, as shown by Bauer.

11 ♘xf3

This position highlights the dangers awaiting Black in the event that he fails to conduct the opening in the most accurate manner. White has not done anything fancy, but already Black is threatened by a pawn avalanche on the queenside and his queen is becoming dangerously short of squares.

11...e5?

Black simply does not have time for this.

11...♗c5! was the only challenging move, although White remains on top after 12 ♕d3! ♔b8 (12...♘xd4? 13 ♘xd4 ♗xd4 14 ♗xd4 e5 15 ♕f5+ wins) 13 a3!, as pointed out by Bauer.

12 a3!

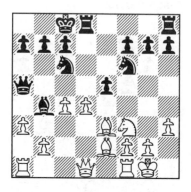

12...exd4

There is nothing better, as bishop retreats would allow 13 b4, winning material.

13 axb4 ♕xb4 14 ♘xd4 ♘xd4 15 ♗xd4

Black is simply a piece down for no

compensation and the game is soon over.

15...a6

Alternatively, 15...c5 loses to 16 ♗g4+.

16 ♗c3!

Escaping the pin and leading to an easy win.

16...♕c5 17 ♕c2 ♖he8 18 b4 ♕e7 19 ♗f3 ♕e6 20 ♗xf6 ♕xf6 21 b5 1-0

The next game will address a couple of Black's rare but interesting 6th-move alternatives.

Game 6
A.Greet-D.Bryson
Glasgow 2011

1 e4 d5 2 exd5 ♕xd5 3 ♘f3 ♗g4 4 ♗e2 ♘c6 5 d4 0-0-0 6 ♗e3

6...♘h6!?

This is a rare move, but it is nonetheless quite a principled and challenging one. The knight is heading for f5, from where it will attack the d4-pawn

while also preparing to eliminate the e3-bishop at a moment's notice.

Two other moves are worth mentioning:

a) 6...e6 7 0-0 ♘f6 transposes to the previous game.

b) 6...♗xf3!? 7 ♗xf3 ♕b5 is similar to the note to move 7 in the last game. Making the exchange a move earlier leads to some slight differences. Once again I recommend the principled 8 ♘c3!? (8 b3 is playable, but the text must be critical), when Black has tested two replies:

b1) 8...♕c4 9 ♕e2!? (this is not the only route to an advantage, but it is certainly one of the safest ways) 9...♕xe2+ 10 ♘xe2 and with two bishops and a space advantage, White had a risk-free edge in D.Wichmann-H.Ochs, German League 2006.

b2) The more challenging 8...♕xb2 was seen in O.Korneev-O.Dolzhikova, Gjovik 2008. At this point I analysed a new and promising continuation for White in 9 ♘a4!?. Black has two possible retreats:

b21) 9...♛b4+ 10 c3 ♛c4 11 ♝e2 (11 ♛b3!? ♛xb3 12 axb3 is also worth considering, with strong positional compensation in the queenless middlegame) 11...♛d5 12 0-0 when White's lead in development and the open b-file add up to promising compensation for the pawn.

b22) 9...♛b5 should be met by 10 ♞c5 when I analysed three tries for Black:

b221) 10...b6?! 11 ♜b1 ♞b4 12 ♝e2 ♛a5 13 c3 ♞d5 14 ♝a6+ ♚b8 15 ♝d2 and Black is under pressure.

b222) 10...♛b4+ 11 ♚f1 when Black has a hard time dealing with the threat of ♜b1.

b223) 10...e6 11 ♜b1 ♛c4 (or 11...♛a5+ 12 ♝d2 ♜xd4 13 ♝xc6 bxc6 14 ♝xa5 ♜xd1+ 15 ♚xd1 ♝xc5 16 ♚e2 and White has the better endgame) 12 ♝xc6 bxc6 13 ♞d3 ♛c3+ 14 ♛d2!? (after 14 ♝d2 ♛xd4 15 0-0 Bauer assesses the position as unclear, which seems reasonable, although it seems to me that Black's position is the more risky) 14...♛xd2+ 15 ♚xd2 when with ♜b3

and ♜hb1 coming, White has fine compensation and will almost certainly regain the sacrificed pawn while keeping some initiative.

Returning to 6...♞h6:

7 ♞bd2

This flexible move seems like the most logical choice to me.

7 c4 has been played a few times, but after 7...♛a5+ I am not impressed with White's position:

a) 8 ♝d2 was played in Y.Gonzalez Vidal-R.Perez Garcia, Havana 2002. Here Black could have obtained a clear advantage with 8...♛f5! 9 ♝e3 ♝xf3 10 ♝xf3 ♞xd4! 11 ♝xd4 ♛e6+ 12 ♝e2 ♛e4. The position is the same as that from the 6 c4 pawn sacrifice variation mentioned in the notes to Game 1, except that Black has gained the free developing move ...♞h6.

b) 8 ♞c3 is better, but after 8...♞f5 9 d5 ♞xe3 10 fxe3 e6 White's dark squares were a bit loose in L.Dominguez Perez-A.Kogan, Havana 2002.

7...♞f5

7...e5?! is worse: 8 c4 ♕a5 9 d5 ♘f5 10 a3 (10 ♘g5!?) 10...♗xf3 11 ♗xf3 ♘cd4 and Black is a tempo down on the main game, which reaches the same position without White having played the useful move a3. After 12 ♗e4 ♔b8 13 0-0 White was clearly on top in Z.Izoria-J.Stopa, Richardson 2007.

8 c3!?

This was a novelty which I made up at the board. Having analysed it at home and compared it to the alternatives, I still consider it an interesting attempt for an advantage. The other options include:

a) 8 0-0 allows 8...♘cxd4 9 ♘xd4 ♗xe2 10 ♕xe2 ♘xd4 11 ♗xd4 ♕xd4 when White should have just enough compensation for the sacrificed pawn, but no real advantage.

b) 8 c4 has been tested in a few games, but I prefer not to rush this move as White is rather soft on the dark squares: 8...♕a5 (Bauer's suggestion of 8...♕d6!? is also interesting) 9 0-0 (or 9 d5 ♗xf3 10 ♗xf3 ♘xe3 11 fxe3 ♘e5 12 0-0 e6 13 ♘b3 ♕b6 and Black

had good counterplay in P.Scharrer-A.Panjkovic, Trento 2008) 9...♗xf3 10 ♘xf3 was K.Spraggett-R.Perez, Figueira da Foz 2008, and now after Bauer's suggestion of 10...e6 Black has a decent position with strong pressure against the d4-pawn.

8...e5

This certainly seems like the most principled idea for Black.

9 c4!

Ironically, after rejecting c2-c4 on the previous move, White plays it a full tempo down! I was quite proud of this novel idea.

9...♕a5 10 d5

The point, of course, is that with ...e6 no longer a possibility, White obtains some much-needed stability in the centre.

10...♗xf3 11 ♗xf3 ♘cd4

A natural move, but it leads to a position with a stable advantage for White.

The critical test of White's idea may well be 11...♘xe3 12 fxe3 ♗c5!? with extremely double-edged play; Black develops quickly and relies on tactics to keep his position together, although there is an obvious risk that if White manages to achieve full coordination, a subsequent a3 and b4 could come with considerable force. Practical tests are needed here, but it looks to me that 13 ♕b3! (13 a3 ♗xe3 14 b4 ♕b6 15 c5 ♕a6 16 ♗e2 b5 is messy, but overall Black seems to be at least equal here; also after 13 ♔f2 f5 14 ♘b3 ♕b6 15 ♘xc5 ♕xc5 16 ♕b3 ♘e7 Black is fine) 13...♘e7 14 0-0-0 is the critical direction.

12 ♗g4

12 0-0 is also good.

12...♔b8

13 0-0

13 a3 c6 14 b4 ♕a6 is rather messy.

13...♕b4

Black hastens to improve his queen before White has time for a3 and b4.

14 ♗xf5 ♘xf5 15 ♕c2 ♘xe3 16 fxe3 ♗c5 17 ♖ae1

The opening has been a success for White, who has a slight lead in development, more space in the centre and the superior minor piece.

17...♕b6 18 ♕d3 f6 19 ♘e4 ♖he8 20 a3

20 b4! would have been marginally more accurate, as taking the pawn would be much too risky for Black. Following 20...♗f8 21 ♖b1 White has a slightly improved version of the game, as his rook is more useful on b1 than e1.

20...♗f8 21 b4 ♕e6!?

Bryson exploits the pin on the d-file to evacuate his queen from the danger zone.

22 ♖d1 ♕g4 23 ♘f2 ♕g6 24 e4 c5!?

Otherwise 25 c5 would have been highly unpleasant for Black.

25 ♖b1?!

Around here I lost the thread slightly. I should explain that this was a local league match with a time control of just one hour for the first thirty moves and I was running low on time. After the correct 25 ♕e3! ♖c8 26 d6! Black would have been in serious trouble.

25...♖d7 26 ♘d1 ♖ed8 27 ♕f3 ♖c8 28 ♘e3 ♗e7 29 ♕f5 ♕xf5 30 ♖xf5 ♗d8 31

♔f1

It was worth considering 31 b5!? ♗a5 32 ♔f2 ♗c3 33 ♔e2 ♗d4 34 g4, intending a minority attack on the kingside.

31...cxb4!? 32 axb4 a5!

Bryson takes the opportunity to clear some space for his rooks. I was a bit annoyed with myself for failing to make the most of my position, but fortunately even here White keeps a slight plus.

33 bxa5 ♗xa5 34 ♔e2 ♗c3 35 ♔d3 ♗d4 36 ♘c2 ♗c5 37 ♖ff1 ♖d6 38 ♖b3 ♖a6 39 ♖a1 ♖xa1 40 ♘xa1 ♔c7 41 ♖b5 ♗g1?

41...b6 was essential.

42 c5!

Presumably Black was expecting the lazy 42 h3, but this pawn is irrelevant as the game will be decided on the queenside.

42...♖a8

42...♗xh2 43 d6+ ♔c6 44 ♔c4 is horrible for Black.

43 ♘b3 b6?

Black's last chance was 43...♖a6! 44 d6+ ♔c6 45 ♖a5 ♗f2 46 ♖xa6+ bxa6 47

♔c4 ♗e1, although after 48 g4 White still has excellent winning chances.

44 ♖xb6 ♖a3

Black played his last move quickly, so perhaps in those brief few seconds he saw the reply 44...♗xc5, but only then noticed the simple refutation, 45 ♖c6+.

45 ♔c4 ♖a4+ 46 ♔b5 ♖xe4 47 d6+ ♔c8 48 ♔c6 1-0

That concludes our coverage of the 3...♗g4 system. Before moving on to lines with kingside castling, let us consider a slightly different way in which Black may prepare for queenside castling.

Game 7
J.Anderson-A.Aasum
Correspondence 2000

1 e4 d5 2 exd5 ♕xd5 3 ♘f3 ♘c6

This time Black develops the knight before the bishop.

The game actually started with the

Nimzowitsch Defence move order of 1...♘c6 2 ♘f3 d5 3 exd5 ♕xd5. I wondered about classifying it under that opening, but eventually decided that the character of the game was more in keeping with the Scandinavian.

4 ♘c3

White steers the game towards a main line (i.e. 3 ♘c3) Scandinavian in which the premature development of the knight on c6 gives White some additional opportunities.

4 d4 is possible, but then White must be ready for 4...e5!? (rather than 4...♗g4 5 ♗e2, transposing to the first six games).

4...♕a5

The main line. Black has tried several other queen retreats, each of which have certain drawbacks, as shown in the following lines:

a) 4...♕d8 5 d4 already leaves Black in some difficulties, bearing in mind that 5...♗g4?! 6 d5! ♘e5? can be refuted by 7 ♘xe5! ♗xd1 8 ♗b5+ c6 9 dxc6 with a winning position, F.Eid-G.Wijesurija, Madras 1995.

b) 4...♕d6 5 d4 ♘f6 6 ♘b5!? ♕d8 7 c4 a6 8 ♘c3 ♗g4 9 ♗e3 (9 d5 ♘e5 10 ♗e2 is also a touch better for White) 9...e6 10 ♗e2 ♗e7 11 0-0 0-0 12 h3 ♗h5 13 a3 left Black struggling for counterplay in T.Airapetian-O.Yuzhakov, Voronezh 2009. See Game 8 for more on positions of this type.

c) 4...♕h5 5 ♘b5! (5 ♗e2 is a good alternative, but it is hard to resist the temptation of forcing the enemy king to move at such an early stage) 5...♔d8 6 d4 and Black has tried three moves here, but none of them come close to equalizing:

c1) 6...a6 7 ♘c3 ♗f5 8 ♗e2 ♕g6 was seen in H.Mecking-A.Fernandez, Las Palmas 1975, and now the simple 9 ♘h4! ♕f6 10 ♘xf5 ♕xf5 11 ♗g4 ♕g6 12 ♗f3 leaves Black in a depressing position.

c2) 6...♘f6 is playable but uninspiring. The simple 7 ♗e2 gives White an excellent position, while Khalifman's suggestion of 7 d5!? is a promising pawn sacrifice.

c3) 6...♗g4 should be met by 7 ♗f4! when the attack on c7 is awkward. Two replies have been tested:

c31) 7...♗xf3 8 ♕xf3 ♕xf3 9 gxf3 a6 10 ♘xc7 ♖c8 11 ♘d5 ♔e8 (11...♘xd4? 12 0-0-0 wins a piece) 12 0-0-0 and White was a pawn up for no compensation in R.Wittmann-G.Moser, Wuerttemberg 2000.

c32) 7...a6 8 d5 (8 ♘xc7 ♖c8 9 d5 is also strong) 8...♗xf3 9 gxf3 (White can even consider 9 dxc6+!? ♗xd1 10 cxb7

♖b8 11 ♗xc7+ ♔d7 12 ♗xb8 with more than enough compensation for the queen) 9...♘e5 10 ♘d4 ♘f6 11 ♕e2 ♘g6 12 ♗g3 ♔c8 13 0-0-0 and Black's position was a disorganized, underdeveloped mess in S.Sop-E.Kaplan, Kayseri 2010.

Returning to 4...♕a5:

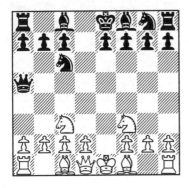

5 ♗b5!

5 d4 can be met by 5...♗g4 followed by castling with interesting play for Black, but White has a more promising way to target the knight on c6.

5...♗d7

5...♗g4 6 h3 ♗h5 7 ♕e2!? (7 g4 ♗g6 8 ♘e5 0-0-0! was somewhat better for White, but still not altogether clear in R.Garside-A.Stewart, correspondence 1988) 7...e6? (7...0-0-0 is better, but 8 ♗xc6 bxc6 9 g4 ♗g6 10 ♘e5 is still excellent for White) was seen in P.Gutierrez Castillo-V.Smirnov, Sydney 2007, and here White overlooked a nice shot: 8 ♕e5! 0-0-0 (White was threatening to win the queen) 9 ♕xh5 a6 when Black narrowly avoids losing a whole piece, but his position remains

hopeless after 10 ♘g5 ♘f6 11 ♕d1 axb5 12 ♘xf7.

6 0-0 a6

Instead 6...0-0-0 7 d4 (7 ♖e1 is a good alternative) 7...e6!? (7...a6 8 ♗xc6 ♗xc6 9 ♘e5 transposes to note 'b' to Black's 8th move, below) 8 a3!? intends ♗e3 followed by b4, embarrassing the black queen. Black has attempted to thwart this plan with 8...♗b4 in a few games, but then the witty 9 ♖b1! ♗xc3 10 bxc3 gave White excellent prospects in V.Cotos-V.Mamonovas, correspondence 2005.

7 ♗xc6 ♗xc6 8 d4

Black has the two bishops, but he is behind in development and the threat of ♘e5 is not easy to meet.

8...f6?!

Black resorts to drastic measures to stop his opponent's idea, but he is playing with fire, making such a move while behind in development. He should have tried one of the following alternatives, not that any of them look particularly appealing:

a) 8...♘f6 is too simplistic and 9 ♘e5

is rather awkward for Black.

b) 8...e6 9 ♘e5 ♗d6 10 ♘xc6 bxc6 11 ♕g4 ♘e7 was seen in M.Rabrenovic-V.Zolotukhin, Budva 2009. At this point it seems to me that White could have safely grabbed the g-pawn and, indeed, after 12 ♕xg7 ♕h5 (or 12...♖g8 13 ♕xh7) 13 g3 ♖g8 14 ♕h6 Black does not have enough compensation.

c) 8...♕h5 9 d5 0-0-0 was tried in R.Felgaer-N.Vlassov, Moscow 2004.

Now 10 ♕d4! ♘f6 (or 10...♔b8 11 ♗e3 b6 12 g4! when the black queen runs out of squares) 11 ♘e5 ♘xd5 12 ♘xc6 bxc6 13 ♕a7 would have put Black in trouble.

d) 8...0-0-0 has been the most popular move, but Black has problems here too after 9 ♘e5 ♗e8 10 b4! ♕b6 (after 10...♕xb4 11 ♕f3 ♕xd4 12 ♖b1 c6 13 ♗f4 White had a huge initiative in A.Vunder-K.Alekseenko, St Petersburg 2008) 11 ♗e3. Black has tried two moves here, but his problems are severe in both cases:

d1) 11...f6 12 ♘d3 ♕c6 13 ♘c5 e6 was reached in S.Zeidler-M.Simons,

British League 2007, and here White should have chosen either 14 ♕e2 or 14 ♕g4, with difficult problems for Black in both cases.

d2) 11...e6 was Black's choice in the most frequently quoted game in this variation, which continued as follows: 12 ♖b1 f6 13 ♘c4 (13 d5 and 13 ♕f3!? both look promising as well) 13...♕c6 14 ♘a5! ♕xc3 15 ♖b3 ♗xb4 16 ♖xc3 ♗xc3. Black has sufficient material for the queen and seems to be surviving, but White's next move shatters any such illusions.

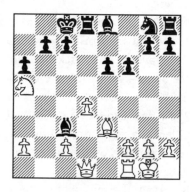

17 ♘xb7! ♔xb7 18 ♕b1+ (18 ♕g4 and ♖b1+ was also crushing) 18...♔a8 19 ♕b3 ♗xd4 20 ♗xd4 ♗b5 21 c4 ♗c6 22 ♕a3 ♗b7 23 ♕c5 ♔b8 24 ♖b1 ♔c8 25 ♕a7 1-0 J.Emms-L.Kristensen, Esbjerg 1996. Returning to 8...f6:

9 d5!

9 ♗e3 and 9 ♕e2 both give White some advantage, but the text move is by far the most energetic continuation. White gives up at least one pawn in order to increase his advantage in development.

9...0-0-0 10 b4!

This is the key idea which justifies White's previous move.

10...♕xb4

10...♕b6 is no better: 11 ♖b1 ♗xd5 (the tactical skirmish will end in White's favour, but Black had no real choice as ♗e3 was a terrible threat) 12 ♘xd5 ♕c6 13 c4 e6 (if 13...♕xc4 14 ♘e3) 14 ♗f4! exd5 15 ♘d4 ♕d7 16 c5! and Black is a pawn up, but he is about to be annihilated on the queenside.

11 ♗d2

Breaking the pin along the d-file while threatening to harass Black's queen.

11...♗b5?!

Allowing White to open additional lines on the queenside. 11...♗d7 was a better try, although 12 ♕e2!? will leave Black hard-pressed to defend against the impending attack along the b-file, but 12 ♖b1 ♕c4 is not so clear.

12 ♖b1 ♕c5 13 ♘xb5 axb5

14 a4!

Beginning a cascade of sacrifices, which sees White losing all his queenside pawns but developing a crushing attack in the process.

14...bxa4

After 14...♕xd5 15 ♖xb5 White will soon break through on the b-file.

15 c4! ♕xc4

At least Black is playing consistently, grabbing every pawn in sight.

15...e6 was no better in view of 16 ♕xa4 ♕a3 17 ♕c2 or 16 ♖b4!? exd5 17 ♖xa4, with a decisive attack in both cases.

16 ♖b4 ♕xd5 17 ♕xa4 e5 18 ♖b5!

This clever move exploits the fact that the queen has no satisfactory escape square.

18...♝c5

Losing without a fight, but the alternatives 18...♛c6 19 ♜c1, 18...♛d6 19 ♝b4, and 18...♛e6 19 ♜a5 were all equally hopeless.

19 ♝e3 b6 20 ♝xc5 ♛b7

Or 20...bxc5 21 ♜fb1 and Black can resign.

21 ♝xb6 cxb6 22 ♜c1+ ♚b8 23 ♛b4 1-0

A great game by Anderson. We will now turn our attention to set-ups in which Black aims for solidity through short castling.

Part 2 – Set-ups with short castling after 2...♛xd5

So far we have focused on variations involving long castling from Black. This is certainly the most critical direction, but there are many players who prefer to avoid a sharp theoretical fight, instead opting to defend a slightly worse position. In the next game a world-class player demonstrates how to make an opponent suffer in just such a situation.

Game 8
A.Grischuk-M.Feygin
European Club Cup,
Ohrid 2009,

1 e4 d5 2 exd5 ♛xd5 3 ♞f3 ♞f6

3...e5?! is a questionable sideline which will be examined in the next game.

4 d4

White's typical plan over the next few moves is unassuming but nonetheless quite promising: the bishop will go to e2 and the king will park itself on g1, while the c-pawn will advance to c4 and the knight will follow behind on c3. It is at this point that the advantage of the present set-up over the 3 ♞c3 Scandinavian becomes clear. In that variation the c3-knight is poorly placed and White will often go out of his way to relocate or exchange it. In the present system White takes his time, but ensures that when the knight does come forwards, it will be to a quality square.

4...c6

Black has several ways of arranging his pieces. In the majority of cases White's next few moves will be roughly the same, as will his general strategy of developing soundly and maintaining his extra space in the centre. Here is a brief summary of the range of set-ups available to Black:

a) 4...♘c6 gives White the option of 5 ♘c3 ♕a5 6 ♗b5 transposing to Game 7, although 5 c4!? followed by a quick d5 may be an even better way of embarrassing the knight.

b) 4...g6 5 c4 ♕d6 (5...♕d8 transposes to Game 10, which reaches the same position via the move order of 2...♘f6 3 ♘f3 ♘xd5 4 d4 g6 5 c4 ♘f6) 6 ♘c3 ♗g7 7 ♗e2 0-0 8 0-0 and White has the better prospects, as illustrated in the following two examples:

b1) 8...a6 9 h3 ♗f5 10 ♗e3 ♘e4 11 ♘d5 ♕d8 12 ♗f4 ♘d6 13 ♘c3 c6 14 ♖e1 b5 15 c5 ♘e4 was M.Malloni-N.Napoli, Rome 2009, and here 16 ♘e5! intending ♗f3 would have been nice for White.

b2) 8...♗g4 9 ♗e3 a6 10 ♕b3 ♘c6 11 ♖fd1 (11 ♖ad1 is equally good) 11...♘a5 12 ♕a4 b6 13 c5! when White has some initiative. After the inaccurate 13...♕d7?! 14 ♕xd7 ♘xd7 15 ♘d5 bxc5 16 h3!? ♗xf3 17 ♗xf3 ♖ab8 of M.Godena-B.Kurajica, Solin 2007, following 18 ♘xe7+ ♔h8 19 b3 cxd4 20 ♗xd4 Black faces a depressing endgame.

c) 4...♗f5 5 ♗e2 e6 (5...c6 reaches the note to Black's fifth move in the main game; here we see Black attempting to save time by doing without this move, but to no great avail) 6 0-0 ♗e7 7 c4 ♕d8 8 ♘c3 0-0 9 ♘h4 ♗g6 10 ♘xg6 hxg6 11 ♗e3 and White has a stable edge thanks to his bishop pair and central control, W.Hoellrigl-K.Roos, Seefeld 1997.

d) 4...♗g4

5 ♗e2 e6 (Black plays just as in the main game, but once again he hopes to gain time by omitting ...c6, perhaps aiming to play ...c5 in one move) 6 0-0 ♗e7 7 c4 ♕d8 8 ♘c3 0-0 9 ♗e3 (White has no reason to alter his development)

9...♘bd7 10 ♕b3!? ♕c8 (or 10...b6 11 ♖ad1) 11 h3 ♗h5 12 ♖ad1 a6 13 ♕c2 (13 g4!? ♗g6 14 ♘h4) 13...c5 14 d5 exd5 15 ♘xd5 ♘xd5 16 ♖xd5 ♘f6 17 ♖d2 ♕c7.

We have been following the game J.Rowson-A.Martin, Southend 2002. Both sides have played consistently and at this point the most logical continuation looks to be 18 ♘h4!? ♗xe2 19 ♖xe2 when White maintains slightly the better prospects.

Returning to 4...c6:

5 ♗e2 ♗g4

The alternative bishop development, 5...♗f5, also falls slightly short of equality: 6 0-0 e6 7 c4 ♕d8 8 ♘c3 ♗e7 9 ♘h4!? (going after the bishop; 9 ♗e3 was a good alternative) 9...♗g6 10 ♘xg6 hxg6 11 ♗e3 ♗d6. This position was reached in P.Dobrowolski-M.Stein, Zakopane 2000, and now 12 g3! would have been the right way to thwart the attack on the h-pawn while restricting Black's remaining bishop.

6 0-0 e6 7 c4 ♕d6

The queen can also go to d8, but the general character of the game remains the same. Compared with the sharp lines in which Black castled on the queenside, here I see no great value in paying close attention to every possible set-up and move order, as the play is generally of a non-forcing character and White's general strategy remains the same in practically all lines. By now we have seen a good selection of illustrative game references, so from this point we will mainly focus on Grischuk's instructive handling of the white position.

8 ♘c3 ♗e7 9 ♗e3

This is White's typical scheme of development. Over the next few moves he will place his queen on d2 (or perhaps b3), followed by the rooks on d1 and e1 in most cases.

9...0-0 10 ♕d2

Another idea is 10 ♘e5!? ♗xe2 11 ♕xe2 ♘bd7, as in M.Kalinina-O.Bulakh, Evpatoria 2007, and now 12 f4 would have been consistent, intending ♖ad1 with a slight edge to White.

10...♗xf3

I am not sure why Black chose to make this exchange at this particular moment. It would probably have been better to wait for a move or two, although the general evaluation of the game remains about the same: White has a slight but pleasant edge and Black will struggle to generate counterplay. Here are a couple of other practical examples:

a) 10...♖e8 11 ♖fd1 (11 ♖ad1!?) 11...♘a6 12 a3 ♗xf3 13 ♗xf3 ♘c7 14 g4!? (14 ♗f4 ♕d7 15 ♗e5 is a good alternative)

14...g6? (Black should have preferred 14...♖ed8, creating an escape square on e8 for the knight) 15 g5 ♘h5 (15...♘d7?? 16 ♘e4 traps the queen) 16 ♘e4 ♕d8 17 ♗xh5 gxh5 18 ♕e2 and Black was already busted in M.Pruja Ramirez de Cartagen-C.Coll Ortega, Vila Seca 2010.

b) 10...♖d8 11 ♖fd1 (11 ♖fe1 and 11 a3!? were decent alternatives) 11...♕b4 12 b3 (another idea was 12 ♘e5!? ♗xe2 13 ♕xe2 ♘bd7 14 f4! with a slight edge) 12...♕a5?! (slightly careless, but

Black had failed to equalize in any case) 13 ♘d5! ♕xd2 (the computer suggests the exchange sacrifice 13...♖xd5!?, although Black would clearly have been struggling here too) 14 ♘xe7+ ♔f8 15 ♘g6+ hxg6 was the course of V.Lezhepekova-A.Rakhmangulova, Herceg Novi 2008. Here the most accurate continuation would have been 16 ♖xd2 intending h3 when Black will be virtually forced to exchange on f3, leaving White with two bishops against two knights, which adds up to a substantial and risk-free advantage.

11 ♗xf3

White's bishop pair gives him a long-term advantage.

11...♖d8 12 ♖fd1 ♘bd7 13 ♖ac1 ♕c7 14 ♕e2 ♖e8

The rook is determined to maintain its distant observation of the white queen.

15 g3 ♖ad8 16 ♗g2

There is no need for White to rush into a direct conflict, so Grischuk wisely spends a few moves tidying up his kingside.

16...a6

Black continues to wait. The attempt to play actively with 16...e5 should be met by 17 d5 when White stands better – compare Game 39 in Chapter Five (Mamedov-Mirzoev).

17 h3 ♗d6 18 a3 e5

19 c5!

19 d5 was a decent alternative, but the text move is the strongest. White gains additional space and creates a dark-squared pawn wedge which restricts the enemy bishop.

19...♗f8 20 b4 exd4 21 ♖xd4 ♘e5 22 ♖cd1 ♖xd4 23 ♖xd4 ♕c8

White has a clear strategic advantage thanks to his two bishops and extra space. Looking ahead to a future endgame, we may note that Black's queenside pawns have already been fixed on light squares.

24 g4!?

For the time being it is difficult to improve White's pieces, so Grischuk decides that a kingside advance is the best way to make progress. It was worth considering 24 f4 ♘g6 25 ♕d3

with the same general idea, but without giving away any dark squares in the centre.

24...h6 25 f4 ♘g6 26 f5 ♘e5 27 ♕f2 ♖d8

Black could have minimized his disadvantage with 27...♗e7! intending ...♗d8-c7.

28 ♕d2 ♗e7 29 ♗f2 ♖d7 30 ♕e2 ♕c7 31 ♖xd7 ♘fxd7 32 ♗g3 ♗f6

It was worth considering 32...a5!? to begin liquidating the queenside pawns, although Black's position would still remain somewhat unpleasant. In the game we see Grischuk maintaining control while gradually creeping forwards:

33 ♘e4 ♕d8 34 ♘d6 b6 35 cxb6 ♕xb6+ 36 ♗f2 ♕b8 37 ♘e4 ♕b5 38 ♘xf6+ ♘xf6 39 ♕xb5 axb5

It is hard to say if this position is technically winning for White, but it is certainly not far off. This is not an endgame book and I have no intention of discovering the ultimate truth of the position here, so I will keep the remaining comments to a minimum.

40 ♗g3 ♘fd7 41 ♔f2 f6 42 ♔e3 ♔f7 43 ♔d4 ♔e7 44 ♗e4 ♔d6 45 ♗c2 ♔e7 46 ♗d1 ♔d8

Presumably Black rejected 46...♘c4 on account of 47 a4 ♘b2 48 axb5 ♘xd1 49 bxc6 ♘b6 50 b5, which indeed looks extremely dangerous for him.

47 h4 ♔e7 48 ♗f4 ♔d8 49 g5 hxg5 50 hxg5 ♔e7 51 g6!

When pressing in an endgame, it is almost always useful to establish a pawn so close to its promotion square.

51...♔e8

51...♔d8? can now be refuted by 52 ♗h6, so Black's movements are even more limited than before.

52 ♗b3 ♔e7 53 ♗g8 ♘f3+ 54 ♔e3 ♘fe5 55 ♔e4 ♔f8 56 ♗b3 ♔e7 57 ♗e3 ♘g4 58 ♗f4 ♘ge5 59 ♗e6 ♔e8

Despite his dominating position, White still has no immediate win, so Grischuk continues to wear his opponent down while gradually preparing to break on the queenside with a4.

60 ♗e3 ♔e7 61 ♗a7 ♔d6 62 ♗f2 ♔e7 63 ♗g3 ♔e8 64 ♔d4 ♘f3+ 65 ♔d3 ♘fe5+ 66 ♔c3 ♔e7 67 ♗f2 ♔d6 68 ♗e3 ♔e7 69 ♔b3 ♘g4 70 ♗g1 ♘ge5 71 a4 bxa4+ 72 ♔xa4 ♘d3 73 ♔a5

White could have put the result beyond doubt by means of 73 ♗xd7! ♔xd7 74 ♗d4 (threatening to take on f6) 74...♔e8 75 ♗c5 when Black's king is paralysed by the need to prevent ♗f8 and he has no good defence against ♔a5-b6.

73...♘7e5 74 ♗b3 ♔d6 75 ♗e3 ♘g4 76 ♗d2 ♘de5 77 ♔b6 ♘d7+?

Feygin has defended stubbornly, but he finally cracks. It was essential to play 77...♘d3 or 77...♘f3, both of which would have left White with plenty of work to do.

78 ♔b7 ♘de5 79 ♗f4!

Zugzwang.

79...♔e7

There was nothing better:

a) After 79...c5 80 b5 the b-pawn decides the issue.

b) 79...♘f2 loses to 80 ♗xe5+ or 80 ♗h6.

c) 79...♔d7 80 ♗e6+ ♔d8 81 ♔b6 ♘d3 82 ♗d6 and White is winning: for instance, 82...♘ge5 83 ♗f8 ♘d7+ 84 ♗xd7 ♔xd7 85 ♔b7 ♔e8 86 ♗xg7 ♔e7 87 ♗h6 ♘xb4 88 ♗e3 when White picks up the c-pawn and Black is unable to sacrifice his knight for White's two remaining pawns.

80 ♔c7 ♘f2 81 ♗xe5 fxe5 82 ♔xc6

White finally wins a pawn and the passed b-pawn decides the game.

82...♘d3 83 b5 e4 84 b6 e3 85 ♗d1 ♘e5+ 86 ♔d5 ♘d7 87 b7 ♔f6 88 ♔d6 ♘b8 89 ♗e2 1-0

The following game is the last in the 2...♕xd5 section. It features a dubious move order which is rarely played, but we should consider it anyway in order to inflict the maximum punishment on any opponent who dares to chance it.

1 e4 d5 2 exd5 ♕xd5 3 ♘f3 e5?!

Black plays the very move which White's third move was designed to prevent! (Compare the position after 3 d4, after which 3...e5 is quite respectable.)

4 ♘c3

White has an improved version of a normal Scandinavian, as he can use the pawn on e5 as a lever to open up the centre and exploit his advantage in development.

Just as in some other games, I have adapted the move order to fit our purposes. In this instance the actual move order was 1...e5 2 ♘f3 d5 3 exd5 ♕xd5?! 4 ♘c3.

4...♕e6 5 ♗e2

White is spoiled for choice with 5 ♗b5+!? being a promising alternative.

5...c5!?

Black makes another non-developing move in an effort to keep the centre closed.

5...♘c6 can be a considered a reversed Centre Game (1 e4 e5 2 d4 exd4 3 ♕xd4 ♘c6, etc) with a full extra tempo for White; a significant asset, considering his development advantage and the awkward position of the enemy queen in the centre. Following 6 0-0 ♗d7 7 d4 exd4 8 ♘xd4 ♘xd4 9 ♕xd4 White was clearly better in A.Kolev-J.Llacuna Roca, Salou 2005.

6 0-0 ♘c6 7 ♗b5 f6 8 d3 ♘ge7

9 ♘d2!

9 ♖e1 is a decent move, but White is playing with a clear plan of opening the f-file.

9...♘f5 10 ♗c4 ♕d7 11 ♘de4 ♔d8?!

Black's position was already difficult, but this was hardly the way to go about improving it.

12 f4!

Simple and strong. Black's play has not been of the highest quality, but when you have a difficult position as early as move 4 these things can happen. I will keep the remaining comments fairly light.

12...h5 13 fxe5 ♘xe5 14 ♗f4 ♘g6

After 14...♘xc4 15 dxc4 ♕xd1 16 ♖axd1+ intending ♘b5 Black has serious problems.

15 ♕d2 b6 16 ♗d5

16 ♖ae1 ♗b7 17 ♘b5 ♘xf4 18 ♕xf4 a6 19 ♗e6!? ♕xb5 20 ♗xf5 was also strong.

16...♗b7 17 ♗xb7 ♕xb7

18 a4!

White has done everything right so far and now he opens a second front of attack.

18...♕d7 19 a5 b5 20 ♕f2 ♗e7 21 ♗e3!

Better than 21 ♘xc5 ♗xc5 22 ♕xc5 ♕d4+ 23 ♕xd4+ ♘xd4 which gives Black some chances to resist.

21...♘xe3 22 ♕xe3 b4 23 ♘e2 ♖c8 24 d4!

Putting even greater pressure on the defender by threatening to open the centre.

24...♖e8 25 ♖ad1 c4 26 ♘2g3 ♗f8 27 ♘xh5

White picks up a pawn without relinquishing any of his other advantages. Black fights hard, but eventually succumbs.

27...♖c6 28 ♘f4 ♘xf4 29 ♕xf4 ♕d5 30 ♘c5 ♖c7 31 c3 b3 32 a6 ♖c8 33 ♕g3 ♕h5 34 ♔h1 ♔e7 35 ♖de1+ ♔f7 36 ♘e4 ♕g6 37 ♕h3 ♖cd8 38 ♘d2 ♔g8 39 ♘xc4 ♖xe1 40 ♖xe1 ♖e8 41 ♖f1 ♖e2

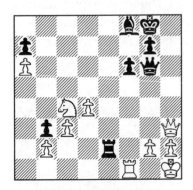

Black seems to have obtained some activity, but White has everything under control. It is important that the knight can maintain its defence of the b2-pawn from a stable position.

42 ♕f3 ♕e8 43 h3 ♕e6 44 d5 ♕e4 45 ♕xe4 ♖xe4 46 ♘a5 ♖e2 47 ♘xb3 ♖xb2 48 ♘d4

White remains two pawns up and the troublesome b-pawn has perished. The rest is easy.

48...♖d2 49 ♖b1 ♗c5 50 ♖b7 ♗xd4 51 cxd4 ♖xd4 52 ♖d7 f5 53 ♔g1 f4 54 ♔f2

🖺d3 55 🖺xa7 🖺xd5 56 🖺c7 🖺a5 57 a7 ♔h7 58 ♔f3 🖺a4 59 h4 ♔h6 60 ♔g4 1-0

With that final minor line out of the way, it is time to move on to Black's other significant second move.

Part 3 – 2...♘f6

Game 10
K.Norchenko-K.Kmiecik
Correspondence 2010

1 e4 d5 2 exd5 ♘f6

Black intends to capture on d5 with the knight, although occasionally he switches plans and reverts back to doing so with the queen. He also tries to lure his opponent into grabbing a pawn with 3 c4, but such a course of action has never interested me.

3 ♘f3

Once again, a note about the move order. This game actually continued 3 d4 ♘xd5 4 ♘f3 g6 5 c4, but I find the 3 ♘f3 move order more convenient. One point is that after 3 d4 Black has an interesting option in 3...♗g4!?. This move is probably not entirely sound, but it forces White to learn another set of variations, which most of us would prefer to avoid if given the choice. Occasionally Black chooses to meet 3 ♘f3 with 3...♗g4?!, but White can maintain an advantage by relatively simple means, as shown in the notes to Game 12.

3...♘xd5

Instead 3...♕xd5 4 d4 was seen in Game 8.

4 d4

Broadly speaking, White's strategy will be the same as we saw in Game 8 and its accompanying notes. White will castle short and play c4 and ♘c3, in one order or another. However, the present variation differs in that Black has some significant ways to sharpen the game, so White must be prepared for a tactical fight should the position on the board demand it.

4...g6

The main alternative of 4...♗g4 is

the subject of Game 11, while 4...♗f5 and other alternatives will be considered in Game 12.

5 c4!

The move order is important; in order to achieve the set-up I have in mind, White must chase the knight from the centre before developing any more kingside pieces.

5...♘b6

5...♘f6 is not a bad move, but the knight blocks the long diagonal and hampers Black's counterplay, so this is rarely seen. After 6 ♘c3 ♗g7 7 h3!? (it is worth investing a tempo to prepare ♗e3 without allowing ...♘g4) 7...0-0 8 ♗e3 White has a slight but stable edge and it is hard to suggest a way for Black to generate counterplay.

6 ♘c3 ♗g7 7 c5!

The point of White's play is to develop the bishop on the active c4-square instead of e2.

7...♘d5

7...♘6d7 8 ♗c4 0-0 9 0-0 gives White easy play: for instance, 9...b6 10 ♖e1 ♗b7 11 ♗g5 ♘f6 12 ♘e5 ♘c6? 13

♗a6! and White won material in Kr.Georgiev-L.Pecot, Maromme 1994.

8 ♗c4 ♘xc3

8...c6 is less challenging and after 9 0-0 0-0 10 ♖e1 Black has a hard time, as demonstrated by the following examples:

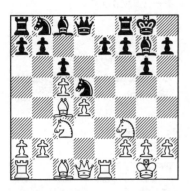

a) I encountered 10...♘xc3 in a blitz game a few years ago: 11 bxc3 b5?! (Black was worse anyway, but he should at least have kept the option of ...b6) 12 ♗b3 ♗g4 13 ♗g5 ♗f6 14 ♗xf6 exf6 15 h3 ♗f5 16 a4! a5 17 ♕e2 bxa4 18 ♖xa4 when White had a huge advantage in A.Greet-H.Stefansson, Beijing (blitz) 2008. I made a complete mess of the position, as can happen in blitz, but eventually picked up a 'rightful' victory after my opponent mishandled a rook endgame while playing for a win.

b) 10...♗g4 11 ♗g5 ♘f6 12 h3 ♗xf3 13 ♕xf3 ♘bd7 14 b4 h6 15 ♗h4 e6 16 ♖ad1 and White was in full control in P.Smirnov-E.Prokopchuk, Nefteyugansk 2002.

9 bxc3

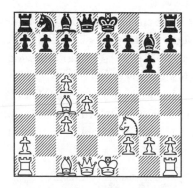

The change in the pawn structure is not unfavourable to White, whose d4-pawn enjoys secure protection.

9...0-0 10 0-0

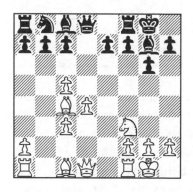

10...♘c6!

Playing for ...e5 looks like the most principled idea for Black.

10...b6 enables White to obtain good play as follows: 11 ♖e1!? bxc5 12 ♗g5 ♗f6 13 ♗h6 ♗g7 14 ♗xg7 ♔xg7 15 ♘e5!, which is a promising sacrifice. After 15...♗e6?! (Black immediately falters; 15...cxd4? 16 ♘xf7 and 15...c6 16 d5! were also difficult for him, so 15...e6 looks best, although 16 ♕f3 c6 17 dxc5 ♕e7 18 ♕e3 gives White excel-

lent chances) 16 ♗xe6 fxe6 17 ♘f3!? (17 dxc5 also gives White a clear plus) 17...♖f6 18 ♘g5 ♕d5 19 ♘e4 Black faced insurmountable problems in Y.Quesada Perez-F.Rodriguez, Cuba 2000.

11 ♖e1 ♗g4 12 ♗g5

Both sides continue to develop rapidly and the game is nearing its critical phase.

12...h6!

Time is of the essence! Indeed, 12...♕d7 is too slow and White gains a comfortable edge after 13 h3 ♗xf3 14 ♕xf3 e6 (also after 14...e5 15 d5 ♘a5 16 c6 bxc6 17 dxc6 ♕f5 18 ♕xf5 gxf5 19 ♗d5 Black has some problems) 15 ♖ab1 ♖ab8 16 h4 h6 17 ♗f6 by when her advantage was becoming quite serious in J.Jackova-A.Koubkova, Klatovy 1998.

13 ♗h4 g5!

Once again Black has no time to lose. He must execute the intended ...e5 as quickly as possible and if he has to weaken his kingside then so be it.

14 ♗g3 e5

The consistent move. Others:

a) 14...e6? is too slow and after 15 ♖b1 the initiative is with White.

b) 14...b6 is not a bad move, although it seems less principled than the text. Here 15 h3 ♗h5 16 ♗e2 e6 (16...bxc5 17 ♕a4 ♘b8 18 ♖ad1! gives White fine compensation, as pointed out by Donev) 17 ♕a4 ♘e7 occurred in N.De Firmian-T.Thorhallsson, Akureyri 1994, and now 18 ♕a3!? looks logical, reinforcing the c5-pawn and keeping the more active position.

15 d5 ♘a5 16 ♗f1

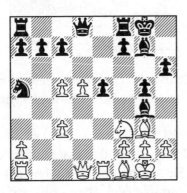

We have reached a critical position, from which Black can try a few different ideas.

16...♖e8!?

Apart from this sensible continuation, we should also consider:

a) 16...e4!? is a reasonable move which has not yet been tested: 17 ♖xe4 ♗xf3 (after 17...f5 18 ♖xg4 fxg4 19 ♘e5 White has great compensation for the exchange) 18 ♕xf3 ♕xd5 19 ♖d1 ♕xc5 20 ♖d7 ♕xc3 21 ♕f5 ♘c6 22 ♗xc7! and White keeps some initiative, as pointed

out by Roiz.

b) 16...c6 17 d6 f6 18 h3 ♗d7 was played in D.Lima-E.Scarella, Buenos Aires 2005. Now 19 ♘d2! looks logical, intending ♘b3.

c) 16...f6 17 h3 (17 ♕a4!? ♗xf3 18 gxf3 is also interesting; Black should respond with 18...b6!, rather than 18...c6 19 d6 b6 20 ♗h3!) 17...♗h5

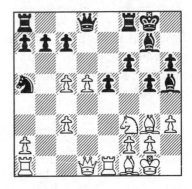

18 ♕d3! c6 was the course of A.Kovalev-D.Pluemer, Dresden 2009. At this point Watson points out the improvement 19 d6! when White has some initiative: for instance, 19...b6 20 ♕f5 bxc5 21 ♖ad1 with more than enough compensation.

17 ♕a4!?

White allows his kingside structure to be damaged, hoping to develop strong play on the light squares. 17 h3 ♗h5 18 ♕d3 looks like a sensible alternative, after which I also prefer White's position – compare note 'c' to Black's last move.

17...♗xf3 18 gxf3 b6

With the positional threat of ...♘b7, forcing the c-pawn to give way, after which the knight can settle on the d6-square. If Black can achieve this then he will stand better, so White must react energetically.

19 &b5! &f8

19...&e7 looks more natural. Presumably Black was put off by 20 &ad1 &b7 21 d6, although the position after 21...&e6 is by no means easy to assess.

20 &ad1

The d5-pawn was en prise.

20...&b7

21 &c6!

This temporary pawn sacrifice enables White to maintain the initiative.

21...&xc5 22 &c2 &b8

The exchange sacrifice 22...f6 23 &xa8 &xa8 looks tempting; the bishop on g3 is entombed and if Black can find time to harmonize his pieces then he will stand better. Fortunately White can throw a spanner in the works with 24 &g6!, after which 24...&e8 25 &xe8 &xe8 26 f4! liberates the bishop and thus gives White excellent winning chances in the endgame.

23 &xe5 &xe5 24 &xe5 &f6 25 &e2

&bd8 26 &d4 &d6 27 &e3

White's extra space and control over the e-file are more significant than his pawn weaknesses.

27...f5 28 &e8!

A remarkable idea. The bishop does not really threaten anything, but it prevents the enemy pieces from using the f7- and g6-squares. Furthermore, I can imagine this move having a strong psychological impact, as there is something unsettling about an enemy piece lodging itself deep in the innermost reaches of one's defensive fortress.

28...&h8 29 c4 &f6 30 &d1 g4?!

Initiating a tactical sequence which favours White.

30...&g8 was better. In this case White retains the upper hand and could slowly aim to open the kingside, but the defender remains solidly placed for the time being.

31 fxg4 &e4 32 gxf5 &c3 33 &xc3 &xc3

Black has picked up an extra exchange in return for two pawns, but White's bishop has become powerful.

34 &g6 &d7

35 ♕e3! ♕xe3

Leading to a difficult endgame, but 35...♕g7 36 ♔h1 ♖e7 37 ♕d2 intending ♖g1 was also unappealing for Black.

36 fxe3 ♖e7

Alternatively after 36...♔g7 37 ♔f2 ♔f6 38 ♔f3 ♔e5 39 ♖d4! White drives the king away.

37 ♔f2 ♖e4 38 ♔f3!

White can afford to let the c-pawn go – it is the central pawns which must be advanced!

38...♖xc4

38...♖h4 39 e4 does not change much.

39 e4 ♔g7 40 e5 ♖c3+ 41 ♔e4 ♖c4+ 42 ♔e3 ♖c5

42...♖d8 would have been met by 43 ♗h5! followed by f6+.

43 ♖g1!

Powerful play from Norchenko, who has seen that he can give up another pawn in order to continue advancing his two passers.

43...♖xd5 44 f6+ ♔h8 45 ♔e4 ♖d2 46 f7! ♖xa2 47 ♔f5 ♖f2+ 48 ♔e6 ♖b8 49 ♔e7 1-0

Black resigned as he is helpless against the plan of e6 and ♔d7.

Game 11
J.Noomen-T.Thomson
Correspondence 2004

1 e4 d5 2 exd5 ♘f6 3 ♘f3 ♘xd5 4 d4 ♗g4

This is Black's second most popular reply, after 4...g6. Black develops the bishop actively in preparation for ...e6, but the downside is that the bishop may become a target, as occurs in the present game.

5 h3

Generally it is useful for White to insert this move, in order to be able to throw in g2-g4 at a moment's notice.

5 c4 has certain advantages, though: for instance, after 5...♘b6 6 c5 ♘d5 (6...♘6d7 should have been preferred) 7 ♕b3 b6?? 8 ♘e5 I picked up an easy point in A.Greet-Jos.Hall, Frome 2006, as the attack on the g4-bishop, combined with the threat of a check on

b5, meant that Black was losing a piece by force.

5...♗h5

5...♗xf3 6 ♕xf3 is hardly worth analysing seriously. White has a space advantage and two bishops, which should be enough to ensure a lasting advantage.

6 c4

Just as in the previous game, White should develop the queenside before deciding what to do on the kingside.

6...♘b6

6...♘f6 is similar to the 2...♕xd5 set-up with short castling and could directly transpose to lines in Game 8 within a few moves. Alternatively, White can contemplate a timely g4 and ♘e5, just as in the present game.

7 ♘c3

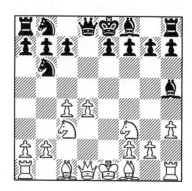

7...e6

Two other moves deserve attention:

a) 7...♘c6?! is premature: 8 d5 ♘e5 9 g4 ♘xf3+ 10 ♕xf3 ♗g6 11 c5 ♘d7 was seen in K.Szabo-J.Harmatosi, Zalakaros 2005, and here 12 ♗e3 looks simplest when White is in full control.

b) The sharp move 7...e5!? demands an equally principled response: 8 g4! exd4 9 ♘xd4 ♗g6 10 ♗g2 c6 11 0-0 ♗e7 12 f4! h6 13 f5 ♗h7. From here White has a pleasant choice:

b1) 14 c5!? is the most aggressive continuation: 14...♘6d7 (14...♗xc5 15 ♖e1+ gives White promising compensation after 15...♔f8 16 ♗e3 ♘a6 17 ♘e4, or 15...♗e7 16 f6 gxf6 17 ♗xh6) 15 g5!! when White obtained a powerful attack and won in fine style in P.Svidler-A.Dreev, Elista 1997.

b2) For those who prefer a more straightforward approach, 14 b3!? 0-0 15 ♗f4 gives White a stable positional advantage thanks to the rotten bishop on h7.

8 g4!

This is the most ambitious and promising way of meeting Black's chosen set-up.

8...♗g6 9 ♘e5

White has an active position and threatens h4, aside from the standard developing moves ♗g2 and ♗e3.

9...♘8d7

This has been the most popular reply. The most-notable alternatives are:

a) 9...♘c6 has been played in several games, but it is hard to believe that this can be a good idea: 10 ♘xc6 bxc6 11 ♗g2 ♕d7 12 ♕f3 0-0-0 was A.Sokolov-H.Ernst, Lenk 2000, and here Khalifman points out that 13 ♗e3 would have given White a clear plus, since 13...♘xc4?! 14 ♕e2! is too risky for Black.

b) 9...c5!? is more challenging and deserves serious attention despite the fact that it has not been played in many games. It is worth considering two responses:

b1) When I encountered this position over the board I tried 10 ♗e3 cxd4 11 ♕xd4 ♕xd4 12 ♗xd4 ♘c6 13 ♘xc6 bxc6 and eventually went on to lose in A.Greet-D.Bryson, Glasgow 2010, although at this stage 14 c5! would have given White some chances to fight for the advantage.

b2) 10 d5! (I believe this is the strongest) 10...exd5 11 ♘xg6 hxg6 12 cxd5 ♗d6 (after 12...♗e7 White might

consider 13 h4!? ♗xh4 14 ♕e2+ ♔f8 15 ♗g2 with a dangerous initiative for the pawn) 13 ♕e2+ ♔f8 (not 13...♕e7?? 14 ♘b5) 14 ♗e3 ♘8d7 15 0-0-0 which has been reached in a couple of games:

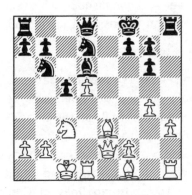

b21) 15...♘e5 was Black's choice in V.Tasic-J.Febland, correspondence 2006. Here the calm 16 ♔b1 looks like a sensible way to preserve White's edge, although he can also consider snatching a pawn with 16 ♗xc5!?.

b22) 15...♕e7 16 ♔b1 ♖e8 17 ♕c2 (17 ♗g2!?) 17...a6 18 ♗g2 ♘c4 19 ♗c1 b5 was M.Zavanelli-P.Spitz, correspondence 2004, and now after 20 b3 (20 ♘e4 also looks tempting) 20...♘cb6 21 ♖he1!? ♕xe1 (or 21...♕d8 22 ♘e4 with some initiative) 22 ♖xe1 ♖xe1 23 ♘e2! followed by ♕d2 White emerges with a material advantage.

Returning to 9...♘8d7:

10 ♘xg6 hxg6

White's bishop pair gives him good prospects, but if Black is given time to organize his position he will not be doing so badly. Thus White must strike while the iron is hot!

11 c5!

Forcing the opponent to make a difficult choice.

11...♘d5

This leads to a disadvantageous position for Black, but at least it enables him to stabilize the situation in the centre. 11...♘c8?! is riskier: 12 ♕b3 ♖b8 13 ♗e3 c6 (this leads to unfavourable complications, but it is hard to suggest a good alternative) 14 ♗f4! e5 15 ♗c4! ♕f6 16 ♗g3 (White has a powerful initiative) 16...♕f3 17 ♔d2! exd4 18 ♖ae1+ ♗e7 19 ♘e4 ♕xb3 20 ♗xb3 ♖a8 21 ♘d6+ ♔f8 22 ♘xf7 ♖h7 was B.Kutuzovic-R.Zelcic, Pula 2000.

Up to this point White's play has been exemplary and he could have sealed his opponent's fate in beautiful fashion, with 23 ♖xe7!!. Now both captures lead to a hopeless situation for Black:

a) 23...♔xe7 24 ♖e1+ ♔f8 (or 24...♔f6? 25 g5+ ♔f5 26 ♗e6 mate) 25 ♘g5 ♖h8 26 ♘e6+ followed by a lethal discovered check.

b) 23...♘xe7 24 ♗d6 ♖e8 25 ♖e1 ♖xh3 26 ♗e6! with a very aesthetic win, as 26...♘f6 is met by 27 ♘e5.

12 ♘xd5 exd5 13 ♕b3 ♕e7+ 14 ♗e3 0-0-0 15 0-0-0

Black has managed to survive the opening, but that is the end of the good news for him. He suffers from a lack of space and his bishop is badly restricted. Moreover, White's bishop pair is a useful asset and he can utilize his space advantage on the queenside to start an attack there at any moment.

15...♘b8

The best chance. After 15...c6 16 ♖e1 White is in full control and will soon play ♕a4 and b4 with a huge attack.

16 ♖e1 ♛d7

16...♘c6 17 ♗b5 ♛d7 18 ♗f4 leaves Black horribly tied up.

17 ♗g5!

Provoking the following pawn move, which restricts Black's bishop even more.

17...f6 18 ♗d2 a6

Preparing ...♘c6 without allowing the pin.

19 ♗g2

White finds a different role for his bishop. From this square it exerts constant pressure against d5 while conveniently keeping h3 defended.

19...♘c6 20 ♛d3 g5 21 ♖e2 g6 22 ♖he1 ♛f7

23 b4!

White has set up his pieces optimally and the time has come to take decisive action.

23...♗g7 24 a4 f5

Black seems to be beginning counterplay in the centre, but White has evaluated the complications perfectly.

25 b5! axb5

25...♘xd4 26 ♖e7 ♛f6 27 bxa6 bxa6

28 ♖7e5! is worse for Black than the game as his king is even weaker.

26 axb5 ♘xd4 27 ♖e7 ♛f6

After 27...♛f8 28 c6! White has a crushing attack.

28 ♖7e5!

Trapping the knight and thus forcing Black's next.

28...♛xe5 29 ♖xe5 ♗xe5 30 ♗xg5

Black temporarily has a slight material advantage of two rooks for a queen, but his loose pieces and unsafe king render his position close to being lost.

30...♘e6?!

30...♖de8 was a bit more resilient, although after 31 ♗e3 ♘e6 32 gxf5 ♘f4 33 ♗xf4 ♗xf4+ 34 ♔c2 Black will not survive in the long run.

31 ♗xd8 ♘f4 32 ♛a3 ♔xd8 33 ♛a8+ 1-0

Black resigned in view of 33...♔e7 34 ♛xb7, after which 34...♘xg2 35 b6 wins easily. He can resist a bit more stubbornly on move 34, but at top correspondence level his position is hopeless.

Game 12
V.Topalov-G.Kamsky
Wijk aan Zee 2006

In this game, the last of the chapter, we will deal with Black's alternatives on moves 3 and 4.

1 e4 d5 2 exd5 ♘f6 3 ♘f3 ♘xd5

Again, note that 3...♕xd5 transposes to Game 8.

The only other noteworthy alternative is 3...♗g4?!, but this move is too optimistic. After 4 ♗b5+! (the clearest route to an advantage) 4...♘bd7 5 h3 Black faces a difficult choice:

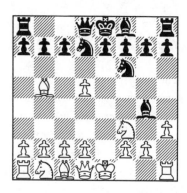

a) 5...♗h5 6 ♘c3 a6 7 ♗e2! redeploys the bishop which has done its job on the queenside. From this position Black can regain his pawn easily enough, but he cannot equalize: for instance, 7...♘b6 8 d4 ♘fxd5 (if 8...♘bxd5 9 ♘xd5 ♕xd5 10 c4 with some initiative) 9 ♘xd5 ♕xd5 10 0-0 e6 11 b3 ♗e7 (or 11...0-0-0 12 ♘e5 ♗g6 13 ♗b2) 12 c4 ♕d8 13 ♗e3 and White had a pleasant edge in B.Macieja-

A.Gershon, Paget Parish 2001.

b) 5...a6!? is a tricky move which forces White to play accurately if he is to maintain his advantage:

b1) 6 ♗e2 has been the most common reaction and has scored 100% for White, but my analysis indicates that it is not the most precise: 6...♗xf3 (not 6...♗h5?! 7 c4) 7 ♗xf3 ♘e5 (7...♘b6 8 d6!) 8 ♘c3 ♕d7 9 d4 ♘xf3+ 10 ♕xf3 was M.Santo Roman-P.Dias, Loures 1997, and here Black should have played 10...♖d8!, regaining his pawn and escaping with only a slight disadvantage.

b2) 6 ♗a4! is stronger when Black has tried two moves, neither of which come close to equalizing:

b21) 6...♗f5 7 ♘c3 b5 8 ♘d4! ♗g6 9 ♘c6 ♕c8 10 ♗b3 and White was clearly better in F.Hernandez Gallardo-J.Herms Agullo, Palma de Mallorca 2009.

b22) 6...♗xf3 7 ♕xf3 b5 8 ♗b3 ♘b6 9 ♘c3 when Black was a pawn down with weak light squares in P.Dias-H.Guetas Sanchez, La Roda 2007.

Returning to 3...♘xd5:

4 d4

Here we will deal with Black's alternatives to the two main lines of 4...g6 and 4...♗g4.

4...♗f5

This is by far the most significant of the said alternatives. Others do not demand much attention:

a) 4...♘c6?! is premature, as after 5 c4 ♘b6 6 d5 the knight must go to an unfavourable square.

b) 4...e6 and 4...c6 are rather passive, and in both cases White can obtain a safe edge with 5 c4 followed by ♘c3, ♗e2 and so on.

5 ♗d3

Exchanging the opponent's active bishop is White's most straightforward course of action.

I spent some time looking at 5 ♘h4!? which works well after 5...♗g6 6 ♘xg6 hxg6 7 g3! when the two bishops give White a stable edge in a position. However, 5...♗c8!? is slightly trickier. The best continuation is probably 6 c4 ♘b6 7 ♘f3, but then 7...♗g4 reaches a position discussed in the notes to the

previous game which is slightly outside the recommended repertoire, although White has reasonable chances to fight for an advantage here too.

5...♗xd3 6 ♕xd3 e6 7 0-0

White should not even think about pawn-grabbing with 7 ♕b5+? ♘c6 8 ♕xb7, as 8...♘db4 gives Black too many threats.

7...♘c6!?

Hoping to generate piece-pressure against White's centre.

7...c6 is more solid but rather passive and White obtains a safe edge with the help of simple development: 8 c4 ♘f6 9 ♘c3 ♗e7 10 ♗f4 0-0 11 ♖ad1 ♘bd7 12 ♕e2!? (12 ♖fe1 is also pleasant for White) 12...♖e8 13 ♖d3 ♕a5 14 ♖fd1 and White was in full control, O.Korneev-F.Carretero Ortiz, Seville 2011.

8 c4 ♘b6 9 ♘c3 ♗e7 10 ♗f4 g5?

Too ambitious. Black should have played more solidly in order to keep his disadvantage within reasonable bounds, as in the following game: 10...0-0 11 ♖ad1 ♕d7 12 ♘e4 ♘b4 13

♕b3 ♘c6 14 ♘c5 ♕c8 15 ♕c3, although White remained on top in A.Dreev-N.Vlassov, Internet 2001.

11 ♗g3!

11 ♗e3 is possible, but Topalov has correctly judged that he can sacrifice a pawn for a powerful initiative.

11...g4 12 ♘e5 ♘xd4

In the event of 12...♕xd4 13 ♕e2 ♕c5 14 ♘e4 ♕b4 15 ♘xc6 bxc6 16 ♗xc7 White regains the sacrificed pawn while keeping a strong initiative.

13 c5!?

Topalov throws another pawn on to the fire in an attempt to increase his initiative.

White could have obtained a stable edge by means of 13 ♖ad1 c5 14 ♘e2!, regaining his pawn while leaving plenty of problems for his opponent to solve.

13...♗xc5 14 ♖ad1

With the threat of ♘e4, winning a piece.

14...0-0!?

A risky decision, but it was arguably the best chance. Indeed, the alternatives were unappealing, for instance:

a) 14...♘c6 15 ♕e2 ♗d6 16 ♘b5! and Black is in trouble.

b) 14...♕e7 15 b4! 0-0-0 16 bxc5 ♘f3+ 17 gxf3 ♖xd3 18 ♖xd3 ♕xc5 19 ♖fd1 when White has too many pieces for the queen, as pointed out by Notkin.

15 ♘e4 ♗e7

16 ♘xg4!

More convincing than 16 ♕xd4 ♕xd4 17 ♖xd4 f5!, although even here White keeps a clear advantage after 18 ♖c1! (18 ♘c3?! c5 19 ♖f4 ♗g5 lets some of White's advantage slip) 18...fxe4 19 ♖xe4 – analysis by Notkin.

16...c5?

Supporting the knight is desirable in principle, but Black simply cannot afford the time for this. It must be said, though, that the alternatives were also highly unpleasant for him:

a) 16...♘f5 loses to 17 ♕c3 ♘d5 18 ♖xd5! exd5 19 ♘ef6+ followed by ♗e5.

b) 16...f5 17 ♘h6+ ♔g7 18 ♗e5+! ♔xh6 19 ♕h3+ ♔g6 20 ♖xd4 ♘d5 and now Notkin mentions 21 ♖d3 as winning, while the computer rates 21 g4! as even more conclusive.

c) According to the machine, the best chance was 16...f6!? 17 ♕xd4 ♕xd4 18 ♖xd4 f5, although Black faces a miserable endgame here.

17 b4?

This keeps a large advantage, but 17 ♗e5! would have won in a few short moves: 17...f6 18 ♘g5! ♘f5 (not 18...fxg5? 19 ♘h6 mate) 19 ♘h6+! ♔h8 (if 19...♘xh6 20 ♕xh7 mate, or 19...♔g7 20 ♘xe6+) 20 ♘gf7+ when White wins the queen and the game, as shown by Notkin.

17...♘d5

Also after 17...♘f5 18 ♕f3 ♘d5 19 bxc5 Black is in deep trouble.

18 bxc5

Again Topalov overlooks 18 ♗e5! with an immediate kill. His position is still overwhelming though.

18...♘f5 19 ♕f3 ♖c8

20 ♗d6

Notkin points out a strong alternative in 20 ♘e3!? ♘fxe3 21 fxe3, bringing the f1-rook into the game and planning ♘d6 next.

20...♘xd6

20...♗xd6 allows a neat refutation: 21 ♖xd5! ♗xh2+ (or 21...exd5 22 ♘ef6+ ♔g7 23 ♕xf5) 22 ♔xh2 ♕h4+ 23 ♔g1 exd5 24 ♘ef6+ ♚h8 25 ♕xf5 when White wins, as analysed by Notkin.

21 cxd6 ♗h4 22 d7!

Despite a few previous inaccuracies, Topalov has done enough to maintain a winning advantage and this precise move practically seals Black's fate.

22...♖c6

22...♖c2 is refuted by 23 ♘d6!: for instance, 23...♕xd7 (23...♗g5 24 h4!) 24 ♘h6+ ♚h8 (or 24...♚g7 25 ♕g4+) 25 ♘hxf7+ ♖xf7 26 ♘xf7+ ♚g8 27 ♘e5, etc.

23 ♘e5 ♖c7 24 ♕g4+ ♚h8 25 ♘d6 1-0

After 25...♖xd7 (25...♕f6 26 ♕h5 ♚g8 27 ♘g4 is crushing) White has a few ways to win, but by far the most attractive is 26 ♖xd5! ♖xd6...

...and now 27 ♕d4!! seals White's victory.

Conclusion

The lion's share of this chapter has been devoted to the 2...♕xd5 variation, specifically the branch beginning with 3 ♘f3 ♗g4 intending long castling. Although by and large the 3 ♘f3 system can be considered a low-maintenance option – at least by comparison to the sharp main lines which occur after 3 ♘c3 – there is no denying that the first seven games contained a great deal of ideas and analysis to digest. Still, I find the overall picture quite encouraging for White and I would expect this variation to become more popular over time.

The other two main branches (2...♕xd5 3 ♘f3 ♘f6, intending short castling, and 2...♘f6) each hold their own challenges, but once again I have faith in White's position, and believe that the recommended repertoire enables the first player to emerge from the opening with healthy prospects.

Chapter Two
Modern Defence

1 e4 g6 2 d4 ♗g7

3 ♘c3

This is my preferred move order. Against the majority of replies, I will be recommending an aggressive set-up with 4 f4, known as the Austrian Attack. I consider this the most principled set-up at White's disposal; since Black has chosen not to contest the central squares over the opening moves, White takes the opportunity to seize additional space, with the prospect of developing an attack later in the middlegame.

From here Black has a number of options:

Part 1 – 3...d6
We will begin by examining **3...d6**, Black's most popular move. Then after **4 f4** Black has several ideas:

Black's most frequently played option is 4...c6, which is usually a prelude to ...♛b6, although Black sometimes uses it to prepare queenside play with ...b5. After the natural reply 5 ♘f3 Game 13 features the main line of 5...♗g4, while Game 14 deals with the tricky sideline 5...♛b6, along with the rest of Black's 5th-move alternatives.

In Game 15 we will look at 4...a6, intending an early counterattack with ...b5. This is quite a challenging system which should be studied carefully. After that we will turn our attention to 4...♘d7 which has the principal aim of preparing ...c5. This plan has fallen out of fashion and Game 16 gives an idea as to why.

Part 2 – Unusual third moves

Next on the agenda are two slightly unusual third moves. In Game 17 we will address the ambitious 3...c5, while Game 18 deals with the even more eye-catching 3...d5.

Part 3 – The 'Modern Caro-Kann'

The final part of the chapter will focus on a very different interpretation of the Modern, in which Black aims for a light-squared strategy based on an early ...c6 and ...d5.

Game 19 shows how White should handle the blocked positions which arise after the sequence 1 e4 g6 2 d4 d6 3 ♘c3 c6 4 f4 d5 5 e5 h5.

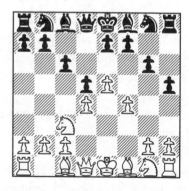

As we will see, Black can and should aim to reach this position with his bishop still on f8, as it has absolutely

no future on g7. Black can also play the position more dynamically and in Game 20 we will consider the system based on 2...♗g7 3 ♘c3 c6 4 f4 d5 5 e5 ♘h6 intending a quick ...f6.

Finally, Game 21 deals with an unusual but slightly tricky move order with 2...c6, against which I recommend an 'Accelerated Austrian' with 3 f4.

Part 1 – 3...d6

Game 13
I.Glek-E.Cekro
Belgian League 2001

1 e4 g6 2 d4 ♗g7 3 ♘c3

It is worth mentioning that the immediate 3 f4 allows Black a couple of attractive options in 3...c5 and 3...d5!?. We will see that both of these moves can also be played against 3 ♘c3, but White is better equipped to deal with them in this case.

3...d6 4 f4 c6

According to the database, this has been Black's most frequently played move here – with the exception of 4...♘f6, which takes us into the next chapter.

5 ♘f3 ♗g4

By pinning the knight, Black continues his policy of fighting for the centre using pieces rather than pawns. This has been the most popular choice, although several alternatives have been tried. These will be seen in Game 14.

6 ♗e3

White logically supports the centre.

6...♛b6

This is the consistent follow-up to Black's previous move. Less forcing alternatives such as 6...♘d7 allow White to obtain easy play with 7 h3 ♗xf3 8 ♛xf3 followed by castling and a subsequent advance in the centre and/or on the kingside.

7 ♛d2 ♗xf3 8 gxf3

White incurs a slight weakening of his kingside pawns. On the other hand, the bishop pair and open g-file are significant assets, especially when one factors in White's lead in development

and central domination.

8...♛a5

This move order is slightly unusual, but we soon transpose back into a normal position. Alternatives include:

a) 8...♘d7 has been more popular. The black queen does not have to move immediately, but nor will she want to remain on b6 indefinitely. For instance, after 9 0-0-0 0-0-0 (9...♛a5 is the main line, after which 10 ♔b1 transposes to the game) 10 ♗c4 Black is unable to play the natural move 10...e6? as then 11 d5 is too destructive.

b) It is worth mentioning that 8...♛xb2? is a bad idea: 9 ♖b1 ♛a3 10 ♖xb7 (the exchange of pawns has clearly benefited White, whose rook stands proudly on the seventh rank) 10...♘d7 (there is also 10...♘f6 11 ♗c4 when White is clearly better) 11 ♖c7! c5? (the lesser evil would have been to jettison the c-pawn, not that Black could hope to obtain any compensation for it) 12 ♗b5 ♖d8 13 e5! ♘h6 14 dxc5 ♘f5 15 cxd6 and with ♖xa7 coming next, White was already winning in M.Dimitriadis-J.Cobb, correspondence 1997.

9 0-0-0 ♘d7

9...b5 10 ♔b1 ♘d7 leads to the same position.

10 ♔b1

White takes a moment to improve the position of his king and defends the a2-pawn in anticipation of ...b5-b4. At this point Black must make an important choice.

10...b5

Cekro elects to start an attack. The strategy entails some risk, as Black's kingside pieces are undeveloped and his king lacks a safe haven. On the other hand, if he plays more solidly he may find it difficult to obtain any active play, as illustrated by the following examples:

a) 10...♘gf6 11 ♖g1 0-0-0 (11...♘h5 12 f5 0-0-0 13 ♗c4 ♖df8 was played in B.Laursen-H.Madsen, correspondence 1999, and now after 14 f4! Black must pay serious attention to the retreat ♗e2, which might even be preceded by e5, taking away the h5-knight's retreat square) 12 f5 ♕c7 13 ♕f2 ♖hg8 14 ♗h3 ♔b8 15 f4 ♘b6 16 ♗c1 ♘c4 17 e5 ♘d5 18 ♘xd5 cxd5 19 e6 ♕b6 20 ♔a1 fxe6 21 fxg6 hxg6 22 ♗xe6 ♖h8 23 ♖xg6 ♗f6 24 ♗xd5 sees White's strategy prevail. He has won a pawn and his light-squared bishop dominates the board, L.Kritz-V.Arapovic, Mallorca Olympiad 2004.

b) 10...0-0-0 11 ♖g1 ♔b8 (for 11...♘gf6 12 f5 see variation 'a') 12 ♗c4!

(White has a couple of decent alternatives available in 12 f5 and 12 ♖g5 ♕c7 13 d5, but I like this developing move the most) 12...e6 (12...d5 was played in J.Brueggemann-C.Meis, German League 1997, and now instead of the strange retreat to f1, White should have preferred 13 ♗b3 e6 14 f5! with a strong initiative, as pointed out by Khalifman) 13 f5! (once again this key resource enables White to get his light-squared bishop working) 13...exf5 14 ♗xf7 ♘e7 15 h4 ♖hf8 16 ♗b3 when with two powerful bishops, a central pawn majority and a clear plan of attack on the kingside, White stood clearly better in I.Smikovski-A.Utkin, St Petersburg 2002.

11 h4!

White begins to soften up his opponent's kingside.

11...♘b6 12 h5!

This method of handling the position can be considered a near-refutation of Black's opening system. In the past it was more common for White to play moves like 12 ♗d3 or even 12 b3 in order to prevent the black knight from hopping to c4. Although these two moves are not bad and offer reasonable chances for an advantage, it turns out that White does have to worry about the knight invasion and can instead press on with his own attack. The results have simply been overwhelming: according to the database, White has scored a massive nine wins, with two draws and no defeats.

12...b4

In one game Black tried the tricky 12...♖b8, but White's reaction was convincing: 13 hxg6 fxg6 (perhaps Black should have considered 13...hxg6, although here too after 14 ♖xh8 ♗xh8 15 ♕h2 ♗g7 16 f5 White's attack looks the faster) 14 ♔a1 (14 b3!?) 14...♘a4 (after 14...♘c4 15 ♗xc4 bxc4 16 f5 ♕b4 17 ♖b1 White defends his king easily, but the same cannot be said for Black) 15 ♘xa4 ♕xa4 (15...♕xd2 16 ♖xd2 bxa4 17 ♗h3 is highly promising too) 16 f5 gxf5 17 ♕g2 ♗f8 18 e5 and White has a crushing attack, M.Pichler-A.Padros Simon, correspondence 1981.

13 ♘e2 ♘c4 14 ♕d3

14...♘xe3

Black can also try 14...d5, keeping his knight on c4. In such situations White's main concern will be defending against the plan of ...♖b8 and ...♘a3+ (or ...♘c3+ in related positions with the knight on a4). Fortunately he has enough pieces in close proximity to the queenside to deal with such 'cheap' tricks, and meanwhile his kingside attack will continue to fire on all cylinders: 15 ♗c1 ♖b8 16 hxg6 hxg6 17 ♖xh8 ♗xh8 18 f5! gxf5 19 ♘g3! and White has a powerful initiative, O.Korneev-K.Movsziszian, Berga 1996.

15 ♕xe3

White no longer has the advantage of the bishop pair, but on the other hand he still has the superior bishop, which forms the basis of a powerful light-squared attacking strategy. White's lead in development and extra space are also important factors of course.

15...♕b6

This seems too slow to be effective, but it is doubtful that Black has a notable improvement – his position is simply bad by this stage. For example:

a) 15...0-0-0?! 16 ♕b3! e6 17 ♗h3! ♔c7 (17...d5 18 f5! smashes Black open on the light squares) 18 f5! exf5 19 exf5 d5 20 fxg6 fxg6 21 ♘f4 and Black was swiftly crushed in R.Basden-L.Kempen, correspondence 2001.

b) 15...♘f6?! 16 h6! ♗f8 17 d5! cxd5 18 e5! ♘d7 19 e6 fxe6 20 ♕xe6 gives White a huge initiative while his opponent's kingside pieces cannot even move, V.Bologan-M.Todorcevic, Las Palmas 1993.

16 hxg6 hxg6 17 Rxh8 Bxh8 18 f5!

White proceeds with the standard attacking plan. The preliminary 18 Bh3 is also good.

18...gxf5 19 Qg5 Kf8

19...Nf6 runs into 20 e5! when White wins material.

20 Bh3!?

Not a bad move, but my recommendation would be the straightforward 20 Qxf5 which gives White a clear plus without allowing any real counterplay.

20...Bf6

20...fxe4?? loses instantly to 21 Rg1.

21 Qg3

21 Qh5!? is also dangerous.

21...e5

White's last move was probably directed against 21...e6, although this might still have been the lesser of the evils for Black:

a) In the event of 22 Qxd6+ Ne7 23 exf5 Rd8 24 Qf4 (24 Qg3 exf5) 24...Nd5 Black gets some counterplay based on the theme of ...Nc3+.

b) Instead White should prefer 22 exf5 e5 23 dxe5 dxe5 (if 23...Bxe5 24 f4 Bf6 25 Rxd6) 24 Nc1 when he keeps some advantage, but Black has some chances to resist.

22 Bxf5 Ne7 23 Qh3!?

Glek decides to sacrifice a pawn. White's position is certainly strong enough to justify it, although simpler moves were possible as well.

23...exd4 24 f4

24 Nf4 also looks promising.

24...Nxf5 25 Qxf5 Bg7 26 Qg4 Re8?

Under pressure, Black blunders. He

should have preferred 26...♕d8, or perhaps the counterattacking 26...d3!? to activate his pieces.

27 ♖g1 ♗f6 28 ♘g3!

Now Black's king is caught.

28...d3

If 28...♔e7 29 ♘f5+ ♔d7 (or 29...♔d8 30 ♘xd6) 30 ♘g7+ White wins easily.

29 ♘f5 dxc2+ 30 ♔c1 1-0

Game 14
I. Martin Alvarez-
K.Movsziszian
Pamplona 2009

1 e4 g6 2 d4 ♗g7

The game actually began with the somewhat unusual sequence 2...d6 3 ♘c3 c6 4 f4 ♕b6 5 ♘f3 ♗g4 6 ♗c4 ♘h6 7 ♗b3 ♗g7 8 ♗e3 d5 9 ♕d2, but I will substitute the standard move order in order to demonstrate some of the other deviations available to Black.

3 ♘c3 d6 4 f4 c6 5 ♘f3

So far everything is the same as the previous game, but Black has a few

other ideas at his disposal.

5...♕b6!?

By shuffling his move order (compared with the plan of 5...♗g4 and 6...♕b6 as seen in Glek-Cekro), Black hopes to inhibit the development of the c1-bishop. The plan is interesting, but we will see that it has certain drawbacks.

Before going any further, we should check some of Black's other options. Only the third of the following lines is of any real significance:

a) 5...d5?! has been played in several games, but after 6 e5 Black has an inferior version of Game 19, having already committed his bishop to g7.

b) 5...♘d7 transposes to note 'b' to Black's sixth move in Game 16.

c) 5...b5 is possible, but the early queenside attack is unlikely to hurt White. The first player should develop quickly and look for an opportunity to attack. After 6 ♗d3 (6 ♗e3 is not bad, but with Black's queenside advance already underway, it looks more logical to castle on the kingside),

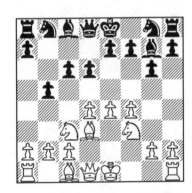

here are some lines to show how the game may develop:

c1) 6...♗g4 (a good rule of thumb is that queenside expansion with ...b5 should generally not be combined with the development of the bishop to g4 – the point is that after the probable exchange of this piece for the knight on f3, Black is liable to become weak on the light squares, as the advancing pawns will leave plenty of holes which can be exploited later on) 7 e5!? (with this active move White wastes no time in opening the h1-a8 diagonal towards Black's weakened queenside; 7 ♗e3 is a reasonable but less incisive alternative) 7...f5?! (Black embarks on a blockading plan on the light squares; positionally it makes some sense, given that he is about to exchange his light-squared bishop, but as things turn out, Black is soon left in a passive position with no counterplay) 8 h3 ♗xf3 9 ♕xf3 d5 10 g4 e6.

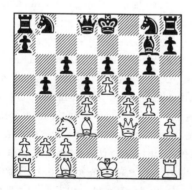

This position was reached in K.Malinovsky-J.Bernasek, Olomouc 2007, and here the strongest continuation looks to be 11 gxf5 ♕h4+ 12 ♔e2 gxf5 13 ♖g1 when White has numerous positional advantages and can develop his initiative on either side of the board.

c2) 6...♘d7 7 0-0 and now:

c21) 7...♗b7 8 e5! sees White's initiative running smoothly.

c22) 7...♕b6 does not achieve much after 8 ♗e3: for instance, 8...e5 (8...♘gf6 should be met by 9 h3!, guarding the g4-square) 9 fxe5 dxe5 10 ♗f2! exd4 11 e5! ♘xe5? (11...♘e7 was better, although after 12 ♘xd4 ♗xe5 13 ♘xc6! ♕xc6 14 ♗e4 White wins material) 12 ♖e1 f6 13 ♘xd4 c5 14 ♗xb5+ ♔f7 15 ♖xe5 fxe5 16 ♗c4+ ♔e8 17 ♕f3 cxd4 18 ♕f7+ ♔d8 19 ♘d5 1-0 T.Chua Zheng Yuan-Wong Meng Kong, Singapore 2009.

c23) 7...♘b6 8 a4!? (we will see the same idea working well in Game 15) 8...b4 9 ♘e2 a5 (after 9...♘f6 10 a5 ♘bd7 11 ♕e1 the b4-pawn is weak) 10 c3 bxc3 11 bxc3 ♘f6 12 ♖b1 0-0 13 f5 and White had a promising initiative in J.Degraeve-E.Cekro, Istanbul Olympiad 2000.

Returning to 5...♕b6:

6 ♗c4!

This seems like the most challenging response, although 6 h3 and 6 a4!? are also not bad.

6...♘h6

The main point of White's last move was to prevent 6...♗g4? which now loses to 7 ♗xf7+!.

7 ♗b3

Covering the b2-pawn and thus facilitating the development of the other bishop.

7...♗g4

We are now directly back in Martin Alvarez-Movsziszian, which started with an unusual move order, as noted at move 2.

8 ♗e3 d5!?

This is practically forced, as if Black makes no attempt to fight for the central light squares, he will have serious trouble justifying the position of the knight on h6.

9 ♕d2!

An important move.

9...dxe4

After 9...♗xf3? 10 gxf3 e6 11 f5 ♘g8 12 fxe6 fxe6 13 ♘a4 ♕c7 14 ♘c5 ♕f7 15 0-0-0 Black's position was already highly suspect in G.Cools-R.Kasimdzhanov, Antwerp 1998.

10 ♘e5

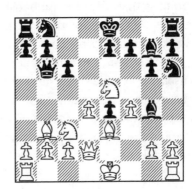

White's pawn sacrifice is likely to be temporary and all his pieces enjoy excellent prospects.

10...♗c8?!

It is hard to believe that Black can solve his opening problems by playing such a move.

10...♗f5 is Black's best try according to both the computer and basic common sense. The position after 11 h3 f6 was reached in E.Andreev-A.Kornev, Tula 2001. At this point I agree with Khalifman's recommendation: 12 g4! fxe5 13 dxe5 ♕d8 (Black had better take the opportunity to exchange queens, but even this does not guarantee him an easy life) 14 gxf5 ♕xd2+ (14...♘xf5 15 ♘xe4 ♕xd2+ 16 ♗xd2 reaches variation 'b' below) 15 ♗xd2. Black has a few ideas here, but none of them are good enough to equalize:

a) 15...gxf5?! 16 ♖g1 ♗f8 17 ♗e3 when Black's kingside pieces are almost stalemated and the b3-bishop is tremendously powerful.

b) 15...♘xf5 16 ♘xe4 ♘d4 17 ♗e3 ♘xb3 18 axb3 ♘a6 19 ♔e2 and White is strong in the centre, whereas Black's bishop is restricted and his queenside weak.

c) 15...e3!? 16 ♗xe3 ♘xf5 17 ♗f2 ♗h6 18 ♘e2 leaves White clearly better thanks to his dominant light-squared bishop.

This analysis, from 12 g4! onwards, is largely based on that of Khalifman.

11 ♘xe4 0-0

12 h3

This is a bit on the slow side. If I had this position over the board I would be more inclined to go for 12 0-0-0 or the direct 12 h4!?.

12...♘f5 13 g4!?

13 ♗f2 was fine, but White decides he does not need his bishop.

13...♘d6

Also after 13...♘xe3 14 ♕xe3 ♘d7 15 ♘xd7 ♗xd7 16 0-0-0 White is some-

somewhat better.

14 ♘f2

14 ♘c5 looks like a more active way to avoid the knight exchange.

14...a5 15 a4 ♘a6 16 h4 ♘c7?

Black should have preferred 16...♕b4, forcing a queen exchange. He is still worse here, but at least he is not about to be mated on the kingside.

17 h5 ♘d5

17...♕b4? 18 hxg6 hxg6 19 ♘xg6 wins a pawn.

18 hxg6 hxg6 19 ♘fd3 ♖d8 20 0-0-0

Already it is doubtful that Black can defend.

20...♘e4 21 ♕h2 ♘ef6

22 ♖de1?

22 f5! would have been crushing: for instance, 22...♘xe3 (22...gxf5 23 gxf5 followed by ♖dg1 is terminal) 23 ♗xf7+ ♔f8 24 ♘f4 and Black can resign.

22...♗xg4

Now the game becomes unclear again.

23 ♘xg4 ♘xg4 24 ♕h7+ ♔f8 25 ♘e5?!

This works out well in the game, but

objectively it was unsound.

25 ♗g1 would have kept the game highly unclear.

25...♘gf6?

This proves to be the fatal error.

After the correct 25...♘gxe3! 26 ♖xe3 ♕xd4! (26...♘xe3?? 27 ♗xf7 wins) 27 ♖f3 e6 White is two pawns down and does not seem to have a convincing way through on the kingside.

26 ♘xg6+! fxg6 27 ♕xg6 e6

From here White makes up for his earlier errors by finishing the game in style.

28 f5! ♘e7

Or 28...♘xe3 29 fxe6 ♕c7 30 ♖xe3 ♕e7 31 ♖f1 when Black has no defence against ♖ef3.

29 ♖h8+! ♘eg8

29...♗xh8 30 ♗h6+ is the end.

30 fxe6 ♕c7 31 ♖f1 1-0

That concludes our coverage of 4...c6. In my view the games and supporting analysis indicate that White has every reason to feel happy here.

Our next game once again sees

Karen Movsziszian in control of the black pieces, but in this particular encounter he favours a different set-up involving a quick ...a6.

Game 15

**J. Fernandez Garcia-
K.Movsziszian**

Mislata 2001

1 e4 g6 2 d4 ♗g7 3 ♘c3 d6 4 f4 a6

This move introduces a dynamic counterattacking system based on the moves ...b5, ...♗b7, ...♘d7, and ...c5. Its greatest exponent is the creative Swedish Grandmaster Tiger Hillarp Persson, who has played it for many years and wrote a book on the system.

5 ♘f3 b5 6 ♗d3

6 ♗e3 is possible, but I consider it more accurate to develop the light-squared bishop first. Indeed, in the main game we will see the queen's bishop being left on c1 for quite some time.

6...♘d7

Usually Black chooses to develop this knight before the light-squared bishop, as it gives him the option of an early ...c5.

6...♗b7 is also possible and indeed the two moves will often transpose. Here, though, is one independent example: 7 a4 b4 8 ♘e2 ♘f6 (8...♘d7 9 0-0 reaches note 'd' to Black's 8th move in the main game) 9 ♘g3 0-0 10 0-0 e6 11 c4!? (11 c3 is slightly better for White) 11...♘bd7. This was T.Luther-T.Paehtz, Stralsund 1988, and here I would suggest the active 12 e5!? intending ♗e4 when White's position looks preferable, although Black's counterattacking chances should not be underestimated.

7 a4!?

White borrows an idea from the 150 Attack. Hillarp Persson regards it as one of White's most promising tries for an advantage and having investigated several of White's options in some detail, I am of the same opinion. The main alternatives are:

a) White's most popular choice has been 7 e5 which can lead to ultra-sharp play, but having analysed the variations in some detail I do not find White's idea fully convincing. Furthermore, you can bet your opponents will have studied this line in detail and will be relishing the wild complications to which it can lead.

b) 7 ♗e3 is worth considering. The main line continues 7...♗b7 8 ♕e2 c5 9 dxc5 ♘xc5 10 ♗xc5! ♗xc3+ 11 bxc3

dxc5 12 e5 ♘h6 when White only has a small advantage.

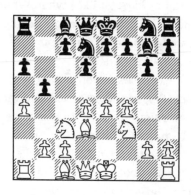

7...b4 8 ♘e2

The knight drops back, intending to re-emerge on the kingside later. The other main point behind White's plan is that he can now meet ...c5 with c3, maintaining a firm grip on the centre.

8 ♘d5 is possible, but after 8...a5 (8...c5!?) 9 0-0 e6 10 ♘e3 ♘e7 the knight is not ideally placed on e3; it is nicely centralized, but it blocks the c1-bishop.

8...c5

Movsziszian decides to strike at the centre without delay; a principled choice, although Black should take care not to open the game too quickly while behind in development.

Several other moves are possible:

a) 8...♘gf6 9 0-0 ♗b7 transposes to variation 'd'.

b) 8...e6 9 0-0 ♘gf6 was played in E.Hermansson-T.Hillarp Persson, Swedish League 2001. At this point Tiger states that 10 f5 would have been problematic for Black, without offering any further analysis. A plausible continuation is 10...exf5 11 exf5 0-0 12 ♘f4 ♗b7 13 c3 bxc3 14 bxc3 when White is somewhat better, although he should not underestimate the latent potential in Black's position.

c) 8...a5!? has been played twice by Hillarp Persson. Black's idea is to vacate the a6-square in order to exchange the light-squared bishops. Here 9 0-0 ♗a6 was S.Narayanan-T.Hillarp Persson, Reykjavik 2008, when I rather like Hillarp Persson's suggestion: 10 ♗b5!? (10 c4!? also looks quite promising) 10...e6 11 c4 (11 f5!?) 11...♘e7. The Swedish Grandmaster opines that White is a little better here and 12 d5 looks like a sensible continuation, intending ♘ed4 with a bind over the light squares.

d) 8...♗b7 has been the most popular alternative to the main line. After 9 0-0 ♘gf6 10 e5 Black has two main options:

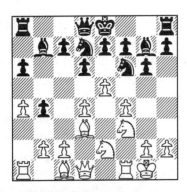

d1) 10...♘d5 is well met by 11 a5! c5 12 ♘g5! cxd4 13 e6 ♘c5 14 ♘xf7 ♕c8, as in J.Hector-T.Hillarp Persson, Goth-

enburg 1997, and here Hillarp Persson points out that 15 ♘xh8 gives White a clear advantage.

d2) 10...♘e4 11 c3 c5 12 ♕c2! (this seems to be strongest, although 12 ♗xe4!? ♗xe4 13 ♘g5 is also interesting: for instance, 13...♗f5 – not 13...♗b7? 14 e6 – 14 ♘g3 h6 15 ♘xf5 gxf5 16 ♘f3 when White's superior structure gives him some advantage) 12...f5?! (12...d5 looks better, although after 13 cxb4 cxb4 14 a5! White has an obvious advantage) 13 exf6 ♘dxf6 14 ♘g5 and Black was already in trouble in V.Kotronias-V.Kotrotsos, Kalamata 2005.

Returning to 8...c5:

9 c3

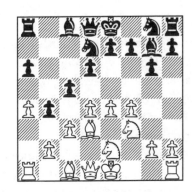

9...e6?!

An unfortunate choice. Black wants to put his knight on e7 and castle, but in the present position he simply does not have the time for it.

More solid is 9...bxc3 10 bxc3 e6 11 0-0 ♘e7, as in N.Ravic-N.Ostojic, Obrenovac 2008. At this point White's best continuation looks to be 12 e5! intending ♘g5-e4 or ♘g3-e4. Black can prevent that plan with ...d5, but then he will have an inferior version of a French Defence, with his bishop poorly placed on g7.

10 cxb4 cxb4 11 ♕b3! a5

11...♖b8 12 f5 does not really change anything.

12 f5!

12...gxf5?

After this weakening move it will be almost impossible for Black to get his king to a safe spot.

Black's only chance was 12...exf5, after which White has a few tempting ideas:

a) 13 exf5 ♘e7 when Black is worse, but at least he manages to castle.

b) 13 ♘g5!? ♘h6 (13...♕e7 14 exf5 ♘gf6 15 0-0 is dangerous) 14 exf5 ♘f6 and Black survives, although the initiative remains with White.

c) 13 ♗c4! looks best: 13...♕e7 14 exf5 ♘gf6 15 0-0 0-0 16 fxg6 hxg6 17 ♘f4 when the threat of ♘xg6 is difficult to meet.

13 exf5 exf5

Black can block the centre with 13...e5, but he will soon be murdered on the light squares: 14 ♘g5 ♕e7 (or 14...♘h6 15 ♘e4! with a strong attack) 15 ♕d5! ♖a7 16 ♘e4 ♗f8 17 ♗b5 ♘gf6 (17...♗b7 18 ♗c6) 18 ♕c6 ♘xe4 (if 18...♔d8 19 ♗g5) 19 ♕xc8+ ♕d8 20 ♕c6 ♘ef6 21 dxe5 dxe5 22 ♗g5 ♗e7 23 ♗xf6 ♗xf6 24 ♖d1 ♖c7 25 ♕d6 and White is winning.

14 ♗c4 ♕e7 15 0-0 ♘b6 16 ♘g3

16 ♗b5+ followed by 17 ♘g3 was also good enough.

16...♔f8 17 ♗f4

17 ♗g5 is also horrible for Black.

17...♗h6

After 17...♘f6 18 ♖ae1 ♘e4 19 ♘xe4 fxe4 20 ♖xe4! ♕xe4 21 ♗xd6+ ♔e8 22 ♖e1 Black's queen perishes and the king will soon join her.

18 ♖ae1

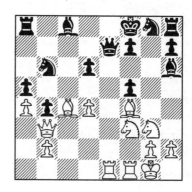

18...♕c7?

In a wretched position Black blunders.

18...♕d8 would have lasted longer, although Black's situation remains virtually hopeless. The most efficient route to victory looks to be 19 ♘h4! (19 ♗xh6+ ♘xh6 20 ♗b5 is also good enough) 19...♘xc4 20 ♕xc4 when Black cannot even win an exchange with 20...♗a6 due to 21 ♕c6! ♗xf1 (21...♗xf4 22 ♖xf4 wins) 22 ♗xd6+ with mate to follow shortly.

19 ♗xh6+ ♘xh6

20 ♕e3! ♘g8

After 20...♘g4 21 ♕e8+ ♔g7 22 ♘h5+ followed by 23 ♕xh8 White wins easily.

21 ♕e8+ ♔g7 22 ♘h5+ 1-0

Overall I would say that the plan involving an early a2-a4 gives White promising play and has the additional benefit of being relatively easy to learn, unlike some of the wild attacking lines at White's disposal.

> ### Game 16
> **D.Strauss-J.Tisdall**
> Lone Pine 1976

1 e4 g6 2 d4 d6 3 ♘c3 ♗g7 4 f4 ♘d7

This move is not particularly fashionable nowadays, but it is worth checking all the same.

I should also mention that occasionally 4...♘c6 is seen. After 5 ♗e3 Black doesn't really have anything better than 5...♘f6 6 ♗e2 0-0 7 ♘f3, transposing to Game 27 in the next chapter.

5 ♘f3

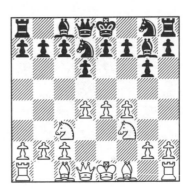

5...c5

Black strikes at the centre, perhaps hoping for a transposition to a Classical Dragon. However, there is a good reason why people generally aim to reach that opening via a Sicilian move order! Indeed, it soon transpires that with accurate play White will obtain excellent chances to punish his opponent's risky opening system.

Before going any further, let us check a few rare alternatives:

a) 5...e5?! 6 fxe5 dxe5 7 dxe5 ♘xe5 8 ♕xd8+ ♔xd8 9 ♗g5+ and Black is already in trouble.

b) 5...c6 6 ♗e3 (6 ♗d3 is also fine) 6...e5 (6...♘gf6 reaches a Pirc in which Black has combined ...♘bd7 with the passive ...c6 instead of the more challenging ...c5 plan) 7 ♕d2 ♕e7 8 0-0-0 when White has a lead in development and the makings of a promising initiative, R.Schuermans-K.Houthoofd, Belgian League 2002.

6 ♗e3! ♘gf6

6...cxd4 is strongly met by 7 ♗xd4!. An exchange of dark-squared bishops would clearly not be in Black's interest, so realistically he has two options:

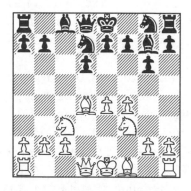

a) 7...e5 is met by 8 fxe5 when Black must make a difficult decision:

a1) 8...♘xe5? leads to serious problems for him: 9 ♗xe5! (9 ♗b5+ ♗d7 10 0-0 also puts Black in trouble) 9...♗xe5? (9...dxe5 was better, although even here White has a pleasant choice between 10 ♕xd8+ ♔xd8 11 ♗c4 and 10 ♗b5+ ♗d7 11 ♗xd7+ ♕xd7 12 ♕xd7+ ♔xd7 13 0-0-0+, with a clearly better endgame in both cases) 10 ♘xe5 dxe5 was J.Choyke-R.Moore, Detroit 1994, and here White could have obtained a huge advantage with 11 ♗b5+!, intending to meet 11...♗d7 with 12 ♕d6!.

a2) 8...dxe5 is the lesser evil, as in

P.Witzschel-M.Krause, correspondence 1998. Here White's most convincing route to an advantage looks to be 9 ♗e3 ♘gf6 10 ♕d6!? when Black has trouble completing his development.

b) 7...♘gf6 8 e5 dxe5 9 fxe5 ♘h5 10 e6! (10 ♕d2 is also good) 10...fxe6 11 ♘g5 e5 (no better is 11...♘e5 12 ♗b5+ ♘c6 13 ♗xg7 ♕xd1+ 14 ♖xd1 ♘xg7 15 ♗xc6+ bxc6 16 0-0 and despite the extra pawn, Black faces a difficult ending due to his numerous pawn weaknesses) was P.Hrvacic-F.Ljubicic, Split 1999, and here the simple retreat 12 ♗e3 would have left Black facing awkward problems.

7 dxc5!

7...♕a5

Recapturing the pawn immediately fails to solve Black's problems:

a) After 7...dxc5 8 e5 ♘g4 9 ♗g1 Black has a difficult position and in the following game he was swiftly crushed: 9...0-0 10 ♕d2 ♕a5 11 0-0-0 (11 ♘d5! would have been even stronger) 11...a6? (11...♗h6 was better, although 12 h4! ♘dxe5 13 ♘xe5 ♘xe5 14 h5 retains White's advantage) 12 ♔b1 ♖e8 13 h3 ♘h6 14 g4 ♔f8 15 ♘d5 ♕xd2 16 ♖xd2 ♖b8 17 ♘c7 1-0 S.Mozaliov-V.Panush, Serpukhov 2003.

b) In the event of 7...♘xc5 White should not hesitate to cede the bishop pair with 8 ♗xc5! dxc5 9 ♕xd8+ ♔xd8 when that minor concession is outweighed by Black's misplaced king. The position after 10 e5 ♘d7 11 ♘g5 ♔e8 was reached in J.Hodgson-I.Jones, Gwbert-on-Sea 2001, and here White could have obtained an overwhelming advantage by means of 12 ♘b5! (12 ♘d5! leads to the same thing) 12...h6 (or 12...♔f8 13 ♘c7 ♖b8 14 ♖d1 with a huge advantage) 13 ♘c7+ ♔d8 (after 13...♔f8 14 ♘xf7 ♔xf7 15 ♗c4+ followed by ♘xa8 White will easily extricate his knight) 14 ♘ge6+! fxe6 15 ♘xe6+ ♔e8 16 ♘c7+ ♔d8 17 ♘xa8 and White is winning.

8 ♕d2 ♘xc5 9 e5

9...dxe5?

In a difficult position Black commits a fatal error. Given the ease with which he has slipped into a precarious posi-

tion, it is small wonder that his opening plan is rarely seen nowadays.

It was essential to choose one of the following two options:

a) 9...♘g4 10 ♗b5+ (also good is 10 ♗d4 0-0 11 h3 ♘h6 12 exd6 ♗xd4 13 ♘xd4 exd6 14 g4! ♖e8+ 15 ♗e2 when White has the better pawn structure and the h6-knight is misplaced) 10...♗d7 11 b4! ♕xb4 12 ♖b1 ♕a3 (or 12...♕xb1+ 13 ♘xb1 ♗xb5 14 ♗xc5 dxc5 15 ♕d5) 13 ♗xc5 ♕xc5 14 ♗xd7+ ♔xd7 15 ♖xb7+ ♔d8 16 ♘d5 when Black was under pressure and was unable to solve his problems in A.Vitolinsh-I.Luckans, Daugavpils 1973.

b) 9...♘fd7 seems to be Black's most resilient defence, although it is still insufficient to equalize: 10 ♘d5 ♕xd2+ 11 ♘xd2 ♘e6 (if 11...♔d8 12 exd6 exd6 13 ♘c4) 12 exd6 exd6?! (12...♗xb2 was better, although after 13 ♖b1 ♗a3 14 f5! gxf5 15 ♘xe7 Black is under pressure) 13 ♘c4 0-0 14 0-0-0 and White is about to win a pawn while keeping a dominant position, S.Nurkic-O.Jovanic, Kastav 2000.

10 b4!

This excellent move effectively ends the contest after a mere ten moves!

10 ♗b5+ ♘cd7 11 fxe5 ♘g4 12 ♘d5 ♕xd2+ 13 ♗xd2 was also excellent for White in S.Voitsekhovsky-V.Filippov, Orel 1992, but the text wins material by force.

10...♕xb4 11 ♖b1 ♘fe4

In the following game Black lost even more quickly: 11...♕a5 12 fxe5!?

(12 ♖b5 is also good enough) 12...♘fd7 13 ♖b5 ♕a3 14 ♖xc5! 0-0 (14...♗xc5 15 ♘b5 wins) 15 ♖b5 ♘b6 16 ♗c5 1-0 M.Smits-G.Mendosa, correspondence 1999.

12 ♖xb4 ♘xd2 13 ♔xd2

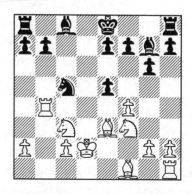

White is a piece up – there is not much more to say.

13...♘e6 14 ♗b5+ ♗d7 15 ♗xd7+ ♔xd7 16 ♘xe5+ ♔e8 17 ♖xb7 g5 18 g3 1-0

According to the computer 18 ♘d5 was even stronger, but the text move was enough to force resignation.

We will now move on to Black's deviations on the third move.

Part 2 – Unusual third moves

1 e4 g6 2 d4 ♗g7 3 ♘c3 c5!?

This respectable sideline is the subject of a recent book by Charlie Storey, who calls it 'The Sniper'.

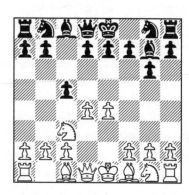

4 dxc5

This is arguably the most principled response, although should White wish it, he can transpose to a few other openings:

a) 4 ♘f3 leaves Black with nothing better than 4...cxd4 5 ♘xd4, reaching a Dragon or Accelerated Dragon.

b) 4 d5 reaches a Schmidt Benoni, as the independent option of 4...♗xc3+?! 5 bxc3 is unattractive for Black.

4...♕a5

4...♗xc3+ is a major alternative and is in fact the recommendation of Storey. After 5 bxc3

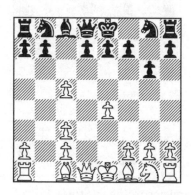

White's c-pawns are tripled, but for the time being he has an extra pawn, and perhaps more importantly his dark-squared bishop has tremendous potential. I would urge the reader to study the following analysis carefully, as the position is rather irregular and both sides will need to play accurately.

Black has three main options:

a) 5...♘f6!? has hardly ever been played, but it is by no means bad. Following 6 e5! (I prefer this over 6 ♗h6) 6...♘e4 7 ♗c4 (7 ♕d4 ♕a5! seems okay for Black) Black has two main options:

a1) 7...♘xc5 (according to the database this is the only move to have been tested) 8 ♘f3 ♕c7 9 0-0 ♘e6 10 ♕e2 was D.Sadvakasov-M.Dougherty, Philadelphia 2006. White's bishop pair, superior development and safer king count for more than the doubled c-pawns.

a2) 7...♕a5 seems like the most natural move. Now White has a choice between two promising continuations:

a21) 8 ♘e2 ♘xc5 9 ♕d5 e6 10 ♕f3 ♘c6

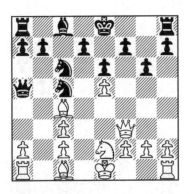

and according to Storey Black is fine

here, but I am not convinced as his dark squares are like Swiss cheese. After 11 0-0 or 11 ♗g5 I prefer White.

a22) 8 ♕f3!? also looks good: for instance, 8...♕xc3+ (after 8...0-0 9 ♗h6 ♘c6 10 ♗xf8 ♘xe5 11 ♕xe4 ♕xc3+ 12 ♔e2 ♔xf8 13 ♘f3 ♕xc4+ 14 ♕xc4 ♘xc4 Black does not have enough compensation for his material deficit) 9 ♕xc3 ♘xc3 10 ♘f3 ♘e4 11 ♗e3 when again I regard White's two bishops and development advantage as more significant than his fractured pawn structure.

b) The idea behind 5...♘c6 is to play ...♕a5 without allowing the reply ♕d4. After 6 ♗b5! (surprisingly this excellent move has hardly ever been played; Storey only mentions the natural 6 ♗e3, which has been the most common choice) Black might try:

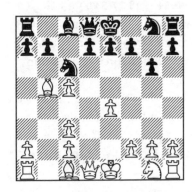

b1) The only game I found on the database from this position (W.Flecker-O.Krassnitzer, Austrian League 1991) continued 6...e5? 7 ♘f3 ♕a5 and now after 8 ♕d3 White has a large plus.

b2) 6...♕a5 is the only sensible move, but after 7 ♗xc6! dxc6 8 ♕d4

♘f6 (8...f6 9 ♘f3 cannot be good for Black) 9 ♗h6 White is a pawn up and has excellent dark square prospects.

c) 5...♕a5 has been Black's most popular choice by far, but with the strong manoeuvre 6 ♕d4! ♘f6 7 ♕b4! White can call his opponent's play into question. Three replies are possible:

c1) 7...♕xb4?! 8 cxb4 ♘xe4 9 ♗b2 0-0 10 ♗d3 was clearly better for White in M.Petrov-L.Dembour, Charleroi 2004.

c2) 7...♘c6!? has hardly ever been played, but it deserves close attention and is the recommendation of Storey. The position after 8 ♕xa5 ♘xa5 9 ♗d3 0-0 was reached in C.Desmarais-J.Fang, Chelmsford 2001. With an extra pawn and two bishops, there is little doubt in my mind that White stands better. However, Black's counterplay connected with the pawn sacrifice ...b6 should not be underestimated.

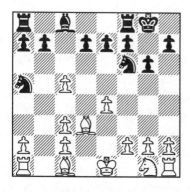

My suggestion is: 10 ♗a3! ♖e8 (in the event of 10...b6!? 11 cxb6 ♘c6 12 bxa7 ♖xa7 13 ♗c5 Black does not have two pawns' worth of compensation) 11 ♘e2 b6 12 f3! when White solidifies his centre and maintains the better prospects. White should endeavour to avoid exchanging on b6, as then Black's a-pawn would come closer to the centre and his rook would become active on the a-file. Instead White should maintain the tension and wait for the exchange on c5, which will not offer his opponent the same benefits.

c3) 7...♕c7 has been the most popular move in the position: 8 ♗b5! (White should not allow ...♘c6 to come with tempo; interestingly the text move has almost never been tested, though) 8...♘c6 9 ♗xc6 ♕xc6 (after 9...dxc6 10 ♘e2 White's extra pawn may not be about to promote any time soon, but the tripled c-pawns help to control several important squares; his pieces are also the more active, so overall he stands better) 10 f3 b6 was seen in E.Rozentalis-A.Payen, Paris 2008. Here White should have played 11 cxb6 axb6 12 ♘e2 with somewhat better chances, although the position remains complex and double-edged.

5 ♗d2 ♕xc5 6 ♘d5!

After this excellent move Black's queen suddenly finds herself in danger. The main threat is ♗b4, meeting ...♕c6 with ♗b5! when the bishop cannot be captured due to the fork on c7.

6...♘a6

Black has surprisingly few playable moves. Here are some examples:

a) The natural developing move 6...♘f6? does nothing to prevent 7 ♗b4 ♕c6 8 ♗b5! winning the queen. One game continued 8...♘xd5 9 ♗xc6 ♘xb4 10 ♗a4 ♗xb2 11 ♖b1 ♗c3+ 12 ♔f1 b6? (12...♘8c6 is better, but White should have few problems converting his material advantage after 13 ♘e2) 13 ♘e2 ♗a6 14 ♖xb4 ♗xb4 15 ♕d4 and Black resigned in H.Scholz-M.Kesik, Seefeld 2005.

b) 6...♔f8?! has been played, but we hardly need to analyse this move seriously. A possible continuation is 7 ♗b4 (7 ♘f3 should also suffice for an advantage, as 7...♗xb2? 8 ♖b1 ♗g7 9 ♗b4 ♕c6 10 ♘d4 is terrible for Black) 7...♕c6 8 ♘f3 d6 (8...♗xb2? 9 ♖b1 ♗g7 10 ♘d4) 9 ♘d4 ♕d7 10 ♗b5 ♘c6 11 0-0 ♘f6 12 ♘xe7!! ♔xe7 13 e5 and White has a huge attack, as pointed out by Khalifman.

c) 6...b6 creates an escape square for the queen on b7, but allows White to build a dangerous lead in development, with 7 ♗b4 ♕c6 8 ♗b5 ♕b7 9 ♕f3! ♗xb2 (taking the pawn was not forced, but if Black refrains from it then he has nothing to counter White's massive development advantage). The present position was reached in E.Rossell-F.Balza, correspondence 2000, and now Khalifman recommends the powerful improvement 10 ♗c3! when Black has two options:

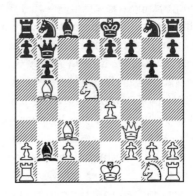

c1) 10...♗xa1 11 ♗xa1 f6 12 e5 and White has a huge attack.

c2) 10...♗xc3+ 11 ♕xc3 f6 (or 11...♘f6 12 ♕e5!) 12 e5! when White has a serious initiative, and this is much stronger than the greedy 12 ♘c7+.

7 ♘f3! ♗xb2?!

This is a principled move, but ultimately it is too risky. Alternatives include:

a) 7...♘f6? can be refuted as follows: 8 b4! ♕d6 9 ♗f4 ♕e6 (9...♕c6? 10 b5) 10 ♘g5 ♕c6, as in J.Sikora Lerch-V.Peresipkin, Strbske Pleso 1978, and several other games. Interestingly, no-one seems to have played the strongest move: 11 ♗e5! when Black has no good defence against 12 b5 (but the immediate 11 b5 allows Black to keep himself in the game with 11...♕c5!).

b) The safest and most common

move is 7...e6, but after 8 &c3 White has an obvious advantage.

8 ♖b1 &g7 9 &xa6!

Khalifman provides lengthy analysis of 9 ♖b5!?. His analysis does look quite convincing, but I disagree with his assessment of the text move as inferior. If anything, I would say that after the game continuation White's advantage is even greater while the supporting variations are much less complicated.

9...bxa6 10 0-0

10...d6?!

This soon leads to trouble, but Black's problems were already bordering on insurmountable, as shown by the following variations:

a) 10...e6 11 ♕e2! is strong, as pointed out by Erenburg

b) 10...♔f8 11 &e3 ♕c6 (11...♕c4 12 ♕d3!) 12 ♘d4 ♕d6 13 ♕d2 and White has a massive position for a meagre pawn, the principal threat being ♕a5.

c) 10...a5 11 &e3 ♕c6 was seen in E.Sveshnikov-E.Ghaem Maghami, Stepanakert 2004. At this point the easiest route to an overwhelming advantage

would have been 12 ♕d2! when Black has no good defence against ♕xa5, e.g.

c1) 12...e6 13 ♘d4 &xd4 (or 13...♕c4 14 ♘b5!) 14 ♕xd4 f6 15 ♘xf6+ ♘xf6 16 ♕xf6 ♖f8 17 ♕g7 and Black will not survive for long.

c2) 12...♘f6 13 ♘e5 ♘xe4 (13...♕d6 14 ♘c4 ♕c6 15 ♘xa5 ♕d6 16 &f4 ♘xe4 17 ♕d3 wins) 14 ♘xc6 ♘xd2 15 ♘c7+ ♔f8 16 &xd2 dxc6 17 ♘xa8 when Black can resign.

11 &b4 ♕c6

11...♕c4 12 &a5 ♔f8 13 ♘c7 ♕xe4 14 ♘d2! reaches the note to Black's next move.

12 &a5!

12...♔d7?!

Black was already losing, but this is hardly the way to improve his situation. The toughest defence was 12...♔f8 13 ♘c7 ♕xe4, although after 14 ♘d2! ♕c6 15 ♕f3 d5 (otherwise White picks up the rook on a8 for nothing) 16 c4! White has a decisive advantage.

13 ♘c7

13 c4!? is also winning, but the text move is simplest.

13...♕xe4

13...♗b7 14 ♘xa8 ♗xa8 15 e5 is virtually hopeless for Black.

14 ♕d3 ♕a4 15 ♕d5

According to the computer 15 ♗c3! was even stronger, although it hardly matters.

15...e6 16 ♕xa8 ♕xa5 17 ♘e8!

This elegant move seals the result.

17...♗f8 18 ♖b8 ♕c5

19 ♘e5+! 1-0

This final flourish puts the exclamation point on a crushing victory.

And now for another exotic third move...

Game 18
S.Karjakin-A.Rakhmangulov
Evpatoria 2007

---

1 e4 g6 2 d4 ♗g7 3 ♘c3 d5!?

This cheeky move is not as bad as it looks. White will obtain an extra pawn, at least in the short term, but if he fails to follow up correctly then his opening advantage could easily evaporate.

4 exd5

Best, since 4 ♘xd5 c6 regains the pawn and gives Black good equalizing chances.

4...♘f6 5 ♗c4

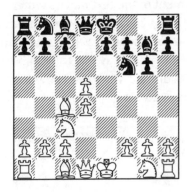

5...♘bd7

Black had better not delay his attempts to recover the pawn.

5...0-0 allows 6 ♘ge2! intending to put the knight on f4 when Black may experience real difficulties regaining his pawn: 6...♘bd7 7 ♗b3 ♘b6 8 ♘f4 a5 9 a4 ♗f5 (after 9...c6 10 dxc6 bxc6 11 0-0 Black had no compensation in B.Chatalbashev-P.Garcia Castro, Mondariz Balneario 2002) 10 0-0 h6 (or 10...♕d7 11 h3! ♖ad8?, as in I.Sorkin-A.Segal, Netanya 1993, and after 12 g4 g5 13 ♘g2 White is winning as the g5-pawn will drop) 11 ♖e1 ♕d7 12 h3 g5 13 ♘h5 ♘xh5 14 ♕xh5 ♗g6 15 ♕d1 when Black has still not managed to regain his pawn and his weakened kingside is an additional source of worry, L.Yudasin-A.Vydeslaver, Beersheba 1992.

6 ♕f3!?

My attention was drawn to this move after a database search revealed that Karjakin and other strong players had used it, with excellent results overall. White's idea is to return the d5-pawn and settle for a slight positional advantage, with more space in the centre and chances for a kingside attack.

The main line is 6 ♗g5 ♘b6 7 ♗xf6 ♗xf6 8 ♗b3 with the idea of hanging on to the extra pawn. This should also be good enough for some advantage, although Black's bishop pair gives him a degree of compensation. To be honest I was rather torn between these two lines, but eventually decided that it would be more interesting to examine the more modern and less thoroughly analysed option.

It is worth mentioning that White can also can begin with 6 ♗b3 ♘b6 (6...0-0 7 ♘ge2 reaches the note to Black's fifth move, above), and only then play 7 ♕f3 to reach the same position as in the game.

Black needs to generate some piece momentum if he is to regain his pawn.

6...0-0? is too slow: 7 h3! ♘b6 8 ♗b3 ♗d7 (8...a5 9 a4 does not change much), as in U.Atakisi-F.Aleskerov, Kusadasi 2006, and now after the simple 9 ♘ge2 c6 10 dxc6 ♗xc6 11 ♕g3 Black has no compensation whatsoever.

7 ♗b3 ♗g4

Black can flick in the moves 7...a5 8 a4 either here or at virtually any point over the next few moves; the timing is unlikely to matter a great deal.

8 ♕g3 ♗f5

In one game Black tried 8...h5?, but soon got into a mess: 9 h3 h4 10 ♕d3 ♗h5 (10...♗f5 11 ♕b5+! is awkward) 11 ♘f3 ♕d7 (11...♘fxd5 12 ♘xd5 ♘xd5 allows White to win a pawn with either 13 ♘xh4 or 13 ♕b5+), and now in K.Richert Goerttler-V.Hoehn, German League 1995, after the simple 12 ♘e5 White's advantage would already have been decisive.

9 ♘f3 ♘bxd5 10 ♘xd5 ♘xd5 11 0-0 0-0

The opening phase is more or less at an end. White has a small but definite

6...♘b6

advantage, with more space and the freer game.

12 ℤe1

12 ♕h4 and 12 c3 have also been played. All three of these moves are likely to feature in White's plans at some point, although it seems correct to develop the rook first.

12...♘f6

After a move like 12...c6 White should play 13 ♕h4 when the ideas of ♗h6 and ♘g5 are on the agenda.

13 ♕h4

13 c3 has also been played, but there is no real reason to destabilize the bishop on b3 just yet, especially as the moves ...a5 and a4 might be inserted at any moment.

13...a5 14 a4 ℤa6!?

Black finds a creative way to develop his rook.

15 h3

Karjakin is in no hurry and settles for a quiet improving move.

15...♕d7 16 ♗c4

Black wants to simplify with ...♗e6, so Karjakin prepares a counter.

16 ♗d2 was a good alternative.

16...ℤb6 17 c3 ♗e6

Black follows his plan.

18 ♘e5 ♕c8

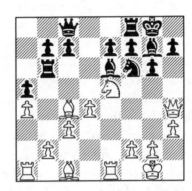

19 b3!?

White allows the bishop exchange, but only on his own terms. Another way to maintain the advantage was 19 ♗b5!? when the rook on b6 is uncomfortably placed.

19...♗xc4 20 bxc4

White's doubled pawns are not weak; on the contrary, they provide him with excellent central control.

20...ℤe8

The computer suggests the brave 20...ℤb3!? intending 21 ♗d2 ℤb2 or 21 ℤa3 ℤb1 when the rook has a certain nuisance value. This would probably have been a better practical attempt than the passive game continuation, although I still prefer White's position.

21 ♗g5

21 ♕f4! looks like a slight improvement, centralizing the queen and pinning the f6-knight. White can consider following up with c5 or even g4!?, gain-

ing more space.

21...♘d7

21...♖b3!? deserved attention once again.

22 ♘g4 f6 23 ♗h6

23...♗h8?!

This looks a bit too slow.

23...♖c6 and 23...e5!? were both more testing, although White should be a little better in both cases.

24 c5! ♖a6 25 ♖ad1

Black's position is becoming distinctly congested.

25...f5

This creates further weaknesses, but Black had to do something to get his pieces working.

26 ♘e3 ♘f6 27 f3!

Preventing Black's plan of ...♘e4 and ...♗f6.

27...♕d7

27...♖c6 would have prevented White's next move, but after 28 ♗f4 or 28 ♘c4 the first player maintains a comfortable plus.

28 d5!

Karjakin gains even more space

while conveniently opening the fourth rank, defending the a4-pawn and creating new opportunities for the white queen.

28...♗g7?

Black commits a tactical error in a difficult position.

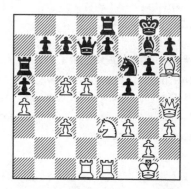

29 ♗g5?!

This maintains a dominant position, but Karjakin has uncharacteristically overlooked a forced win.

A cleaner kill could have been achieved by 29 c6! bxc6 (29...♕c8 30 cxb7 ♕xb7 31 ♘xf5! is also crushing) 30 ♕c4! ♕c8 31 d6+! ♔h8 32 ♗xg7+ ♔xg7 33 d7! ♘xd7 34 ♖xd7 ♕xd7 35 ♕xa6 when White emerges with an extra piece and an easily won game.

29...♔h8 30 ♕c4 h6 31 ♗h4 g5?!

Black's position was horrible in any case, but weakening the f5-pawn is unlikely to improve it.

32 ♗f2

White could have punished his opponent's last move even more convincingly with 32 c6! ♕c8 33 cxb7 ♕xb7 34 ♗f2. The f5-pawn is mortally weak and if 34...f4 35 ♘f5 Black is toast.

32...♖f8?

32...♕c8 was the last chance to prolong the game, although White remains in total control.

33 c6! ♕c8 34 cxb7 ♕xb7 35 ♘xf5

Black loses an important pawns and his position is in ruins.

35...♖f7 36 d6 1-0

Part 3 – The 'Modern Caro-Kann'

In the next three games we will deal with Black's set-up involving an early ...c6 and ...d5, intending a light-squared strategy in the centre.

Game 19
Le Quang Liem-H.Danielsen
Dresden Olympiad 2008

1 d4

White opened with the queen's pawn in this game, but we will be back in e4-territory soon enough.

1...d6

Sometimes Black goes for the same kind of set-up using the move order 1...g6 2 e4 ♗g7 (2...d6 3 ♘c3 c6 reaches the present game) 3 ♘c3 c6 4 f4 d5 5 e5, with two main possibilities:

a) White should be happy to see 5...h5?!, for reasons that will be explained in the note to Black's fifth move below.

b) In positions with the black bishop already on g7, it is more logical for him to concentrate on rapid development

with 5...♘h6, intending ...f6 in the near future. This approach is featured in Game 20.

2 e4 g6 3 ♘c3 c6 4 f4 d5!?

With this move Black loses a tempo... but gains two in return! The reason will be explained shortly.

5 e5 h5

This is the most common and consistent move, and the one which provides the most justification for Black's decision to play ...d5 in two moves rather than one. The point is that with the centre blocked, Black's bishop has absolutely no future on g7 and in most games he will voluntarily retreat this piece to f8 where it will have better prospects. In other words, Black may have lost a tempo by playing ...d7-d6-d5, but he has avoided losing two moves with ...♗f8-g7-f8.

Before moving on, I should briefly mention that 5...♘h6 is occasionally played. Then after 6 ♘f3 we have:

a) 6...♗g7? makes no sense, as after 7 ♗e3 Black is a full tempo down on Game 20.

b) 6...♗g4 is better. White's most energetic response is 7 h3! (after 7 ♗e3 ♕b6 8 ♖b1 ♘f5 9 ♗f2 e6 10 ♗e2 c5 Black may not have equalized fully, but he has certainly gone a long way towards justifying his opening play, S.Rublevsky-V.Bologan, Dortmund 2004) 7...♗xf3 8 ♕xf3 ♘f5 (8...♕b6 should also be met by 9 ♘e2) 9 ♘e2 ♕b6 10 c3 e6 (it is too late to restrain the g-pawn, as shown by 10...h5 11 g4 ♘g7 12 ♘g3 with the better prospects for White) 11 g4 ♘h4 12 ♕f2 ♗e7 13 ♘g3 ♘d7 14 ♗e3 by when White has the bishop pair and a space advantage while the knight on h4 is misplaced, C.Casares Cabanas-M.Manolache, Vilagarcia de Arousa 2006.

6 ♘f3

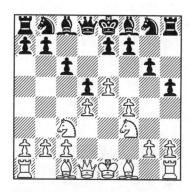

Regardless of whether the bishop is on g7 or f8, White has the better prospects, as demonstrated by the course of the main game along with the accompanying notes. Should you reach the same position with the bishop on g7 (via the move order given in the note to Black's first move), you should handle the position in exactly the same way, while feeling extra-confident in the knowledge that you will effectively be a tempo up on the present game, as the black bishop will usually retreat from g7 to f8 at some point.

6...♘h6

6...♗g4 hardly changes anything: 7 h3 ♗xf3 8 ♕xf3 e6 9 ♗e3 h4 10 ♗d3 ♘h6 11 0-0 and play will almost certainly transpose to the main game after a subsequent ...♘f5 and ♗f2.

7 ♗e3 ♗g4

Black prepares to swap off his light-squared bishop, in preparation for completing his light-squared pawn chain with ...e6. Naturally there are a few other ideas available to him:

a) A move like 7...♘f5? makes absolutely no sense, as after 8 ♗f2 Black is unable to exchange any pieces, and White will easily prepare a kingside expansion with g3, h3 and eventually g4.

b) Some players have tried the disruptive move 7...♕b6, but this also fails to equalize.

Let us follow the instructive play of Karjakin for a model demonstration of White's chances: 8 ♘a4! ♕a5+ 9 c3 ♗g4 10 ♘c5 (White should avoid allowing ...♗xf3 at a time when gxf3 would be forced, as his kingside pawns would lose their fluidity) 10...♕c7 11 h3 ♘f5 12 ♗f2 ♗xf3 13 ♕xf3 b6 (otherwise: 13...e6? 14 g4 gives White everything he could wish for; and 13...h4 14 e6! b6 15 exf7+ ♔xf7 16 ♘d3 gave White a obvious advantage in M.Kuznecov-O.Efimova, Moscow 2006) 14 ♘d3 h4 15 e6!! (this far-sighted positional sacrifice sets Black difficult problems, although the modest 15 ♗e2 would also have given White a slight plus) 15...fxe6 (after 15...f6 16 0-0-0 ♕d6 17 ♖e1 ♘a6 – 17...a5 18 g4 hxg3 19 ♗xg3 ♘a6 20 ♖g1 ♘c7 21 ♗f2 ♘xe6 22 ♖xg6 is also very good for White – 18 ♕g4 ♖h6 19 ♘e5! fxe5 20 dxe5 ♕xe6 21 ♗xa6 White keeps a clear advantage according to Avrukh's analysis) 16 ♕g4 ♖h6 17 ♘e5 ♘d7 18 ♗d3!? (also promising is 18 ♘xd7 followed by ♗d3, intending to pile up on the e-file) 18...♗g7 (the computer suggests 18...♘xe5, but fails to recognize that after 19 fxe5 Black's bishop is in a cage and will have serious trouble getting into the game) 19 0-0 ♗xe5 20 fxe5. In S.Karjakin-P.Kotsur, Chalkidiki 2002, Black's extra pawn was meaningless and White won smoothly after a timely c4 opened the way for his rooks and light-squared bishop.

Returning to 7...♗g4:

8 h3!

This is a standard move, but to the uninitiated it might seem like a positional error, as White allows his kingside pawns to be fixed. The subsequent course of the game will show that this is of no great concern.

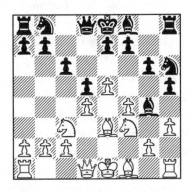

8...♘f5

8...♗xf3 9 ♕xf3 ♘f5 10 ♗f2 h4 11 ♗d3 e6 is just another route to the same position.

9 ♗f2 ♗xf3 10 ♕xf3 h4

I hardly need state that if Black allows his knight to be driven back by g2-g4, then his opening will have been an abject failure.

11 ♗d3 e6 12 0-0

White has completed his development and over the next few moves he will follow a standard plan which can be played against virtually anything Black might try. White will begin by retreating his knight to e2, which serves two purposes:

a) The first is to open the way for c2-c4, which will usually be supported by b2-b3. With these moves White begins to cramp his opponent on the queenside. Later he can bide his time before deciding whether to exchange with cxd5 or gain additional space with c5.

b) White's second major idea involves a regrouping of his kingside pieces with ♔h2, ♘g1, ♕e2 and ♘f3. This will improve his general coordination while also developing pressure against the h4-pawn. This is all the more significant when one considers the possibilities of ♕e2-e1 and ♗xf5, which can be played at any moment White wishes.

All in all, Black is rather passive and will have a hard time defending against the threats on both flanks.

12...a5

Black anticipates his opponent's plan and hopes to benefit from the opening of the a-file. Black has a number of slightly different ways of handling the position, but none of them really alter the general assessment of the position.

A logical alternative is 12...♘d7 13 ♘e2.

Here are few examples to show how the game may develop:

a) 13...♗e7 14 b3 ♔f8 15 c4 ♔g7 16 ♖fc1 ♕a5 17 a3 ♖hc8 18 b4 ♕d8 19 c5 ♕c7 20 a4 (another highly promising plan was the kingside regrouping beginning with 20 ♔h2!, intending ♘g1, ♕e2 and ♘f3 when the h4-pawn will become seriously weak) 20...b6 21 b5 ♘b8 22 ♔h2 ♕d8 23 ♖c2 a6?! 24 cxb6 ♕xb6 25 a5 ♕b7 26 b6 and White had a huge advantage in D.Schneider-A.Kireev, Pardubice 2007.

b) 13...b5 14 b3 b4 15 c4 bxc3 16 ♖ac1 ♕b6 17 ♗xf5!? gxf5 18 ♘xc3 ♗a3 19 ♖c2 ♕a6 20 ♘a4 ♖c8 21 ♖d1 ♘b6 22 ♘c5 ♕b5 23 ♕e3 ♘d7 24 ♘d3 a5 25 ♕e1 ♗e7 26 ♖c3 when Black was under pressure and the subsequent error 26...♗b4? soon led to a losing position after 27 ♘xb4 axb4 28 ♖c2 ♔d8 29 ♗xh4+ ♔c7 30 ♗e7 in A.David-J.Kvamme, Berlin 1997.

13 ♘e2 a4

Let us see one more instructive example of how to conduct White's position. In the following game Black developed his knight in a slightly unusual way and he was again unable to solve his problems: 13...♘a6 14 c3 ♗e7 15 ♔h2! (once more we see the same thematic regrouping) 15...♔f8 16 b3 ♔g7 17 ♘g1 ♘c7 18 ♕e2 a4 19 ♘f3 ♕g8 20 c4! (having arranged his kingside pieces in the optimal way, White switches back to the queenside) 20...♕h7 21 c5 ♕h6 22 ♕d2 axb3 23 axb3 ♖hb8 24 ♖a4 ♔f8 25 ♖fa1 ♖xa4 26 ♖xa4 (26 bxa4!? is also promising, as Black will experience unpleasant pressure along the b-file) 26...♔e8 27 ♖a7 when White was in full control and went on to win in T.Michalczak-U.Dresen, German League 2010.

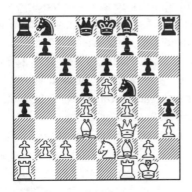

14 ♖fd1

I consider this move to be slightly inaccurate, although it does not jeopardize White's advantage. It is hard to see the rook having much of a future on d1 and in any event I see no point in placing it there so soon, so I would instead recommend one of the following alternatives:

a) 14 b3 ♕a5 15 ♖ab1 axb3 16 axb3 when Black has obtained the use of the a-file, but he can do little with it, and

White is ready for c4 with the usual queenside pressure.

b) White can also play the move 14 ♔h2, refusing to clarify the situation on the queenside just yet and instead planning the standard kingside regrouping.

14...♕a5 15 ♔h2!

White gets back on track with a more purposeful move than his previous one.

15...♘d7 16 ♖ab1

Le Quang decides to build his position on the queenside before returning to the kingside plan.

16...♗e7 17 b3 axb3 18 axb3 ♔f8

The question of where to put the king is a common problem for Black in this variation. If he wants to connect his rooks then he will have to put it on g7, but later it could become vulnerable there, especially if the h4-pawn eventually falls.

19 c4

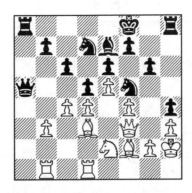

19...♗b4?!

Danielsen decides to activate his bishop, although there is an obvious risk of the h4-pawn becoming weak.

19...♔g7 would have been a better try when White has a number of ideas:

a) 20 ♘g1 looks slightly inaccurate, as 20...♕a2! inhibits the plan of ♕e2 for the time being.

b) 20 c5 looks tempting, but after 20...b5! Black has decent chances to hold.

c) White should go for a more flexible option such as 20 ♖dc1, improving his position slightly and keeping all his options open. (Of course this underlines the fact that his 14th move was not the best.) Here 20 ♗e1!? is also interesting.

20 ♘g1!

White continues his plan.

20...♕a2!?

Black anticipates the planned ♕f3-e2, which would now allow a queen exchange and so ease Black's defence.

21 ♗xf5!

Usually White would not make this exchange so soon, but thanks to Black's last move, White needs to free a different square for his queen.

21...gxf5 22 ♕e3

22 cxd5 cxd5 23 ♖bc1 also looks promising, as White takes over the c-file.

22...♔e8?!

Black decides the kingside is not such a safe haven after all. He is right, but still the text move does not make a good impression.

22...♕c2!? looks more resilient, although after 23 ♖dc1 (23 cxd5 ♖a2!) 23...♕e4 24 ♖a1 followed by ♘f3 Black is under pressure.

23 ♘f3 ♗e7 24 ♕e1!

And just like that, the h4-pawn is a goner.

24...♕c2

Black cannot defend with 24...♗b4 25 ♕f1 ♗e7?? due to 26 ♖a1.

25 ♖a1!?

White could have simply grabbed the pawn with 25 cxd5 cxd5 26 ♗xh4, but he decides to take control over the a-file first.

25...♖b8 26 c5!

The h-pawn is not going anywhere, so White takes a moment to seal off the queenside and restrict his opponent's pieces, especially the queen which is now noticeably short of squares.

26...♕e4?

The queen makes an unfortunate step into an inescapable prison cell.

26...♕xb3? was also hopeless due to 27 ♕d2! followed by ♖db1 trapping the queen.

Black should have played some kind of waiting move, as White is not yet threatening to win the queen by force. Nevertheless, White is completely dominating and can improve his position with b4, before deciding whether to collect the h4-pawn or continue with his queenside attack.

27 ♕d2!

The door is locked on the wandering black queen.

27...b6 28 ♖e1

Black's queen is trapped and the rest is easy.

28...bxc5 29 ♖xe4 fxe4 30 ♘g5 cxd4 31 ♕xd4 ♗c5 32 ♕d2 ♗b4 33 ♕c2 ♖c8 34 ♖a6 c5 35 ♖a7 ♖d8 36 ♕e2 1-0

This game and the accompanying examples shows that White has a relatively easy time against the blocking set-up involving an early ...h5. In the next game we see a more challenging set-up, involving faster development and a rapid ...f6 from Black.

> ### Game 20
> ### D.Mastrovasilis-D.Svetushkin
> ### Greek Team
> ### Championship 2004

1 e4 g6 2 d4 ♗g7 3 ♘c3 c6 4 f4 d5

There is one other version of the blocked pawn centre which deserves some attention, namely 4...♕b6 5 ♘f3 d5!? (5...d6 6 ♗c4 was covered in Game 14) 6 e5! (after 6 exd5 ♗g4 Black has reasonable compensation) 6...♗g4 7 ♗e2.

Due to the presence of the queen on b6, White is more or less forced to put his bishop on this less than ideal square, unless he is willing to accept doubled f-pawns, which in my view would be a far greater concession. Here are a few examples to show how the game may develop:

a) 7...♗xf3 8 ♗xf3 e6 9 ♘a4 ♕a5+ 10 c3 ♘d7 11 b4 ♕c7 12 ♗e3 ♘e7 13 0-0 a5 14 a3 0-0 15 ♘c5 axb4 16 axb4 b5 17 ♕b1 ♘b6 18 ♖f2 ♖xa1 19 ♕xa1 ♖a8 20 ♖a2 ♖xa2 21 ♕xa2 ♘ec8 22 g4 ♘c4 23 ♗c1 ♕a7 24 ♕xa7 ♘xa7 25 ♗e2 and White kept some advantage in the endgame, A.Greet-P.Constantinou, British Championship, Torquay 2009.

b) 7...♘h6 gives White a couple of possibilities:

b1) The rare 8 ♘g5!? ♗xe2 9 ♘xe2 should give White decent chances for an edge.

b2) 8 ♘a4 is the typical way to drive the queen away from b6, eliminating the pressure on the b2- and d4-pawns, and thus enabling White to complete his development. After 8...♕a5+ (with 8...♕c7 9 ♗e3 White develops smoothly and the knight is by no means badly placed on a4; White's plan involves b3, c4 and ♖ac1, and later the knight can switch to c5, c3, or possibly via b2 to d3) 9 c3 ♘d7 10 0-0 b5 (another approach is 10...f6 11 b4 ♕c7, as in M.Zumsande-J.Hodgson, German League 2003, and now after 12 h3 ♗e6 13 g4 White's space advantage gives him a definite plus) 11 ♘c5 ♘xc5 12 b4 ♕a4 13 bxc5 ♕xd1 14 ♖xd1 ♔d7 15 a4 a6 16 h3 ♗f5 17 ♖d2 ♔c7 18 g4 ♗d7 19 ♖da2 ♔b7 20 ♔f2 Black faces an unpleasant defensive task in this queenless middlegame, D.Howell-S.Cicak, Stockholm 2007.

Returning to 4...d5:

5 e5

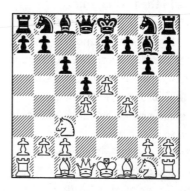

5...♘h6

5...h5?! has been the most-common move, but to me it makes no sense in this position. Let me reiterate the point made in the note to Black's fifth move in the previous game: after 6 ♘f3 Black is virtually a tempo down on Le Quang Liem-Danielsen, as following the standard continuation of 6...♘h6 7 ♗e3 ♗g4 8 h3 ♘f5 9 ♗f2 ♗xf3 10 ♕xf3 h4 11 ♗d3 e6 12 0-0 the black bishop has absolutely no future on g7 and in most games it has retreated to f8 at some point over the next few moves.

6 ♘f3 ♗g4

Black has a number of different move orders available. Should he try a different sequence, the best he can achieve is to transpose to the main game, whereas if he tries to deviate then he will soon find himself in a worse position. Here are some examples to illustrate this point:

a) 6...0-0 7 ♗e3 ♗g4 (7...f6 is variation 'b3', below) 8 ♗e2 ♘f5 (8...f6 9 0-0 transposes to the main game) 9 ♗f2 f6 10 0-0 reaches the note to Black's 9th move in the main game.

b) 6...f6 7 ♗e3 and now:

b1) Black's soundest is 7...♗g4, which transposes to the main game.

b2) 7...♕b6 should as usual be met by 8 ♘a4! ♕a5+ 9 c3 when Black's queenside demonstration has achieved nothing.

b3) 7...0-0 is well met by 8 h3!. After this accurate move Black will pay the price for delaying the development of his light-squared bishop, which now lacks a decent square: 8...♘f7 9 ♘e2! (White's number one priority is to stabilize his centre; once that has been achieved he will easily catch up on development, while Black will struggle to generate counterplay) 9...fxe5 10 fxe5 c5 11 c3 ♘c6 12 ♕d2 cxd4 13 cxd4 ♗f5 14 ♘g3 (14 ♘c3 also looks good) and White has a comfortable plus, O.Korneev-E.Fernandez Romero, Albacete 2001.

7 ♗e3

This move is actually a slight inaccuracy. Should you reach this position over the board, I recommend that you choose one of the following move orders:

a) If you are aiming for the position reached in the main game, then 7 ♗e2 is the best way, as it enables White to bypass the possibility mentioned in the note to Black's next move. For example:

a1) 7...f6 8 ♗e3 transposes to the game.

a2) 7...♘f5 8 0-0 (8 ♘g5!? is also interesting) is safe enough for White, as 8...♕b6 can be met by 9 ♘a4!.

b) Against the particular move order chosen by Black in the present game, White can consider 7 h3!? ♗xf3 8 ♕xf3 with good chances for an advantage. However, I do not want to dwell on this option too much, as Black can easily avoid it: for instance, with 6...f6 7 ♗e3 ♗g4, transposing to the game without allowing White this extra possibility.

7...f6

7...♕b6!? would have more or less

forced the passive 8 ♖b1, as the generally desirable 8 ♘a4?! can be met by 8...♕a5+ 9 c3 ♗xf3! forcing the inconvenient 10 gxf3.

8 ♗e2 0-0

In this position 8...♕b6 can be met by the standard response of 9 ♘a4! ♕a5+ 10 c3: for instance, 10...♘d7 11 b4 ♕c7 12 0-0 0-0 (O.Gutierrez Castillo-M.Cabrera Peinado, Malaga 2000) 13 h3 ♗xf3 14 ♗xf3 ♘f5 15 ♕d3!? with a slight plus for White.

9 0-0

This is the key position of the variation, which can be reached via several different move orders.

9...♘d7

The main alternative is 9...♘f5 10 ♗f2 ♗h6 (10...♗xf3?! 11 ♗xf3 leaves Black virtually a tempo down on the game), when White has tried numerous moves. In my view there are two main contenders:

a) Khalifman recommends the interesting 11 exf6 when Black may try:

a1) 11...♖xf6 12 ♕d2 ♘d7 13 ♖ae1 ♕c7 14 ♘e5 ♗xe2 15 ♖xe2 ♘xe5 16

dxe5 ♖ff8 17 g4 d4 18 ♘e4 ♘e3 19 ♗xe3 dxe3 20 ♕xe3 and White remains on top.

a2) After 11...exf6 12 ♘h4! ♗xe2 13 ♕xe2 ♘xh4 14 ♗xh4 the point of White's idea is that Black has no good way of preventing f4-f5.

However, it is not clear how big a problem this is for him:

a21) Khalifman mentions the line 14...♖e8 15 ♕d3 ♕d6 16 f5 ♖e3 17 ♕d1 ♘d7 18 ♕g4 with some initiative for White.

a22) A better try is 14...♘a6! as played in A.Bezemer-R.Hartoch, Wijk aan Zee 2005. From here the most logical continuation seems to be 15 f5 ♖e8 (if 15...♕e8 16 ♕g4) 16 ♕g4 ♗e3+ 17 ♗f2 ♗xf2+ 18 ♖xf2 ♕d7 when White's position is certainly a bit more comfortable, but I am not convinced that his advantage is anything serious. Black will block the kingside with ...g5 at an opportune moment, and can double his rooks on the e-file to create counterplay and keep White from building a truly dangerous attack.

b) In view of the above, the more ambitious 11 ♘h4!? is my recommendation. White exchanges a pair of bishops in order to relieve the pressure on his centre and maintain his space advantage. After 11...♗xe2 12 ♕xe2! (12 ♘xe2 has been played in a few games, but it turns out that White does not have to defend the f4-pawn and can instead play more actively) Black has tried three moves:

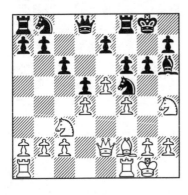

b1) 12...♗xf4?! was tried in M.Schuster-T.Baerwinkel, Binz 1995, but after 13 ♘xf5 gxf5 14 exf6 Black is struggling.

b2) 12...♘g7 13 exf6 exf6 14 f5! (White has an improved version of variation 'a2' above) 14...♖e8 15 ♕d3 g5 16 ♕d2!? b5 (16...♘d7 might be a slight improvement, but after 17 g4 intending ♘g2 the evaluation is about the same). This position was reached in M.Orlinkov-A.Gorbatov, Moscow 2000, and now after the logical 17 g4 ♘d7 18 ♘g2 White is better.

b3) 12...fxe5 13 fxe5! (I checked the other recaptures as well, but in the end I strongly prefer this natural move which maintains White's space advantage and creates some attacking chances on the f-file), and here I analysed the following possible continuations:

b31) After 13...♘xh4 14 ♗xh4 Black lacks counterplay and the pressure on the e7-pawn is annoying for him.

b32) With 13...e6 14 ♘f3! White avoids exchanges and is ready to play g4 next.

b33) 13...♘d7 14 ♘f3 when White consolidates his space advantage and keeps a slight edge.

b34) 13...♘g7 14 ♗e3 ♗xe3+ 15 ♕xe3 ♘d7 16 b3!? anticipates ...♕b6.

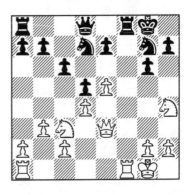

After 16...e6 17 ♖xf8+ ♕xf8 18 g4! c5 19 ♘e2 cxd4 20 ♘xd4 White keeps a slight plus thanks to the offside knight on g7.

b35) 13...♕b6 appears critical, but it meets with a convincing response: 14 ♘f3! ♕xb2 (Black is not forced to take this pawn, but if he refuses then what was the point of putting his queen on b6?) 15 ♕d3 ♕a3 (after 15...♘a6 16

⌶ab1 ♕a3 17 ⌶b3 ♕a5 18 g4 Black loses material) 16 ⌶ab1 (less accurate is 16 g4 ♘a6!) 16...♕a6 17 ♕xa6 bxa6 (if 17...♘xa6 18 ⌶xb7) 18 ♘a4 when White has a promising initiative in the endgame and Black's extra pawn is virtually meaningless.

Returning to 9...♘d7:

10 h3 ♗xf3 11 ♗xf3 ♘f5

11...fxe5 12 fxe5 does not really change anything, as the knight has no better square than f5.

12 ♗f2 fxe5

13 fxe5

13 dxe5 has been tried successfully in a couple of games, but I believe

White should recapture with the f-pawn unless there is a truly compelling reason not to.

13...e6 14 ♘e2!

White prepares to support his centre with c3.

14...♕g5

Perhaps Black should have considered 14...♗h6 15 ♕d3 ♕g5 16 ♗g4 when a few moves have been tried:

a) 16...♕e7 was seen in D.Barria Zuniga-V.Komliakov, Internet (blitz) 2004, and now after 17 ♘g3 c5 18 c3 White keeps a slight plus.

b) 16...⌶ae8 was played in O.Simon-P.Petitcunot, French League 2008. At this point I think White should have played 17 ♔h2!? anticipating the following knight jump: 17...♘e3 18 ♗xe3 ♕xe3 19 ♕xe3 ♗xe3 20 h4 and the weakness on e6 is slightly more significant than the one on d4, although I would be the first to admit that White's advantage is not huge.

15 c3 ⌶f7

After 15...♘e3 16 ♗xe3 ♕xe3+ 17 ♔h1 White no longer has the two-bishop advantage, but he keeps a slight edge as his remaining bishop has better prospects than its dark-squared counterpart. The former can attack the weak pawn on e6, whereas the latter is currently being shut out of the game by the d4-e5 pawn wedge.

16 ♕c1 ♕e7

After 16...♕xc1 17 ♘xc1 ♗h6 18 ♘d3 the knight finds an ideal square and White keeps a slight edge.

17 ♗e3!?

Once again White is happy to allow the exchange of his dark-squared bishop for the enemy knight.

17...♖af8

In the event of 17...♘xe3 18 ♕xe3 ♖af8 19 ♗g4 White keeps a slight plus.

18 ♗g5 ♕e8 19 ♕d2 h6

Up to now both sides have played logically and consistently, with White maintaining a modest edge thanks to his space advantage. On the next move, however, both players go slightly astray.

20 ♗e3

Should you reach the same position over the board, I would recommend 20 ♗f4! as the most accurate continuation. The logical response is 20...c5 (20...g5?! just weakens the light squares, and White is better after both 21 ♗h2 and 21 ♗g3!?) 21 ♗g4 ♘b6 when it is worth mentioning two ideas:

a) Khalifman offers 22 ♗xf5 ♖xf5 23 ♘g3 ♘c4 24 ♕c1 ♖5f7 25 b3 ♘a5 26 ♗xh6 ♖xf1+ 27 ♘xf1, but seems to overlook the riposte 27...♖xf1+! when Black wins two pieces for a rook and reaches an unclear endgame.

b) Instead I recommend the simple 22 b3! when White maintains control of the position and keeps a slight plus.

20...h5?!

This weakens the kingside needlessly.

Black should have preferred 20...♘b6 or 20...c5, with a decent position in either case.

21 ♗g5 ♔h7

22 ♖f2

It was worth considering 22 g4!? hxg4 (22...♘d6 23 ♘f4) 23 hxg4 ♘g3 24 ♘xg3 ♖xf3 25 ♖xf3 ♖xf3 26 ♔g2 ♖f7

27 ♘e2 with an edge for White.

22...♗h6! 23 ♗xh6 ♘xh6

Black should be okay from here. The rest of the game is not particularly important for our study of the opening, so I shall offer only light commentary.

24 ♖af1 ♕e7 25 g3 c5 26 ♗g2 ♖xf2 27 ♖xf2 ♖xf2 28 ♔xf2 cxd4 29 cxd4 ♘b8 30 a3

30 h4!? was worth considering.

30...♘c6 31 b4 ♘f5 32 h4?!

32 ♕c3 ♕f8 33 ♔e1 was better.

32...♕f8! 33 ♔g1 a5!

Developing strong counterplay.

34 ♗h3!

White correctly avoids the trap 34 b5? ♘cxd4! 35 ♘xd4 ♕c5.

34...axb4 35 ♗xf5 ♕xf5

After 35...exf5 36 axb4 ♕xb4 37 ♕c1 White has enough compensation for the pawn.

36 axb4 ♕b1+ 37 ♔f2 ♕f5+

37...♕xb4?! 38 ♕xb4 ♘xb4 39 ♘f4 can only be dangerous for Black.

38 ♘f4

38...♕f7?

38...♔g7 would have maintained

the balance. After the text move White takes over.

39 ♕c3! ♕d7 40 ♕c5 ♔g7 41 b5 ♘d8 42 ♕d6?

Correct was 42 ♔e3! ♗h7 (or 42...♕e8 43 ♕c2! ♔h6 44 ♕c7!) 43 ♕c2 ♕f7 44 ♘xh5 when White is winning.

42...♕xd6 43 exd6 ♔f6 44 ♔e3 ♘f7 45 d7 ♔e7 46 ♘xg6+ ♔xd7 47 ♘f4?

Better was 47 ♔f4! ♘d6 48 ♔e5 ♘c4+ (not 48...♘f5? 49 ♘f8+) 49 ♔f6 ♔d6 and now the elegant 50 ♘h8! should be winning for White.

47...♘d6 48 ♘xh5 ♘f5+ 49 ♔d3 b6!

Now Black is okay and he succeeds in holding the draw.

50 ♘f4 ♘xg3 51 h5 ♘f5 52 ♘g6 ♔e8 53 ♘e5 ♔f8 54 ♘d7+ ♔g7 55 ♔c3 ♘d6 56 ♔b4 ♘f5 57 ♔c3 ♘d6 58 ♔b4 ♘f5 59 ♘xb6 ♘xd4 60 ♘d7 ♘xb5 ½-½

In the next and final game of the chapter, we will consider a different way for Black to head for the same types of positions, by using a slightly tricky move order.

Game 21
N.Kosintseva-P.Blatny
MOSCOW 2004

1 e4 g6 2 d4 c6!?

Here it is. Black hints at a ...d5 setup without having committed his bishop to g7, while also avoiding the ...d6-d5 tempo loss seen in Game 19.

3 f4!?

Against the usual options of 2...♗g7 and 2...d6 I have recommended 3 ♘c3, but I have made an exception for the present move order. The point is that in the blocked positions resulting from ...d7-d5 and e4-e5, the white knight is not particularly well placed on c3 and the present game shows how White can deploy it in a more favourable way.

In fact that is not the end of the story and after 3 ♘c3 d5 White has good chances to fight for the advantage with the help of 4 h3!, the point of which is to prepare ♘f3 without permitting the reply ...♗g4. Although the theoretical picture is decent enough for White, I do not consider it to be an especially pragmatic choice, as the level of theoretical knowledge required is somewhat disproportionate to its low level of popularity.

After pondering the various options available, I decided that the text move would be the best all-round solution. Let us now see how the game may develop and why I favour the early advance of the f-pawn.

3...d5

The alternative is 3...♗g7 4 ♘f3 when Black may play:

a) 4...d5?! 5 e5 gives Black an inferior version of the game, as his bishop has committed itself to the unfavourable g7-square.

b) 4...d6 5 ♘c3 transposes to Games 13 and 14. Alternatively, White could try to exploit his opponent's move order with 5 ♗d3!?, retaining the option of supporting his centre with c3.

4 e5 h5

If Black tries the alternative plan of ...♗g7, ...♘h6 and ...f6, White will have an improved version of the previous game, as his knight will have the option of going to d2 (and possibly recapturing on f3), instead of the undesirable c3-square.

5 ♘f3 ♗g4

5...♘h6 6 ♗e3 ♗g4 7 ♘bd2 reaches the same position.

6 ♗e3 ♘h6 7 ♘bd2!

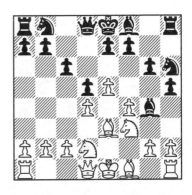

This is White's idea. It all makes sense when you think back to the regrouping manoeuvre seen in Game 19

(as well as several of the examples mentioned in the notes to that game). Recall how White would move his queen from f3 to e2, king from g1 to h2, and his knight from e2 to g1, all so that the knight could finally re-emerge on the ideal f3-square. In the present game Kosintseva takes advantage of the much more direct route from b1-d2-f3, thereby saving considerable time. Of course we should not forget that Black has saved some time by playing ...d7-d5 in one move, while also avoiding the misplacement of his bishop on g7. Nevertheless, in the grand scheme of things, it is White who is making the bigger gain.

7...♘f5

7...e6 8 h3 ♗xf3 was played in D.James-C.Majer, British League 2010, and now for some reason White rejected the logical 9 ♘xf3 which supplies some advantage and can be compared with the main game.

8 ♗f2 e6

Black is in danger of falling into a clearly worse version of Game 19, for reasons already explained. If he is to prevent this from happening, then he will need to find a way to disrupt White's smooth development over the next few moves. Blatny has a particular concept in mind, but there are a few other ideas to consider as well:

a) Two years earlier he had tried 8...♕b6 in R.Biolek-P.Blatny, Ostrava 2002. He was successful in that encounter, but chose not to follow the same path in the present game, perhaps on account of the improvement 9 ♕c1! ♗h6 10 h3 ♗xf3 11 ♘xf3 when White consolidates his position and obtains a stable advantage.

b) 8...♗h6!? is another interesting attempt, but in the following game White navigated the opening expertly: 9 h3! (Black was hoping for 9 g3 h4! with counterplay) 9...♗xf3 10 ♕xf3 (White has been prevented from recapturing with the knight, which would have been generally desirable, but on the other hand Black's bishop is not ideally placed on h6 in such positions) 10...♕b6 (or 10...h4 11 ♗d3) 11 ♘b3 a5.

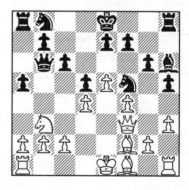

Usually White castles short in these positions, but in this specific case going long works perfectly: 12 0-0-0! h4 13 ♗d3 a4 14 ♘c5 ♘g3? (a mistake in a worse position) 15 ♗xg3 hxg3 16 e6! f5 17 ♕xg3 a3 18 b3 ♕b4 19 ♗e2 ♖g8 20 ♖hf1 when White has a winning position and after the further mistake 20...b6? in B.Laurusaite-A.Balcaite, Panevezys 2009, he could have ended the game immediately with the cute 21

♘b7! followed by c3 trapping the black queen.

9 h3 ♗xf3 10 ♘xf3

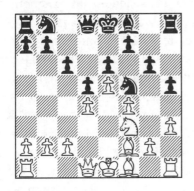

10...♕b6!

This is the only way in which Black can attempt to justify his opening.

The more sedate 10...♗e7?! 11 ♗d3 h4 12 0-0 ♘d7 was played in S.Videki-B.Vlaic, Pula 2000. At this point White should have played 13 b3! intending c4, just as in Game 19, except that here he already has his knight on the ideal f3-square.

11 ♗d3!

Kosintseva correctly sacrifices the b-pawn, having seen that defensive moves on the queenside would be met by either a troublesome check or a quick ...c5 with strong counterplay.

11...♕xb2

Black snatches a pawn, although it is obvious that White will obtain promising compensation.

The only other logical idea is 11...c5, which should be met by 12 0-0! and now:

a) 12...c4 13 ♗xf5 gxf5 14 b3! gives

White some initiative.

b) 12...♘c6 can safely be met by 13 c3, as 13...♕xb2?! 14 ♖b1 is too risky for Black.

c) 12...cxd4 was played in D.Moldovan-D.Suciu, Baile Tusnad 2000, and here my choice would be 13 ♗xf5!? gxf5 14 ♘xd4 ♗c5.

At this point there are two promising paths for White: 15 a4 looks like one sensible idea, intending to meet 15...♘c6 with 16 ♘b5!, and the aggressive 15 c4!? is also tempting. In both cases White keeps the better chances, thanks primarily to his safer king. And if Black makes it as far as the endgame, his broken kingside structure might come into play.

12 0-0

12 ♖b1 is a logical alternative which has been tested in a couple of games:

a) 12...♕xa2 13 ♖xb7 ♕a5+ 14 ♔e2 ♗e7 15 g4 ♘h6 16 ♕b1 ♘d7 was A.Popov-R.Sichinava, Voroshilovgrad 1989, and here both 17 ♘g5 and 17 gxh5 gxh5 18 ♕a1!? leave Black under unpleasant pressure.

b) 12...♕c3+ 13 ♔e2 b5 14 g4 ♘e7 (perhaps 14...♘g7!? should have been preferred) 15 a4 ♘d7 (15...a6!?) 16 axb5 (16 ♖b3 ♕a5 17 axb5 cxb5 18 ♖xb5 would have gained some extra time for White) 16...cxb5 17 ♖xb5 a5 18 ♕a1 ♕xa1 19 ♖xa1 hxg4 20 hxg4 ♘c6 21 ♖b7 0-0-0 22 ♖ab1 ♗b4 23 ♗a6 ♘db8 24 ♖7xb4+ ♘xa6 25 ♖b6 ♘ab8 was G.Piesina-G.Sarakauskas, Radviliskis 1995, and here the cute 26 ♗e1! would have won the a5-pawn.

I suspect that Black's play can be improved in both of the above examples. Nevertheless, as a general rule I believe that in all these lines White has full compensation for a mere pawn.

12...♕b6

Another idea is 12...♕a3, hoping to block the queenside. Here I found a nice riposte: 13 ♕b1! b5 14 c4! dxc4 15 ♗xc4 ♘d7 (15...bxc4? 16 ♕b7) 16 ♗d3 when White has succeeded in opening the position and Black has a difficult defence in store.

13 c4!

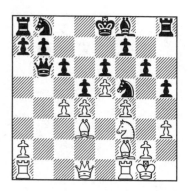

In return for the sacrificed pawn,

White has a space advantage, the two bishops, and a lead in development. With her last move she ensures the clearing of additional lines for her attack.

13...♗e7?

After this weak move White's attack quickly gathers huge momentum.

More solid would have been 13...♕c7!?, anticipating the impending attack on the b-file. Following 14 cxd5 (White can also consider 14 ♕b3 without exchanging yet) 14...cxd5 15 ♕b3 White has promising compensation, but the position is not as one-sided as it becomes in the game.

14 cxd5 cxd5

Forced, as 14...exd5? 15 e6! fxe6 16 ♕e2 is crushing.

15 ♖b1 ♕c7 16 ♕b3 b6 17 ♖fc1

Thanks to Black's inaccuracy, White has been able to bring all three of her heavy pieces into play with gain of tempo.

17...♕b7 18 a4

18 ♖c2 intending ♖bc1 was also highly unpleasant for Black.

18...♔f8

The king cannot remain on e8 forever. One illustrative line is 18...♘d7 19 a5 ♖c8 20 a6! ♕b8 21 ♗b5 when the knight is trapped in a fatal pin.

19 a5 ♔g7 20 ♕a4!

White could have regained her pawn by means of 20 axb6 axb6 21 ♕xb6 with a clear advantage, but it is even more unpleasant to set up a queenside bind.

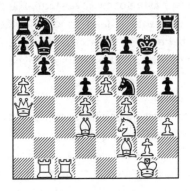

20...h4 21 a6 ♕d7 22 ♕xd7

White was spoilt for choice, with 22 ♗b5 ♕d8 23 ♖b3 being equally grim for the defender.

22...♘xd7 23 ♖c7 ♖hd8

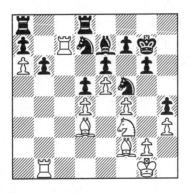

24 ♗b5

This does not spoil anything, but the most effective route would have been 24 ♖b7! with the threat of ♖c1 and ♖cc7. Black is helpless: e.g., 24...♖ac8 (or 24...♔f8 25 ♖c1) 25 ♖xa7 ♖c3 26 ♗b5 ♘b8 27 ♖a1! and White is winning, such as with 27...♖b3 28 ♖xe7, etc.

24...♘f8 25 ♖bc1

25 ♖xe7! ♘xe7 26 ♗xh4 looks to be winning.

25...g5!

Black was almost paralysed, so Blatny makes a final roll of the dice in an effort to activate his kingside pieces.

26 fxg5 ♘g6

White should still be winning this position, but Black continues to fight and later he almost manages to save himself. The rest of the game is not relevant to the opening, so I will keep the annotations fairly brief.

27 ♔f1

27 ♖b7 ♖dc8 28 ♖xc8 ♖xc8 29 ♖xa7 would have been good enough, despite Black's apparent counterplay: 29...♖c1+ 30 ♔h2 ♘d6!? (or 30...♖c2 31 ♗e1) 31 ♗d3 ♘e4 32 ♗xh4 and White should win.

27...♗a3

After 27...♘g3+ 28 ♔e1 ♗b4+ 29 ♔d1 ♘e4 30 ♗e3 Black's counterplay comes to an end.

28 ♖1c2 ♘g3+ 29 ♗xg3 hxg3 30 ♗c6 ♖ac8 31 ♗d7 ♖xc7 32 ♖xc7 ♘f8 33 ♗b5 ♘g6

34 ♘e1?!

The most accurate continuation

was 34 ♖xa7 ♖c8 35 ♘e1 ♖c1 36 ♔e2 ♘h4 37 ♗e8 ♗b4 38 ♖xf7+ ♔h8 39 ♘d3 ♖c2+ 40 ♔f1! ♘xg2 41 ♖f3! and White is winning.

34...♗b2 35 ♘c2?

Better was 35 ♖xa7 ♗xd4 36 ♖b7 ♘xe5 37 a7 ♖a8 38 ♘f3 ♘xf3 39 gxf3.

35...♖h8?

Black could have obtained serious counterplay by means of 35...♘f4! 36 ♘b4 ♖h8!, with the idea of 37 ♖xa7?? (37 ♘d3 is necessary) 37...♖xh3! when it's Black who wins!

36 ♔e2 ♖h4?!

36...♘h4 was a better try.

37 ♖xa7 ♖e4+ 38 ♔f3

38 ♔d1! would have been a bit more accurate.

38...♗xd4 39 ♘xd4 ♘xe5+ 40 ♔xg3 ♖xd4

The time control has been reached and despite the mutual errors, White's advantage has just about remained intact. From this point on Kosintseva finishes the game efficiently.

41 ♖xf7+! ♘xf7 42 a7 ♖b4 43 ♗a6 ♖b3+ 44 ♔h2 ♖a3 45 a8♕ d4 46 ♕b7 d3 47 ♕xb6 d2 48 ♗e2 ♖d3 49 ♕xe6 d1♕ 50 ♗xd1 ♖xd1 1-0

Conclusion

The foundation of this chapter has been the Austrian Attack with an early f2-f4. I believe this to an excellent choice for players at all levels; aside from being objectively strong, White's play is direct and easy to understand. The term 'controlled aggression' sums it up nicely: in many of the featured games we have seen White launching an attack from a position of strength, based on his space advantage and healthy central control. This was equally true in both the traditional Modern set-up with ...d6 and the blocked centre which results from the ...c6 and ...d5 plan. Black's unusual third moves lead to different kinds of struggles, but White has every reason to feel happy there too.

Chapter Three
Pirc Defence

1 e4 d6 2 d4 ♘f6 3 ♘c3 g6

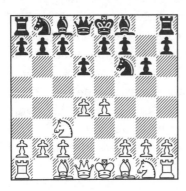

The Pirc Defence can be considered a close cousin of the Modern from the previous chapter. Again Black gives his opponent free reign over the centre, in the hope that his g7-bishop will help him to generate dynamic counterplay.

4 f4

Just as in the previous chapter, I am recommending the Austrian Attack, which is arguably White's most promising try for an opening advantage.

4...♗g7

Black gains nothing from delaying the development of this piece.

5 ♘f3

From here Black must make a fundamental choice:

Part 1 – 5...0-0

The first part of this chapter will be devoted to the natural **5...0-0**, after which I have chosen to recommend **6 ♗e3**, an aggressive option which is often associated with long castling. The material has been organized as follows:

Black's main line of 6...b6, intending to support ...c5 at some point, is the subject of Games 22-24.

A different way of preparing ...c5 is 6...♘bd7, which is seen in Game 25.

Another popular move is 6...c6, for

which see Game 26.

6...♘c6 leads to a position that can also be reached via a Modern move order and is considered in Game 27.

Finally, 6...♘a6 will be considered in Game 28, along with the rest of Black's unusual 6th-move alternatives.

Part 2 – 5...c5 and rare alternatives

The second part of the chapter will concentrate on **5...c5**, striking at White's centre immediately.

White has a number of possible replies, but my research has led me to the conclusion that the rarely played 6 dxc5 ♕a5 7 ♕d4!? poses difficult questions, as shown in games 29 and 30.

Part 1 – 5...0-0

> ### Game 22
> ### A.Shirov-C.McNab
> Gibraltar 2006

1 e4 d6 2 d4 ♘f6 3 ♘c3 g6 4 f4 ♗g7 5 ♘f3 0-0 6 ♗e3 b6

This is Black's most-popular and highest-scoring response to White's sixth move. The second player prepares to fianchetto the queen's bishop, while also facilitating ...c5 to fight for the centre.

7 ♕d2 ♗b7

Black can also strike at the centre immediately with 7...c5, for which see Game 24.

8 e5!

White should not shy away from an immediate confrontation. The more reserved 8 ♗d3 allows Black to obtain a satisfactory game after 8...c5 or 8...♘a6.

8...♘g4

This is clearly the most natural move and the alternatives are almost never seen:

a) 8...♘e4 9 ♘xe4 ♗xe4 10 ♘g5 ♗f5 (10...♗b7 is well met by 11 e6) was seen in P.Craciun-A.Dragomirescu, Predeal 2006, and now 11 g4! would have forced the bishop to lose time retreating, as 11...♗xg4? loses to 12 ♕g2 ♗d7 13 e6! (13 ♕xa8? ♗c6) 13...fxe6 14 ♖g1!, threatening both ♕xa8 and ♘xh7.

b) 8...dxe5 does not look so bad, although I could only find one example of this move: 9 dxe5! ♘g4 (after 9...♕xd2+ 10 ♔xd2 ♘e4 11 ♘xe4 ♗xe4 12 0-0-0 White is more comfortable in this queenless position) 10 ♗d3 (10 h3!?) 10...♘a6 11 0-0-0 (11 h3 ♘xe3 12 ♕xe3 ♘b4 13 0-0-0 also looks decent) 11...♘b4 12 ♕e1 ♘xd3+ 13 ♖xd3 ♕c8 was Z.Lanka-P.Jaracz, Bad Wiessee 2002, and now I would suggest 14 h3! ♘xe3 15 ♕xe3 when White's extra activity and space outweigh the power of Black's bishop pair: for instance, 15...♖d8 16 ♖xd8+ ♕xd8 17 e6! and White retains some initiative.

9 0-0-0

White should not waste time retreating the bishop, as it is more important to focus on development. Besides, an exchange on e3 will help to clear the d-file – a common theme in the 6 ♗e3 variation.

9...c5

This undermining move must be considered the critical test of White's play. The main alternative 9...dxe5 will be considered in Game 23, along with a few minor options.

10 dxc5

This is the only serious way to challenge Black's set-up. White grabs a pawn and challenges his opponent to demonstrate compensation.

10...bxc5

We should also consider a couple of alternatives:

a) In a couple of subsequent encounters McNab turned to 10...♕c8?! 11 cxd6 exd6, but with no improvement in the overall result on either occasion:

a1) The first encounter continued 12 h3 ♘xe3 13 ♕xe3 dxe5 14 fxe5 ♘c6 15 ♗b5! (intending to re-route the bishop to b3, from where it will exert serious pressure against f7) 15...a6 16 ♗a4 ♘a5. At this point in M.Mahjoob-C.McNab, Turin Olympiad 2006, I like the following suggestion of Vigus: 17 ♘d5! ♘c4 18 ♕e2 ♕c5 19 b4! ♗h6+ 20 ♔b1 ♘a3+ 21 ♔a1 (or 21 ♔b2 ♕c4 22 ♘f6+ ♔g7 23 ♕e1 a5 24 ♖d4) 21...♕c4 22 ♕xc4 ♘xc4 23 ♗b3 when White's endgame advantage should prove decisive.

a2) A year later McNab followed the same path, which suggests that he had an improvement in mind, although I have not been able to find anything special for Black in the above line. In any case, White deviated with 12 ♗g1 and once again obtained an excellent position: 12...dxe5 13 h3 ♘f6 14 fxe5 ♘e4 15 ♘xe4 ♗xe4 16 ♗d3 (16 ♘g5!?) 16...♗xd3 (Black is not helped by 16...♗xf3 17 gxf3 ♗xe5 18 f4 ♗f6 19 ♗e4 ♖d8 20 ♕e2 ♖xd1+ 21 ♕xd1, winning an exchange; his best chance may have been 16...♖d8 17 ♕e3 ♗xf3 – 17...♗xd3 18 ♖xd3 ♖xd3 19 ♕xd3 ♘c6 20 ♗h2 sees White retain his extra pawn – 18 gxf3 ♕e6 19 b3 ♕xe5 20 ♕xe5 ♗xe5 21 ♗e3 when Black has regained his pawn, but faces a difficult ending against the opponent's powerful bishop pair) 17 ♕xd3 ♘c6 18 ♗h2 ♖e8 19 ♖he1 ♕e6 20 ♕b3. This was G.Jones-C.McNab, London 2007, in which White had consolidated his extra

pawn and went on to convert his advantage.

b) Another second-rate alternative is 10...♘xe3?! 11 ♕xe3 bxc5. This avoids any immediate loss of material, but enables the first player to start a venomous attack by means of 12 h4! (12 ♗c4 is a good alternative, but there is no reason not to go for the jugular!), when Black has tried a couple of ideas:

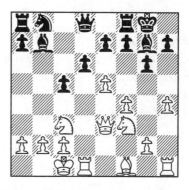

b1) 12...h5 13 f5! ♗xf3 (13...gxf5 14 ♕g5) 14 gxf3 ♘c6 was seen in N.Yaremko-M.Kozakov, Lvov 2006, and now both 15 e6 and 15 f4!? ♘d4 16 fxg6 fxg6 17 ♖g1 look tempting.

b2) After 12...♕b6, the following game was pretty much a model attacking effort from White: 13 h5 ♗xf3 14 gxf3 (14 ♕xf3 is also strong) 14...♘c6 15 hxg6 hxg6 16 ♘d5 ♕b7 17 c3 dxe5 18 fxe5 ♘d4 19 ♗c4 ♖ab8 20 ♖d2 ♘f5 21 ♕g5 ♖fd8 22 e6! fxe6 23 ♕xg6 exd5 24 ♕h7+ ♔f8 25 ♕xf5+ ♗f6 26 ♖h8+ ♔f7 27 ♖h7+ and Black resigned in T.Airapetian-V.Tarasova, Herceg Novi 2006, in view of 27...♔e8 28 ♕g6+ ♔d7 29 ♕xf6.

Returning to 10...bxc5:

11 ♗xc5 ♕a5

Once again, this is certainly not the only playable move:

a) 11...♕c7 does not appear to have been tested, but it seems fairly sensible. Still, White should keep an edge: 12 ♗d4 dxe5 (12...♘c6? 13 exd6 is no good for Black: for instance, 13...♕xd6 14 ♗xg7 ♕xd2+ 15 ♖xd2 ♔xg7 16 ♖d7 with what should be a simple technical conversion) 13 ♘xe5 ♘xe5 14 ♘b5! (winning a pawn, temporarily at least; both 14 fxe5 ♖d8 and 14 ♗xe5 ♗xe5 15 fxe5 ♕xe5 are not so impressive) 14...♕c6 15 ♗xe5 ♗xe5 16 fxe5 ♕e6 17 ♕c3! ♖c8 (Black is not helped by 17...♕xa2 18 ♗c4 ♕a4 19 e6 f6 20 b3 followed by ♘c7) 18 ♘c7 ♕xa2 19 ♗c4 ♕a1+ 20 ♔d2 ♕a4 21 e6 f6 22 b3 ♕a3 23 ♘xa8 when White still has some work to do thanks to his unsafe king, but overall I doubt that Black has enough for the exchange here.

b) 11...♘d7!?, as played in G.Figlio-M.Umansky, correspondence 2003, deserves attention:

b1) A couple of games have continued 12 ♗a3?! ♘dxe5! (this is the clever point behind Black's last move) 13 fxe5 ♗h6 14 ♘g5 ♘xe5 with good counterplay for Black as ...f6 is on the way.

b2) Therefore I agree with Vigus's proposed improvement of 12 ♗g1!. The point is that if Black executes the same idea of 12...♘dxe5? 13 fxe5 ♗h6 14 ♘g5 ♘xe5, the response 15 ♗e3 spoils all of his fun. Therefore he must settle for something like 12...♖c8 when Vigus opines that Black does not have quite enough for the pawn, although the position remains very complicated. A possible continuation is 13 h3 ♘h6 14 h4!? ♘f5 15 ♖h3 h5 16 ♗d3 ♘h6 17 ♘g5 ♕a5 18 ♗e4 ♗xe4 19 ♘gxe4 intending ♕d5 when Black's compensation remains insufficient.

12 ♗a3 dxe5 13 ♘d5!

By forcing a queen exchange White has eliminated most of the opponent's counterplay. Furthermore, it is in the endgame that his extra queenside pawns will really come into their own.

The alternative 13 h3 leads after

13...♗h6! 14 ♘g5 exf4 15 ♘xf7 ♖xf7 16 hxg4 ♗g5 17 ♘e4 ♕xd2+ 18 ♘xd2 f3 to unclear complications.

13...♕xd2+ 14 ♖xd2 ♗xd5 15 ♖xd5

15...♘e3

This has been criticized by some commentators, but it seems to me that Black's chances are worse after other moves too. That being said, in several lines White needs to play with great resourcefulness and precision, so I suggest you pay close attention to the following alternatives, as well as the game continuation.

a) 15...e4!? is suggested by Vigus and also mentioned by Gershon and Nor in *San Luis 2005*. White responds with 16 ♘e5 and now:

a1) Vigus gives 16...♘e3 17 ♖d4 ♘xf1 18 ♖xf1 f6 intending ...f5 when Black seems to be doing fine. However, it turns out that White has a major improvement available in 18 ♖xe4!, picking up the crucial e4-pawn while the knight on f1 remains trapped. Black has nothing better than 18...♘xh2 19 ♖xh2, reaching an ending where White

enjoys a clear advantage despite the equal material. His pieces are much the more active and his three versus one majority on the queenside can advance much more easily than Black's four versus two on the kingside.

a2) Best, therefore, is 16...♘xe5 17 fxe5 ♘c6 18 ♗b5 ♘xe5 19 ♗xe7 ♖fc8 20 c3 as analysed by Gershon and Nor. The position is rather complicated, but I believe White's bishop pair ought to count for something.

b) 15...♗h6!? is another interesting move, and was tested in the game M.Perunovic-D.Leskur, Mataruska Banja 2008. Now instead of the game's 16 ♔b1, I recommend 16 ♗xe7! ♗xf4+ 17 ♔b1 ♖e8 18 ♗g5 ♘e3, reaching the following critical position:

Here I found a strong idea: 19 ♗b5! (19 ♖c5 has been suggested, but without going into too many details, I think Black should be fine after 19...♘d7!). The main idea of the text move is to avoid losing time moving the rook (for the moment at least), while preserving the important light-squared bishop, as well as restricting the development of the knight on b8. Here are some lines I analysed:

b1) 19...♖c8 20 ♖d2 a6 (inferior are 20...h6 21 ♗xf4 exf4 22 g3! and 20...♗xg5 21 ♘xg5 f5 22 ♖e1 f4 23 g3!) 21 ♗d3 with two possibilities:

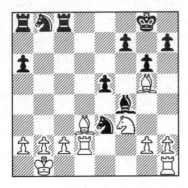

b11) 21...♘c6 22 ♖e2 ♗xg5 (or 22...h6 23 ♘xe5 ♗xg5 24 ♘xc6 ♖xc6 25 ♗e4 ♖cc8 26 h4) 23 ♘xg5 ♘d5 (if 23...♘f5 24 c3) 24 ♗c4 ♘ce7 25 ♗b3 f6 26 ♖d1 fxg5 27 ♖xe5 with an easily winning ending.

b12) 21...♗xg5 22 ♘xg5 ♘c4 23 ♗xc4 ♖xc4 24 ♖d8+ ♔g7 25 ♘f3 (if 25 ♖hd1 ♖g4) 25...f6 26 ♖hd1 with a near-decisive advantage due to the awkward pin along the eighth rank.

b2) 19...♘xd5 20 ♗xe8 with a final split:

b21) 20...e4 21 ♗xf4 exf3 (21...♘xf4 22 ♘g5) 22 ♗h6 fxg2 23 ♖g1 and with two bishops against two knights, White has excellent winning chances.

b22) 20...♘e3 21 g3 ♗xg5 22 ♘xg5 f5 23 ♖e1 f4 24 ♗a4 ♘a6 25 ♘e6 and White wins a pawn.

b23) 20...♔f8 21 ♗a4 ♗xg5 (after 21... ♘b6 22 ♗xf4 exf4 23 ♗b5 a6 24 ♗e2 White's better pawn structure and superior minor piece give him excellent chances) 22 ♘xg5 f6 (22...h6? 23 ♘xf7!) 23 ♖d1 ♘c7 (not 23...♘b6? 24 ♘e6+ ♔e7 25 ♘c7) 24 ♘e4 and once again White's active pieces make his pawn majority more dangerous than that of his opponent.

After that lengthy yet necessary diversion, let us now return to the game:

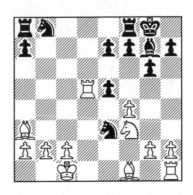

16 ♖d2?!

Although this leads to success in the game, it is not the most accurate for reasons that will become apparent.

If you reach this position over the board, I recommend the improvement 16 ♖d3!, as suggested by Gershon and Nor. I have found no fault with their analysis, so I will reproduce it more or less as it appears in their book:

a) 16...♘xf1 17 ♘xe5! is clearly better for White.

b) 16...♘c4 17 ♗xe7 ♖e8 18 ♖d8 ♖xd8 19 ♗xd8 with a favourable endgame.

c) 16...exf4 17 ♗xe7 ♖c8 (17...♖e8 18 ♗g5) 18 c3 ♘c6 19 ♗d6 ♗h6 20 ♖g1 and White will soon unravel his kingside, after which his queenside majority should be more potent than Black's kingside one.

d) 16...♘xc2!? is perhaps the best chance to complicate the game, but White still keeps the advantage: 17 ♗xe7! (but not 17 ♔xc2? e4) 17...♖c8 18 ♖c3! ♘c6 (or 18...♖xc3 19 bxc3 ♘e3 20 ♘xe5 ♗xe5 21 fxe5 ♘xf1 22 ♖xf1 and Black is clearly worse) 19 ♗a6!. Black has two possibilities here, but neither is good enough to equalize:

d1) 19...♘2d4 20 ♗c5 ♖e8 21 ♘xe5 and at this point 21...♘xe5? 22 ♗xd4 leaves White with a healthy extra pawn, so Black is forced to play 21...♗xe5 22 fxe5 ♖xe5, after which the two white bishops should outrun the enemy knights in the wide-open position.

d2) 19...♘xe7 20 ♗xc8 ♘b4 21 ♗b7 ♖b8 22 ♖c7 ♘ed5 23 ♗xd5 ♘xd5 24 ♖d7 ♘xf4 25 ♖hd1 ♘e6 when Black is by no means dead and buried, but at the same time I find it doubtful that his compensation for the exchange can really be sufficient.

16...♘xf1?

With this error Black's position becomes critical. In theoretical terms, none of the following is relevant to us, since we have already seen the most accurate way for White to handle the position. However, it is still interesting to consider the following possibilities in order to appreciate the resources available to both sides:

a) First, let us briefly note that both 16...e4 17 ♘g5 f5 18 ♗b5! and 16...exf4 17 ♗xe7 ♖e8 18 ♗d6 are unsatisfactory for Black, as pointed out by Gershon and Nor.

b) A year before the present game, a top-level encounter soon reached a similar type of ending to that seen in the main game: 16...♘c6 17 ♗b5 ♖fc8 18 ♗xc6 ♖xc6 19 ♘xe5 ♗xe5 20 fxe5 ♘c4 21 ♗xe7 ♘xd2 22 ♔xd2 ♖b8. This was R.Kasimdzhanov-P.Svidler, FIDE World Championship, San Luis 2005. From this position several commentators have pointed out that the obvious 23 b3! would have given White excellent winning chances.

c) And now for the fly in the ointment. The reason why it was necessary for White to improve on the previous turn is that Black has a serious improvement available in 16...♗h6!, which should enable him to solve all his problems.

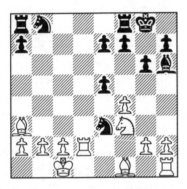

For example, 17 ♗xe7 ♘xf1 18 ♖xf1 (with the rook on d3 White would just capture on f8 here) 18...♗xf4 19 ♗xf8 ♔xf8 20 ♔d1 ♗xd2 21 ♔xd2 ♘c6 is equal, while after 17 ♗d3 ♘c6 18 ♗e4 ♖ac8 19 ♗xc6 ♖xc6 20 ♘xe5 ♖c7 21 g3 ♖fc8 Black wins back his pawn by force, with at least equal chances, as pointed out by Gershon and Nor.

Returning to the misguided 16...♘xf1:

17 ♖xf1 ♘c6

17...exf4 18 ♗xe7 ♖e8 19 ♗g5 wins a pawn.

18 ♘xe5 ♘xe5 19 fxe5 ♗h6

After 19...♗xe5 20 ♗xe7 ♖fe8 21 ♗d6 White is simply a pawn up.

20 ♗xe7

Winning a second pawn. True, White is about to lose the exchange, but his splendid bishop and powerful queenside majority should provide excellent winning chances. In view of the improvements noted previously, the remainder of the game is not so relevant to our study of the opening, so I will limit myself to a few light annotations. That being said, I would certainly suggest that you play through the rest of the game in order to observe Shirov's masterful endgame technique.

20...♖fb8 21 ♖ff2 ♖b5

22 ♗f6

The bishop is perfectly placed on this square, from where it protects the e5-pawn, controls the d8-square, and restricts the enemy king.

22...♖d5 23 c4 ♖c8 24 b3 ♖c6 25 g4

Threatening to break the pin with g5.

25...♖xd2 26 ♖xd2 ♗xd2+ 27 ♔xd2 ♔f8 28 ♔c3

Intending b4.

28...♖a6 29 a4 ♔e8

The pressure against the a4-pawn prevents its neighbour from advancing, but the inconvenience is temporary.

30 c5 ♔d7 31 ♔c4 ♔c6 32 ♗e7 ♖a5

32...h5 33 gxh5 gxh5 34 h4 changes nothing; Black will soon have to give way on the queenside.

33 g5 ♖a6 34 ♗d6 ♖a5 35 ♔b4 ♖a6 36 h4 ♔b7 37 ♔b5 ♖c6 38 b4 a6+ 39 ♔c4 ♖c8 40 ♔d5

All of White's pieces are optimally placed and Shirov wraps things up efficiently.

40...♖e8 41 c6+ ♔b6 42 ♗c5+ ♔c7 43 a5 ♔b8 44 ♗d6+ ♔a7 45 ♔c5 ♖e6 46 b5 axb5 47 ♔xb5 ♖e8 48 c7 1-0

This game, along with the sometimes deep accompanying variations, showcased some of the most critical lines in the entire 6 ♗e3 variation. Fortunately our next game is rather more digestible, while still providing an instructive example of how to handle Black's alternatives on the 9th move.

Game 23
K.Spraggett-O.Jakobsen
Andorra 2007

---

1 e4 d6 2 d4 g6 3 ♘c3 ♗g7 4 f4 ♘f6 5 ♘f3 0-0 6 ♗e3 b6 7 ♕d2 ♗b7 8 e5 ♘g4 9 0-0-0

So far the opening moves have been the same as in Shirov-McNab.

9...dxe5

Apart from the main line of 9...c5, as examined in the previous game, we should briefly consider a couple of rare alternatives. The problem with both these moves is that they fail to put White's centre under any immediate pressure:

a) 9...♘d7 10 h3 (10 ♗g1!?) 10...♘xe3 11 ♕xe3 c5 was seen in A.Grischuk-G.Seul, Mainz (rapid) 2004, and now the simplest route to an advantage would seem to be 12 d5, increasing White's space advantage and shutting the b7-bishop out of play.

b) Occasionally Black has tried 9...♕c8?!, planning ...c5 while avoiding the pin along the d-file, but this plan turns out to be too slow: 10 ♗g1!? (10 h3 is also promising and after 10...♘xe3 11 ♕xe3 c5 12 d5 ♗a6 13 g4 ♗xf1 14 ♖hxf1 White had a clear initiative in E.Paehtz-A.Dragomirescu, Dresden 2004) 10...c5 11 d5 dxe5 12 h3 ♘h6 13 fxe5 ♘f5 14 ♗h2 a6 15 g4 ♘d4 16 ♘xd4 cxd4 17 ♕xd4 by when White had an extra pawn and a dominant centre in J.Dworakowska-A.Borsuk, Bled Olympiad 2002.

10 ♘xe5!

It is important to recapture in the correct way. Instead 10 fxe5 c5! gives Black promising counterplay.

10...♘xe3

In the event of 10...♘xe5 White's simplest answer is 11 dxe5 ♕xd2+ (or 11...♘c6 12 ♕f2 ♕c8 13 h4) 12 ♖xd2, reaching a position in which his extra space, active pieces, and control over the open d-file add up to a stable advantage. One example continued 12...♘c6 13 ♗e2 ♗h6 14 ♘d5 ♖ac8 15 ♗f3 ♗a8 16 ♖hd1, leaving White fully mobilized and firmly in control, M.Carlsen-K.Lahno, Wijk aan Zee 2004.

11 ♕xe3 ♘d7

The alternative 11...e6 has so far scored 100% for Black, but it is safe to say that this in no way reflects the true state of the position. Play continues 12 h4! and now:

a) 12...♘d7 13 h5 ♘f6 14 hxg6 fxg6 15 ♕h3 ♕e7 16 ♗c4 ♘h5 17 ♗xe6+ ♔h8 was M.Mrdja-A.Dunnington, Cannes 1995, and now 18 ♘d5 ♗xd5 19 ♗xd5 would have brought White a huge advantage.

b) 12...♕e7 13 h5 ♘d7 14 ♗d3 (14 hxg6 is also promising, but in some positions it might be useful to retain the option of advancing with h6) 14...♖fd8 15 ♗e4 ♘xe5 was seen in G.Kubach-Z.Nyvlt, correspondence 2002, and now 16 dxe5 would have maintained a pleasant advantage for White.

12 h4

Starting a dangerous attack, although White arguably has an even more promising alternative available in 12 ♗b5!? ♘f6 (12...♘xe5 13 dxe5 ♕b8 14 ♘d5 ♗xd5 15 ♖xd5 ♕b7 16 ♖hd1 is clearly better for White, as pointed out by Belov) 13 d5! ₩d6 14 ☐he1 with strong central pressure.

From here Black has tried:

a) 14...☐ad8 15 ②c6 ②g4 (15...♗xc6 16 dxc6 ₩b4 17 ☐xd8 ☐xd8 18 a3 ₩a5 19 ₩xe7 ☐e8 20 ₩xe8+ ②xe8 21 ☐xe8+ ♗f8 22 ☖b1! is a nice variation given by Vigus, the point being that Black must inevitably lose the queen: for instance, 22...☖g7 23 ☐xf8 ☖xf8 24 ☖a2 followed by b2-b4) 16 ②xe7+ ☖h8 17 ₩f3 ②e5 (17...②xh2 18 ₩g3) 18 fxe5 ₩xe7 19 ₩g3 when White had an extra pawn and a positional advantage to boot, J.Stopa-M.Szczepinski, Koszalin 2005.

b) 14...a6 15 ♗c6 ♗xc6 (or 15...☐ab8 16 g4 with a clear advantage to White) 16 dxc6 ₩e6 17 ₩f3 ₩c8 18 ②d7 saw Black getting completely smothered in D.Campora-E.Torre, Moscow 1994. The remaining moves were: 18...☐e8 (18...②xd7 19 cxd7 ₩d8 20 ₩c6 is clearly better for White) 19 g4 e6 20 g5 ②h5 21 ②e4 a5 22 ②g3 ②xg3 23 hxg3 ₩a6 24 ₩e2 ☐ed8 25 c4 a4 26 a3 ₩a5 27 ☐h1 ₩f5 28 ₩h2 h5 29 gxh6 ♗f8 30 g4 ₩a5 31 ₩h4 1-0.

12...②xe5

Black has also avoided the exchange with 12...②f6, as in A.Berelovich-F.Cuijpers, German League 2001. At this point the most straightforward response seems to be 13 ♗e2 intending h5 (the game continuation of 13 h5 ②xh5 gave White reasonable compensation for the pawn, but nothing conclusive). Play might continue 13...h5 (13...♗xg2 seems too risky in view of 14 ☐h2 ♗b7 15 h5 with a venomous attack) 14 ♗f3 ♗xf3 15 ₩xf3 when White remains on top, thanks to his central control and attacking possibilities based on a timely g4.

13 dxe5 ₩c8 14 h5

White's attack is already well underway, while Black is struggling to coordinate his forces.

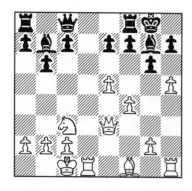

14...₩e6 15 hxg6 hxg6 16 ♗d3 ☐fd8

16...♗xg2 looks too risky. After the natural 17 ☐h2 ♗b7 White breaks through with 18 f5! ₩xe5 (18...gxf5 19 ☐g1) 19 ₩h3 ☐fd8 20 fxg6. It is doubtful that Black's exposed king will be able to survive from here. I analysed the following line, which illustrates his difficulties quite nicely: 20...♖d6 21 ♔b1! (White can afford to spend a tempo improving his king and avoiding any defences based on a check on e3, f4 or g5) 21...♖f6 (21...♔f8 22 ♖f2 f6 may hold out for longer, but Black's position is grim nonetheless) 22 ♖e2 ♕f4 23 ♖xe7 fxg6 24 ♕d7 ♕h6 (24...♔f7 loses to 25 ♕e6 intending ♖f1 or ♗c4) 25 ♘d5 ♖f2 (25...♖d6 26 ♕xc7) 26 ♖xg7+! ♕xg7 27 ♘e7+ and White wins.

17 ♕g3 ♖d4 18 ♖h3 ♖ad8 19 ♖dh1 f5

Black cannot do without this move for long, in view of the threatened ♖h7 followed by ♕g5 and ♖xg7+.

20 ♕g5 ♔f7 21 ♖h7 ♖g8

Black is making a reasonable attempt to defend, but he is fighting a lost cause.

22 ♖g1

A more conclusive route to victory was 22 ♖1h6!, which virtually forces the desperate sacrifice 22...♖xd3 (the threat was ♗e2! followed by ♖xg6 and/or ♗h5) 23 cxd3 when White has an extra exchange as well as a domi-

nant position.

22...♗e4

The threat was g4 and presumably Black found 22...♗c8 too depressing a move to contemplate.

23 ♗xe4 fxe4 24 g4 ♔f8

The best practical chance was 24...e3, although White keeps a big advantage here too: 25 ♖e1 ♕c4 26 ♖h3! (26 f5 ♖xg4 27 fxg6+ ♔e6 is not quite so clear, although White must be doing well) 26...♖gd8 (26...♖xf4 27 ♘d5!) 27 ♖hxe3 ♖xf4 28 ♘e4 ♖f1 29 b3 and Black remains under heavy pressure.

25 ♖h3!?

Having provoked a weakening of the enemy structure, White sets about rounding up the weak e-pawn.

25...♖h8 26 ♖xh8+ ♗xh8 27 ♖e1 ♗g7

After 27...♕c6 28 ♕h4 ♗g7 29 ♕h3 the e-pawn is a goner.

28 a3 ♕c6

29 ♔b1!

Preventing any counterplay based on ...e3.

29...a6

29...e3 30 ♖xe3 ♕h1+ achieves

nothing after 31 ♔a2.

30 f5!

White must remain vigilant. Indeed, 30 ♕h4? would have squandered a significant part of his advantage after 30...e3!, with an awkward counterattack against f4: for instance, 31 ♕g3 ♕c4!.

30...♗xe5 31 fxg6

With an exposed king and loose pieces, Black's position is lost.

31...♕f6

31...♗g7? 32 ♕f5+ wins immediately.

32 ♕h6+ ♕g7 33 ♖f1+ ♔g8 34 ♕g5 ♖d6

35 ♘d5!

This final tactical blow seals Black's fate.

35...♖xd5 36 ♖f7 ♕h8

Giving up the queen would have led to a hopeless endgame, but the text is hardly any better.

37 ♕xe7 ♕h1+ 38 ♔a2 ♕h6 39 ♕e8+ 1-0

This was an excellent performance from Spraggett. Overall I would assess

the positions after 9...dxe5 10 ♘xe5 as distinctly favourable to White, who can quickly launch a powerful and easy-to-handle attack.

Our next game also features a dangerous attacking scheme, although this time the play is rather more double-edged as White must be willing to sacrifice some material. Fortunately the potential rewards more than justify the risk.

Game 24
J.Polgar-I.Smirin
Istanbul Olympiad 2000

1 e4 d6 2 d4 ♘f6 3 ♘c3 g6 4 f4 ♗g7 5 ♘f3 0-0 6 ♗e3 b6 7 ♕d2 c5

7...♗b7 was seen in the previous two games. The text move is an important alternative, for which White should be well prepared.

8 0-0-0

This is the most interesting response, although readers who find the game continuation too wild may wish to investigate 8 d5, which also offers good chances for an opening advantage.

8...cxd4 9 ♗xd4!

9 ♘xd4 is not a bad move, but the non-stereotypical move seen in the game is the best way to put the opponent under pressure.

9...♘c6

In the event of 9...♗b7!? (A.Ashton-C.Beaumont, British League 2007), the most consistent response is 10 h4! when possible replies include:

a) The e-pawn is poisoned, as revealed by the variations 10...♗xe4?? 11 ♗xf6 ♗xf3 12 ♗xg7 ♗xd1 13 ♗xf8, and 10...♘xe4?? 11 ♘xe4 ♗xe4 12 ♗xg7 ♗xf3 13 ♗xf8 ♗xd1 14 ♗h6 ♗h5 (if 14...♗g4 15 ♕d4) 15 g4! ♗xg4 16 ♕d4 e5 (16...f6 17 ♕d5+) 17 fxe5, when White wins in each instance.

b) 10...h5 weakens the kingside and 11 f5! offers White good attacking chances.

c) 10...♘bd7 11 e5 (11 h5!? also looks interesting, although I was unable to find anything conclusive after

11...♘xh5 12 ♗xg7 ♔xg7) 11...dxe5 12 fxe5 ♘g4 (also promising for White are both 12...♘d5 13 h5 and 12...♘e4 13 ♘xe4 ♗xe4 14 h5) 13 e6 ♘de5 (or 13...♗h6 14 ♘g5 ♘de5 15 ♕e2) 14 ♘xe5 ♘xe5 15 h5 with some initiative for White.

10 ♗xf6! ♗xf6 11 h4!

The point behind White's 9th move is revealed. It is worth 'sacrificing' the valuable dark-squared bishop for a knight in order to gain time for the attack.

11...♗g4

11...h5!? was suggested by Polgar, but has not yet been tested. The strongest continuation looks to be Vigus's suggestion of 12 f5! when Black must tread carefully: for instance, 12...gxf5? 13 ♕h6 fxe4 14 ♘xe4 ♗g7 15 ♕xh5 ♕c7 16 ♗d3 and White's threats are already unstoppable.

12 h5

The most energetic, although the untested 12 ♘d5!? also looks interesting: for example, 12...♗g7 13 ♘e3 ♗e6 14 h5!? (14 ♔b1 is of course not bad either) 14...♗xa2 15 hxg6 hxg6 16 ♕e1! with good attacking chances.

12...♗xh5

This is the only move to have been tested; presumably most players would reason that if one is going to face a strong attack regardless, then one may as well grab some material and hope for the best. Other possibilities fail to equalize:

a) Black is certainly not helped by 12...♘b4?! 13 hxg6 hxg6 14 ♗c4 ♖c8 15 ♗b3 followed by ♕f2-g3 with strong pressure, as noted by Finkel.

b) 12...gxh5 is not ridiculous, as the bishop on g4 helps to glue the black kingside together. The line 13 ♘d5 ♗g7 14 ♗b5 was mentioned by Polgar, who presumably believes White is doing well here. Extending this line a little further, play might continue 14...♖c8 15 e5!? e6 (if 15...dxe5 16 ♗xc6 ♖xc6 17 ♘f6+) 16 ♗xc6 ♖xc6 and from here 17 ♘b4 ♖c4 18 b3 ♖c7 19 ♕xd6 ♕xd6 leads to a murky endgame, so 17 ♘e3! looks like the right way to preserve White's initiative.

13 ♖xh5! gxh5 14 ♕d5

White has sacrificed a considerable amount of material, but in return she has succeeded in wrecking the opposing king's protective barrier. Her last move wins a tempo to transfer the queen to the danger zone.

14...♖c8?!

This natural move is not the best, so Black should investigate the second of the following alternatives:

a) 14...♕c8 15 ♕xh5 and now:

a1) 15...♗xc3?? 16 ♘g5 1-0 was the embarrassing end to J.Van Mechelen-N.Bernard, Belgian League 2001.

a2) Instead of this unfortunate blunder, 15...♗g7 was essential, although 16 ♘d5 maintains a powerful initiative for White. Please note that the natural 16...e6? loses by force after 17 ♘g5! h6 18 ♘f6+! ♔h8 (18...♗xf6 19 ♕xh6 ♗xg5 20 ♕xg5+ ♔h7 21 ♗d3 and ♖h1 leads to mate) 19 ♕xf7! ♘e7 20 ♖xd6 and so on.

b) 14...♗xc3!? looks like the best chance to make Black's opening viable: 15 bxc3 ♕c8 (Polgar mentions the line

15...♘a5 16 ♕xh5 f6 17 e5 ♕e8 18 ♕h4 which looks promising for White) 16 ♕xh5 ♕e6 was seen in J.Copley-D.Kraszewski, correspondence 2001. Now instead of the game's 17 f5, I recommend 17 ♗b5! when Black has three plausible replies:

b1) With 17...♘d8? Black hopes to use the knight on the kingside, but this plan seems too clumsy. My main line runs 18 ♖h1 ♕g6 19 ♕h4 f6 20 g4! ♔h8 21 f5! ♕g7 22 g5 fxg5 23 ♘xg5 h6 24 ♖g1 ♖f6 25 ♘h3! intending ♘f4; it is doubtful that Black can defend.

b2) 17...♘a5 18 ♖h1 ♕g6 19 ♕h4 was mentioned by Polgar. Black's position looks precarious: for instance, 19...♖fc8 20 ♖h3 ♕f6 (20...♔h8 21 f5 ♕g7 22 ♘g5 ♔g8 23 ♖g3 ♔h8 24 f6! exf6 25 ♘f3 wins for White) 21 ♖g3+ ♔h8 22 ♘g5 ♕g7 23 ♘xh7! ♕xh7 24 ♕xe7 ♖g8 25 ♖h3 and White should win the ending.

b3) 17...♖fc8! looks best when White must make a tough decision:

b31) The first point to note is that White definitely has at least a draw to

fall back on: 18 ♖d5 ♘d8 (18...♘a5? is worse: 19 ♗d7! ♕f6 20 ♖g5+ ♔f8 21 ♕xh7 e6 22 ♖g8+ ♔e7 23 ♗xc8 ♕xf4+ 24 ♔b1 and White is winning)

19 ♘d4 (19 ♗d3 ♖xc3 seems okay for Black, who can always sacrifice on d3 if the bishop threatens anything terrible) 19...♕xe4 20 ♖g5+ ♔h8 21 ♗d3 ♕e1+ 22 ♔b2 ♕xc3+ 23 ♔b1 ♕e1+ and the game ends in perpetual check.

b32) There are other ways for White to play the position, but to tell the truth I have not found anything absolutely convincing: for example, after 18 ♗xc6 ♖xc6 19 ♘d4 ♕xe4 (if 19...♖c5 20 ♕xc5 bxc5 21 ♘xe6 fxe6 22 ♔d2) 20 ♕g5+ ♔f8 21 ♘xc6 ♕xc6 22 ♖d3 it seems doubtful that White can hope for any more than a draw, as his exposed king will be vulnerable to checks.

b33) Another idea is 18 ♘h4!?, which leads to unclear play after 18...♕f6 19 ♘f5 e6 20 ♘xd6 ♕xf4+ 21 ♔b2. I doubt that White is really better here, but the game goes on.

In conclusion, it is possible that

Black can narrowly maintain the balance with precise play. Should this dissuade you from playing this line with White? It depends on your own outlook, but unless your opponent is exceptionally well-prepared, I would say it is unlikely to matter much. Naturally too I would encourage the reader to conduct his own research and look for improvements in the above lines. If he is still unsatisfied, there are plenty of other ways to fight for the advantage, such as the untested 12 ♘d5!? as well as the earlier deviation 8 d5, both of which were noted earlier.

We now return to 14...♖c8:

15 ♕xh5

15...♗g7

This looks forced, as the threat was e5 followed by ♗d3.

It is worth noting that 15...♗xc3?? 16 ♘g5! wins at once, as pointed out by Finkel.

16 e5!

The imminent ♗d3 remains a serious concern for Black.

16...♕e8

Perhaps Black's most resilient defence would have been 16...h6!?, although he is clearly struggling here too: 17 ♘h4! e6 18 ♖xd6 ♕e8 (18...♕e7? 19 ♘d5! is crushing) 19 ♗b5. Polgar chose to end her analysis here, but I would like to extend it a little further: 19...a6 20 ♗xa6 ♖d8 21 ♘e4 ♖xd6 22 ♘xd6 ♕a8 23 ♗b5 ♘e7 24 ♔b1 and Black is alive, but he is clearly struggling.

17 ♕h3!

Sidestepping any defences based on ...f5, which would have threatened a queen exchange.

17...h6

Black has no time for 17...dxe5, in view of 18 ♘g5! h6 19 ♕f5! hxg5 20 ♗d3 with a mating attack.

18 ♗d3

Threatening ♕f5 and mate.

18...♘b4

18...e6 does not solve Black's problems after 19 ♘e4 ♘b4 (or 19...dxe5 20 ♘f6+! ♗xf6 21 ♕xh6) 20 ♘f6+ ♗xf6 21 exf6 ♘xd3+ 22 ♖xd3 ♔h7 23 ♘g5+ ♔g6 24 ♘e4 – analysis by Finkel.

19 ♗e4!

Naturally this valuable attacking piece must be preserved.

19...e6

Black needs to stop ♕f5 somehow. Hopeless are both 19...d5? 20 ♘xd5 ♘xd5 21 ♕f5 and 19...♕d8? 20 ♕f5 ♖e8 21 e6 fxe6 22 ♕xe6+ ♔h8 23 ♘g5 with mate to follow shortly.

20 f5!

The humble foot soldier charges to the front-line.

20...♖xc3

Black desperately tries to distract his opponent from the attack, but to no avail.

Instead 20...dxe5 21 f6! ♗xf6 22 ♕xh6 wins immediately and the other desperate attempt, 20...♘xa2+, soon loses after 21 ♘xa2 ♕a4 22 ♖d4! ♕xa2 23 f6 ♕a1+ 24 ♔d2.

21 f6!

One cannot help but admire Polgar's complete single-mindedness in executing her attack.

21...♕b5?

Not the most resilient defence, but there was little chance of saving the game in any case:

a) 21...♘xa2+ 22 ♔b1 achieves nothing.

b) The best try was 21...♕a4, but after 22 bxc3 ♘xa2+ 23 ♔b2 ♘xc3 (23...♕xe4 24 ♕g3 ♕g6 25 ♕xg6 fxg6 26 fxg7 wins, as pointed out by Vigus) 24 ♖d4! Black has no good defence, as shown by Polgar.

22 ♕g3! 1-0

Black resigned, as he will soon run out of checks after 22...♖xc2+ 23 ♗xc2 ♘xa2+ 24 ♔d2 ♕b4+ 25 ♔e3 ♕c5+ 26 ♖d4.

This was a model attacking display from Judit Polgar. Despite the improvement noted on Black's 14th move, I cannot imagine many Pirc players lining up to defend Black's position.

Having devoted three games to Black's main line of 6...b6, we will now turn our attention to his other options on the sixth move, beginning with a logical knight development.

Game 25
T.Stoere-B.Hanison
Correspondence 1990

1 e4 d6 2 d4 ♘f6 3 ♘c3 g6 4 f4 ♗g7 5 ♘f3 0-0 6 ♗e3 ♘bd7

This comes with Vigus's seal of approval. Just as with 6...b6, Black's main idea is to prepare ...c5, but this time he does so by developing a piece. In most lines of the Austrian Attack, Black would be ill-advised to deploy his knight to this square, as the automatic response e4-e5 would leave the knight on f6 without a convenient retreat square. However, the fact that the bishop has already been developed on e3 means that Black will be able to gain a tempo with ...♞g4, which makes the e5 plan a lot less attractive for White.

9...♞fe4

This has been the usual choice, although I also found a game featuring a different knight move: 9...♞g4 10 ♗xc5 (10 ♗g1 b6 11 0-0-0 ♗b7 is unclear according to Vigus) 10...dxc5 was tried in S.Dvoirys-G.Zaichik, Kharkov 1985, and here I believe White should have played 11 0-0-0 ♛xd2+ 12 ♖xd2 when his lead in development looks more significant than Black's bishop pair. Play might continue 12...♞e3 (otherwise ♞d5 may be awkward) 13 ♗d3 ♗g4 14 ♗e4 ♞c4 15 ♖e2 and White keeps a slight plus.

10 ♞xe4 ♞xe4 11 ♛b4

7 ♛d2

Proof of the previous comment is seen after 7 e5?! ♞g4 8 ♗g1 c5 when White is already struggling to hold his centre together.

7...c5 8 dxc5!?

This is an important moment. The most popular move has been 8 0-0-0, but after 8...♞g4! 9 ♗g1 cxd4 10 ♞xd4 e5 Black has reasonable chances to equalize. The text move has not been as heavily investigated, but to my eyes it appears promising.

8...♞xc5

8...dxc5? is never played; with good reason as Black is clearly struggling after 9 0-0-0.

9 e5

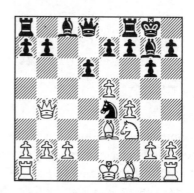

Now Black must decide how to deal with the threat to the knight. Note that the greedy 11 ♕d5?! ♘c5 12 ♗xc5 ♗e6 13 ♕xb7 dxc5 is not at all attractive for White.

11...d5

Two other moves have been tried:

a) 11...♘c5 12 0-0-0 ♕c7 13 exd6 exd6 14 ♗d4 gave White a pleasant edge in S.Dvoirys-G.Laketic, Chelyabinsk 1991.

b) 11...♗f5 12 ♗d3 d5 13 ♘d4 e6 14 0-0 ♕c7 was seen in A.Bangiev-H.Jongman, correspondence 1987, and now after 15 c4!? dxc4 16 ♖ac1 White has a useful space advantage and the more active pieces, while the knight on e4 isn't very stable.

12 ♗d3

12 ♖d1!? also deserves serious consideration, intending c2-c4.

12...b6 13 0-0 ♕c7

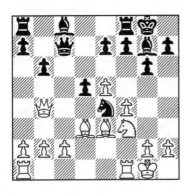

14 a4!

Improving over a previous battle between two bigger names, which continued as follows: 14 ♖ae1 ♗b7 15 ♖e2 e6 16 ♗d4 ♗h6 17 ♕e1 ♕e7 18 ♘d2 ♖fd8

19 ♗xe4 dxe4 20 ♕f2 ♗xf4 21 ♘xe4 ♗xe4 22 ♖xe4 ♗h6 when White failed to achieve anything and the game was subsequently drawn, A.Khalifman-Z.Azmaiparashvili, Kiev 1986.

The idea of breaking up the black queenside is much more potent.

14...♘c5 15 a5 ♗g4 16 ♘d4

White should not allow this valuable knight to be exchanged for the much weaker enemy bishop.

16...♘xd3

Perhaps Black could have considered preserving the knight on c5, where it would at least help to shield the b6-pawn from diagonal attacks. Nevertheless, there is no question that the initiative lies with White.

17 cxd3

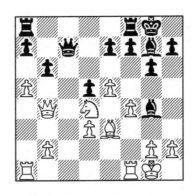

17...bxa5

Not an easy decision to make, but Black was probably worried about ♖fc1 with the idea of meeting ...♕b7 with a6.

18 ♕xa5 ♕b7 19 b3

It was also worth considering 19 b4!? intending b5, with an even more powerful grip over the queenside.

19...f6

19...罝fc8 20 罝fc1 maintains the pressure, so Black tries to fight back in the centre.

20 e6!

Obviously White should avoid pawn exchanges, which would open the position for the enemy bishops.

20...f5

Otherwise White have played either f5 or h3, leading to total domination. After the text move, however, the offside bishop on g4 remains a serious concern for Black.

21 罝fc1 罝ac8 22 h3 兔h5 23 b4 兔f6?!

23...a6 was essential, although Black is still in trouble.

24 b5

Completing the bind over the queenside. Black has almost no active moves at all.

24...罝xc1+ 25 罝xc1 豐b6 26 豐xb6

The computer wants to play 26 豐a4 intending 罝c6, which is also more than good enough, but the ending is clearly winning so there is no special reason to

avoid it.

26...axb6 27 罝c6 罝a8!?

Black abandons the b-pawn in a desperate bid for counterplay.

27...罝b8 would have been met by 28 罝c7 intending ②c6.

28 罝xb6 罝a3 29 罝b8+

With this move White starts to make the winning process a little more complicated. 29 ②c6! 罝xd3 30 兔c5 was more conclusive. White will win the e7-pawn, after which the two passed pawns, combined with some possible threats against the black king, should make the win a formality: for instance, 30...兔h4 (threatening ...兔g3) 31 ②xe7+ 含g7 32 罝b7 含f6 33 ②c6

33...含xe6 (not 33...兔g3 34 罝f7+ 含xe6 35 ②d8 mate) 34 ②e5 罝d1+ 35 含h2 (threatening mate on b6) 35...d4 36 罝d7 and Black has no defence against the threats of 兔f8 followed by 罝d6 mate, and 罝d6+ immediately followed by a discovered check.

29...含g7 30 b6 罝xd3 31 b7 罝xe3 32 罝g8+ 含xg8 33 b8豐+ 含g7 34 豐e8

Material is approximately equal,

but Black's weak e7-pawn and vulnerable king give him problems. The remainder of the game is not so important for us, but White was eventually able to convert his advantage as follows.

34...♔h6 35 ♕f8+ ♗g7 36 ♘xf5+! gxf5 37 ♕xf5 ♗f6 38 g4 ♖g3+ 39 ♔h2 ♗g6 40 g5+ ♗xg5 41 fxg5+ ♖xg5 42 ♕f8+ ♔h5 43 ♕xe7

Black is unable to build a fortress.

43...♖e5 44 ♕d6 ♖e2+ 45 ♔g1 ♔h6 46 ♕xd5 ♖e4 47 ♕d2+ ♔h5 48 ♕d6 ♔g5 49 ♕d8+ ♔h5 50 e7 ♔h6 51 ♔f2 ♔h5 52 ♕d5+ ♔h6 53 ♕xe4 1-0

Overall it seems that the slightly unusual 8 dxc5!? is an excellent try for an advantage. We will now move on to a third option for Black on move six.

Game 26
D.Pavasovic-N.Mrkonjic
Croatian Team
Championship 2010

---

1 e4 d6 2 d4 ♘f6 3 ♘c3 g6 4 f4 ♗g7 5 ♘f3 0-0 6 ♗e3 c6

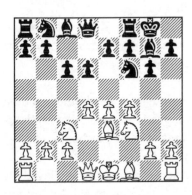

This is the most-frequently played of Black's alternatives to 6...b6. Instead of aiming for ...c5, Black bases his counterplay on ...b5 or occasionally ...d5.

7 h3!?

I find this slightly offbeat move to be one of the most promising at White's disposal. The main idea is to prepare e5 without allowing the reply ...♘g4. Here is a quick round-up of the alternatives:

a) 7 ♕d2 is possible, although after 7...b5 Black's counterplay is already underway; he is threatening to win a pawn and his early queenside activity renders long castling unappealing for White.

b) 7 ♗d3 is a decent move, against which Black has numerous possible replies. One interesting game continued 7...♘a6!? 8 ♗xa6 bxa6 9 h3 ♖b8 10 ♖b1 d5?! (Vigus recommends the improvement 10...♘e8!? intending ...f5) 11 e5 ♘e4 12 ♘xe4 dxe4 13 ♘d2 when Black had too many pawn weaknesses and went on to lose in V.Kotronias-

V.Tseshkovsky, Vrnjacka Banja 2005.

7...b5

Black has tried several other moves. Here is a summary of the most significant ones:

a) 7...♘a6?! 8 ♗xa6 bxa6 9 0-0 gives White an extra tempo over the Kotronias-Tseshkovsky game noted above.

b) 7...♘bd7 8 e5 dxe5 (8...♘h5 leaves the black knight in trouble after 9 ♘e2 or 9 ♔f2!?) 9 dxe5 ♘d5 10 ♘xd5 cxd5 11 ♕d2 ♘b6 was A.Donchenko-A.Gavrilov, Moscow 1995, and now after 12 b3 White has the better chances, as Black's minor pieces do not coordinate very well.

c) 7...♕a5 8 ♗d3 ♘bd7 9 0-0 e5 10 ♕e1 and White has a slight plus, as he controls the centre and has good chances to develop a kingside attack.

Interestingly Pavasovic reached this position five years prior to the present game and won in fine style then too: 10...exd4 (10...♘h5 11 dxe5 dxe5 12 f5 gave White a promising kingside initiative in Y.Masserey-R.Schmaltz, Alten-

steig 1994) 11 ♗xd4 ♖e8 12 ♕f2 ♘c5 13 e5 ♘xd3 14 cxd3 dxe5 15 fxe5 ♘d5 16 ♘e4 ♗e6 17 ♘fg5 ♕c7 18 ♘xh7!? (White could also have kept some advantage by calmer means with 18 ♘d6 followed by ♕h4) 18...♔xh7 19 ♕h4+ ♔g8 20 ♘g5 c5 21 ♖ac1 b6 22 ♕h7+ ♔f8 23 ♕xg6 ♕e7? (23...♕d7! was the best defence, after which 24 ♖f3? runs into 24...♘f6!) 24 ♖f3! cxd4 25 ♖cf1 ♔g8 26 ♖xf7 ♗xf7 27 ♖xf7 ♕xf7 28 ♕xf7+ ♔h8 29 ♕xd5 ♖ac8 30 ♘f7+ ♔h7 31 e6 ♗f6 32 ♕h5+ ♔g8 33 ♘h6+ ♔g7 34 ♘f5+ 1-0 D.Pavasovic-A.Graf, Deizisau 2005.

8 e5

One of the advantages of delaying ♕d2 is that Black does not have the option of meeting the text move with ...b4.

8...♘d5 9 ♘xd5 cxd5 10 ♗d3

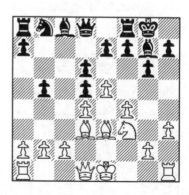

White's powerful central pawn wedge gives him the better chances. The tension between the pawns on e5 and d6 also favours the first player. If Black exchanges on e5, then the reply fxe5 will open the f-file and the c1-h6

diagonal, both of which lead towards Black's king. If, on the other hand, Black leaves the pawns as they stand, he must constantly remain mindful of the possibility of exd6.

10...a6

In the following game Black also failed to solve his problems: 10...♞c6 11 0-0 (obviously 11 ♗xb5?? is impossible due to 11...♛a5+) 11...♛b6 (11...a6 transposes to the main game) 12 ♛e1 f6?! (this creates too many weaknesses) 13 exd6! exd6 (Black would normally prefer to meet the capture on d6 with 13...e6, but having already played ...f6 the resulting pawn formation is rather soft and after 14 h4! Black is under pressure) 14 f5! ♗xf5 15 ♗xf5 gxf5 16 ♞h4 ♞e7 17 ♞xf5 ♞xf5 18 ♖xf5 ♖ae8 19 ♛d2 and Black had too many weaknesses and soon went down in J.Aubel-P.Van Hoolandt, Belgian League 1997.

11 0-0 ♞c6

12 ♛d2

12 ♛e1 is a decent alternative.

12...♗f5!?

The bishop lacked a useful role so

Black decides to exchange it, although the weakening of his kingside carries an obvious risk.

13 ♗xf5 gxf5 14 ♖ae1 ♛a5

A queen exchange would obviously suit Black.

15 c3

15 exd6!? e6 16 ♞e5 also looks promising, as after 16...♛xd2 17 ♗xd2 ♞xd4? 18 c3 ♗xe5 19 fxe5 ♞c6 20 ♗h6 Black's dark-squared weaknesses will prove fatal.

15...b4?!

This is too ambitious. Black should have settled for a defensive move such as 15...e6 when his position is somewhat worse, but still playable. White can choose between the solid 16 a3, followed by kingside play with ♗f2-h4, perhaps combined with a rook lift to g3, or the more aggressive 16 g4!? fxg4 17 hxg4, with the makings of a strong attack.

16 exd6!

White should only play this move when the circumstances are particularly favourable, otherwise Black will simply respond with ...e6 followed by rounding up the loose pawn. In the present position, Pavasovic has correctly judged that Black's poor coordination will prevent him from carrying out this plan in a satisfactory way.

16...bxc3 17 bxc3 e6

17...exd6 leaves the f5-pawn chronically weak and after 18 ♘h4 ♘e7 19 ♗f2 Black has a horrible position.

18 ♘e5 ♖ac8

Black is not helped by 18...♖fc8 19 ♖b1 when the vulnerability of the f7-pawn might come into play.

19 ♖b1!

White takes advantage of his opponent's queenside demonstration by utilizing the recently opened b-file.

19...♕d8 20 ♕d3

There was an even stronger continuation available: 20 c4! dxc4 (after 20...♘xe5 21 fxe5 ♖xc4 22 ♖b7 material is equal, but positionally Black is busted) 21 ♘xc4 ♘a7 22 ♖fc1 ♘b5 23 ♕b4 ♖c6 (or 23...♘xd4 24 ♔h2! when the disappearance of the d4-pawn could prove helpful to White, as the

more important d6-pawn can now be supported along the open d-file) 24 d5! exd5 25 ♘e5 ♖xc1+ (25...♖xd6 26 ♗c5) 26 ♖xc1 ♘xd6 27 ♗c5 and White will win the exchange for a pawn; combined with Black's weak kingside structure, this ensures him of excellent winning chances.

20...♘b8?

Black should have cut his losses with 20...♕xd6 21 ♕xa6 when he may be a pawn down, but his pawn structure and piece coordination remain in reasonable shape. Best play looks to be 21...♖a8! 22 ♕xc6 (22 ♕b5 ♖fc8) 22...♗xe5 23 ♖b6 ♕xc6 24 ♖xc6 ♗f6 when White is still better, but it will not be easy to convert his extra pawn.

21 c4! f6

After 21...♕xd6 22 c5 ♕c7 23 ♖b6 White is in complete control.

22 cxd5! exd5

In the event of 22...fxe5 both 23 dxe5 and 23 fxe5 leave White with a hugely powerful central pawn mass.

23 ♘f3

White could even have left the

knight en prise with 23 ♗d2!? in order to prevent the capture on d6.

23...♕xd6 24 ♘h4 ♖c4 25 ♘xf5

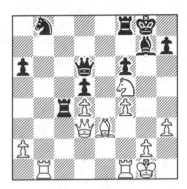

Black is a pawn down, but that is the least of his worries. The knight on f5 is exceptionally powerful.

25...♕d7 26 ♖b6

There is nothing wrong with this, although the direct 26 ♖f3! would have been even better.

26...♖fc8

After the alternative 26...♘c6 27 ♖fb1 Black has to worry about the seventh rank.

27 ♗d2 ♖4c6 28 ♖fb1 ♖xb6 29 ♖xb6 ♘c6 30 ♖xa6

Another pawn drops. Black struggles on for a while longer, but his situation is hopeless.

30...♗f8 31 ♖b6 ♕c7 32 ♖b5 ♕d7 33 ♕b1 ♘a7 34 ♖b7 ♖c7 35 ♖xc7 ♕xc7 36 ♕b3 ♕c4 37 ♕xc4 dxc4 38 ♘e3 ♘b5 39 ♘xc4 ♘xd4 40 ♗e3 ♘e2+ 41 ♔f2 ♘c3 42 a3 f5 43 ♗d4 ♘a4 44 ♘b2 ♘xb2 45 ♗xb2 ♔f7 46 g4 ♗c5+ 47 ♔f3 ♔g6 48 a4 ♗b4 49 ♗d4 ♗a5 50 ♔e3 fxg4 51 hxg4 h5 52 f5+ 1-0

1 e4 d6 2 d4 ♘f6 3 ♘c3 g6 4 f4 ♗g7 5 ♘f3 0-0 6 ♗e3 ♘c6

This move is slightly unusual but should definitely be considered, especially as it can be reached via a Modern move order, as was the case in the present game.

7 ♗e2

The game actually began with the opening moves 1...g6 2 d4 d6 3 ♘c3 ♗g7 4 f4 ♘c6 5 ♗e3 ♘f6 6 ♗e2 0-0 7 ♘f3, but I have taken the liberty of modifying the sequence to fit in with the present chapter.

The development of the bishop on e2 appears timid and indeed it would not normally be our first choice, but this particular variation is a rare exception. White intends to meet ...e5 with dxe5, so he avoids placing the bishop on the typically more desirable d3-square in order to keep the d-file open.

An example of a more energetic but not necessarily more promising approach is 7 e5 ♘g4 8 ♗g1 dxe5 9 dxe5 f6 10 ♗c4+ ♚h8 11 h3 ♘h6 when Black is okay.

7...e6

Black reverts to a kind of Hippo formation. A number of alternatives have been tried, the most important being the following:

a) 7...♗g4 8 e5 dxe5 9 dxe5 ♘d7 (9...♕xd1+ 10 ♖xd1 ♘h5 was K.Kopczynski-J.Blaszczyk, correspondence 1991, and now 11 ♘d4! ♗xe2 12 ♘cxe2 is good for White) 10 h3 ♗xf3 (in the event of 10...♗f5 11 g4 ♗e6 12 ♘g5! ♘b6 13 ♘xe6 fxe6 14 g5! Black is in trouble as his bishop is trapped in a cage) 11 ♗xf3 ♘b6 12 0-0 and with more space and a pair of great bishops, White has an obvious advantage.

b) 7...e5 is playable, but it does not equalize: 8 dxe5 (8 fxe5 dxe5 9 d5 ♘e7 is playable, but I prefer the text) 8...dxe5 (8...♘g4 9 ♗g1 reaches variation 'c' below) 9 ♕xd8 ♖xd8 10 fxe5 ♘g4 11 ♗g5 ♖d7 12 ♘d5 h6 13 ♗h4

♘gxe5 (after 13...g5 14 ♗g3 ♘cxe5 15 ♘xe5 ♘xe5 16 0-0 f5 17 ♗xe5 ♗xe5 18 ♗c4 ♚g7 19 exf5 Black dropped a pawn for insufficient compensation in Baldizzone-Fiorentini, correspondence 1983) 14 ♘xe5 ♗xe5.

This position was reached in A.Beliavsky-E.Cekro, Sarajevo 1982. Now Vigus points out the line 15 ♘f6+ ♗xf6 16 ♗xf6 ♖d6 when White is slightly better thanks to his powerful dark-squared bishop. A plausible continuation is 17 e5 ♖d5 (17...♖d4 18 ♗f3) 18 ♗f3 ♖c5 19 ♗xc6 ♖xc6 20 0-0-0 when the opposite coloured bishops certainly do not guarantee a draw for Black, and White can press for a win without taking the slightest risk.

c) Black can also advance his e-pawn after the preliminary knight lunge 7...♘g4: 8 ♗g1 e5 9 dxe5 (I prefer this to 9 fxe5 dxe5 10 d5 ♘e7 11 h3 ♘f6) 9...dxe5 10 h3 ♘f6 (alternatively, there is 10...♘h6 11 ♗c5 ♖e8 12 ♕xd8 ♖xd8 13 ♘d5 exf4 14 0-0-0 ♖d7 15 ♘xf4 ♘e5 16 g4 ♚h8 as seen in B.Naeter-K.Walsh, correspondece 1998, and now after 17 ♖xd7 ♗xd7 18 ♖d1 ♗c6 19 ♘d5 White keeps some initiative) 11 ♕xd8 ♖xd8 12 fxe5 ♘d7 (12...♘e8 13 ♗h2! ♘b4 14 ♗d1 ♗e6 15 a3 ♘c6 was R.Pfretzschner-K.Piersig, correspondence 1990, and here I suggest 16 ♗e2 when Black will not have an easy time regaining his missing pawn) 13 0-0-0 (13 ♘d5!? ♘dxe5 14 c3 also looks promising) 13...♘dxe5 14 ♘d5 ♗e6 15 ♘xc7 (15 ♗h2 has also been played, but I prefer the immediate capture) 15...♖xd1+ 16 ♗xd1 ♖d8 17 ♘xe6 ♗h6+. We have been following the game A.Vitolinsh-I.Chikovani, Riga 1975. Now after the most precise 18 ♘fg5! fxe6 19 h4 ♖f8 20 b3 ♖f4 21 ♗e3 ♗xg5 22 hxg5 ♖xe4 23 ♖h3 we reach an endgame where White's two bishops are obviously superior to Black's knights.

Returning to 7...e6:

8 ♕d2 ♘e7

Preparing to meet e5 with ...♘fd5.

The main alternative is 8...b6 9 0-0-0 ♗b7 (9...♘e7 transposes to our main game), to which White should respond

with the direct 10 e5 ♘g4 11 h3 (11 ♗g1? does not work here due to 11...dxe5 12 dxe5 ♗h6! with awkward pressure against f4 and e5) 11...♘xe3 12 ♕xe3. I only found one game from this position, which continued 12...♘e7 13 g4 f6 14 ♗c4 (14 exf6 and 14 h4!? both deserve attention) 14...♗xf3 (14...d5 was wiser, when Black is only a little worse) 15 ♗xe6+ ♔h8 16 ♕xf3 fxe5 17 dxe5 ♗xe5 18 ♘e2 and White kept some advantage thanks to his kingside attacking chances and strong outpost on e6, J.Nunn-S.Kindermann, Wiesbaden 1981.

9 0-0-0 b6

McNab attempts to improve on 9...a6, which he had played eleven years earlier without success: 10 e5 ♘fd5 11 ♘xd5 exd5 (after 11...♘xd5 12 h4 b5 13 h5 ♗b7 14 hxg6 hxg6 15 ♘g5 Black was already facing strong kingside threats in A.De Vriendt-J.Voth, correspondence 1990) 12 h3 f6 (the following change in the pawn structure does not help Black, but he was worse anyway) 13 exf6 ♖xf6 14 g4 ♕f8 15 ♖de1 ♗d7 16 ♘h4 c5?! (in a difficult situation Black tries to change the course of the game, but only succeeds in worsening his position) 17 dxc5 ♖c8 18 g5 dxc5?! 19 gxf6 ♕xf6 20 c3 ♕xh4 21 ♗g4 ♗xg4 22 hxg4 ♕f6 23 f5 and Black soon had to resign in P.Wolff-C.McNab, London 1989.

10 e5!

There is no reason for White to delay his attack. The plan is simple: drive away the defensive knight, then advance the h-pawn up the board.

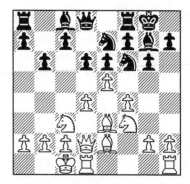

10...♘fd5

10...♘g4 was played in I.Nataf-F.Nijboer, Mondariz 2000, and here the simplest way for White to maintain an advantage is with 11 ♗g1, intending to play against the misplaced knight with h3 and g4.

11 ♘xd5 ♘xd5

11...exd5 has been tried by a few players, including none other than McNab once again. Play continues 12 h3 c5 (compared with the variation beginning with 9...a6 above, the pawn on b6 supports this undermining move; it does not solve Black's problems, though) 13 g4 when Black has tried two moves:

a) 13...cxd4 was played in D.Bryson-C.McNab, Troon 1982, and here the simplest path to an advantage would have been 14 ♗xd4!, intending to meet 14...♘c6 with 15 e6! ♘xd4 (15...fxe6? loses a piece to 16 ♗xg7 ♔xg7 17 ♕c3+) 16 exf7+ ♖xf7 17 ♘xd4 ♕f6 18 ♖hf1 with a huge positional plus.

b) 13...dxe5 14 fxe5 ♕c7 15 ♗h6 ♗e6 16 ♗xg7 ♔xg7 17 ♕f4 and White kept a pleasant initiative in J.Gallagher-J.Hickl, Pula 2000.

12 h4

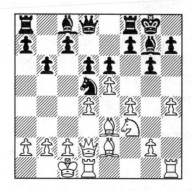

12...♘xe3

After 12...h5 13 ♘g5 (13 ♖hg1!?) 13...f6 14 exf6 ♕xf6 15 g3 ♗b7 16 ♗f2 a6 17 ♖he1 b5 18 ♗f1 ♖ae8 19 ♗h3 ♗c8 20 ♖e4 White was in full control, I.Bardos-J.Long, correspondence 2004.

13 ♕xe3 ♗b7 14 h5 dxe5

In the following game Black avoided this pawn exchange, but soon succumbed to a crushing attack: 14...♕e7 15 hxg6 hxg6 16 ♘g5! ♗xg2 17 ♖h2 (17 ♖h7!?) 17...♗b7 18 ♗d3 ♖fd8 (18...f6? 19 ♕h3 wins) 19 ♕h3 dxe5 20 ♗xg6! fxg6 21 ♕h7+ ♔f8 22 ♕xg6 ♕e8 23 ♘xe6+ ♔e7 24 ♕xg7+ ♔xe6 25 ♕xe5+ ♔d7 26 ♖h7+ 1-0 N.Fercec-S.Kosanski, Pula 1998.

15 dxe5 ♕e7 16 hxg6 hxg6

16...fxg6 was possible, but the e6- and h7-pawns are both weak, and White remains clearly better after 17 ♘g5 h6 18 ♘e4.

17 ♘g5 ♖fd8

17...♗xg2 18 ♖h2 (18 ♖h7!?) 18...♗b7 19 ♗d3 is similar to the note to move 14 above.

18 ♗d3 ♖d7 19 ♖h4 f6

Unsurprisingly, the greedy 19...♗xg2 meets with a swift refutation in 20 ♖d2 ♗d5 21 ♕h3 ♕c5 22 ♖h2! ♔f8 23 ♖h7! when there is no good defence to ♖xg7.

20 exf6 ♗xf6

20...♕xf6 would have lasted a bit longer, but after 21 ♕xe6+ ♕xe6 22 ♘xe6 Black is close to defeat, as shown by Vigus with the following short variations: 22...♗xg2 (or 22...♔f7 23 ♗xg6+ ♔xe6 24 f5+ ♔e7 25 f6+) 23 ♘xg7 ♖xg7 24 ♗c4+ ♔f8 25 ♖g1 ♗b7 26 f5! and White wins.

21 ♖h6

With the g6-pawn about to fall, Black's position is on the verge of collapse.

21...♗d5 22 ♖xg6+ ♗g7 23 c4

Now the e6-pawn drops as well. White was spoilt for choice, though, as 23 ♖h1 was also devastating.

23...♗xg2 24 ♖xe6 ♕d8 25 ♖g6 ♕e7 26 ♘e6 ♖e8 27 ♕g3 1-0

By now we have dealt with Black's four most important options on move six. In the following game, our last in the 6 ♗e3 system, we will deal with the less common options at his disposal.

1 e4 g6 2 d4 ♗g7 3 ♘c3 d6 4 f4 ♘f6 5 ♘f3 0-0 6 ♗e3

6...♘a6

Here is a summary of Black's remaining 6th-move alternatives:

a) 6...♘g4?! is premature: 7 ♗g1 c5 (after 7...e5 8 dxe5 dxe5 9 h3 ♘h6 10 ♕xd8 ♖xd8 11 ♘xe5 ♗xe5 12 fxe5 White had a big advantage in S.Maus-J.Eriksson, Gausdal 1990) 8 dxc5 ♕a5 9 ♕d2 dxc5 10 ♘d5 ♕xd2+ 11 ♘xd2 ♘c6 12 h3 (12 c3!?) 12...♘f6 13 ♗xc5 and

Black had no real compensation for the missing pawn in U.Goy-M.Pruess, Porz 1991.

b) 6...a6 7 e5 (White might also consider 7 h3!? by analogy with Game 26) 7...♘g4 8 ♗g1 b5 9 ♕e2 c5 10 0-0-0 (White concentrates on rapid development, although the materialistic 10 dxc5!? also looks like a decent try for an advantage) 10...cxd4 11 ♘xd4 dxe5 was tried in A.Khalifman-P.Svidler, Moscow 1995, and here the strongest continuation would have been 12 ♘f5! ♗xf5 13 ♖xd8 ♖xd8 14 h3 ♘f6 15 g4 with some advantage for White. With ♗g2 on the way, Black does not have sufficient compensation for the missing queen and he will have to worry about avoiding further material losses.

c) Finally, 6...c5 is not such a bad move, although it is not by accident that most experts choose to prepare it with one of the alternatives examined earlier in the chapter: 7 dxc5 ♕a5 (7...dxc5? 8 ♕xd8 ♖xd8 9 ♗xc5 ♘c6 10 ♗b5 just leaves Black a pawn down for nothing) 8 ♗d3 ♘g4 (in principle Black should generally try to recapture with the queen to reach a Sicilian structure; 8...dxc5 is playable, but White retains a pleasant edge with 9 ♗d2, as well as the rare 9 ♘e5!?) 9 ♗d2 ♕xc5 10 ♕e2 ♘f6 (10...♘c6? is a blunder: 11 h3 ♘f6 12 ♘a4 ♘d4 13 ♘xd4 ♕xd4 14 c4! left Black without a good answer to the threats of ♗c3 and ♗e3 in L.Erben-L.Stemmler, Torgelow 2006) 11 0-0-0 (11 ♗e3 ♕a5 12 0-0 transposes to a line

of the Austrian that is usually reached after 5...c5, but castling immediately is undoubtedly better: the queen is misplaced on c5, so there is no point in driving it away).

Here we will consider two options for Black:

c1) The problem with the queen's position can be seen after 11...♘c6 12 ♘a4! ♘d4 13 ♕e3 (13 ♘xc5 ♘xe2+ 14 ♗xe2 dxc5 15 e5 also looks like an edge for White) 13...♘g4 14 ♘xc5 ♘xe3 15 ♗xe3 dxc5 16 ♗xd4 cxd4 17 e5 and White has a good ending as the d4-pawn is likely to drop, J.Timman-R.Hartoch, Leeuwarden 1981.

c2) 11...♗g4 12 h3 ♗xf3 13 ♕xf3 ♘a6 (once again 13...♘c6?? is a blunder in view of 14 ♘a4 ♕h5, as in G.Quattrocchi-O.Thal, Correspondence 1996, and after 15 g4 White wins) 14 ♔b1 and White kept the better prospects in A.Mikhalchishin-J.Rukavina, Hastings 1985/86. He has more space, a pair of bishops and promising attacking chances.

Returning to 6...♘a6:

7 e5 ♘g4

7...♘d7 is rather passive and after 8 ♕d2 c5 9 0-0-0 White was the better mobilized in M.Paragua-A.Kakageldyev, Beijing (blitz) 2008.

8 ♗g1!

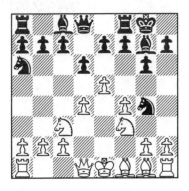

On this occasion White should keep his bishop. One reason is that this piece will play a useful role in defending his centre after the imminent ...c5. More importantly, in this particular variation White has a strong plan involving h3, driving the enemy knight back to the passive h6-square, followed by g4, after which the knight will have a hard time finding its way back into the game.

8...c5 9 h3

White wastes no time in executing his plan. There will be time to catch up on development later.

9...cxd4

This is Black's usual choice, although he sometimes prefers 9...♘h6 10 g4 with two options:

a) 10...cxd4 11 ♕xd4 will closely resemble the game after White castles.

b) The interesting 10...♕b6!? was

played in V.Nevednichy-F.Manca, Kusadasi 2006.

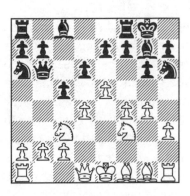

White responded with 11 ♖b1 and eventually won, but the game was not totally convincing, and it seems to me that the defensive rook move is a concession, especially as White will no longer be able to castle on the queenside. There are a few ways in which White can sacrifice the b-pawn and obtain interesting play, but it is all rather murky. Having checked the various options, my recommendation is the calm 11 a3!?, protecting the b-pawn indirectly and effectively asking Black how he plans to justify the position of his queen, which is hardly ideally placed in the firing line of the bishop on g1.

10 ♕xd4!

Naturally White recaptures with the queen in order to facilitate castling.

10...♘h6 11 0-0-0

11 g4!? is another valid move order, but since ...♘f5 is not yet a genuine threat, most players have preferred to castle first.

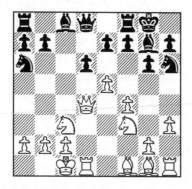

11...♗e6

This is not the only playable move:

a) 11...♘f5 has never been tested, and with good reason. White should respond with 12 ♕f2!, covering the g3-square, followed by g4 when the knight will be forced to retreat to its previous dismal post on h6.

b) A more important alternative is 11...♕a5 12 g4 when Black has tried the following moves:

b1) 12...♗e6 13 ♕a4! transposes to the note to Black's 12th move in our main game.

b2) 12...dxe5 13 fxe5 ♘b4 (B.Socko-M.Dzhumaev, Istanbul Olympiad 2000) 14 a3 ♘c6 15 ♕e3 transposes to variation 'b4' below.

b3) 12...♗d7 13 ♘d5!? (13 ♖h2!? is a sensible alternative) 13...♕xa2 14 ♘xe7+ ♔h8 was V.Tseshkovsky-L.Vadasz, Malgrat de Mar 1978. In this rich position White has several possibilities, but my preference would be 15 ♕c3!? ♕a4 (most other moves would be met by ♗d4, with powerful threats for White) 16 ♔b1 (now 16 ♗d4 can be

met by 16...♖ac8! 17 ♘xc8 ♖xc8 18 b3 ♖xc3 19 bxa4 ♖xf3 with a rather unclear endgame) 16...♗e6 17 b3 when the position remains messy, but White's chances are higher.

b4) 12...♘b4 13 a3 ♘c6 14 ♕e3 (14 ♕d5!?) 14...dxe5 15 fxe5 ♗e6 (15...♘xe5?? loses to 16 ♖d5!) 16 ♗h2 ♔h8 17 ♗d3 (17 ♔b1!? was worth considering, either here or over the next few moves) 17...a6 18 ♗e4 when White controls more space and his pieces are considerably more active, while the knight on h6 remains an ongoing problem for Black, G.Sigurjonsson-W.Zbikowski, German League 1983.

12 g4!

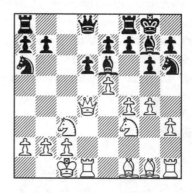

Aside from its primary purpose of restricting the enemy knight, this move fulfils a few other purposes. Firstly, it may facilitate the development of the king's rook via h2, as well as of the light-squared bishop to g2. Secondly, it sets up the tactical motif of f5, intending to meet ...gxf5 with g5 when the knight on h6 will be trapped.

12...♖c8?

This overoptimistic move is refuted by White's accurate response.

The best chance was 12...♕a5, although after 13 ♕a4! ♕xa4 14 ♘xa4 practice has shown that Black does not equalize:

a) 14...♘b4 15 a3 ♘d5 was S.Ali-M.Saud, Abu Dhabi 1999, and here the most accurate continuation would have been 16 exd6 exd6 17 f5! ♗d7 (17...gxf5? 18 g5) 18 ♖xd5 ♗xa4 (the evaluation is similar after 18...♗c6!? 19 ♖d3 ♗xa4 20 f6!) 19 ♗b5! ♗xb5 20 ♖xb5 b6 21 f6! and White is winning.

b) 14...dxe5 15 fxe5 ♘b4 16 a3 ♘c6 17 ♘c5 ♗c8 18 ♗e3 b6 19 ♗b5! ♘xe5 20 ♘xe5 bxc5 21 ♘c6 when White had a powerful initiative in E.Bareev-M.Todorcevic, Marseille 1990.

c) 14...♖fc8 15 ♗xa6 bxa6 16 exd6 exd6 17 ♗d4 ♗xa2!? 18 ♘c3 ♗c4 19 ♗xg7 ♔xg7 20 ♖xd6 and White kept a clear advantage in V.Kotronias-A.Kakageldyev, Bled Olympiad 2002.

13 ♕xa7!

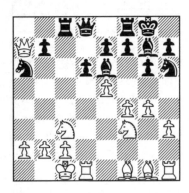

13...♖xc3!?

This sacrifice is not fully sound, but it was the best practical chance. Avrukh demonstrates that the following two alternatives are hopeless:

a) 13...♘c5 14 ♗xc5 ♖xc5 15 ♕xc5 dxc5 16 ♖xd8 ♖xd8 17 ♘g5 and White's extra pawn should decide the endgame.

b) 13...♘b4 14 a3 ♖xc3 (or 14...♘c6 15 ♕xb7 ♕a5 16 ♗b6!) 15 bxc3 ♘d5 16 f5! gxf5 17 g5 when the knight on h6 is trapped, and in the resulting position Black will be a rook down for insufficient compensation.

14 bxc3 ♕a5 15 ♗xa6 bxa6 16 ♗d4!

From this square the bishop effectively glues White's whole position together, by defending the c3-pawn, neutralizing the bishop on g7, and blocking the d-file, thus allowing the king to shelter on d2. Black tries his best to create some attacking chances, but his position is already beyond salvation.

16...♗d5 17 ♖hf1 dxe5 18 ♘xe5 ♕xa2

Avrukh mentions the line 18...f6 19 ♘d3 ♕xa2 20 ♘b4! when White wins.

19 ♖fe1!

Preventing ...♗e4. Despite the

slightly shaky appearance of his king's fortress, White is in no real danger and it is only a matter of time before he forces further exchanges.

19...♖a8 20 ♕b6 ♕a3+ 21 ♔d2 ♕a4 22 ♖a1 ♕e8 23 ♖xa6 ♖c8

Black is trying desperate to avoid simplification, but the white rooks will soon team up to hurt him.

24 ♖a7 ♖d8 25 ♕c7 f6

26 ♘xg6! 1-0

Black resigned in view of 26...hxg6 27 ♖xe7. It's worth noting too that since retreating to the h6-square on move ten, the black knight never got another chance to move.

Part 2 – 5...c5 and rare alternatives

> ### Game 29
> ### A.Van Herwaarden-
> ### C.De Saegher
> Dieren 2006

Our two protagonists are not well known; according to the database Black was rated a little over 2200 at the time of the game, while White was not even rated at all, although at the time of writing these words he has ascended to the 2100+ ranks. Despite the sub-grandmaster pedigree of this game, it is of considerable theoretical importance, as the players followed what I believe to be a critical line for my recommended variation.

1 e4 d6 2 d4 ♘f6 3 ♘c3 g6 4 f4 ♗g7 5 ♘f3

5...c5

The immediate central strike is a serious option, which has been seen in approximately half as many games as 5...0-0. Serious Pirc players rarely deviate from these two main moves.

Here is a brief summary of a few rare alternatives:

a) After both 5...♘c6 6 ♗e3 and 5...♘a6 6 ♗e3 it is doubtful that Black has anything better than 6...0-0 transposing to Games 28 and 27 respectively.

b) Following 5...♗g4 6 h3 ♗xf3 7

♕xf3 White will continue with ♗e3 followed by castling and a timely e5.

c) 5...c6 6 ♗e3 b5 (6...0-0 7 h3 transposes to Game 26) 7 e5 (7 ♗d3 should also give White an edge) 7...♘g4 8 ♗g1 is seldom played and I do not see much point in analysing it in detail, but rest assured White's chances are higher.

6 dxc5

The big main line is 6 ♗b5+ ♗d7 7 e5 (7 ♗xd7+ intending 8 d5 is a decent alternative), but I believe that the text gives at least as many chances for an advantage without being anywhere near so theoretically demanding.

6...♕a5

Nothing else is playable.

The endgame arising after 6...dxc5? 7 ♕xd8+ ♔xd8 is simply bad for Black: 8 e5 ♘h5 9 ♗e3 ♘c6 10 0-0-0+ ♔c7 11 ♘d5+ ♔b8 12 ♗xc5 ♗g4 was F.Winiwarter-J.Kurasch, Feffernitz 1996, and now after 13 ♘xe7 ♘xe7 14 ♗xe7 ♘xf4 15 ♖d4 ♗xf3 16 ♗d6+ ♔c8 17 gxf3 White should win comfortably.

7 ♕d4!?

An important moment. By far the most popular continuation is 7 ♗d3 ♕xc5, but it seems to me that the text move poses more difficult problems for the defender.

7...dxc5

This seems safest, although a few other options have been tried:

a) The most principled move is arguably 7...0-0!?, but as we shall see in Game 30, Black has his share of problems there as well.

b) Black must definitely avoid 7...♕xc5? 8 ♕xc5 dxc5 9 e5 ♘g4 10 ♘d5 (Vigus), when his difficulties are already bordering on the insurmountable.

c) The only other option worth considering is 7...♘c6 8 ♗b5 with a choice for Black:

c1) 8...♕xb5 is strongly met by 9 ♕xf6! ♗xf6 10 ♘xb5 0-0 11 cxd6 exd6 12 c3 ♖d8, as in L.Milov-H.Henderikse, Haarlem 2004, and now 13 ♘c7 ♖b8 14 ♗e3 would have left Black a pawn down for very little.

c2) 8...♗d7 9 ♕a4! (9 ♗xc6?! ♗xc6 10 cxd6 exd6 11 0-0 0-0 gives Black excellent compensation), with a further division:

c21) 9...♕xa4 does not appear to have been tried. Here is my analysis: 10 ♗xa4 ♘b4 (if 10...dxc5 11 e5) 11 ♗b3 dxc5 12 0-0 c4 (otherwise White's strong centre and active pieces would guarantee a pleasant advantage) 13 ♗xc4 ♘xc2 14 ♖b1 ♖c8 15 ♗b3 ♘b4 (15...♘a3?! 16 bxa3 ♖xc3 17 e5 looks risky for Black) 16 ♗e3 with a pleasant position for White.

c22) 9...♕c7 10 ♘d5 (10 cxd6 exd6 gives Black some compensation) 10...♕a5+ (trying to force matters with 10...♘xd5 11 exd5 ♕a5+ is no better, as 12 ♗d2 ♕xa4 13 ♗xa4 ♘d4 14 ♗xd7+ ♔xd7 15 ♘xd4 ♗xd4 16 cxd6 ♔xd6 17 ♗b4+ turns out badly for Black) 11 ♕xa5 ♘xa5 12 ♘xf6+ (better than 12 ♘c7+ ♔d8 13 ♘xa8 ♗xb5 14 e5 dxe5 15 ♘xe5 ♗e8) 12...♗xf6 13 ♗xd7+ ♔xd7.

with 14 cxd6 exd6 15 ♔e2! ♖he8 16 ♔d3. The king does a superb job here and after 16...♖ac8 17 ♖e1 Black does not have enough for the sacrificed pawn.

c3) After 8...0-0 9 ♕a4! Black has tried two moves:

c31) The pawn sacrifice 9...♕c7!? is interesting but probably not fully sound: 10 0-0 (White can also obtain a slight plus with 10 ♗e3 intending long castling, as in D.Howell-M.Mitchell, Hastings 2009/10, but it seems safer for the king to go short) 10...a6 11 ♗xc6 bxc6 12 cxd6 exd6 13 ♗e3 c5 was T.Maslowski-A.Stolarczyk, Polish Team Championship 2007, and now after the natural developing move 14 ♖ae1 I do not believe Black has enough compensation for the missing pawn.

c32) 9...♕xa4 has been more popular, but White is doing well here too. Indeed, after 10 ♗xa4 Black faces a difficult task.

This position was reached in C.Hanley-S.Detienne, Charleroi 2006. At this point I see no reason for White not to preserve his material advantage

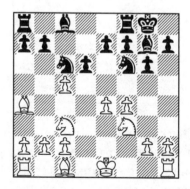

In the following lines, the absence of queens seems to favour the first player:

c321) 10...dxc5?! loses a pawn: 11 e5 ♘d7 (another game continued 11...♘e8 12 ♘d5 e6 13 ♗xc6 exd5 14 ♗xd5 ♘c7 and now in V.Shapiro-W.Meissner, Troisdorf 2005, 15 ♗e4 would have been clearly better for White) 12 ♘d5 e6 was reached in P.Anisimov-A.Voinov, Krasnoyarsk 2007, and now 13 ♗xc6 exd5 14 ♗xd5 ♘b6 15 ♗e4 leaves White with a clear extra pawn.

c322) 10...♘d7 11 cxd6 ♗xc3+ 12 bxc3 exd6 gives Black good chances to regain his pawn, but he has paid a high price in exchanging his prized dark-squared bishop for an enemy knight. P.Garbett-A.Ker, Auckland 2008, continued 13 0-0 ♖e8 14 ♗b3 ♘c5 (14...♖xe4 allows 15 ♗xf7+!) and now 15 ♗a3! would have brought White an excellent game.

Black will regain his pawn, but he is still behind in development, and White's dark-squared bishop has enormous potential. Here are two possible continuations:

c3221) In the event of 15...♘xe4 White has the powerful riposte 16 ♘g5! ♘xg5 (or 16...♖e7 17 ♗xf7+! ♖xf7 18 ♘xe4 d5 19 ♘d6) 17 fxg5 when Black will lose the d-pawn.

c3222) Therefore 15...♖xe4 looks like the best chance. Now White has several tempting continuations, of which the simplest is probably 16 ♗xc5 dxc5 17 ♗xf7+ ♔g7 18 ♘g5 ♖e3 19 ♗d5 ♖xc3 20 ♖ae1 with strong pressure: for instance, 20...♗d7 21 ♖f2!? and Black still has plenty of problems in front of him.

After that lengthy but necessary diversion, let us return to the game continuation to see how White should fight for an edge against the straightforward recapture of the pawn on c5:

8 ♕c4!

Amazingly I was only able to find three games in which this promising move was played.

Note that 8 ♗b5+?! would be ineffective, as after 8...♕xb5 9 ♕xf6 ♗xf6 10 ♘xb5 ♘a6 Black will be able to complete development without difficulty, after which his bishop pair should come into its own.

8...0-0

Two other moves have been tried:

a) 8...a6 9 e5 ♗e6 10 ♕a4+ (10 exf6!? ♗xc4 11 fxg7 ♖g8 12 ♗xc4 looks interesting, though hardly necessary) 10...♕xa4 11 ♘xa4 ♘fd7 12 ♗e3 b6 13 0-0-0 was E.Sharapov-E.Koscielny, Lubawka 2009, where White had obtained an advantage which is rather typical for queenless positions with this pawn structure. He won easily, although the 500-point rating differential also probably had something to do with it.

b) 8...♘c6 was played in B.Lindberg-T.Hillarp Persson, Stockholm 2007. Now instead of Lindberg's 9 e5, White should consider 9 ♕b5!?, angling for a favourable queenless position (9 ♗d2!? is a decent alternative, but it seems to me that the main line should bring White a slight edge with little risk). After 9...♕xb5 (9...♕c7 10 ♕xc5 is a safe extra pawn) 10 ♗xb5 ♗d7 11 ♗e3 b6 12 0-0-0 White has a little more space in the centre and slightly the more active pieces, so he can feel quite content with the outcome of the opening.

9 e5

9 ♕b5!? could be worth a try.

9...♘g4

The untested 9...♗e6 has been recommended by a few sources, but I doubt that it is sufficient to equalize. After 10 ♕b5 (10 ♕a4!? ♕xa4 11 ♘xa4 ♘fd7 12 ♗e3 looks interesting, but having analysed both moves I prefer the text) 10...♕xb5 I checked two moves:

a) 11 ♘xb5? ♘d5 12 a3 a6 13 c4 axb5 14 cxd5 ♗xd5 15 ♗xb5 is apparently analysis from Martin (cited by Vigus). I am not impressed by White's eleventh move.

b) A clear and obvious improvement is 11 ♗xb5 ♘d5 12 ♘xd5 ♗xd5 13 ♗e3.

It seems to me that Black still has to work to equalize:

b1) 13...b6 14 0-0-0 is excellent for White. Note that in the event of an exchange on f3, White's better development and powerful light-squared bishop would more than make up for his weakened kingside.

b2) Black is not obliged to play 13...c4 immediately, since ♗xc5 can presently be met by ...♖c8 with an attack on c2. Nevertheless, he will have to address the threat sooner or later, and the text looks like a principled attempt to question the placement of the bishop on b5. Following 14 ♖d1!? (the more natural-looking 14 0-0-0 is not at all bad, but there is something to be said for short castling; the rook on f1 will guard against ...♗xf3 ideas, while it could be useful for the king to avoid the c-file which might soon become open)

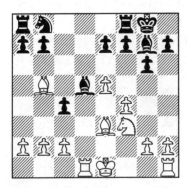

14...e6 (or 14...♗xf3 15 gxf3 when in addition to the aforementioned factors regarding the exchange of bishop for knight, Black also has to worry about his c-pawn: for instance, 15...♖c8 16 ♖d4 c3 17 bxc3!? with some advantage for White despite his dodgy pawn structure) 15 b3 cxb3 16 axb3 ♘c6 (16...f6 17 exf6 ♗xf6 18 0-0 is nice for White) 17 0-0 White has a pleasant advantage thanks to his extra space, more active pieces, and the useful possibility of c2-c4 at an opportune moment.

Returning to 9...♘g4:

10 h3 ♘h6 11 ♗e3 ♘a6 12 ♕b5!

There was nothing wrong with 12 0-0-0, but since the queenless position works well for White, it makes sense to force the issue.

12...♕xb5 13 ♗xb5 b6

13...♘f5 14 ♗f2 achieves nothing for Black just now. He still has to defend his c-pawn and must now add the

g2-g4 advance to his list of worries.

14 ♗c6!?

14 0-0-0 was fine as well, but White instead decides to impede the development of the enemy bishop to b7.

14...♖b8 15 a3!

Preventing Black from driving away the bishop with ...♘b4.

15...♗b7 16 ♗xb7 ♖xb7 17 0-0-0 f6

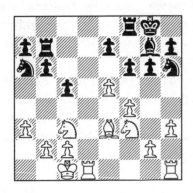

18 exf6

There is also 18 g4!? fxe5 19 ♘xe5 ♘f7 20 ♘xf7 ♖xf7 21 ♘e4 when White keeps a slight plus.

18...exf6 19 ♘d5

Another possibility was 19 ♖he1 when all five of White's pieces are more actively placed than their black counterparts, which ought to count for something. Play might continue 19...♖e8 20 ♗f2 ♖xe1 21 ♗xe1 and White will follow up with g4 in the near future, with ongoing pressure.

19...♘b8

19...♖e8 may have been a slight improvement, although the general evaluation of the position remains the same.

20 g4 ♔f7 21 ♗d2

The computer points out the interesting possibility of 21 f5!? gxf5 (other moves might be met by fxg6+ and ♖hf1) 22 g5 ♘g8 23 h4!? with interesting compensation. There is no particular need for such a speculative approach though.

21...♖d8 22 ♗c3?

22 c4! would have preserved a significant plus.

22...♖bd7 23 ♘e3

Now that the knight has been forced to retreat, Black is close to equal.

23...♘c6 24 ♖xd7+ ♖xd7 25 ♖d1 ♖xd1+ 26 ♔xd1 ♘g8 27 ♔e2 ♘ge7 28 ♔d3 ♔e6

The remainder of the game is not so important. Suffice to say that, having failed to make the most of his trumps, White has very little advantage here.

29 b3 ♘b8 30 ♗b2 ♘d7 31 c4 ♗h6 32 ♘g2 f5 33 g5 ♗f8 34 ♘e3 ♘c6 35 ♘d5 ♗d6 36 ♗c1 ♘a5 37 ♔c2 b5 38 ♔c3 a6 39 ♗d2 ♘b8 40 ♗e3 ♘d7 41 ♘h2 ♘e5!? 42 ♘b6 ♘ec6

The game seems to be heading for a

draw, but now an unfortunate blunder gifts Black the full point.

43 ♘d5??

43 ♘f3 would have kept the game equal.

43...bxc4

43...♘xb3!? may have been even stronger, with the point 44 ♔xb3 ♘a5+ followed by 45...♘xc4.

44 bxc4 ♘xc4!

This is the trick that White had overlooked.

45 ♘c7+

45 ♔xc4 ♘a5+ would be hopeless for White.

45...♔xc7 46 ♔xc4 ♗d6 47 ♘f3

47 ♗xc5? ♗xf4 hardly helps White.

47...♘a5+ 48 ♔c3 ♔d5 49 ♘d2 ♗f8!

The 'Pirc bishop' returns to its favourite long diagonal, sealing White's fate in the process.

50 ♗f2 ♗g7+ 51 ♔d3 c4+ 52 ♔c2 ♘c6 53 ♗b6 ♘d4+ 0-1

The next game features a more combative approach from Black. This seems like a logical reaction to White's early queen sortie, but we will see that here too the second player has plenty of problems.

Game 30
G.Pilavov-Y.Zimmerman
Sochi 2007

1 e4 d6 2 d4 ♘f6 3 ♘c3 g6 4 f4 ♗g7 5 ♘f3 c5 6 dxc5 ♕a5 7 ♕d4 0-0!?

This pawn sacrifice has been tested a few times. I doubt that it is completely sound, but White must be prepared to react in a resolute way. In certain cases this may actually involve returning the material with interest, in order to develop a powerful attack.

8 cxd6!

White must react in a principled way. Anything else would allow Black to solve his problems with ease.

8...♘xe4

This must be critical. Moreover, the alternatives are nothing to worry about:

a) 8...♘c6 9 ♕d2! exd6 10 ♗d3 and Black does not have enough compensation.

b) 8...exd6 does not seem to have been tried. It seems to me that the simplest reaction would be 9 ♗d2 (9 ♕d2 has also been recommended) 9...♘c6 (9...♖e8 10 ♗d3 ♘c6 11 ♕f2 is good for White) when White can either play 10 ♕e3, or even the computer-like 10 ♕c4!? ♗e6 11 ♕b5 ♕c7 12 ♗d3 (12 ♘g5!? is also interesting), intending to meet 12...a6 with 13 ♕g5, when the queen makes a safe getaway, or 12...h6 with 13 ♗e3, so that the queen can go to b6 if attacked.

9 ♕xe4 ♗xc3+

Now if White were forced to play 10 ♔f2 his position would be a little shaky, despite the computer's confidence. Fortunately there is a much stronger continuation.

10 bxc3!

This exchange sacrifice effectively refutes Black's seventh move, unless a massive improvement can be found for the second player.

10...♕xc3+ 11 ♔f2 ♕xa1 12 dxe7 ♖e8 13 ♗c4!

In this critical position White's tremendous e7-pawn combined with his opponent's chronically weak dark squares outweighs the extra exchange.

13...♕f6

This is the only way for Black to stay in the game. The point is that most alternatives will allow a lethal sacrifice on f7, for example:

a) 13...♘d7? 14 ♗xf7+! ♔xf7 15

♕d5+ ♔g7 16 ♗e3 is the end, as 16...♕xh1 17 ♗d4+ ♘f6 18 ♕e5 leads to mate.

b) 13...♘c6? 14 ♗xf7+! ♔xf7 15 ♕c4+ ♔g7 (if 15...♔xe7? 16 ♗a3+, or 15...♗e6 16 ♘g5+) 16 ♕b3! and there is no satisfactory defence against ♗b2+: for example, 16...♗e6 17 ♗b2+ ♔h6 (17...♘e5 18 ♕c3) 18 ♕b5 ♕xb2 19 ♕xb2 and White is winning.

c) Finally, please note that Black cannot defend f7 with 13...♕g7? on account of 14 ♘g5 ♗f5 15 ♕e3 when his kingside collapses.

14 ♗a3

In this position 14 ♘g5?? is, of course, no good because of 14...♖xe7.

14...♘c6

The other natural move is 14...♗f5, but this also fails to solve Black's problems: 15 ♕e3 (15 ♕xb7 is also quite decent, but in principle I would prefer not to be distracted from the kingside) 15...♘c6 16 ♘g5 ♖xe7 17 ♗xe7 ♘xe7 18 ♗xf7+ ♔g7 19 ♖e1 and White is a pawn up for nothing. After, for instance, 19...♘c6 20 ♗d5 h6 21 ♘e4

♗xe4 22 ♕xe4 he has good chances to win the ending.

15 ♘g5 ♗f5 16 ♕d5

16...♖xe7

Vigus points out the following interesting line: 16...♗e6?! 17 ♘xe6 fxe6 18 ♕xe6+ ♕xe6 19 ♗xe6+ ♔g7 20 ♗b2+ ♔h6 21 ♖e1. Vigus ends his analysis here, pointing out the threat of ♖e3 followed by mate on h3. Extending the line a little further leads to the following beautiful finish: 21...g5 22 g4! (not the only way to win, but by far the most elegant and effective) 22...gxf4 (after 22...♘xe7 23 h4! gxf4 24 ♗f7 it is all over) 23 ♗f7! ♖xe7 24 h4!!.

Black must give up too much material in order to avoid mate.

17 ♗xe7 ♘xe7 18 ♕xf7+ ♕xf7 19 ♗xf7+ ♔g7 20 ♖e1

With an extra pawn and the more active pieces, White should win without too many problems, notwithstanding the split queenside pawns.

20...♘c6 21 ♗d5 h6 22 ♖b1

There is nothing wrong with this, although the computer's suggestion of 22 ♘e6+ ♔h8 23 c3 looks even more compelling. The rest of the game is not hugely important for our study of the opening, so I will limit myself to a few brief comments.

22...♘d8 23 ♘f3 ♖c8

Black obviously did not like the look of 23...♗xc2 24 ♖c1 followed by ♖c7+.

24 ♘d4 ♔f6 25 ♖b2 b6 26 c4

White finds a way to put the isolated c-pawn to good use.

26...♘e6 27 ♘xf5 ♔xf5 28 g3 ♖c5 29 h4 ♘c7 30 ♖d2 b5 31 ♖d4 ♔f6 32 ♔e3 a5 33 g4 b4 34 g5+ hxg5 35 hxg5+ ♔g7 36 ♗e4

Pilavov has increased his advantage skilfully and is now set to win another pawn on the kingside. Combined with the threats to the black king, it is all too much for the defender to handle.

36...a4 37 ♖d7+ ♔f8 38 ♗xg6 ♘e6 39 ♖f7+ ♔g8 40 ♖b7 ♘xg5 41 fxg5 ♖xg5 42 ♗e4 1-0

To summarize, it seems that the rarely played 7 ♕d4!? represents quite a potent threat to the 5...c5 variation. Most of the lines mentioned have not yet received extensive practical testing, so it remains to be seen whether my evaluations will stand the test of time. For the time being though, all I can say is that the future looks bright!

Conclusion

There is little doubt in my mind that the Austrian Attack is White's most principled attempt to fight for the advantage against the Pirc Defence. White's aggressive set-up leads to rich middlegame positions, with a diverse range of potential pawn structures and plans available to both sides. Sometimes a direct kingside attack will be the order of the day, while in other lines White will strive for an early queen exchange, relying on his space advantage to provide a positional advantage in the endgame. There are a number of sharp lines that need to be learned, but in my view the rewards are well worth the effort.

Chapter Four
Philidor and Czech Pirc

1 e4 d6

This move is not always the prelude to the Pirc or Modern, and there are a number of other important set-ups at Black's disposal.

2 d4 ♘f6

The rare and unpromising 2...e5 is covered in Game 37.

3 ♘c3

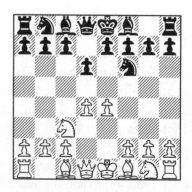

From this basic starting position I have divided the chapter into two.

Part 1 – Philidor with 3...e5
3...e5

Although the Philidor is usually classified as a 1 e4 e5 opening, the pre-

sent move order is the most fashionable way of reaching it nowadays (unless Black is specifically aiming for a line that can only arise via 1 e4 e5).

4 dxe5

The largest theoretical branch of the opening lies with 4 ♘f3 ♘bd7, but I believe that the early queen exchange is promising for White.

4...dxe5 5 ♕xd8+ ♔xd8 6 ♗g5 ♗e6

The other main move is 6...c6, which has been favoured by numerous strong players. This will be considered in Game 33, along with a few other 6th-move alternatives.

7 g3!?

This venomous and slightly unusual move offers White good prospects. From here Game 31 deals with the main line of 7...♔c8, while 7...h6 will be covered in Game 32.

Part 2 – Other set-ups

Apart from the Modern Philidor, Black has a few other systems that we should consider.

3...c6

This variation is known as the Czech Pirc.

3...♘bd7 is another idea, playing for a Philidor without allowing an early queen exchange. This can be found in Game 36.

4 f4

Generally I favour this space-gaining move whenever the opportunity arises to play it.

4...♕a5 5 ♗d3 e5 6 ♘f3 ♗g4 7 ♗e3

From here the main line of 7...♘bd7 will be covered in Game 34, while Black's various alternatives between moves 4 and 7 will form the subject of Game 35.

Part 1 – Philidor with 3...e5

1 d4 d6 2 e4 ♘f6 3 ♘c3 e5 4 dxe5 dxe5 5 ♕xd8+ ♔xd8 6 ♗g5 ♗e6

7 g3!?

The vast majority of games have featured the natural 7 0-0-0+ and indeed who could possibly resist such a move? However, the problem is that the f2-square can become a target in some lines, so there is a good argument for postponing castling. The main theoretical lines feature a quick f4 from White after castling. Although this is a perfectly valid approach, the positions featuring an isolated e-pawn are not always easy to navigate. Overall I find the idea of supporting the f4-push with 7 g3 to be just as challenging, and the fact that it is slightly unusual only increases its effectiveness as a practical weapon.

7...♚c8

This is the main line, although a number of alternatives have also been tested – see the next game for details.

8 f4 ♝b4

On his Philidor DVD Viktor Bologan recommends a different solution for Black, but I do not find it particularly convincing: 8...exf4 9 gxf4 ♝b4 10 ♝xf6 (this is certainly not forced and 10 ♝d3 deserves attention too) 10...gxf6 11 ♞ge2 ♜d8.

Now Bologan gives 12 a3 ♝f8 with a decent position for Black, but 12 ♜g1 is a better move which keeps some initiative for White.

9 ♝d3

In some games White has exchanged on f6, but I prefer to keep the tension for the time being.

9...♞a6!?

Not a typical square for the knight in this opening, but it seems to meet the demands of the present position. The knight is heading for c5 and the d7-square was off-limits, as the bishop on e6 would have got trapped after f5.

Black has tried two other moves from this position:

a) 9...h6 was seen in A.Kornev-Y.Shabanov, Moscow 2007. Here 10 ♝xf6 looks sensible and after 10...♝xc3+ 11 bxc3 gxf6 12 ♞f3 White keeps a slight initiative.

b) 9...♞e8!? looks a little strange, but is not easy to refute. I.Popov-I.Khairullin, Ulan Ude 2009, saw 10 fxe5 (this must be the critical test) 10...h6 11 ♝f4 g5 12 ♝e3 ♞d7 13 ♞f3 ♝f8.

An interesting situation has arisen. If Black is given time to play ...♝g7 and ♞xe5 then he will have no problems whatsoever. I think the right plan for White is to prod on the kingside, with 14 ♝e2!? ♝g7 15 h4! g4 (after 15...gxh4 16 ♜xh4 the h-pawn will be an easy target) 16 ♞d4 ♞xe5. Now I analysed the following line, which is obviously not forced, but represents sensible and consistent play from both sides: 17 ♞xe6 fxe6 18 0-0-0 ♞d6 19 ♝c5 ♜d8 20 h5! (fixing the g4-pawn as a weakness) 20...b6 21 ♝xd6 ♜xd6 22 ♝a6+ ♚d7 23 ♞b5 ♜xd1+ 24 ♜xd1+ ♚e7 25 ♞xc7 and White has won a pawn.

10 ♘ge2

Instead 10 fxe5 ♘d7 11 ♘f3 ♗g4 is nothing for White.

10...♘c5

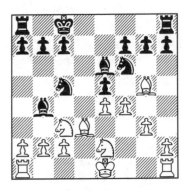

11 0-0

This natural move allows Black to equalize.

Should you reach this position over the board, I suggest that you try the following continuation: 11 ♗xf6!? gxf6 12 f5 (by blocking the centre, White creates an environment in which his knights will not be inferior to the enemy bishops) 12...♗d7 (12...♘xd3+ 13 cxd3 ♗d7 14 ♔f2 is similar) 13 a3 (13 0-0-0 c6 14 a3 ♘xd3+ 15 ♖xd3 is another idea, when the rook might swing to h3 later) 13...♘xd3+ 14 cxd3 ♗f8 15 ♔f2. Both sides have certain trumps here, but in this fairly blocked position I would take White's knights and superior pawn structure over the black bishops.

11...♘g4

Black could have equalized by means of 11...♗h3! 12 ♗xf6 (White is

more or less forced to insert this exchange, as 12 ♖fd1 is met by 12...♘xd3, or 12...♘cd7 with ideas of a check on c5 followed by ...♘g4) 12...gxf6

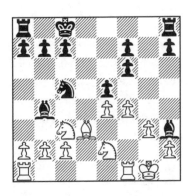

13 ♖f3 (otherwise, 13 ♖f2 ♘xd3 14 cxd3 ♗c5 15 d4 exd4 16 ♘a4 ♗b4 17 ♘xd4 ♖e8 is good for Black and 13 ♖fd1 ♗g4 leaves White with no real improvement over 14 ♖f1, repeating) 13...♗g4 14 ♖ff1 (if 14 ♖f2?! ♘xd3 15 cxd3 ♗c5, while 14 ♖e3 loses the exchange to 14...♘e6 or 14...♘d7 followed by ...♗c5) 14...♗h3, with a repetition. Obviously if White was feeling stubborn he could avoid this with a move like 15 ♖fc1 (or 13 ♖fc1 earlier), but this is hardly an ideal solution and after 15...c6 Black should be fine.

12 f5

The bishop on g5 was starting to run short of squares and in any case it is useful to gain space on the kingside.

12...♗d7 13 ♘d5

13 ♗c4!? was an interesting alternative. Play might continue 13...♗c6 14 ♗d5 ♗xd5 15 exd5 (not 15 ♘xd5? ♘xe4) 15...h6 16 ♗c1, intending to

drive the black minor pieces away and mobilize the queenside majority with c4 and b4. Nevertheless, I prefer the game continuation overall.

13...♘xd3 14 cxd3 ♗c5+ 15 ♔g2

The position bears a certain resemblance to that reached in the note to White's 11th move, although the absence of the ♗xf6 exchange is of course a significant difference. White has 'sacrificed' a bishop for a knight, but in return he has established a powerful pawn chain from d3 to f5 which restricts Black's unopposed bishop. The rest of White's pieces enjoy an edge in terms of coordination and his king is slightly happier too.

15...h6 16 ♗d2 ♗c6 17 ♖ac1 ♗f8?

Black wants to keep both his valuable bishops, but he has overlooked his opponent's next move.

17...♗xd5 was better, although after 18 ♖xc5 ♗c6 (18...♗xa2?? 19 ♖a1) 19 ♘c3 White keeps a pleasant advantage.

18 f6!

After this powerful shot it is hard to find a satisfactory defence.

18...♗xd5

Others are no better:

a) 18...g6? 19 h3 wins the knight.

b) 18...♘xf6 19 ♘xf6 gxf6 20 ♖xf6 and Black will shortly lose a pawn on the kingside: for instance, 20...♖h7 21 ♖f5 followed by ♗c3 if necessary.

19 fxg7 ♗xg7 20 exd5 ♘f6

20...♖f8 also fails to hold Black's position together: 21 ♖c4! f5 (21...♘f6 22 ♗xh6!) 22 ♘c3! ♔d7 23 h3 ♘f6 24 ♖xf5 and the extra pawn should be enough to decide the game.

21 ♘c3 ♖d8 22 ♘e4

22 ♖ce1 was also strong.

22...♘xd5 23 ♖xf7

23...&f8?

23...&d7 would have been more resilient, although there is no reason why White should fail to convert his extra pawn – that is, as long as he avoids 24 &cf1?? &f4+! when suddenly the tables are turned.

24 &cf1

White could have wrapped up the game more efficiently with 24 &f6! &e7 (24...&d6 25 &xd5) 25 &b4, but the text move is good enough.

24...&e7 25 &1f5 1-0

Perhaps it was a little early to resign, but Black is about to lose at least one more pawn without gaining any counterplay whatsoever.

In the next game we will look at Black's other options on move 7.

Game 32
R.Hasangatin-P.Neuman
Pardubice 2006

1 e4 d6 2 d4 &f6 3 &c3 e5 4 dxe5 dxe5

5 &xd8+ &xd8 6 &g5 &e6 7 g3 h6

This rather provocative move has been almost as popular as 7...&c8, but it has scored much worse: a mere two wins for Black, with nine losses and no draws. Three other moves deserve close attention too:

a) 7...&e7 8 f4 h6 9 0-0-0+ (9 &h4!? has been tried by Khenkin, but it leads to rather murky complications), and both king moves have been tested here:

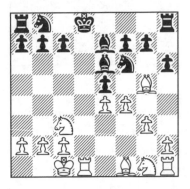

a1) 9...&e8 10 &xf6 gxf6 (10...&xf6 looks more logical; now 11 &b5!? is interesting and after 11...&d8 12 &f3 or 11...&a6 12 f5 &d7 13 &f3 White keeps some initiative) 11 &f3 &d6 12 f5 &c8 13 &b5 &e7 14 &d2 &d7 15 &xd6 cxd6 16 &c4 &c6 17 &g2 &d8 18 &d2 b5 19 &a5 a6 20 &hd1 and White obtained a commanding positional advantage in V.Malakhov-A.Miltner, Bad Wiessee 2002.

a2) 9...&c8 10 &xf6 &xf6 11 &f3 exf4 12 gxf4 &xc3 13 bxc3 g6 was J.Kountz-S.Schmidt Schaeffer, Hockenheim 1994. White has an advantage in development and he must put it to good use before Black can get coordinated.

I think the right way is 14 ♘d4! ♗d7 15 e5! when White has various attacking ideas based on ♗c4 followed by e6 and/or f5, opening the kingside and creating a target on f7 or g6.

b) 7...♗b4 should be met by 8 0-0-0+ when Black has tried two moves:

b1) 8...♚c8 9 ♗xf6 gxf6 10 ♘d5, which Khenkin has had in two games:

b11) The first continued 10...♗xd5?! 11 exd5 ♗c5 and here in I.Khenkin-K.Urban, Koszalin 1998, the most incisive continuation would have been 12 ♗h3+ ♚d8 13 ♘e2! with a clear advan-

tage to White, as 13...♗xf2 14 ♖hf1 ♗e3+ 15 ♚b1 ♗g5 16 ♘c3 gives him more than enough for a pawn.

b12) In the second he faced 10...♗c5, but after 11 ♘xf6 ♗xf2 12 ♗h3 it was clear that White had won the opening battle, even though he eventually lost the war in I.Khenkin-J.Koscielski, Bad Wiessee 2000.

b2) 8...♘bd7 9 ♗xf6+ gxf6 10 ♘d5 ♗d6 (10...♗e7 was played in A.Jakab-G.Lorscheid, Budapest 2003, and here 11 f4! looks like the right move) 11 ♗h3 ♖g8 (11...c6? 12 ♗xe6 fxe6 13 ♘xf6 ♘xf6 14 ♖xd6+ ♚e7 15 ♖d2 left Black a pawn down for nothing in V.Malakhov-A.Gelman, Ekaterinburg 1996) 12 f3 ♚e8

13 ♗f5! (playing for domination on the light squares) 13...h5 14 ♘h3 ♖c8 was the course of M.Zhai-N.Unapkoshvili, Kemer 2007. So far White has done a nice job of building his position and at this point the right way to continue improving it would have been 15 ♖d3!, not only planning to double on the d-file, but perhaps

also to use the rook on the third rank to provoke additional weaknesses.

c) With 7...♘bd7 Black prepares to hit the bishop without incurring doubled pawns. After three natural moves from both sides, 8 f4 h6 9 ♗xf6+ ♘xf6 10 0-0-0+ ♚c8, White must decide whether to pursue the advantage in an open or (semi-)closed position. The choice is largely a matter of personal taste, so we will consider both approaches:

c1) 11 ♘f3 exf4 12 gxf4 g6 13 f5! (White should undertake quick action before his opponent's bishop pair becomes a serious force) 13...gxf5 14 exf5 ♗xf5 15 ♘e5 ♗c5 (15...♗e6?? 16 ♘xf7! ♗xf7 occurred in M.Santo Roman-J.Chabanon, Nantes 1993, at which point Black resigned without waiting for 17 ♗h3+ winning easily) 16 ♘xf7 ♖f8 17 ♗c4 ♘g4 18 ♖hf1 ♗d7. We have been following the game E.Cosma-T.Shumiakina, Timisoara 1994. At this point 19 ♖f3! would have maintained some initiative for White. The threat is ♖fd3 and 19...♘e3? runs into 20 ♘e4!

♖e8 (20...♘xd1 21 ♘fd6+ wins) 21 ♘xc5 ♘xd1 22 ♘xd7 ♚xd7 23 ♖d3+ when White should win the endgame.

c2) 11 f5 ♗d7 12 ♗c4 ♘g4!? (also after the continuation 12...♗e8 13 ♘f3 ♗d6 Black is just slightly worse) 13 ♘f3 ♗d6 (13...♘f2? 14 ♖xd7 ♚xd7 15 ♘xe5+ is too risky for Black, as is 13...♘e3? 14 ♖xd7).

Now in N.Matinian-S.Yudin, Saratov 2006, White should have played 14 ♖he1! (the game continuation of 14 ♗xf7!? ♘f2 15 ♖xd6 cxd6 16 ♖f1 gave him sufficient compensation for the exchange, but nothing more) 14...♖f8 15 h3 ♘f6 (15...♘f2? only leads to trouble for Black after 16 ♖d2 ♘xh3 17 ♖h1 ♘g5 18 ♘xg5 hxg5 19 ♗xf7! ♖xf7 20 ♖xd6) 16 ♗b5!?, exchanging the better of his opponent's two bishops. Thus White keeps a slight edge thanks to his more active pieces and the possibility of a kingside pawn advance.

Returning to 7...h6:

8 0-0-0+

8 ♗xf6+ is likely to come to the same thing.

8...♞bd7?!

This natural move leads to quite unpleasant problems for Black.

8...♚c8 would have been preferable. The resulting position is somewhat similar, except that Black will not have to worry about his bishop being trapped after f4-f5: 9 ♝xf6 gxf6

10 f4! (White follows the standard plan of playing on the kingside) 10...exf4 (another game saw 10...c6 11 ♞f3 b5 12 fxe5 fxe5 13 ♞xe5 ♝g7 14 ♞d3 ♞d7, E.Vorobiov-D.Chuprov, Tula 1999; Black has a degree of compensation for the sacrificed pawn, but after the accurate 15 ♞e2! ♚c7 16 ♞ef4 I

doubt that it is enough, as White is ready to eliminate one of the dangerous bishops, either with ♞xe6 directly, or ♝h3) 11 gxf4

11...c6 (11...f5? is too ambitious and after 12 ♝h3 ♝d6 13 ♞ge2 ♜e8 14 exf5 ♝d7 15 ♜hg1 Black was in trouble in E.Cosma-M.Sheremetieva, Timisoara 1994) 12 ♞f3 ♚c7 13 f5! (if White has to play 'anti-positional' chess to develop his initiative, then so be it) 13...♝d7 14 ♝c4 ♝e8 15 e5 (White is playing with a lot of energy, but Black's position remains sound despite the apparent awkwardness of his pieces) 15...fxe5 16 ♞xe5 ♞d7 17 ♞xd7 ♝xd7 18 ♜hf1 ♝d6 (after 18...f6 19 ♞e4 ♝e7 20 ♜d2! ♜ad8 21 ♜g2 White keeps the advantage, as shown by Erenburg) 19 ♝xf7 ♝xh2 20 ♞e4 (20 ♝e6!? ♜ad8 21 ♞e4 was also worth considering) 20...♜hf8 21 ♝g6 and despite the simplification, White kept some advantage thanks to his active pieces and more dangerous passed pawn in E.Prokopchuk-P.Kazakov, Nefteyugansk 2002.

9 ♗xf6+ gxf6 10 f4!

This thematic move creates real problems for the defender. The threat is simply f5, against which Black lacks an ideal solution.

10...exf4

10...♗g4 11 ♗e2 h5 was tried in G.Drzymala-R.Lubczynski, Krakow 2003, and here I would suggest the simple 12 h3 ♗xe2 13 ♘gxe2 when White keeps the upper hand.

11 gxf4 f5

Once again after 11...♗g4 12 ♗e2 h5, as in J.Gomez-N.Nguyen, Kuala Lumpur 2006, I recommend the same solution, 13 h3 ♗xe2 14 ♘gxe2, with excellent chances for White, based on his development advantage, superior pawns, and the prospect of installing a knight on the dominating f5-square.

12 ♗h3!

Black's position is already rather unpleasant.

12...♗d6

Black has tried three other moves, none of which come close to solving his problems:

a) 12...f6 was played in A.Zaharov-M.Suleimanov, Kolontaevo 1997, and here the simplest route to a huge advantage would have been 13 ♘ge2! intending ♘d4 or ♘g3.

b) 12...fxe4 13 f5! ♗c4 14 f6 ♗e6 15 ♗xe6 fxe6 16 ♘xe4 (the f6-pawn is huge, and Black quickly succumbs) 16...♔e8 17 ♘f3 ♘c5? 18 f7+! ♔xf7 19 ♘e5+ ♔e8 20 ♘f6+ ♔e7 21 ♖hf1 h5 22 ♘g6+ ♔f7 23 ♘xf8 1-0 R.Hasangatin-F.Dinger, Pardubice 2007.

c) More recently Black tried 12...♗c5, but lost even more quickly: 13 exf5 ♗c4 14 b3 ♗a6 15 f6 ♗d6 16 ♘e4 ♗xf4+ 17 ♔b1 ♗b5 18 ♘e2 ♗d6 19 ♘d4 ♗a6 20 ♘f5 1-0 I.Schneider-J.Stuhler, Bad Wiessee 2010.

13 e5

Not the only good move, but the simplest. The f5-pawn is now a chronic weakness, which White will capture with minimal fuss.

13...♗c5 14 ♘ge2 c6

15 ♖hf1

By guarding the f-pawn White takes the sting out of ...♗e3+, thereby facilitating ♘g3. The idea is sensible enough, but the text move was not the best way of accomplishing the goal:

a) White tried 15 ♘d4 in J.Lerch Gallemi-J.Mellado Trivino, Spain 1992, but here 15...♗xd4 16 ♖xd4 ♚c7 would have given Black some chances to resist.

b) The strongest continuation of all would have been 15 ♔b1!. This was a better way of pre-empting the bishop check, for reasons that will soon become clear: 15...♚c7 (15...f6 is impossible due to 16 ♘e4!) 16 ♘g3 f6 17 ♗xf5 ♗xf5 18 ♘xf5 fxe5 19 ♘g7! and Black is in real trouble, as compared with the game continuation, he does not have the resource of ...♗e3+ and ...♗xf4. Therefore he has nothing better than 19...exf4 20 ♘e6+ ♚c8 21 ♖xd7 (21 ♘e4!?) 21...♚xd7 22 ♘xc5+, reaching an endgame with good winning chances for White.

15...♚c7

15...f6 16 ♘g3 is similar.

16 ♘g3 f6

Black has to fight back, otherwise he will lose a pawn for nothing.

17 ♗xf5 ♗xf5 18 ♘xf5 fxe5

19 ♘g7

19 ♘e4! would have been a bit more accurate. The threat is ♖xd7+, so Black is more or less forced to retreat with 19...♗f8, after which 20 fxe5 ♘xe5 21 ♘f6 leaves White with ongoing pressure, though admittedly no clear win.

19...♗e3+

This is the reason why the king should have gone to b1 on move 15!

20 ♔b1 exf4 21 ♘e6+ ♚c8 22 ♘e4!

Despite a few inaccuracies White is still in the driving seat. He can win back his pawn at any point and Black must search for a way to bring his pieces into play, all the time while watching out for tactics based on knight forks.

White was wise to resist the temptation to regain his pawn immediately with 22 ♘xf4 ♗xf4 23 ♖xf4, after which 23...♖h7! followed by ...♚c7 solves most of Black's problems.

22...♖h7

Black could have got closer to a draw with 22...♘e5!? 23 ♘d6+ ♚d7!

(23...♔b8 24 ♘xf4 ♗xf4 25 ♖xf4 keeps some initiative) 24 ♘xf4 ♗xf4 25 ♖xf4 ♔c7, although this would not have been easy to find over the board.

23 ♖d6!

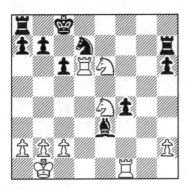

Preventing ...b6 and introducing the possibility of doubling on the d-file.

23...♗b6

Another idea was 23...a5!? 24 ♖fd1 ♖f7! (24...a4? 25 ♘f6!), although White maintains some pressure after 25 ♘4c5 ♗xc5 26 ♘xc5 or 25 ♖xc6+ bxc6 26 ♘d6+ ♔b8 27 ♘xf7.

24 ♖xf4 ♗c7?

Black has been under pressure for some time and it is hardly surprising that he eventually slips up.

The right move was 24...a5!, the main purpose of which is to create a square for the king on a7, although it is not impossible that Black might also seek to activate his rook by means of ...a4 and ...♖a5. From here a logical continuation would be 25 ♘f8 ♖e7 26 ♘xd7 ♖xd7 27 ♖f8+ ♗d8 28 ♖h8 when White wins a pawn, although victory would still be a long way off.

25 ♖g4!

Planning a deadly invasion on g8.

25...b6

Black had no choice, as 25...♖h8 26 ♖g7 was hopeless for him.

26 ♖xc6 ♘e5 27 ♖g8+

27 ♘xc7 ♘xc6 28 ♘xa8 ♔b7 29 ♘xb6 was also winning.

27...♔b7 28 ♖xc7+ ♖xc7 29 ♖xa8

29...♖e7?

Losing immediately. 29...♖c4! was essential, although after 30 ♘d6+ ♔xa8 31 ♘xc4 ♘xc4 32 b3 there is no reason why White should not go on to convert his extra pawn.

30 ♖e8! 1-0

In the next game we will deal with the various alternatives to 6...♗e6.

> ## Game 33
> **I.Khenkin-F.Bellini**
> Bratto 2004

1 d4 d6 2 e4 ♘f6 3 ♘c3 e5 4 dxe5 dxe5 5 ♕xd8+ ♔xd8 6 ♗g5

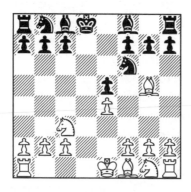

6...c6

This is the main alternative to 6...♗e6 and the first choice of several Philidor connoisseurs. Naturally Black has tried some other moves as well:

a) 6...♘bd7 7 0-0-0 will almost certainly transpose to a line considered elsewhere. For instance, 7...c6 8 ♘f3 is the main game, while 7...♗d6 8 ♘f3 and 7...♗e7 8 ♗c4 are respectively lines 'b' and 'c' below.

b) 6...♗d6 7 0-0-0 ♘bd7 (7...♗e6?! 8 f4! is strong) 8 ♘f3 ♔e8 (8...♔e7 9 ♘h4! is strong) 9 ♘b5! (attempting to exploit the omission of ...c6) 9...a6 10 ♘xd6+ cxd6 11 ♘d2 h6 12 ♗e3 b5 13 f3 ♘c5

14 ♘b1! ♔e7 15 ♘c3 ♗e6 16 g4 and White kept the upper hand in A.Timofeev-L.B.Hansen, Skanderborg 2005. Sooner or later he will drive the knight away from f6 and cement his control over the d5-square. Needless to say, the bishop pair is also an important asset.

c) 6...♗e7 7 0-0-0+ ♘bd7 8 ♗c4 ♔e8 9 f4!? (this aggressive thrust seems quite promising; 9 ♘f3 can be compared with the main game and might even transpose if Black follows up with the thematic plan of ...c6 and ...♗d8-c7) 9...h6 10 ♗xf6 ♗xf6 and now:

c1) 11 ♘f3 exf4? (taking the pawn is too dangerous; 11...c6! is the critical reply when Khalifman offers the line 12 f5 b5 13 ♗d3 ♘c5 14 g4 intending h4 with some initiative on the kingside, but Black is not without his trumps, boasting two bishops and a healthy position on the queenside) 12 e5 ♗xe5?! (12...♗d8 was the best chance, although Khalifman points out that after 13 e6 fxe6 14 ♗xe6 ♘b6 15 ♗b3 ♗f5 16 ♖he1+ ♔f8 17 ♘b5, intending

♘bd4 and ♘e5, White has more than enough for the sacrificed pawn) 13 ♖xd7 ♗xd7 (if 13...♗xc3 14 ♖xc7 ♗f6 15 ♖xf7) 14 ♘xe5 ♗e6. We have been following the game A.Alekhine-A.Aviles, Nogales (simul) 1932, and at this point White could have secured a decisive advantage with the straightforward 15 ♗xe6 fxe6 16 ♘b5!.

c2) Depending on how one evaluates the improvement noted in 'c1' (11 ♘f3 c6), 11 ♘d5!? could be considered a possible improvement. Khalifman then analyses 11...♗d8 12 ♘f3 c6 13 ♘e3 ♗c7 14 ♘f5 ♘b6 15 ♗b3 ♗xf5 16 exf5 exf4 17 ♖he1+ ♔f8 18 a4, concluding that White has a dangerous initiative. He certainly has fine compensation for a mere pawn and a doubled one at that.

Returning to 6...c6:

7 0-0-0+

7 ♘f3 could transpose after 7...♘bd7 8 0-0-0, but Black has an additional option in 7...♗d6!? intending ...♔e7.

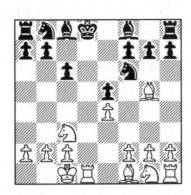

7...♘bd7

Alternatives have little independent value:

a) 7...♔c7? 8 ♗c4 ♗e6 9 ♗xe6 fxe6 is just bad for Black. Place his bishop on d6, king on e7, and pawn back on c7, and he would be doing fine. But in the absence of a magic wand, he is stuck in an inferior version of the thematic doubled e-pawn structure: 10 ♘f3 (10 f3 is also promising, intending ♘h3-f2-d3) 10...♘bd7 11 ♗h4 and Black had a real problem with the e5-pawn in G.Mandelli-F.Franciosi, Bratto 2008.

b) 7...♔e8 is a popular alternative, but it usually just transposes to the main game: 8 ♘f3 ♗g4!? (a rare independent alternative to 8...♘bd7, which reaches the standard position for this line) 9 ♗e2 (White could consider the provocative 9 h3!? ♗xf3 10 gxf3 when one can argue that his bishop pair is more relevant than the fractured kingside) 9...♘bd7 10 h3 ♗xf3 11 ♗xf3 ♗c5 12 ♗h4 ♗e7.

This position was reached in A.Scerbo-V.Georgiev, Cutro 2003. At this point I think White should have played 13 ♗g3 in order to safeguard his bishop from being exchanged. Black's position is just mildly uncomfortable (remember he cannot castle!), and in the long run White can aim to put his bishop pair to good use.

8 ♘f3

8...♔e8

Once again, this is the main line by a wide margin.

8...♔c7 is occasionally seen, although most players prefer to keep the king close to the f7-pawn. Black has enough time to defend it, but still his set-up feels a bit suspicious. One game continued 9 ♗c4 ♗b4 10 ♖he1 (10 ♗xf7 ♖f8 11 ♗xf6 ♘xf6 12 ♘xe5 ♘d7 13 ♘xd7 ♗xd7 gives Black enough compensation) 10...♗xc3 11 bxc3 ♖f8 and in H.Wirtz-H.Westenberger, German League 1995, White's bishop pair and active pieces were more important than his damaged queenside structure. Here both 12 a4 and 12 ♗h4 would have kept some advantage for him.

9 ♗h4!

This clever move combines both active and prophylactic ideas. The former include ♗g3 to attack the e5-pawn and ♗c4 followed by ♘g5 to hit f7. The latter relates to the move ...♘g4, which will no longer threaten f2. The following game illustrates the last point: 9 ♗c4 ♘g4!? 10 ♖hf1 f6 11 ♗h4, T.Lochte-O.Hirn, German League 1997. Now after 11...♘h6 Black has succeeded in supporting the e5-pawn; his knight will slot back to f7 and perhaps later d6, and the bishop lacks any real purpose on h4.

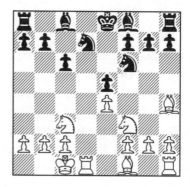

9...♗b4

This active move has been Black's most popular reply, although we should also consider a couple of other bishop moves:

a) 9...♗e7? is just a mistake, as 10 ♗g3 leaves Black without a good way to defend e5.

b) 9...♗c5 is a reasonable alternative. The position after 10 ♗c4 ♗b6 11 ♖d2 ♗c7 12 ♖hd1 is rather typical for the whole variation. Black's position is sound and, given enough time, he should be able to unravel and equalize.

Nevertheless White's position is easier to play and Black has a smaller margin for error. One could argue that both players have reason to feel happy with the outcome of the opening.

Here are a couple of practical examples from this position:

b1) The time-wasting move 12...h6? is a luxury that Black can ill-afford (remember the comment about margin for error?): 13 ♗xf6 gxf6? (missing White's next move; 13...♘xf6 was the best chance, although 14 ♘xe5! ♗e6 15 ♗xe6 ♗xe5 16 ♗d7+ ♔f8 17 ♖d3 still leaves Black in difficulties) 14 ♗xf7+! and White won material in V.Durnev-Y.Sanotsky, Lviv 2011.

b2) 12...♔e7 is a better move. The following game featured pretty logical play on both sides: 13 a3 h6 14 b4 ♖e8 15 ♘e1 ♘b6 16 ♗b3 g5 17 ♗g3 ♘h5 18 ♘d3 f6 19 ♘c5 ♖d8 20 ♖xd8 ♗xd8 21 f3 and White's position remained a bit more pleasant, although Black eventually managed to hold the draw, V.Malakhov-B.Damljanovic, Chalkidiki 2002.

10 ♗c4

White continues developing in an active manner.

10...♗a5

The bishop transfer to c7 is a typical manoeuvre, which covers both the d6-square and the e5-pawn.

Two other moves have been tested:

a) 10...♔e7 was played in R.Londyn-J.Pribyl, Prague 2006. Here I would suggest the direct 11 a3!? ♗xc3 (11...♗a5 resembles the main game) 12 bxc3 when White's bishop pair counts for more than his damaged queenside.

b) 10...♗xc3 11 bxc3 b5 (11...♘xe4? 12 ♘xe5 is winning) 12 ♗b3 c5. This rather adventurous and risky plan was tried in I.Videnova-S.Bednikova, Dupnitsa 2010.

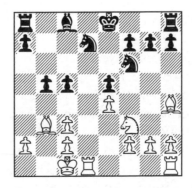

Here White could have obtained some advantage with the following resolute continuation: 13 c4! ♘b6 (13...bxc4 14 ♗a4! is awkward for Black, while 13...a6 can be met by the calm 14 ♖he1!? intending ♗g3) 14 ♘xe5 ♗e6 15 cxb5! c4 16 f3 cxb3 17 axb3. With three healthy pawns and the initiative in return for the piece, White is clearly better.

11 a3

This often turns out to be a useful improving move in such positions. White creates an escape route for his bishop and may consider a queenside expansion with b4, as in the Malakhov-Damljanovic game noted above.

11...h6

Black often plays this move at some point; the need for it is revealed by the first of the following variations:

a) 11...♗e7?! is risky due to 12 ♘g5! when Black has a problem with his kingside pawns.

b) One of the few other games to have reached this position continued with 11...♗c7, after which a couple of ideas deserve consideration:

b1) One logical idea is 12 ♖d2 when 12...♔e7 13 ♖hd1 transposes to note 'b2' to Black's 9th move, above. However, Black might be able to improve with 12...b5!? 13 ♗a2 a5 when the queenside counterattack gives him decent prospects.

b2) In H.Jurkovic-Z.Jovanovic, Sibenik 2005, White also borrowed a manoeuvre from Malakhov: 12 ♘e1 ♔e7 13 ♘d3 ♖e8 14 f3 ♘f8 and now 15 ♖d2! looks like the most logical way to improve White's position; the rook vacates the d1-square not just for the other rook, but maybe even for the knight. For instance, after 15...♗e6 (15...b5? can be strongly met by 16 ♗xb5, and 16 ♘b4! is even better) 16 ♗xe6 ♘xe6 17 ♘d1! the knight is coming to e3 and Black still has certain problems to solve.

12 ♗xf6!

White gives up one of his important bishops in order to damage the enemy kingside. This can often prove a rather double-edged idea, but Khenkin obviously decided that the potential reward justified the risk. Perhaps Black's last move had something to do with it; now if White can establish a knight on f5, it will tie one of the black pieces to the defence of the h6-pawn, whereas with the pawn on h7 this would not have been an issue for Black.

12 b4 gave White a tiny edge in S.Rosic-Z.Jovanovic, Neum 2005, but the text move is more interesting and it is definitely the one I would prefer.

12...gxf6

Forced, as otherwise the e5-pawn would hang.

13 ♘e2!

The knight had no future on c3, so Khenkin wastes no time in shifting it towards the key f5-square.

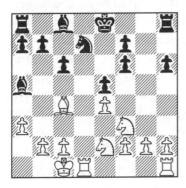

13...b5 14 ♗a2 ♗c7 15 ♘h4 ♘b6 16 ♘g3

One of the nice features of this structure is that White gets to play a number of easy moves: just send the knights towards f5 and see how Black plans to solve his problems.

16...♗e6 17 ♗b3!

A nice way to deal with the tension on the diagonal.

17...h5

Preventing the knight from coming forwards. After 17...♗xb3 18 cxb3 Black not only has a headache arriving on the f5-square, but might experience problems on the c-file as well.

18 ♘gf5 ♖g8

Black had to prevent the check on g7.

19 ♖d3!

By bringing the rook into play, White creates a new set of problems for his opponent.

19...♖d8 20 ♖g3 ♔f8

Alternatives were also demoralizing for Black:

a) After 20...♖xg3 21 hxg3 the h-pawn will soon fall.

b) 20...♖g5 21 ♘g7+ ♔e7 22 ♘hf5+ ♗xf5 23 ♘xf5+ and Black's position is unpleasant.

21 ♖xg8+ ♔xg8 22 ♘e7+ ♔f8 23 ♘xc6

The pressure pays off and White deposits a pawn in the bank.

23...♖a8 24 ♘b4

I am not sure why White rejected the simple 24 ♖d1!, bringing his last piece into play. In that case he would have been in full control, with both a material and a positional advantage.

24...♘c4

24...a5 was a better try, although Black is still struggling.

25 ♗xc4 bxc4 26 ♘d5 ♗xd5 27 exd5

Apart from his extra pawn, White has a strong passed d-pawn and a bind over the light squares. Bellini fights as best he can, but it is a losing battle.

27...♔g7 28 ♖d1 ♗b6 29 ♘f5+ ♔g6

30 ♘e3

30 ♘e7+ ♔g5 31 d6 ♖d8 32 d7 ♗d4 33 h4+! would have won fairly easily.

30...c3!? 31 bxc3 ♗c5 32 ♘c4

32 d6! would have wrapped things

up more quickly; the a3-pawn is not really relevant.

32...e4 33 ♖d2 ♖d8 34 a4 f5 35 ♔d1 f4 36 ♔e2

36 ♘a5! was a good move, intending ♘b3 and c4-c5, and because 36...♗xf2? does not work due to 37 ♘c6.

36...♔f5 37 ♖d1 ♖g8 38 g3 f3+ 39 ♔e1

White has not conducted the endgame in an optimal way, but he has done just enough to maintain a winning margin.

39...h4 40 d6 hxg3 41 hxg3 ♔e6 42 d7 ♗e7 43 ♖d4 f5 44 g4!

44...♖h8?

Losing quickly.

44...fxg4 45 ♖xe4+ ♔xd7 46 ♘e5+ will take a while to win, but White should get there eventually.

45 gxf5+ ♔xf5 46 ♘d6+ ♔e6 47 ♘xe4

We have reached something similar to the previous note, except that the d7-pawn is still on the board – quite a serious difference.

47...♖d8 48 ♔d2 ♖xd7 49 ♖xd7 ♔xd7

The minor piece ending is trivial

and the rest can pass without comment.

50 ♔e3 ♔c6 51 ♔xf3 ♔b6 52 c4 ♗a5 53 c5 ♗d8 54 ♔f4 ♔xa4 55 ♔e5 ♔b4 56 ♔d6 a5 57 ♔d7 a4 58 ♔xd8 a3 59 c6 a2 60 c3+ ♔b3 61 c7 a1♕ 62 c8♕ ♕a5+ 63 ♔e7 1-0

Part 2 – Other set-ups

In the first two games of this section we will consider a defensive set-up based on 3...c6.

> ### Game 34
> ### Y.Yakovich-M.Romero Garcia
> Seville 1999

1 d4 d6 2 e4 ♘f6 3 ♘c3 c6

This opening is known as the Czech Pirc. Black keeps a flexible position in the centre and waits for the enemy knight to come to f3 so that he may pin it with ...♗g4. Depending on how White reacts, Black may challenge for the centre with ...e5 or ...d5.

4 f4

Just as against the Pirc and Modern, I favour this aggressive space-gaining move.

4...♕a5

Black makes use of his previous move to attack the e4-pawn while preparing ...e5 without allowing a queen exchange.

5 ♗d3 e5 6 ♘f3 ♗g4

Black usually makes this pinning move when permitted in the Czech Pirc; the bishop hardly has anything better to do.

7 ♗e3 ♘bd7

Once again this natural developing move has been the most popular choice by far. Of course a number of different ideas have been tried, including 7...♕b6?!, a risky attempt to grab a pawn. This move will be considered in the next game, along with all of Black's main alternatives between moves 4 and 7.

8 0-0

8 h3!? ♗xf3 9 ♕xf3 is another possible move order, which retains the option of long castling. Here 9...♕b4? is certainly not an issue due to 10 a3! when 10...♕xb2? 11 ♔d2! leaves Black in serious trouble. A sounder reply is 9...♗e7 when 10 0-0 transposes to the game, but White can also consider the more aggressive 10 0-0-0!?.

So far so good, but there is a small drawback. Black has a more critical reply in 8...exf4!? 9 ♗xf4 ♗xf3 10 ♕xf3 ♕b4! when White must sacrifice a pawn for less than certain compensa-

tion, S.Keskinen-J.Haanpaa, Turku 1997.

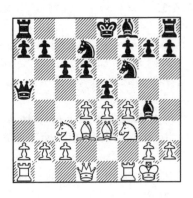

8...♗e7

Black's main alternatives are all connected with the idea of attacking the b2- and d4-pawns, but none of them bring him much joy:

a) 8...♕b4? is useless in view of 9 a3! when the queen must retreat as 9...♕xb2?? 10 ♘a4 leaves her trapped.

b) 8...♕b6 can be met by 9 ♕e1 (another equally strong reply is 9 ♘a4!? followed by 9...♕c7 10 h3 or 9...♕a5 10 c4) 9...exf4 (9...♗xf3? 10 dxe5) 10 ♘a4! ♕c7 11 ♗xf4 when White stays in control.

c) After 8...exd4 9 ♗xd4 Black has given up his foothold in the centre and 9...♕b4 10 ♘e2 keeps everything in order for White.

d) Releasing the central tension only really makes sense if Black can mount a serious attack on the d4-pawn, but he is in no position to profit from 8...exf4 9 ♗xf4:

d1) 9...♕b6 10 ♘a4 (10 ♘e2 is also good) 10...♕a5 (or 10...♕c7 11 h3) 11 c4

♘b6?! (this leaves both the queen and the knight misplaced after White's obvious response) 12 ♘c3 ♗e7 was Z.Veroci-N.Hoiberg, Espergarde 1992, and here the most effective way of increasing White's advantage would have been 13 ♖b1 or 13 a3 with the unpleasant threat of b4.

d2) With 9...♕b4 10 a3! this time White makes a genuine sacrifice:

10...♕xb2 (10...♕b6 is safer, but 11 ♘a4 just gives White a slightly improved version of the previous variation) 11 ♕d2 ♕b6 12 ♖ab1 ♕c7 13 e5! ♘h5 14 exd6 ♗xd6 15 ♗xd6 ♕xd6 16 ♘e4 ♕e7 17 ♖xb7 ♗xf3 (17...0-0 18 ♘e5 ♗e6 19 ♕e2! g6 20 g4 wins a piece) 18 ♖xf3 (18 ♘c5!? ♗g4 19 ♘xd7 is also devastating) 18...0-0 was M.Gagunashvili-Z.Azmaiparashvili, Izmir 2002. Here White's simplest route to victory would have been 19 ♖f5! (now the knight is trapped, whereas the game continuation of 19 ♖h3 allowed Black to resist with 19...f5!), since 19...g6 is refuted trivially by 20 ♖xh5 gxh5 21 ♖xd7.

Returning to 8...♗e7:

9 h3 ♗xf3

At first glance this seems like an automatic choice, but retreating the bishop is quite playable too: 9...♗h5 10 ♕e1 (10 g4 exf4 avoids the loss of a piece) 10...♗xf3 (10...exf4 11 ♗xf4 ♗g6 is risky: 12 e5 dxe5 13 dxe5 ♘d5 14 e6 ♕b6+ 15 ♔h1 fxe6 16 ♗xg6+ hxg6 17 ♗g5 ♘5f6 18 ♕xe6 ♕xb2 was W.Browne-J.Benjamin, Modesto 1995, and here 19 ♘e4! ♘f8 20 ♘d6+ ♔d8 21 ♕f7 ♗xd6 22 ♕xg7 would have left Black in a hopeless situation) 11 ♖xf3.

The situation on the board resembles that which occurs in the main game, but the position of the rook on f3 instead of the queen will lead to some small differences. After 11...0-0 12 a3!? (preventing any ...♕b4 ideas while giving White the option of b4 in certain positions) here are three examples of how the game might continue:

a) 12...c5 was played in D.Baramidze-D.Curic, Essen 2002. Here White could have put his last move to full use with 13 b4! cxb4 14 axb4 (14

♘b5 is also promising) 14...♕xb4 15 ♖a4 ♕b2 16 ♘b5 and the black queen is in trouble.

b) 12...♘h5 is rather risky: 13 fxe5 dxe5 14 ♖f5 g6 15 ♖xh5 gxh5 16 ♗h6 (threatening an immediate mate) 16...♗f6 17 ♗xf8 ♖xf8 18 d5 when material was equal, but Black had no compensation for his busted kingside, M.Gerzina-L.Cederloef, correspondence 1999.

c) A more recent encounter continued 12...♕c7 13 ♕f2 exd4 14 ♗xd4 ♘c5?! (allowing White to force a favourable change in the pawn structure) 15 ♗xc5 dxc5 16 e5 ♘d7 (after 16...♘d5 17 ♘e4 the evaluation is similar) 17 ♘e4 b5 18 c4 f5?! 19 exf6 ♘xf6 20 ♘g5 bxc4 21 ♗xc4+ ♔h8 22 ♘e6 and White won an exchange and soon after the game, E.Sveshnikov-P.Toulzac, Malakoff 2009.

10 ♕xf3

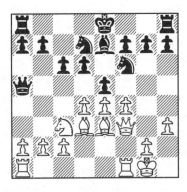

10...0-0

In some games Black has tried 10...exd4, but after 11 ♗xd4 0-0 12 ♖ae1 White has an obvious advantage.

Instead 10...0-0-0 is understandably rare and after 11 ♖ab1, intending b4-b5, Black will face a strong attack.

11 ♘e2!

An important regrouping move. White prepares c3 to support the centre and the knight will be deployed on the kingside.

11...c5

With 11...♖fe8 12 c3 c5 Black's play is similar to the main game, but by waiting for c2-c3 he prevents the white knight from using that square as a springboard to get to d5 (note too that 12...♗f8 should be met by 13 ♘g3, instead of 13 g4 which allows Black to obtain full counterplay with 13...d5!). Now 13 dxe5 dxe5 occurred in J.Chabanon-C.Bauer, Meribel 1998, when it is worth considering two paths for White:

a) In the game White chose 14 ♗c4, but Black could have initiated a tactical sequence, with not unfavourable consequences: 14...b5! 15 ♗xf7+! ♔xf7 16 fxe5 ♘xe5 17 ♕h5+ ♔g8! (Yudasin noted 17...♘g6 18 e5 when White keeps some initiative, but Black does better to retreat his king to safety) 18 ♕xe5 ♕b6! when Black intends ....♗f8 to win back his pawn, and White will be hard-pressed to find a convincing counter.

b) Instead I believe the most promising continuation to be 14 f5! intending a kingside pawn storm. The following illustrative line is mentioned by Yudasin: 14...h6 15 g4 ♘h7 16 ♕g3 ♕d8 17 ♗f2 when Black fails to blockade the kingside and after completing development with ♖ad1, White will transfer his knight to f3, followed by h4 and g5.

12 dxe5 dxe5 13 ♘c3!

The knight makes a hasty return, having become aware of some new and important business on the c3-square.

13...♗d6

13...♖ac8 14 ♗b5 c4 (14...exf4?! 15 ♗xf4 ♘b6 16 e5 ♘e8 17 ♕xb7 was rotten for Black in O.Renet-V.Moskalenko, St Martin 1991) 15 ♖ad1 ♖fd8 16 ♘d5 ♘xd5 17 ♖xd5 ♘f6 was G.Flear-C.Papatryfonos, Plovdiv 2003, and here 18 ♖xd8+ ♖xd8 19 ♗xc4 would have bagged a safe extra pawn for White.

14 f5 ♘b6 15 ♕e2

Maintaining the blockade.

15 ♘b5 ♗e7 16 c4 a6 17 ♘c3 ♘a4! is irritating, as a knight exchange would make it almost impossible for White to utilize the d5-square. 18 ♘d1!? is possible, but it feels a bit cumbersome.

15...♖fd8

15...♖ac8 is well met by 16 ♘b5! and with ♗d2 coming, Black has problems.

16 a3

Also interesting is 16 ♗c4!? ♘xc4 17 ♕xc4 ♕b4 18 b3.

16...♖ac8 17 ♗c4 ♘xc4 18 ♕xc4

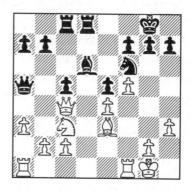

18...a6

Interestingly Yakovich had reached the identical position five years earlier. That game continued 18...♗f8 19 ♗g5 ♖d4 20 ♕e2 ♘e8 21 ♗e3 ♖d7 22 ♖ad1 ♖xd1 23 ♖xd1 ♕b6 24 ♕b5 ♕xb5 25 ♘xb5 a6 26 ♘c3 and White kept a clear positional advantage, Y.Yakovich-K.Mokry, Pardubice 1994.

19 ♗g5!

Forcing a favourable minor piece exchange.

19...b5 20 ♕e2 ♗e7 21 ♗xf6 ♗xf6 22 ♘d5

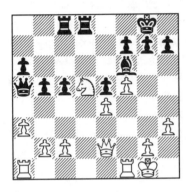

White has a permanent positional advantage thanks to the superiority of his dominant knight over the passive enemy bishop.

22...♖d6 23 ♖ad1 ♕d8 24 a4

The strong knight cannot win the game by itself, so White begins chipping away at the queenside. 24 c4!? was another way of doing so, which would also have been rather troublesome for Black.

24...c4

Shielding the b5-pawn while increasing the scope of the bishop.

After 24...bxa4 25 ♕c4 White will soon regain the pawn and Black's queenside has been damaged irreparably.

25 ♕g4

Taking on b5 first would have prevented the next suggestion for Black.

25...♔f8

With the white queen far away on the kingside, it was worth considering 25...bxa4!? intending ...♖b8 when it is

not so easy for White to maintain full control over the queenside.

26 axb5 axb5 27 ♔h1

Yakovich points out that 27 ♖a1 gives Black the opportunity for 27...♖xd5!? 28 exd5 ♕xd5 with some chances to hold.

27...♖a8

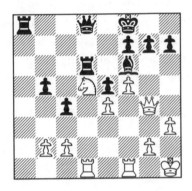

28 c3

Yakovich elects to keep the queenside closed, but it was also worth considering 28 b3!? when Black will be left with a weak pawn on c4 or b5.

28...♖a7 29 ♕g3 ♖a2 30 ♕f2 ♕c8 31 ♘b4

31 ♘xf6!? ♖xf6 32 ♖d5 wins a pawn while keeping a positional advantage; on the other hand, it is never easy to bring oneself to exchange such a knight for such a bishop, so Yakovich continues manoeuvring in order to wear down his opponent.

31...♖xd1 32 ♖xd1 ♖a8 33 ♕b6 ♕e8

33...♖b8 34 ♕d6+ ♔g8 35 ♘c6 ♖a8 36 ♘xe5 is a safe extra pawn.

34 ♘c6 ♖c8 35 ♘a7 ♖b8 36 ♕c7 ♔g8 37 ♖d7 b4 38 ♘c6 ♖c8 39 ♕d6

39 ♘e7+ ♗xe7 40 ♖xe7 followed by ♕xe5 wins a pawn, but Black may have some chances to hold the major piece endgame.

39...bxc3 40 bxc3 ♖a8

Black should have preferred 40...h5 to avoid meeting his end on the back rank.

41 ♘e7+ ♔h8

41...♗xe7 42 ♖xe7 ♕b8 43 ♕xb8+ ♖xb8 44 ♖xe5 g6 45 ♖c5 leads to a rook ending with two extra pawns. The level of harmony in White's position is not ideal, but he should be able to win eventually.

42 ♘d5 ♗g5

42...♗h4 43 ♔h2 prevents all counterplay.

43 f6!

Having improved his position to more or less the maximum extent possible, the time has come for White to take decisive action.

43...gxf6?

Losing quickly.

43...♕f8 44 ♕xe5 and 43...♗xf6 44 ♘xf6 gxf6 45 ♕xf6+ ♔g8 46 ♖e7 ♕f8

47 ♕xe5 were both losing for Black, but both would have offered greater resistance than the game continuation.

44 ♘c7 ♖a1+

44...♕b8 45 ♘xa8 ♕b1+ does not work, as White has 46 ♕d1.

45 ♔h2 ♗f4+

45...♕g8 46 ♖d8 ♗f4+ 47 g3 ♗xg3+ 48 ♔g2 wins.

46 g3 ♗xg3+ 47 ♔g2

And obviously not 47 ♔xg3?? ♕g8+ when it is Black who wins.

47...♖a2+ 48 ♔f3 1-0

The next game deals with Black's early deviations in the Czech Pirc.

> ## Game 35
> ## S.Karjakin-A.Ivanov
> Russian Team
> Championship 2010

1 e4 d6 2 d4 ♘f6 3 ♘c3 c6 4 f4 ♕a5

This is the main line by far, but three other moves deserve a mention:

a) 4...g6 is just a Pirc where Black has committed himself to ...c6 prematurely.

b) 4...♗g4 should be met by 5 ♕d3! when the bishop will soon be driven away, and the attempt to force matters in the centre backfires horribly: 5...d5?! (5...g6 and 5...♘a6 are preferable, although in both cases 6 h3 followed by ♗e3 leaves White in control) 6 e5 ♘e4? (6...♘g8 7 h3 ♗d7 8 ♘f3 is obviously not good for Black, but this was the lesser evil) 7 ♘xe4 ♗f5?? 8 ♘d6+ and White wins a piece.

c) 4...♕b6 should be met by the energetic 5 e5! with the following possibilities:

c1) 5...dxe5 6 fxe5 ♘d5 7 ♘xd5 cxd5 8 ♗d3 when White is doing well, with an impressive central wedge and the open f-file.

c2) 5...♘g4 6 h3 ♘h6 7 g4 with a huge space advantage.

c3) 5...♗g4 can be met by 6 ♕d3!? as in variation 'a' above, and 6 ♗e2 ♗xe2 7 ♕xe2 ♘d5 8 ♘xd5 cxd5 9 e6!? is also interesting.

c4) After 5...♘d5 6 ♘xd5 cxd5 7 ♗d3 (7 c3 ♗f5 is less accurate) 7...g6 (or 7...♘c6 8 c3) 8 c3 White's strong central pawn wedge is an important asset which promises him good chances.

Here are a few examples:

c41) 8...♗g7 9 ♕f3!? (9 ♘f3 is also fine) 9...♗e6 10 ♘e2 ♘d7 11 ♕g3 (threatening f5) 11...♗f8 12 0-0 ♗f5 13 ♗xf5 gxf5 14 b3 and White kept a pleasant edge in G.Kaidanov-G.Zaichik, Connecticut 2003.

c42) 8...♗f5 9 ♗xf5 gxf5 10 ♕h5! (10 ♘h3 h5! is not so clear) 10...e6 11 ♘f3 ♘c6 12 ♘g5 ♘d8 13 g4! ♗e7 14 gxf5 exf5 15 ♘xf7 ♘xf7 16 e6 ♖f8 17 ♖g1 and Black was in trouble in P.Wells-N.Rashkovsky, London 1990.

5 ♗d3

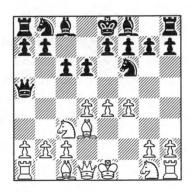

5...e5

In the event of 5...♗g4, White should once again avoid exchanges: 6 ♕d2! g6 (if 6...e5? 7 dxe5 dxe5 8 f5) 7 h3 ♗d7 8 ♘f3 and White has a clearly favourable version of a Pirc.

Instead 5...d5!? 6 e5 ♘e4 7 ♗xe4 dxe4 leads to quite an irrational position which deserves some attention. White has a strong centre and the e4-pawn is weak, but the light-squared bishop is a significant casualty. After 8 ♗d2!? (8 ♕e2 has been much more popular, but I like the idea of playing dynamically and increasing White's development advantage more than the simple attack on the e-pawn) 8...♕b6 9 ♘ge2 f5 White has two promising paths, leading to completely different types of position:

a) 10 ♘a4 ♛c7 11 c4 e6 12 ♖c1 gives a closed position with better chances for White, I.Ibragimov-A.Young, Minneapolis 2005. Black is short of space and it is tough to suggest a useful role for his bishops.

b) The more dynamic option is 10 exf6 exf6 11 ♘xe4.

Igor Glek has won two games from this position:

b1) 11...♛xb2?! (it is too risky for Black to worry about pawn-counting when he is so far behind in development) 12 0-0 ♗e7 13 f5 ♘a6 14 c4 ♛b6 15 ♔h1 0-0 16 ♖b1 ♛c7 17 ♖b3 ♖d8 18 ♛e1 ♗f8 19 ♛h4 ♛f7 20 ♖h3 h6 21 ♖g3 and White had built up a decisive attack by simple means in I.Glek-A.De Santis, Castellaneta 1999.

b2) 11...f5 12 ♘g5 ♛xb2?! (falling into the same trap as in the previous example) 13 0-0 ♗e7 14 ♖f3! ♛b6 15 ♖e3 (now Black's king will never escape the centre) 15...c5 16 ♘c3 ♛d8 17 ♛h5+ g6 18 ♛h6 ♛d7 19 ♖ae1 1-0 I.Glek-M.Scekic, Rethymnon 2003.

6 ♘f3 ♗g4

Establishing this pin is a knee-jerk reaction for most Czech Pirc players, but there are two notable alternatives:

a) After 6...exd4 7 ♘xd4 Black has two main ideas:

a1) 7...♛b6 8 ♗e2 sees both sides having lost a tempo, but the black queen is in rather an uncomfortable spot, and will have to move again after White arranges to put his bishop on e3: 8...♘bd7 9 0-0 (this entails a pawn sacrifice which White should be delighted to offer) 9...♘c5 10 ♗f3 ♘e6 11 ♗e3 ♛xb2 (11...♛c7 12 ♛d2) 12 ♛d2 ♛b4?! (12...♛a3 was better, although 13 ♖ab1 still leaves White with excellent compensation) 13 ♖ab1 ♛a5 14 e5 and White had a huge initiative in Y.Dembo-E.Kostopoulos, Korinthos 2004.

a2) 7...g6 8 0-0 ♗g7 9 ♔h1 0-0 10 f5! gives White the simple but effective attacking plan of ♛e1-h4, ♗h6, and ♘f3-g5 mating. Here is one an example from grandmaster praxis: 10...♘bd7 11 ♛e1 ♘c5 12 ♛h4 ♛b4 13 ♘f3 ♘xd3 14 cxd3 ♘d7 15 ♗h6 f6 16 ♗xg7 ♔xg7 17 d4!? (17 ♖f2 ♘e5 enables Black to simplify, thus solving his problems to some degree) 17...♘b6 (17...♕xb2 gives White full compensation after 18 ♖fc1 or 18 ♕e1!? intending ♖b1-b3), L.Dominguez Perez-W.Arencibia Rodriguez, Havana 2005.

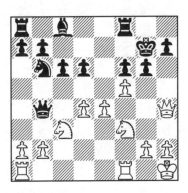

Call me boring, but I would prefer not to have to think about ...♕xb2 on every move, and so here I would recommend the calm 18 ♖f2, guarding the loose pawn while preparing to double on the f-file.

b) 6...♘bd7 is a significant sideline which deserves some attention: 7 0-0 ♗e7 8 ♗e3 (8 ♔h1 has been the overwhelmingly most popular choice, but moving the king is not yet essential, and White may be able to do without it altogether) 8...0-0 (8...♘g4 9 ♗d2 is nothing to worry about) 9 ♕e1 ♘g4 (alternatively: 9...♖e8 10 ♘d5! and White will eliminate the bishop on e7 to obtain a pleasant advantage, with or without queens; or 9...♕c7 when it looks logical to play 10 ♖d1, planning to meet ...♘g4 with ♗c1) 10 ♗d2 exd4 11 ♘d5! ♕d8 12 ♘xe7+ ♕xe7 13 ♘xd4

♘c5 14 b4 ♘xd3 15 cxd3 and White kept the more active position in S.Beshukov-V.Bachin, Tomsk 2001.

7 ♗e3

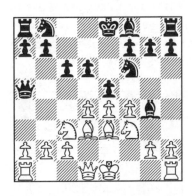

So far we have followed the same path as the previous game, which featured the main line of 7...♘bd7. Now it is time to finish our round-up of the less common alternatives.

7...♕b6

Alternatively:

a) 7...d5?! is too optimistic: 8 fxe5 ♘xe4 (after 8...dxe4 9 exf6 exd3 10 fxg7 ♗xg7 11 ♕xd3 Black's bishop pair is not enough to compensation for his missing pawn and damaged kingside) 9 0-0 ♘xc3 10 bxc3 ♘d7 (10...♕xc3 11 ♕b1 ♕b4 12 ♘g5 gives White too much activity for a pawn, while 10...♗e7 is met by 11 ♕e1 ♘d7 12 ♕g3) 11 ♕b1! ♕b6 12 ♕e1! and White had a dangerous initiative, L.Ondok-J.Dostan, Hungarian League 2006.

b) 7...exf4 8 ♗xf4 and now Black has a couple of ways of targeting the d4-pawn, but neither of them works well for him:

b1) 8...♕b4? is just bad: 9 a3 ♕b6 (if 9...♕xb2?? 10 ♘a4, while 9...♗xf3 10 axb4 ♗xd1 11 ♔xd1 was clearly better for White in R.Patterson-J.Simon, Bermuda 2002) 10 ♗e3! and Black's opening has been a failure; he has wasted time moving his queen around and the b2-pawn is still poisoned.

b2) 8...♕b6 9 ♘e2! (9 ♕d2 ♗xf3 10 gxf3 ♕xd4 11 0-0-0 is a fairly promising pawn sacrifice, but the text keeps a pleasant edge while keeping White's important central pawns intact) 9...♗xf3 10 gxf3 ♕xb2 (principled, but extremely risky) 11 ♖b1 ♕xa2 12 ♖xb7 gives White tremendous compensation for a pawn, A.Shirov-M.Rivas Pastor, Manila Olympiad 1992.

c) 7...exd4 8 ♗xd4 ♕b4 (8...♘bd7 9 0-0 ♕b4 10 ♘e2 gives White comfortable play) 9 ♗e2! offers a promising pawn sacrifice:

9...♘xe4 (consistent but risky; even worse, though, would have been 9...♕xb2? 10 ♘d5) 10 0-0 d5 11 a3 ♕e7 12 ♘xe4 dxe4 13 ♘g5 (13 ♘e5 is also good) and White had a strong initiative

for the pawn in M.Brodsky-A.Rakhmangulov, Nikolaev 1995.

The game continuation, 7...♕b6, is a slightly different incarnation of the attempted pawn-grabbing strategy. The evaluation is similar to most of the above lines – Black is risking too much and should not be wasting time moving his queen again.

8 fxe5!?

Usual has been 8 ♕d2, but Karjakin decides he prefers the f-file open.

8...dxe5 9 ♕d2

9...exd4

9...♗xf3 would commit Black to a queen sacrifice: 10 dxe5 ♕xb2 11 ♖b1 ♘xe4 (11...♕a3?! 12 exf6 is horrible for Black) 12 ♗xe4 ♕xb1+ 13 ♘xb1 ♗xe4 14 0-0 when Black has enough material for the queen, but he has a serious problem with his lagging development. **10 ♗xd4 ♕d8**

Otherwise, 10...c5? 11 ♗b5+! followed by ♗xf6 is nasty and 10...♕a5 11 e5 ♘d5 12 ♘g5!? is dangerous, as 12...h6 is met by 13 e6! with a serious attack.

11 0-0-0 ♗xf3 12 ♗xf6 ♕xf6 13 gxf3

Another game proceeded with 13 e5!? ♕h4 14 gxf3 ♗e7 15 ♖hg1 ♘d7 16 ♖g4 ♕h6 17 ♕xh6 gxh6 18 f4 h5 19 ♖g7 ♗f8 20 ♖g5 and here the players agreed a draw in R.Haataja-A.Kuzenkov, correspondence 2002, although in the final position White is clearly better and is about to win a pawn.

13...♗b4

13...♕xf3?? is of course suicidal and 14 ♗c4 is the easiest refutation. Instead 13...♘d7!? looks like Black's best chance to survive the opening, intending to park the king on the queenside.

14 e5 ♕h4?!

The queen would have been less exposed on e7.

15 ♖hg1 g6 16 f4?!

A small slip, as 16 ♖g4 ♕e7 17 ♖xb4! ♕xb4 18 ♗xg6! ♕e7 19 ♗f5 would have been crushing.

16...♗xc3?

It is surprising to see an experienced grandmaster pawn-grabbing in such a naive way.

16...0-0 would have survived for longer, although Black is clearly skating on thin ice.

17 ♕xc3 ♕xf4+ 18 ♔b1

Black's position simply looks ridiculous and Karjakin makes short work of him.

18...♖f8

19 e6! fxe6 20 ♕b3

20 ♖gf1 ♕d6 21 ♕g7 ♖xf1 22 ♖xf1 was also devastating.

20...♔e7

20...♕f7 is met by 21 ♗c4 and ♗xe6 with annihilation on the central files.

21 ♕xb7+ ♘d7 22 ♗b5! ♖fd8 23 ♗xc6 ♖ab8 24 ♖xd7+ ♔f8 25 ♖xd8+ ♖xd8 26 a4 ♔g8 27 ♕xa7 1-0

A bad day at the office for Ivanov, but this kind of disaster is hardly an isolated occurrence when Black indulges in an early bout of pawn-hunting with ...♕b4 or ...♕b6.

Having concluded our business with the Czech Pirc, let us now move on to a couple more variations of the Philidor theme.

Game 36
A.Dreev-A.Kveinys
Vienna 1996

1 d4 d6 2 e4 ♘f6 3 ♘c3 ♘bd7

Black aims for a Philidor, without allowing a queen exchange. Black would get his wish after 4 ♘f3 e5, but White can instead opt for a more aggressive set-up in order to question the position of the d7-knight.

4 f4

The other fashionable continuation is 4 g4!? h6 5 h3 e5 6 ♗g2, intending ♘ge2 and later f4, when White's extended fianchetto offers him good chances. I would evaluate the two lines as equally promising, but eventually decided that the early f4 would be a more consistent repertoire choice, having already recommended it against the Modern, Pirc, and Czech Pirc systems.

4...e5

Black needs to secure a foothold in the centre while preventing e4-e5, which would embarrass the knight – a clear drawback of the early ...♘bd7.

4...c5 is a riskier and less common way of challenging in the centre: 5 e5 cxd4 6 ♕xd4 ♘g4 7 exd6 (White can also consider 7 ♘f3 dxe5 8 fxe5 ♘dxe5 9 ♕xd8+ ♔xd8 10 ♘xe5 ♘xe5 11 ♗f4 with good play for a pawn, V.Lupynin-Y.Lavrentyev, correspondence 2006) 7...exd6 8 ♘f3 ♘gf6 was J.Randviir-A.Peterson, Riga 1960, and here it looks

promising to prepare long castling with 9 ♗d2: for instance, 9...♗e7 10 g4! 0-0 11 g5 ♘e8 12 0-0-0 and White is clearly on top.

5 ♘f3 exd4

Sometimes Black leaves the e5-pawn for the taking, but this is a risky business as the following lines demonstrate:

a) 5...♗e7 6 dxe5 dxe5 7 fxe5 ♘g4 8 ♗f4 ♗c5 9 ♕d2!? when Black can invade with either piece on f2, but neither one does him much good:

a1) In G.Malbran-M.Tempone, Buenos Aires 1997, Black chose 9...♘f2 10 ♖g1 ♘g4. In this position White chose 11 ♖h1, after which Black spurned the repetition with 11...♗f2+ and went on to lose. See line 'a2' below for coverage of the bishop check – with the move number two behind of course. However, White can do much better than repeating moves in the first place: 11 0-0-0! ♗xg1 12 ♘xg1 gives White a huge initiative for a tiny material investment. Indeed, it is hard to suggest a good way for Black to get his pieces out and make it through the middle-game.

a2) 9...♗f2+ 10 ♔e2 ♗c5 11 h3 ♘h6 was reached in the aforementioned game after the move repetition. At this point the best of several strong continuations would have been 12 ♘d5! when the threats of ♗g5 and e6 are too much for the defence.

b) 5...c6 has been tried by a few strong players, but it leads practically by force to a queenless position where White enjoys a clear advantage in terms of development and mobility: 6 dxe5 dxe5 7 fxe5 ♘g4 8 e6 fxe6 9 ♘g5 ♘de5 10 ♕xd8+ ♔xd8 11 h3 ♘h6 12 ♗f4 ♘g6 (12...♘hf7 is safer, although 13 0-0-0+ ♔e8 14 ♘xf7 ♘xf7 15 ♗c4 gave White an ongoing initiative in A.Alpern-H.Perelman, Buenos Aires 1992) 13 0-0-0+ ♔e8.

Now for a striking demonstration of the power of a development advantage: 14 ♘b5!! (this spectacular lunge leads to a winning position by force) 14...cxb5 15 ♗xb5+ ♔e7 16 ♗c7 ♔f6 17 h4! ♗c5 (or 17...♘xh4 18 ♖xh4 ♔xg5?

19 ♗d8+) 18 e5+ ♔e7 19 ♗d6+ ♗xd6 20 exd6+ ♔f6 21 d7 ♖d8 22 dxc8♕ ♖axc8 23 ♗d7 and White had recouped the sacrificed material with interest in N.Ong-W.Oaker, correspondence 2004. From here the most resilient continuation would have been 23...♗c7, but then 24 ♖df1+! ♔e7 25 ♗xe6 leaves White a pawn up and winning.

Returning to 5...exd4:

6 ♕xd4

Naturally White takes with the queen in order to take a step towards long castling.

6...c6

Preparing ...d5 is the most dynamic and critical way for Black to handle the position.

The most significant alternative is 6...♘c5, but after 7 ♗e3 Black has trouble developing any counterplay, as the following examples demonstrate:

a) 7...g6 is rather slow and allows White to launch an immediate attack: 8 e5 ♘e6 9 ♕c4 ♘g4 10 ♗d2 c6 11 h3 ♘h6 12 exd6 (12 g4 d5 13 ♕e2 is also good) 12...♘f5 13 ♘e4 ♘xd6 14 ♘xd6+

♗xd6 15 0-0-0 ♕f6 16 g3 0-0 17 h4 h5 18 ♗c3 ♕e7 19 f5 gxf5 20 ♗h3 when White was clearly better and went on to win in *Shredder-Komodo*, Trier 2010.

b) 7...♗e7 8 0-0-0 0-0 9 e5 ♘fd7 (or 9...♘g4 10 ♗g1 ♗e6 11 h3 ♘h6 12 g4 f5 13 ♗c4 ♔h8, as in E.German-M.De Freitas, Fortaleza 1951, and now after 14 exd6 cxd6 15 g5 ♘f7 16 ♗f2 intending ♖he1 White has an obvious advantage) 10 ♘d5 dxe5 11 ♘xe5

11...♗d6 (11...♘xe5 12 ♘xe7+ ♕xe7 13 ♕xc5 ♘c6 14 ♕xe7 ♘xe7 15 ♗c5 is winning for White, as shown by Golubev) 12 ♘c4 ♘e6 13 ♕c3 ♗c5? (a mistake, but Black was already clearly worse) 14 f5 ♗xe3+ 15 ♕xe3 ♘ec5 16 ♘e7+ ♔h8 17 ♘e5 ♕e8 18 ♘5g6+! fxg6 19 ♘xg6+ hxg6 20 ♕h3+ ♔g8 21 ♗c4+ ♖f7 22 fxg6 ♘e5 23 gxf7+ ♘xf7 24 ♗xf7+ 1-0 M.Feygin-M.Muse, German League 2009.

7 ♗e3 d5

Several other moves have been tried, but the text is clearly the most challenging.

Here is one example in which Black conducted the opening more timidly: 7...♗e7 8 ♕d2!? (retreating the queen from the centre is a sensible prophylactic measure) 8...0-0 9 ♗d3 ♖e8 10 0-0-0 ♕a5 11 ♔b1 ♗f8 12 ♖he1 and White had the better position, with healthy central control and all his pieces in play, K.Mokry-M.Mikas, Pardubice 1994.

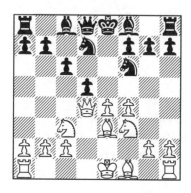

8 e5

With this move White gains space in the centre and aims for a positional advantage, although sometimes he can play for an attack as well.

It is worth mentioning that the game continuation is not the only good one and 8 exd5!? deserves attention as well. One game continued 8...♗c5 9 ♕d3 ♕e7 10 ♘d4 ♘b6 11 dxc6 0-0 12 0-0-0 bxc6 13 ♗g1 and Black had insufficient compensation, J.Polgar-M.Rivas Pastor, Dos Hermanas 1993.

8...♘g4 9 ♗g1 ♗c5 10 ♕d2 ♗xg1 11 ♖xg1 ♕b6

The last few moves have been natural and logical for both sides, but now White must make an important decision.

12 ♘a4!?

I like this straightforward move, which steers the position towards a favourable endgame. Once again the decision is partly a matter of taste, so I will mention a couple of alternatives which may appeal to aggressively-minded players:

a) 12 h3 ♘h2 13 ♘d4 ♘xf1 14 ♖xf1 ♕xb2 15 ♖b1 ♕a3 16 ♖f3 with promising compensation for White, J.Palkovi-A.Miltner, German League 1992.

b) 12 0-0-0 ♘xh2 13 ♘d4 ♘xf1 14 ♖dxf1 0-0 15 g4 ♖e8 16 ♘f5 ♘f8 17 ♘d6 ♖e6 18 g5 and once again White's attack was quite venomous in M.Palas-S.Schmidt, Münich 1992.

12...♕e3+

12...♕c7 hardly solves Black's problems after 13 h3 ♘h6 14 g4 when White's pawns are strong and the h6-knight is misplaced.

13 ♕xe3 ♘xe3 14 ♗d3

The queens are off, but Black is still some way from equality. White has better pieces and the more potent pawn majority.

14...b5

14...♘b6 was preferred in R.Alias Franco-F.Izeta Txabarri, Euskadi 1996. White responded by exchanging on b6 and although his position remained somewhat favourable, I see absolutely no reason to help Black by opening the a-file. Instead 15 ♘c5! would have preserved a pleasant advantage without conceding anything.

15 ♘c3 ♘b6

Another game continued 15...♘c5 16 ♔d2 (16 ♔e2 is also good) 16...♘c4+ 17 ♗xc4 dxc4 18 ♔e3 with an excellent endgame for White, A.Dobrowolski-J.Orzechowski, Wroclaw 2007. The position resembles something from the Berlin Defence, but White's coordination is excellent and Black's queenside has more holes than a doughnut shop.

16 a3 0-0

With the queens off Black would ideally prefer to keep his king in the centre, but it is hard to suggest a safe place for it there.

17 b3

Not a forced move, but certainly a

useful one.

17...♖d8?!

It is hard to believe that this can be the way to solve Black's problems.

17...f6!? has been proposed, but after 18 ♔d2 ♘f5 (no better is 18...♘g4 19 h3 ♘f2 20 ♘d4 fxe5 21 fxe5) 19 g4 ♘e7 20 exf6 ♖xf6 21 f5 ♗d7 22 a4!? (22 ♖ae1 is also good) 22...b4 23 ♘e2 White stands clearly better; the plan is ♘f4 and ♖ae1 when his pieces will start to look quite menacing.

18 ♘d4 ♗b7 19 ♔f2

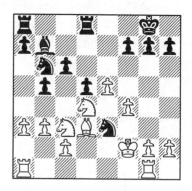

19...♘ec4!?

Of course the knight is indirectly defended here, but apart from that it accomplishes nothing and White can easily just ignore it.

Chekhov mentions the alternative 19...♘g4+ 20 ♔f3 ♘h6 (20...♘xh2+? 21 ♔g3) 21 g4 when White dominates.

20 ♘ce2 g6!?

Black renews the indirect defence, as bxc4 will now be met by ...bxc4 when the bishop is trapped. Kveinys seems eager to provoke some kind of disruption in the balance of the position, but

Dreev refuses to take the bait – at least not in the way his adversary had hoped.

21 a4!

Excellent! Now Black faces a crisis on the queenside.

21...♘b2

This fails to offer much resistance, but it was hard to offer much advice by this stage:

a) Chekhov points out the line 21...a6 22 a5 ♘d7 23 c3 ♘b2 24 ♗c2 ♘c5 25 ♔e3 when Black loses as the knight is trapped.

b) The only way to prolong the game was 21...bxa4! 22 bxc4 c5! 23 cxd5 ♗xd5 when, amazingly, Black avoids the loss of a piece. However, after the correct continuation of 24 ♘b5! c4 25 ♘c7 cxd3 26 ♘xa8 ♗xa8 27 cxd3 ♖xd3 28 ♖gd1 White is the exchange up and should win the endgame without much fuss.

22 a5!

22 axb5 wins a pawn but the text does so in an even more favourable way which effectively shuts down

Black's entire position.

22...♘xd3+ 23 cxd3 ♘d7 24 a6! ♗c8 25 ♘xc6 ♖e8 26 ♘c3 1-0

Faced with a miserable position plus the loss of another pawn, Black had had enough.

Game 37
M. Narciso Dublan-
P.Garcia Castro
Mondariz 2002

---

1 d4 d6 2 e4 e5

This move is rare, but it could be seen as another way of playing for a Philidor while inviting a slightly different type of queenless middlegame from that seen in Part 1 of the chapter.

3 dxe5 dxe5

3...♘c6? is just unsound and after 4 exd6 ♗xd6 5 ♘c3 ♘f6 6 ♘f3 intending ♗d3 and 0-0, Black has no compensation.

4 ♕xd8+ ♔xd8 5 ♗c4

I would evaluate this queenless middlegame as more favourable for

White than the version we saw in Games 31-33, as the knight should be able to find a more purposeful square than c3.

5...f6

The position after 5...♗e6 6 ♗xe6 fxe6 illustrates the previous point quite well. In the analogous position with the respective knights already on c3 and f6, the white knight does nothing useful and can often become target for Black's counterplay with ...b5-b4. However, in the present position White can obtain a nice advantage with 7 ♗e3 ♘f6 8 f3 intending ♘h3-f2-d3 (or ♘e2-c1-d3) and ♘d2-c4 when the knights will help to generate strong pressure against the e5-pawn.

6 f4!

If Black is given time to catch up in development and exchange a few pieces, it is unlikely that he will have too many problems. Instead Narciso Dublan provokes an immediate confrontation in the hope of exploiting the opponent's slightly exposed king and backward development.

6...♗d6

With this provocative move Black tempts his opponent into luring his bishop into the centre.

6...♘d7 is a safer alternative when play may continue 7 ♘f3 ♗d6 8 f5 (8 g3!? is a decent alternative, but gaining space on the kingside looks quite appealing) 8...c6 9 ♗e3 ♔c7 10 a4 ♘e7. This was H.Pfeil-L.Vogt, Neukieritzsch 1968, and here the most logical continuation looks to be 11 g4 with some initiative for White.

7 fxe5!

A good decision. White does not mind taking on an isolated pawn, as his active pieces provide more than enough compensation for it. This only works here because Black is forced to recapture with his bishop as opposed to a knight, which would have made a much better blockader on e5.

7...♗xe5 8 ♘f3 ♘d7

Black has tried two other moves, but his position remains unpleasant in all variations:

a) 8...♘c6 9 ♘c3 ♗g4 10 ♗e3 ♘ge7 11 0-0-0+ ♔e8 12 h3 ♗h5 13 g4 ♗g6 14 ♘b5! (White hurries to create direct threats before Black can catch up on development) 14...a6 15 ♘xe5 axb5 16 ♘xg6 hxg6 17 ♗xb5 ♖xa2 18 ♔b1 ♖a5 19 c4 ♔f7 20 ♖d7 and Black was unable to solve his problems in D.Bronstein-A.Beni, Munich Olympiad 1958.

b) 8...♗d6 9 ♘c3 c6 10 e5! (10 ♗e3 would have given White a pleasant edge, but this energetic pawn sacrifice creates major problems for the defence) 10...♗xe5 (or 10...fxe5 11 ♘g5 ♘h6 12 ♘ce4) 11 ♘xe5 fxe5. This position was reached in N.Fercec-D.Vretenar, Rabac 2003, and here the most accurate continuation would have been 12 0-0! (better than the game's 12 ♗g5+ ♘f6 13 0-0, for reasons that are about to become clear) 12...♘f6 13 ♗h6! when Black has serious problems.

9 ♘c3

A few other moves have been tried, but I like this flexible knight development. It is useful for White to retain the option of castling on either side.

9...c6 10 ♘e2!

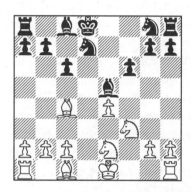

Preparing to deploy the knight on d4 or f4, or perhaps the bishop on f4.

10...♘e7 11 ♘f4 ♘c5

11...♗xf4 12 ♗xf4 ♘g6 13 ♗g3 ♖e8 was recommended as Black's best try by Andrew Martin, who mentions the continuation 14 ♘d2 when Black's position is indeed rather solid. However, White can do better by sacrificing a pawn with 14 0-0-0! ♖xe4 15 ♗g8 and here 15...h6 16 ♗h7 ♖g4 17 ♖he1, 15...♘gf8 16 ♗d6, and 15...♘f4 16 ♗xf4 ♖xf4 17 ♖he1 all see Black facing severe problems.

12 ♘xe5 fxe5 13 ♘h5

The opening has been a success for White, who has the two bishops and an ongoing initiative, and without suffering from an inferior pawn structure.

13...♗e6 14 ♗e3!

This excellent move increases

White's advantage. He will no longer have the bishop pair, but he will have the superior bishop.

14...♗xc4 15 ♗xc5 ♖g8 16 0-0-0+ ♔e8 17 ♖d2

17 ♘g3! would have been even stronger, the point being that the move ...♘g6 can now be met by ♘f5. The game continuation is still tough for Black though.

17...♘g6

For the time being 17...♖d8 would lose a pawn, so Black has to attempt to cover all the invasion squares along the d-file while gradually unravelling his pieces – not an easy task.

18 ♖hd1 ♗e6

19 h3

Preventing ...♗g4.

19 ♘g3!? was once again a tempting alternative, intending ♘f5.

19...♘h8?

Under serious pressure, Black allows an instant knockout.

It was necessary to chase the bishop away with 19...b6 20 ♗e3 c5, in order to meet 21 ♖d6 with 21...♔f7 22 ♗g5

♖ge8 when Black succeeds in holding his position together. However, White can do better with 21 ♗g5! when the threat of ♖d6 is quite nasty.

20 ♖d6 ♗f7 21 ♖d7 1-0

The invasion on the seventh rank is absolutely crushing, so Black decided to call it a day.

Conclusion

Of the openings examined here, the Modern Philidor is arguably the most theoretically significant and robust. By taking on e5 and exchanging queens White makes no attempt to refute his opponent's play, but instead settles for a lead in development and a generally more comfortable game. Get to know this variation well and you should win more than you lose with it.

The Czech Pirc is a decent system which has been tested in thousands of games. Still, White's three-pawn set-up provides him with a good deal of space in the centre, which can lead to promising attacking chances later in the game – especially if Black indulges in the kind of pawn-hunting we saw in Game 35.

The 3...♘bd7 Philidor has the benefit of preventing an early queen exchange for those that wish to avoid it, but committing the knight at such an early stage carries drawbacks as well, as was highlighted in Game 36 after the active 4 f4. Finally, 2...e5 isn't really a serious opening and after studying the example of Game 37 you should have no problems meeting it over the board.

Chapter Five
Alekhine's Defence

1 e4 ♘f6 2 e5 ♘d5

Rare alternatives will be considered in the final game of the chapter.

3 d4 d6

Black's entire opening is based around the concept of undermining this central pawn and since Black can hardly do without this move indefinitely, I will not waste time checking any offbeat alternatives.

4 ♘f3

From here the chapter will be divided into three main sections.

Part 1 – 4...dxe5 5 ♘xe5

The immediate exchange on e5 has more or less taken over as Black's main line in recent times. The most important continuation nowadays is:

5...c6

The provocative 5...♘d7 is the subject of Game 43, while 5...g6 is considered in Game 42.

6 ♗e2

Now the most common continuation is:

6...♗f5

Black can also challenge the knight immediately with 6...♘d7, which can be found in Game 40. Alternatively 6...g6 is featured in Game 41.

7 0-0 ♘d7 8 ♘f3

Black has two main moves here: 8...h6 is the subject of Game 38, while 8...e6 can be found in Game 39.

Part 2 – 4...♗g4

This is the traditional main line of the Alekhine. It has lost some ground to 4...dxe5 in recent years, but it remains a viable option.

5 ♗e2

White should break the pin.

5...e6

This natural move is the main line, but Black has plenty of other options: 5...c6 is covered in Game 46, and 5...♘c6 can be found in Game 47, while 5...dxe5?! and Black's other minor lines form the subject of Game 48.

6 0-0 ♗e7 7 c4 ♘b6 8 ♘c3 0-0 9 ♗e3

From here the popular but inaccurate 9...d5?! is covered in Game 44. The sounder 9...♘8d7 is considered in Game 45, along with Black's alternatives between moves 6-9.

Part 3 – Other lines

The most significant of Black's 4th-move alternatives is:

4...g6

The provocative 4...♘c6!? is the subject of Game 51, while 4...♘b6 and other minor 4th moves can be found in Game 52.

5 ♗c4

Now 5...♘b6 is considered in Game 49 and 5...c6 in Game 50.

Finally, the quirky 2...♘g8 will be analysed in Game 53 along with the dubious 2...♘e4?!.

Part 1 – 4...dxe5 5 ♘xe5

We have a lot to get through, so without further ado let's begin with our first game, an explosive encounter in which White introduced a venomous exchange sacrifice in a critical line.

Game 38
D.Smerdon-M.Grunberg
Paks 2007

1 e4 ♘f6 2 e5 ♘d5 3 d4 d6 4 ♘f3 dxe5 5 ♘xe5 c6

It could be argued that this has taken over as the main line of the Alekhine in recent years. Black fortifies his position in the centre and prepares to challenge his opponent's strong knight with ...♘d7, without allowing any ♘xf7 ideas.

6 ♗e2

Several other moves have been tried, but this is the one I like best. It has a fine pedigree, having been used by several leading players including Anand.

6...♗f5

This is the most frequent choice in the position, although 6...♘d7 is almost as popular, and 6...g6 has also been tried by some strong players. These moves will be examined in Games 40 and 41 respectively.

7 0-0 ♘d7

There is no point in Black delaying this move. In the event of 7...e6 White can already consider 8 g4!? ♗g6 9 c4 (9 f4!?) 9...♘f6 (or 9...♘b4 10 a3 ♘4a6 11 ♘c3) 10 f4 with a strong initiative.

8 ♘f3!

This retreat may appear surprising, but we will see throughout the chapter that it is a standard idea. The reasoning is straightforward: Black has less space, so it follows that White should avoid exchanges where possible.

8...h6

8...e6 will be considered in the next game. The text is something of a waiting move, although it is also specifically directed against the impending c2-c4, which Black now intends to answer with ...♘b4. (We will see in the notes to Mamedov-Mirzoev that the same idea is less attractive in the position after 8...e6.) Unfortunately for the second player, White's play in the present game calls the whole plan into question.

9 c4!?

It took a while before anyone realized that this could be used to fight for an advantage. The critical continuation involves a promising exchange sacrifice, which was first played in the present game.

It should be mentioned that if

White is feeling less ambitious, he can aim for a slight plus with the more modest continuation 9 a3 e6 10 c4 ♘5f6 11 ♗f4!? (preventing the enemy bishop from occupying its preferred square; 11 ♘c3 ♗d6 gives Black a reasonable game) 11...♘h5!? (11...♗e7 12 ♘c3 0-0 13 d5!? gives White some initiative, as mentioned by Khalifman) 12 ♗e3 ♗d6 13 ♘c3 (White might also consider 13 ♖e1!?, intending to meet 13...♘f4 with 14 ♗f1, preserving the bishop pair) 13...♘f4 14 d5 ♘xe2+ 15 ♕xe2 cxd5 16 cxd5 e5 (16...0-0 17 ♘d4 is pleasant for White, as pointed out by Khalifman) 17 ♘d2 by when White's strong passed pawn and active prospects on the queenside counted for slightly more than Black's bishop pair in G.Kjartansson-D.Madsen, Hastings 2005/06.

9...♘b4

10 ♘c3!

White continues to develop his pieces towards the centre. 10 ♘e1 is not completely stupid, but it is nowhere near as much fun as the text.

10...♘c2

Black has no choice – without this move his previous play would make no sense at all.

11 ♖b1 ♘b4 12 ♗e3!

Hitherto the only practical encounter had resulted in a quick move repetition after 12 ♖a1 ♘c2 and ½-½ in H.Hoeksema-S.Loeffler, Hoogeveen 2004. Instead Smerdon simply allows the rook to be taken – a good decision, as White's initiative turns out to be quite potent.

12...♗xb1 13 ♕xb1

Black is the exchange up with no weaknesses, but White has a serious lead in development. It is too early to give a definitive theoretical verdict, but practice has shown that Black faces the more difficult problems.

13...e6?!

This has been Black's choice in the majority of games, but I find it hard to believe it can be the right move, as White gets an immediate chance to open the centre. Others:

a) One recent game saw a new approach in 13...g5!? 14 a3 ♘a6 15 d5 (15 h4!?) 15...c5 (15...♗g7 16 ♘d4 looks promising for White). This was T.Baron-L.Piasetski, Jerusalem 2009, and here it looks logical for White to continue with either 16 ♘e4 ♗g7 17 ♘g3, intending ♘f5, or 16 h4 g4 17 ♘d2 h5 18 ♘de4, with a strong initiative in either case.

b) I find it surprising that no-one has tried 13...g6, which looks like the most logical way to go about completing development without giving White an easy way to open the position. The best answer looks to be 14 ♘h4!, creating an immediate threat before Black has time to castle.

In the absence of any practical encounters, I will mention a few sample lines:

b1) 14...♗g7? 15 ♘xg6 fxg6? 16 ♕xg6+ ♔f8 17 ♗h5 ♕e8 18 ♕f5+ wins.

b2) 14...g5 15 ♘g6 ♖g8 16 ♘xf8 ♘xf8 17 d5 looks very dangerous for Black.

b3) 14...♕a5 is well met by 15 ♘xg6! fxg6 16 ♕xg6+ ♔d8 and now 17 ♖d1!, calmly developing the last piece and

preparing a timely opening of the position with d5. Black is a rook for two pawns up, but his pieces are in utter disarray; I suspect that White is close to winning.

b4) 14...♕c7 15 a3 ♘a6 16 ♘xg6!? (once again this sacrifice looks promising, although the calmer 16 b4 also leaves White with a fine position, as Black will struggle to find a safe spot for his king) 16...fxg6 17 ♕xg6+ ♔d8. In this position both 18 ♘e4 and 18 c5 look excellent for White. There is no outright mating attack and we could spend pages analysing the various possibilities, but I think it is reasonable to stop here and say that Black faces an uphill struggle to survive.

14 a3 ♘a6 15 d5!

Here we see the problem with Black's 13th move. White immediately blasts open the centre before Black can complete development.

15...e5

This is the only move to have been tested. The most natural alternative looks to be 15...cxd5 16 cxd5 e5, trying to keep the centre closed. Here White has two ways to break the defence:

a) The calm option is 17 ♗b5 ♗d6 18 ♕f5 ♕e7 (or 18...g6 19 ♗xd7+ ♕xd7 20 ♕f6 ♖f8 21 ♘e4 ♗e7 22 ♗xh6! ♗xf6 23 ♘xf6+, leading to an ending with at least one extra pawn for White) 19 ♘e4 ♘c7 (there is nothing better) 20 ♕xd7+ ♕xd7 21 ♘xd6+ ♔e7 22 ♗xd7 ♔xd6 23 ♗a4 ♘xd5 24 ♖d1 and White should win this ending without too much trouble.

b) The flashier method is 17 ♘xe5!? ♘xe5 18 ♗b5+ ♘d7 (18...♔e7 19 ♗d4 f6 20 f4 is crushing) 19 ♖e1 ♗e7 and now White keeps a big advantage with 20 ♗g5! hxg5 21 d6 ♘ac5 (or 21...0-0 22 dxe7 ♕c8 23 exf8♕+ ♘xf8 24 ♖e8) 22 ♖xe7+ ♔f8 (22...♕xe7 23 dxe7 should also be winning for White) 23 ♕f5 ♘f6 24 ♕xc5, retaining a huge attack for a tiny material investment, with the principal threat being ♗c4.

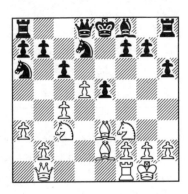

16 ♖d1

Also not bad is 16 dxc6 bxc6 17 ♖d1 ♕c7 as in W.Hendriks-A.Green, Hastings 2008/09, and here 18 b4! would

have given White a powerful initiative.

16...c5

Black is desperately trying to keep the position closed.

16...cxd5 is probably no worse than the text, although Black is still in trouble after 17 ♘xd5 ♗c5 18 b4 ♗xe3 19 ♘xe3.

17 d6!

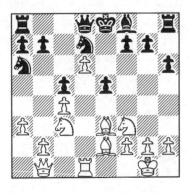

17...g6

After 17...♕b6 the strongest continuation looks to be 18 ♘e4 0-0-0 (18...f5 is well met by 19 ♘c3! g6 20 ♘h4 ♖g8 21 ♘xg6!) 19 b4 with a continuing attack.

18 b4!

Black is not given a moment's respite. Now he must worry about the pawn advancing to b5. Three games have reached this position, with White scoring 100%.

18...f5

A more recent game continued 18...♖c8 19 ♕e4 ♗g7 20 ♕xb7 ♘ab8 21 ♘d5 ♖c6 22 ♘c7+ ♔f8 and here in A.Reshetnikov-Y.Prokopchuk, Moscow 2010, the simplest winning continuation looks to be 23 ♕xa7 intending b5 when Black's position is hopeless.

19 bxc5 ♕c8

No better is 19...e4 20 ♕xb7 ♗g7 (20...♘axc5 21 ♗xc5 ♘xc5 22 ♕c6+ ♘d7 23 ♘e5 wins) 21 c6 0-0 22 cxd7 f4 23 ♘xe4 fxe3 24 ♕xa6 exf2+ 25 ♘xf2 1-0 G.Papp-S.Loeffler, Austrian League 2008.

20 ♘h4!

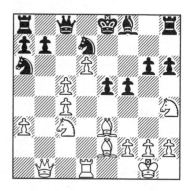

Having made inroads on the queenside, White now switches his attention to the kingside. A few simple sacrifices are all it takes to smash through Black's flimsy barriers.

20...♔f7

20...♖g8 runs into 21 ♘xg6 ♖xg6 22 ♗h5.

21 ♘xg6

White could have won more quickly with 21 ♗h5!, but the move played should not affect the outcome.

21...♔xg6 22 ♗h5+ ♔f6?

The only chance to prolong the game was 22...♔g7, although it is clear that Black is on his last legs. My main line runs 23 ♕xf5 ♖g8 24 ♘d5 ♔h8 25

♘e7 ♗xe7 26 dxe7 ♕c6 27 g3 ♘axc5 28 ♗xc5 ♘xc5 29 ♕xe5+ ♔h7 30 ♖d6 ♖g5 31 ♕f6 ♕xd6 32 ♕xd6 ♖xh5 33 ♕d8 with an easily winning endgame.

23 ♘d5+ ♔e6 24 ♗g4 1-0

A nice way to kick off the chapter! Let's now see a more recent example where Black played less provocatively.

Game 39
N.Mamedov-A.Mirzoev
Baku 2010

1 e4 ♘f6 2 e5 ♘d5 3 d4 d6 4 ♘f3 dxe5 5 ♘xe5 c6 6 ♗e2 ♗f5 7 0-0 ♘d7 8 ♘f3 e6

This is more solid than 8...h6. Black focuses on normal development, without trying to be too clever.

9 c4

9...♘5f6

9...♘b4?! is risky and in fact White has more than one good answer:

a) 10 ♘c3!? ♘c2 was seen in R.Zelcic-E.Rozentalis, Dresden Olympiad 2008, and here White should have played 11 ♖b1 ♘b4 12 ♗g5! f6 (12...♗e7 13 ♗xe7 ♕xe7 14 ♖c1 gives White a pleasant edge) 13 ♗e3 ♗xb1 14 ♕xb1 with promising compensation for the exchange, as pointed out by Taylor. The situation is not entirely dissimilar to that from the previous game.

b) 10 a3 ♘c2 11 ♖a2 and Black has tried two moves here:

b1) 11...c5? was played in L.Vogt-S.Loeffler, Austrian League 2002, and here White could have won more or less by force with 12 dxc5! ♘xc5 (12...♗xc5 is met by 13 ♘c3 intending b4, winning material; 12...♘f6 13 b4 ♕xd1 14 ♗xd1 ♘xb4 15 axb4 ♗xb1 16 ♗a4+ intending ♖d2 is winning for White, as pointed out by Khalifman) 13 b4 ♕xd1 14 ♗xd1 ♘xb4 15 axb4 ♗xb1 16 ♖d2 ♘d7 17 ♗a4 0-0-0 18 ♖fd1 and wins – analysis by Khalifman.

b2) 11...♘xd4 12 ♕xd4 ♗xb1 (12...c5 13 ♕c3 ♗xb1 14 ♗g5 f6 15 ♖xb1 fxg5 16 ♕e3 ♗e7 was M.Carlsen-D.Madsen, Trondheim 2004, and now after the straightforward 17 ♕xe6 Black is in a mess and will almost certainly have to shed a pawn) 13 ♗g5 f6 14 ♖xb1 fxg5 15 ♖d1 ♗e7 was seen in T.Gharamian-A.Barthel, Böblingen 2007, and here the simplest continuation looks to be 16 ♕xg7 ♗f6 17 ♕h6 ♕e7 18 ♘d2 0-0-0 19 ♘e4 when White benefits from a better structure and safer king, and will soon solve the problem of the wayward rook with b4 and ♖d2.

10 ♘c3 ♗d6 11 ♘h4!

Compared with the previous game, the absence of the move ...h6 has certain drawbacks, most notably the lack of a retreat square for the light-squared bishop.

11...♗g6 12 g3

White delays capturing, just in case Black gets any ideas about utilizing the open h-file for an attack. Besides, the text move will be useful in its own right as it helps to restrict what will soon be Black's sole remaining bishop.

12...0-0

In another game Black tried to do without castling, with painful results: 12...♘e4 13 ♘xg6 ♘xc3 14 bxc3 hxg6 15 c5!? (it was possible to play more patiently with 15 ♖e1, but there is no reason to refrain from the direct approach) 15...♗c7 16 ♖b1 ♖b8 (16...b6 17 ♗f3 is awkward) 17 ♗f3 ♕f6?! (presumably Black found the prospect of 17...0-0 18 ♕a4 unappealing, but the text move leads to even greater difficulties) 18 h4 ♕f5? 19 ♗g5 and in view of the threats to trap the queen, Black was forced to jettison material in N.Guliyev-S.Loeffler, Vienna 2009.

13 ♗f3 a6?!

It is hard to guess the motivation for this time-wasting move.

13...e5 was more to the point, although White still keeps an edge after 14 ♘xg6 hxg6 15 d5.

14 ♘xg6 hxg6 15 ♗g2 e5

Black needs to try and free his position at some point. The other typical break for such a position would be ...c5, but here Black wants to restrict the bishop on g2.

16 d5

16...c5

16...cxd5 would open the diagonal for the unopposed bishop and after 17 ♘xd5 ♖c8 18 b3 White keeps an edge.

17 ♖e1 ♕c7 18 ♕d3 ♖fe8 19 ♗d2 ♖ad8 20 ♖ad1 ♘f8

Another natural-looking idea was 20...♘h7 intending ...f5. Play might continue 21 ♔h1 (just about any reasonable alternative is possible, but it is the next move that really matters) 21...f5 and here it is essential for White to play 22 f3!, preventing Black from freeing his position with ...e4 and

...♘e5. Black has no real counterplay and White can take his time to prepare g4, with the ultimate aim of exploiting some of those juicy light squares.

21 ♖e2 ♘8h7 22 ♖de1 ♕d7 23 a4 g5!?

Fed up with waiting passively, Black embarks on an active plan – an understandable though somewhat risky policy.

24 h3 g4 25 hxg4 ♕xg4 26 ♘e4

Usually in positions with this material balance, White would prefer to keep his remaining knight on the board, but otherwise here ...♘g5 would have been mildly annoying.

26...♘xe4 27 ♕xe4

27...♕xe4

This leads to a difficult ending, although it is hardly surprising that Black was not attracted by the position resulting from 27...♕d7 28 a5, when the combination of pressure against the e5-pawn and potential kingside threats involving the open h-file would spell serious problems for the defender.

28 ♗xe4 g6 29 ♗c2 ♖e7 30 ♗c3 ♘f6?

After this Black's position crumbles

to dust. The only chance to resist was 30...♘f8 31 f4 (31 ♗xe5? ♖de8) 31...f6, not that this would have been much fun for Black either.

31 f4 ♖de8 32 fxe5 ♘d7 33 e6 fxe6 34 ♖h2 1-0

34 ♗xg6 would have been even stronger, but the move played was good enough to force resignation. The finish might have been 34...e5 35 ♗xg6 ♖f8 36 ♗e4 ♘f6 37 ♖h6 when White keeps an extra pawn and full control over the position.

In the next two games we will turn our attention to set-ups where Black delays the development of the c8-bishop.

> ### Game 40
> **Z.Efimenko-L.D. Nisipeanu**
> European Championship,
> Rijeka 2010

1 e4 ♘f6 2 e5 ♘d5 3 d4 d6 4 ♘f3 dxe5 5 ♘xe5 c6 6 ♗e2 ♘d7

This time Black challenges the knight immediately.

7 ♘f3!

Once again we see this thematic retreat, avoiding exchanges for the time being.

7...g6

The kingside fianchetto is quite logical, although a few other ideas have also been seen:

a) The rare 7...♕c7 8 0-0 e6 was seen in V.Anand-S.Mamedyarov, Nice (blindfold) 2008, and now 9 ♖e1 looks sensible, intending c4 and meeting a possible ...♘f4 with ♗f1.

b) 7...♘7f6 is possible and after 8 0-0 Black must decide where to develop his bishop:

b1) 8...♗f5 9 ♘h4 (9 a3 intending c4 also looks good) when Black can play:

b11) 9...♗d7 10 c4 ♘b6 11 ♘c3 g6 was seen in V.Meribanov-D.Danilenko, Moscow 2009, and now the simplest route to an edge looks to be 12 h3 ♗g7 13 ♘f3 when Black's queenside pieces are less than ideally placed.

b12) 9...♗g6 10 c4 ♘b6 11 ♘c3 e6

12 g3 ♗e7 13 ♗e3 ♕c7 14 ♘xg6 hxg6 15 ♕b3 ♖d8 16 ♖fd1 0-0 17 ♖ac1 sees White obtain a pleasant edge thanks to his space advantage and two bishops.

We will follow the game for a while longer, as Anand's play is highly instructive: 17...e5 (Black decides his best chance is to aim for counterplay on the dark squares) 18 d5 (threatening d6, winning a piece) 18...♘bd7 19 ♗f3 ♗c5 20 ♗xc5 ♘xc5 21 ♕a3 b6 22 b4 e4 23 ♗e2 ♘b7 (23...♘cd7 is well met by 24 d6 followed by c5, with a mighty passed pawn) 24 ♕xa7 (24 dxc6 ♕xc6 25 ♘d5 was also strong, but the text leads practically by force to a winning ending) 24...♖a8 25 d6 ♖xa7 26 dxc7 ♖c8 D 27 c5! bxc5 28 b5 cxb5 29 ♘xb5 ♖xa2 30 ♗f1 and White had no problem converting his advantage in V.Anand-M.Carlsen, Nice (blindfold) 2008.

b2) 8...♗g4 9 ♘e5!? (this should leads to a slight edge; nevertheless, there was also nothing wrong with 9 h3 ♗xf3 10 ♗xf3 e6 11 c4 ♘b6 12 b3 ♗e7 13 ♗b2 0-0 14 ♘d2 when the

bishop pair gave White a slight plus in S.Karjakin-M.Carlsen, Nice (rapid) 2008) 9...♗xe2 10 ♕xe2 e6 11 c4 ♘e7 12 ♖d1 ♘g6 13 ♘c3 ♕c7 14 g3 and now:

b21) 14...♗e7 15 h4 0-0 16 ♗g5 and White had a pleasant initiative in K.Sasikiran-E.Rozentalis, Warsaw 2008.

b22) The untested 14...♗d6!? seems like a more principled way to develop, although in his annotations Sasikiran shows that White keeps an edge here as well: 15 ♘xg6 hxg6 16 d5 0-0! (or 16...0-0-0 17 ♗e3! with some initiative for White) 17 ♗e3!? (17 dxe6 ♖ae8 18 exf7+ ♕xf7 offers Black some compensation) 17...exd5 18 cxd5 ♖fe8 (after 18...♖ae8 19 dxc6 bxc6 20 ♕f3 ♖e6 21 ♖ac1 the c-pawn is a permanent weakness) 19 dxc6 ♕xc6 20 ♕b5 ♕xb5 21 ♘xb5 ♗e5 22 ♘d6 ♖e7 (22...♗xd6 23 ♖xd6 ♘g4 24 ♗d4 is a similar story) 23 ♘c4 ♘g4 24 ♘xe5 ♖xe5 25 ♗d4 ♖e2 26 h3 ♘f6 27 ♖ac1 and White's superior minor piece gives him the better chances in the ending. (This analysis is taken from Sasikiran's excellent annotations.)

Returning to 7...g6:

8 0-0 ♗g7 9 c4

9...♘5f6

9...♘c7 has been played more frequently, although it seems doubtful that Black can equalize here: 10 ♘c3 0-0 11 ♗f4 ♘e6 12 ♗e3 (White is happy to lose a tempo as the knight on e6 prevents Black from freeing his game with ...e5) 12...♘f6 13 h3 ♕c7 (in the event of 13...b6, as in C.Bauer-S.Mamedyarov, Merida 2005, I would suggest 14 ♕d2 followed by centralizing the rooks, with a typical slight plus) 14 ♕d2 ♖d8 15 ♖fd1 ♘h5 16 ♕e1 ♘ef4 17 ♗f1 h6. This position was reached in C.Lupulescu-M.Grunberg, Bucharest 2008, as well as the subsequent game A.Bokros-M.Grunberg, Austrian League 2009. At this point it looks quite promising for White to play 18 d5!. White increases his space advantage and sets up the threat of g4, intending to meet ...♘f6 with d6, winning material. A possible continuation is 18...e5 (after the sequence 18...g5 19 ♗d4! g4 20 ♗e5 ♗xe5 21 ♕xe5 ♕xe5 22 ♘xe5 gxh3 23

g3 Black has real problems) 19 dxc6! (White can keep an edge with a simple move like 19 ♖d2, but it is even better to open the position before Black catches up in development) 19...♖xd1 20 ♖xd1 ♕xc6 (if 20...bxc6 21 ♗c5)

21 ♘xe5! (this small combination nets a pawn) 21...♗xe5 (21...♘xh3+ 22 gxh3 ♗xe5 23 ♗xh6) 22 ♗xf4 ♗xf4 23 ♖d8+ ♔h7 (23...♔g7? 24 ♕e7 is even worse) 24 ♕e7 ♕f6 25 ♕e8 ♕g7 26 ♖xc8 ♖xc8 27 ♕xc8 when White has good winning chances in the ending.

10 ♘c3 0-0 11 ♗f4 ♘h5

The bishop was rather irritating on the h2-b8 diagonal and I suppose Nisipeanu wanted to drive it away before White could secure its position with h3.

12 ♗g5!

Provoking a barely perceptible weakening of the black kingside.

12...h6

With the benefit of hindsight Black may have done better to refrain from this move, although in any case it is obvious that he has failed to equalize from the opening.

13 ♗e3 ♕c7 14 ♕d2

Here we see the first benefit of White's 12th move: he wins a tempo for development.

14...♔h7 15 ♖ad1 ♖d8?

As incredible as it may sound, this is already a decisive error!

16 g4!!

White could have maintained a pleasant edge with the straightforward 16 ♖fe1, but the text move yields a huge advantage.

16...♘hf6 17 ♗f4!

Before cracking open the kingside, White first drives the enemy queen to an unfavourable square.

17...♕b6 18 g5 ♘h5

18...hxg5 19 ♘xg5+ ♔g8 is refuted by 20 c5! when it transpires that Black is in trouble on both sides of the board: 20...♕a5 21 b4! (21 ♘d5!? ♕xd2 22 ♘xe7+ ♔f8 23 ♖xd2 is also strong, but the text should win outright) 21...♕xb4 22 ♗c7! And White wins, as apart from the attack on the d8-rook, he also threatens to trap the enemy queen.

19 gxh6 ♗f6 20 ♘e4

Threatening to carve open the kingside with ♘fg5+ followed by ♗xh5.

20...♘xf4 21 ♕xf4

The loss of the bishop pair is of no consequence, as White's attack is too powerful.

21...♖f8 22 c5!

Making room for the bishop to join the action.

22...♕xb2

After 22...♕b4 White might have increased the pressure with 23 ♖fe1 or even 23 b3!?, intending ♗c4.

23 ♗c4 ♔h8 24 ♘fg5 ♗xg5

Exchanging this valuable defender looks suicidal, but how else could Black attempt to defend f7? Instead 24...e5 25 dxe5 ♕xe5 26 ♕xe5 ♘xe5 27 ♘xf6 ♘xc4 28 ♘xf7+ forces mate.

25 ♘xg5 f6 26 ♘f7+ ♔h7 27 ♖fe1

After this move all five of White's remaining pieces are actively participating in the attack, not to mention the pawn on h6. Compare Black's scattered forces, with the queen marooned on b2 and two of his queenside pieces having not even moved. It is hardly surprising that the game is soon over.

27...♖e8 28 ♘g5+ ♔h8

29 ♘e6

White could have crushed all resistance immediately and in fine style with 29 ♕d6!, but the text move is good enough to get the job done.

29...b5 30 ♗b3 a5 31 ♘c7 a4 32 ♗f7 e5 33 ♕g3 1-0

Game 41
P.Svidler-A.Baburin
Bunratty 2009

1 e4 ♘f6 2 e5 ♘d5 3 d4 d6 4 ♘f3 dxe5 5 ♘xe5 c6 6 ♗e2 g6

This bears a close resemblance to the Kengis variation (5...g6), which will be examined in the next game. Since the early ...c6 has rendered Black's development a little slower than it would usually be in that line, White can conduct the opening more aggressively than normal. First he drives the enemy knight away from the centre.

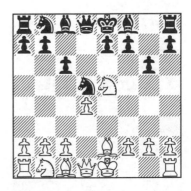

7 c4 ♘c7

Highlighting one of the points behind Black's fifth move.

8 ♘c3 ♗g7 9 ♗e3 0-0

Here White can try something a little more adventurous than usual:

10 f4!?

White should never play such a move lightly against Alekhine's Defence, as committal, space-gaining moves can often overextend White's position and play into the hands of the defender. The present case is an exception and a good example of what I would call 'controlled aggression'.

That being said, I should mention too that the quieter 10 0-0 ♘d7 11 ♘f3 should also suffice for a slight plus. The position is the same as was reached in the note to Black's 9th move in the previous game, except that the black knight is on c7 instead of e6. Black has tried several moves here, but in most cases White keeps a pleasant edge with natural moves. The most principled option looks to be 11...e5 and now it seems promising for

White to try the untested 12 ♕c2!?, maintaining the central tension. Play might continue 12...exd4 (after 12...♖e8 White can continue to strengthen his position with 13 ♖ad1) 13 ♘xd4 intending ♖ad1 when White keeps a slight pull.

10...♘d7 11 0-0

11...♘xe5

11...♘e6 should be met by 12 ♗g4 when Black has tried two moves:

a) 12...♘b6 was seen in V.Durarbeyli-D.Bulanov, Sibenik 2007, and here White could have kept control with the simple 13 b3.

b) 12...♘xe5 was played in Y.Vovk-E.Miroshnichenko, Cappelle la Grande 2009, and here the ambitious continuation would have been 13 fxe5 (the game continuation of 13 dxe5 f6 14 exf6 ♗xf6 was not too dangerous for Black). Perhaps White was concerned about 13...c5, but it seems to me that after 14 d5 (14 ♗xe6!? ♗xe6 15 d5 ♗f5 16 ♗f4 also looks pretty good) 14...♘d4 15 ♗f4! White keeps an edge. However, it should be noted that after 15 ♗xc8

♖xc8 16 ♗xd4 cxd4 17 ♕xd4 ♕c7 Black regains his pawn with a reasonable game.

12 fxe5

12...c5?!

Undermining the centre is the primary strategic aim which underlies Black's whole opening, but in this particular position White's pieces are much better equipped to deal with the change in the position. Black could have minimized his disadvantage with one of the following alternatives:

a) 12...f6 13 exf6 exf6 14 d5 ♖e8 15 ♕d2 cxd5 16 cxd5 ♗f8 was seen in Y.Vovk-H.Streit, Vlissingen 2009, and here 17 ♗c4 ♗d6 18 ♗d4 would have given White a strong initiative.

b) The safest continuation seems to be 12...♗e6 13 ♘e4 (13 ♕d2 also looks reasonable) 13...♗f5 (13...f6 can be met by 14 exf6 exf6 15 ♘c5), as played in T.Stepovaia Dianchenko-T.Chekhova Kostina, Elista 1994. At this point White should have continued 14 ♗f3, maintaining a slight plus.

13 dxc5!

13 d5 ♗xe5 14 ♗xc5 was good enough for a slight edge, but Svidler's choice is more dynamic and just a stronger move.

13...♗xe5 14 ♕e1

From here Black will have real trouble coordinating his position.

14...♗d4?!

This exchanging manoeuvre costs valuable time.

The best chance was 14...♘e6 15 ♖d1 ♕a5 when White can choose between two advantageous though not yet decisive continuations:

a) 16 ♗f3 ♗xc3 17 bxc3 reaches a position in which White's bishop pair and active pieces are more relevant than his dubious queenside structure.

b) After 16 ♘d5 ♕xe1 17 ♘xe7+ ♔g7 18 ♖fxe1 ♗xb2 19 ♗f3 ♗c3 20 ♖e2 ♖d8 21 ♖xd8 ♘xd8 22 c6 bxc6 23 ♘xc6 we have reached an ending in which Black will soon drop a pawn, although the win is still a long way off for White.

15 ♗f3 e5

15...♘e6 fails to solve Black's prob-

lems after 16 ♖d1 ♗xe3+ 17 ♕xe3 ♕a5 18 c6 bxc6 19 ♗xc6 ♖b8 20 ♘d5.

16 ♖d1

From this point on, it is hard to offer much advice to Black.

16...a5?!

This slow move does not help, but even after the superior 16...♘e6 White increases his initiative by simple means: 17 ♘b5 (17 ♗xd4 exd4 18 ♘d5 is also strong) 17...♗xe3+ 18 ♕xe3 ♕e7 (now White wins a pawn with a forcing sequence) 19 ♘d6 f6 20 c6 bxc6 21 ♗xc6 ♖b8 22 ♘xc8 ♖fxc8 23 ♖d7 ♕c5 24 ♕xc5 ♘xc5 25 ♗d5+ ♔h8 26 ♖xa7 f5 27 b3 and the endgame should be an easy win.

17 ♗xd4 exd4 18 ♕e5 ♘e6 19 ♘b5 ♕e7 20 ♘d6

20...♕c7

After 20...♕g5 21 ♕xg5 ♘xg5 22 ♖xd4 White is a pawn up with a dominating position.

21 ♗d5 ♖a6

21...♕xc5 is refuted by 22 ♘xf7!.

22 ♔h1

Black is virtually paralysed, so

Svidler takes a sensible precaution before preparing a final assault.

22...h5 23 ℤf6 1-0

Black resigned as he is helpless against the simple plan of doubling on the f-file.

That concludes our coverage of the fashionable 5...c6 variation. We will now move on to some of Black's alternatives on the fifth move, beginning with the solid kingside fianchetto.

Game 42
G.Kasparov-M.Adams
Linares 1997

1 e4 ♘f6 2 e5 ♘d5 3 d4 d6 4 ♘f3 dxe5 5 ♘xe5 g6

This variation bears the name of the Latvian Grandmaster Edvins Kengis, who used it with considerable success in the 1990s. His games and ideas have played an important role in shaping the modern-day understanding of the resulting positions.

6 ♗c4

This has been White's most popular choice, although there has been some debate as to his most promising continuation. The other move that I strongly considered recommending was 6 g3, when the soon-to-be fianchettoed bishop will help White to exert positional pressure. If the reader wishes to investigate this option in more detail, I will just mention that the most relevant high-level game, and the best starting point for any analysis, is the encounter V.Anand-M.Adams, Linares 1994. To be honest I consider 6 ♗c4 and 6 g3 to be equally promising and the decision to recommend the former was partially influenced by the fact that the aforementioned Anand-Adams game has been analysed in detail by numerous other commentators, and it was tough to find anything new to contribute.

6...c6

This has been Black's choice in the great majority of games, although a few other moves have been tried.

a) Black should certainly avoid 6...♗g7? 7 ♘xf7 ♔xf7 8 ♕f3+ ♔e8 (8...♔e6? 9 ♕e4+ ♔f6? 10 ♗xd5 e6 was K.Gentes-D.Herkert, Winnipeg 2005, and now 11 ♕f3+ ♔e7 12 ♗g5+ wins the queen) 9 ♗xd5 ℤf8 10 ♕b3 c6 11 ♗f3 ♕xd4 12 0-0 when White had an obvious advantage in R.Ramesh-M.Mishra, Jalandhar 2000.

b) 6...♗e6!? is playable, although the most likely outcome will be a transposition to note 'b' to Black's 9th move in the main game. With 7 0-0 (White can also consider playing more aggressively with 7 ♘c3 ♗g7 8 ♘e4, although without going into too many details, I doubt that this is objectively any better than the calmer course of action I am recommending) 7...♗g7 8 ♖e1 0-0 9 ♗b3 White continues just as in the main Kasparov-Adams game.

I seriously doubt that Black can benefit from omitting ...c6 indefinitely, for instance: 9...♘d7 (9...c6 is the aforementioned transposition) 10 ♘f3 ♘7f6 (10...c6 11 ♘g5 is awkward), as in W.Hendriks-A.Matthaei, Münster 1993, and here White could have obtained some advantage by means of 11 c4 (11 ♖xe6!? fxe6 12 ♕e1 is also interesting; White should always keep an eye open for exchange sacrifices whenever the black bishop appears on e6) 11...♘b6 12 ♖xe6!? (12 d5 should also suffice for an edge) 12...fxe6 13 ♕e1 with promising compensation.

7 0-0 ♗g7 8 ♖e1 0-0

We have reached a standard type of

position, in which White's d4-pawn gives him slightly more space and central control. In principle this should make his position a little easier to handle. On the other hand, if he plays without conviction then the defender will have excellent chances to neutralize his initiative by means of a well-timed ...c5 break, after which the g7-bishop may come into its own. Experts such as Kengis have practically made a career out of executing precisely that type of strategy. In the present game and accompanying notes I will endeavour to show you how White can maintain control of the position and nurture his slight opening edge into a more tangible advantage.

9 ♗b3

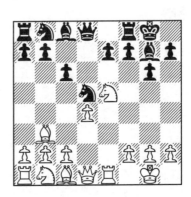

White retreats the bishop from its slightly exposed position and waits to see how Black intends to arrange his pieces.

9...♘d7

Here are a few other examples to show how the game might unfold:

a) 9...a5 10 c4!? (in certain positions

White may prefer to stabilize his centre with c3, but since Black's last move failed to develop a piece, the more active approach does not look out of place) 10...♘b6 11 ♘c3 ♗e6!? (Black is playing rather provocatively, but by no means badly) 12 d5 ♗f5 13 ♗f4 cxd5 14 cxd5 ♘a6 was seen in O.Wegener-J.Palkovi, Budapest 2000. So far White's play has been absolutely logical and at this point it seems to me that the most principled approach would have been 15 g4!? ♗c8 (15...♗d7 16 ♗g5! is awkward for Black) 16 d6!? (White can also keep an edge through quieter means with 16 a3 ♘c5 17 ♗a2 when his active pieces are a more significant factor than his slightly loose kingside) 16...♕xd6 (16...exd6? 17 ♘xf7! ♖xf7 18 ♗xd6 is horrible for Black) 17 ♕f3! (after 17 ♕xd6 exd6 18 ♘xf7 ♖xf7 Black survives).

In this complex position White maintains a dangerous initiative which easily makes up for the sacrificed pawn. The computer's main line continues 17...e6 18 ♘c4 (but obviously not 18 ♘xg6?? fxg6! when the bishop is pinned along the newly opened f-file) 18...♕d8 19 ♖ad1 ♘d5 and at this point both 20 ♗d6 and 20 ♘e3 look excellent for White.

b) According to Taylor 9...♗e6 is Black's most precise move. He may well be right, although I doubt that the second player can achieve full equality in any case. Black's main idea is to exchange the light-squared bishops, in order to rob the white position of some of its dynamism. This idea makes a good deal of sense, especially when we consider that Black's main strategic idea is to prepare ...c5. After 10 ♘d2 I considered two branches of analysis:

b1) The immediate 10...♘c7 should be met by either 11 ♘df3 or 11 ♘e4. Please pay attention to the following point: if Black wishes to exchange the light-squared bishops, then we should endeavour to make sure that the exchange takes place on the b3-square rather than e6. The subsequent axb3 will benefit White by opening the a-file for his rook, as well as subtly increasing his central control by bringing the a-pawn closer to that crucial area of the board.

b2) 10...♘d7

11 ♘ef3! (as is customary for the Alekhine, White does not mind retreating his knight from the centre in order to avoid unnecessary exchanges, which would relieve the congestion in Black's position) 11...♘c7 (11...a5 should be met by 12 c3 when White will soon be ready to start thinking about ♖xe6 ideas; it is a little too early, though, for 12 ♖xe6?! fxe6 13 ♘g5 ♗xd4 when White's compensation is questionable) 12 ♘e4 ♗xb3 (perhaps Black should have avoided this move, although the tension between the bishops was preventing the c7-knight from moving, while the d7-knight was having to remain in place to prevent ♘e4-c5; the best response to 12...a5 is once again 13 c3! ensuring that any bishop exchange will take place on b3) 13 axb3 ♘e6 14 c3 ♖e8 15 h4! ♘f6 16 ♘eg5 ♘xg5 17 hxg5 saw White has permit the exchange of a few pieces, but only

on his own terms, with both exchanges helping him to improve his pawn structure. Black had failed to obtain any counterplay and was gradually outplayed in M.Adams-Tu Hoang Thong, Yerevan Olympiad 1996.

Returning to 9...♘d7:

10 ♘f3

10...♘7f6

Another game continued 10...♖e8 11 ♗g5 ♘7f6 12 ♘bd2 h6 13 ♗h4 ♗g4 14 h3 ♗xf3 15 ♘xf3 when White's bishop pair gave him a pleasant edge in L.Yudasin-Rasmussen, Calgary 1996.

11 c4 ♘c7

11...♘b6 is also possible. Just as in the main game White should respond with 12 h3 when Black must decide how to develop the c8-bishop:

a) 12...♗e6 rather invites the thematic sacrifice 13 ♖xe6!? (13 ♘bd2 and 13 ♕e2 are both decent alternatives) 13...fxe6. Now Taylor mentions the plausible continuation 14 ♘c3 ♕d7 15 ♕e2 ♘h5 16 ♕e4 ♘f6 17 ♕h4 ♘h5 18 ♗e3 when White maintains excellent compensation.

b) 12...♗f5 13 ♘c3 ♕c7 14 ♗g5 ♗e6 15 ♕e2 (Taylor notes that 15 ♖xe6!? is possible here as well, but the game continuation demonstrates that White can also improve his position without the exchange sacrifice) 15...♖fe8 16 ♗e3 ♘c8 17 ♘g5 ♖f8? (I am at a loss to explain this dreadful move; 17...♗d7 was necessary when White keeps a clear advantage after 18 ♖ad1, but the win would be a long way off) 18 ♘xe6 fxe6 19 ♗g5 and White soon triumphed in J.Gallagher-G.Lukasiewicz, Bern 1990.

12 h3!

It is useful to prevent ...♗g4. Compared with the note to Black's 10th move above, the big difference here is that the d4-pawn can no longer be bolstered by c2-c3, so White should be careful about allowing the f3-knight to be exchanged. Now Black will have a hard time finding a meaningful role for his light-squared bishop.

12...c5

12...b5!? was mentioned as an interesting alternative by Psakhis and subsequently received a practical test in 2003: 13 ♘e5 (the computer suggests 13 ♕e2 ♗e6 14 ♘a3 bxc4 15 ♘xc4 ♗d5 16 ♘ce5 with a plus for White; nevertheless, there is something appealing about forcing Black's light-squared bishop on to the unfavourable b7-square) 13...♗b7 14 ♘c3 ♘d7 15 ♘g4!? (15 ♗g5) 15...e6. This was J.Aguera Naredo-J.Rodriguez Fernandez, Oviedo 2003, and at this point my own preference would be 16 c5!, securing an outpost on d6 and burying the b7-bishop for the foreseeable future. Alternatively 16 ♗h6!? would force the exchange of Black's best piece while maintaining more fluidity in the centre.

13 ♘c3

13 dxc5 and 13 d5 were decent alternatives, but Kasparov's choice works well.

13...cxd4 14 ♘xd4

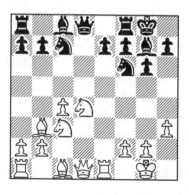

The position resembles that from the next game, Lutz-Tischbierek. The pieces are arranged slightly differently on both sides, but the core characteristics are the same: the pawn structures are practically identical and, just as we will see in Game 43, White's active pieces enable him to make more effective use of his queenside majority.

14...♘e6

14...♕d6 fails to equalize after 15 ♗e3 ♖d8 16 ♘db5 ♘xb5 17 ♘xb5, as noted by Psakhis.

15 ♗e3 ♘xd4 16 ♕xd4 ♗e6

In the event of 16...♕xd4 17 ♗xd4 Black faces a difficult defensive task.

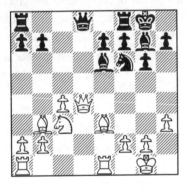

17 ♕h4!?

17 ♖ad1 looks more natural, but it turns out that Kasparov has cooked up a typically imaginative way to utilize the rook's presence on the a-file.

17...♕a5 18 c5! ♗xb3

Perhaps this was too cooperative. Psakhis suggests 18...♗d7!? 19 ♗d4 ♖fe8 as an improvement, although White keeps an edge here too after 20 ♖ad1 ♖ad8 21 ♗c4.

19 axb3 ♕c7 20 b4 a6

This is rather slow, although Black was clearly worse in any case. The rook was exerting unpleasant pressure

along the open a-file and ♘b5 was a constant worry.

21 ♗f4!

With most of the action taking place on the queenside over the past few moves, it was easy to forget that the e7-pawn was also vulnerable.

21...♕c6

Psakhis points out that 21...♕d7? was unplayable due to 22 ♖ad1 ♕e8 23 ♗d6 and White wins.

22 ♖xe7 ♘d5

This is the only decent attempt to stir up problems for White.

23 ♘xd5 ♕xd5 24 ♕g4!

This excellent move is the best way for White to maintain control. It is instructive to observe how Kasparov is in no way desperate to preserve his extra pawn and instead focuses on improving his pieces, specifically by preparing ideas such as ♖d1 and/or ♕d7.

24...♖ae8?!

This leads quickly to a lost endgame. Alternatives were:

a) 24...♗xb2 was also unsatisfactory due to 25 ♖d1 when White's pieces are far too active and Black will soon be forced to shed material.

b) A better chance was 24...♖ad8!? (Psakhis), preventing White's two main threats of ♖d1 and ♕d7. From here a sensible continuation would be 25 ♗d6 ♖fe8 (or 25...♗xb2 26 ♖d1 ♕c6 27 ♖b1 intending ♖c7) 26 ♖xe8+ ♖xe8 27 ♕d7 ♕e4 28 f3 when White will pick up the b7-pawn and should ultimately win, but care would still be required.

25 ♕d7!

Now the win is relatively simple – the queens are forced from the board, and the b7-pawn's days are numbered.

25...♕xd7 26 ♖xd7 ♗xb2

26...♖e4 loses even more quickly after 27 ♗d6 ♖xb4 28 c6! – Psakhis.

27 ♖ad1

The computer prefers 27 ♖a2!, keeping the a6-pawn as a target. Nevertheless, the text move is still good enough.

27...♖e4 28 ♗d6 ♖c8

Once again 28...♖xb4 29 c6! is the end.

29 ♖xb7 ♗c3 30 ♖b1 ♖c4?!

This allows a tactical finish. Black could have resisted more stubbornly with 30...h5, although there is no question that White's extra pawn should suffice for victory in the long run.

31 ♖c1! ♖xb4 32 c6

The rampant c-pawn, combined with the vulnerability of Black's pieces, is too much for the defender to bear.

32...♖d4

Alternatives are equally futile, one example being 32...♖c4 33 c7 ♔g7 34 ♖xc3, winning.

33 c7 1-0

A possible finish is 33...♖xd6 34 ♖b8 ♖c6 35 ♖xc8+ ♔g7 36 ♔f1 ♔f6 37 ♔e2 ♔e7 38 ♔d3 ♔d7 39 ♖f8 etc.

The next game features a notoriously provocative choice from Black.

Game 43
C.Lutz-R.Tischbierek
German League 1999

1 e4 ♘f6 2 e5 ♘d5 3 d4 d6 4 ♘f3 dxe5 5 ♘xe5 ♘d7

This move is pretty rare, and with good reason. Black will have to memorize a mountain of hard analysis to meet the infamous 6 ♘xf7 sacrifice, but at the same time he will rarely get to use it as most opponents will avoid it anyway. There is also the issue of White having a forced draw available.

6 ♘f3!

This simple retreat should lead to a slight edge while demanding little theoretical knowledge, making it by far the most pragmatic choice for the great majority of players. Given the rarity with which you are likely to be confronted by this variation, I see no value whatsoever in attempting to refute Black's last move with 6 ♘xf7. I will say no more about this unfathomably complicated variation here, apart from highlighting the important practical point that White can, if he wishes, force a draw after 6...♔xf7 7 ♕h5+ ♔e6 8 ♕g4+ (8 c4 is the big theoretical move, leading to massive complications and still no clear verdict) 8...♔f7 (the attempt to play for a win with 8...♔d6? backfires after 9 c4 when Black will have to return his extra piece while remaining with a ridiculous king position) 9 ♕h5+ with perpetual check.

6...e6

This is the most natural and popular move, although a few alternatives have been tried from time to time. In general White's plan will remain more or less the same: c4, ♘c3, ♗e2, and short castling, with a slightly easier

position. For example:

a) After 6...c6 White can choose between 7 c4 ♘c7 8 ♘c3 with a slight plus and 7 ♗e2 transposing to Game 40 (which featured the move order 5...c6 6 ♗e2 ♘d7 7 ♘f3).

b) 6...♘7f6 (it looks a little early to determine the position of this piece) 7 c4 ♘b6 8 ♘c3 ♗g4 (Black's idea was to develop this bishop actively before playing ...e6, but White finds a convincing response) 9 h3 ♗h5 10 g4! ♗g6 11 ♘e5 e6 12 ♗g2 ♕c8.

This was N.Ninov-J.Graf, Odessa 1990, and here White could have secured a huge advantage with 13 g5! ♘fd7 (13...♘g8 14 c5) 14 ♘xg6 hxg6 15 c5 when Black must lose a pawn.

c) 6...g6 7 c4 with two choices for Black:

c1) 7...♘5b6 8 ♘c3 c6 (8...♗g7?? 9 c5) 9 ♗e2 ♗g7 10 0-0 0-0 11 ♗f4 was a little better for White in B.Proeschold-A.Von Kap, Münster 1995.

c2) 7...♘5f6 8 ♘c3 ♗g7 9 ♗e2 0-0 10 0-0 c5 11 d5 and with more space in the centre and slightly the more harmonious pieces, White obviously stands a little better.

I found a couple of examples in the database:

c21) 11...♘e8 12 ♗g5 ♘d6 13 ♖e1 ♗xc3!? (13...♘b6 14 ♕b3) 14 bxc3 f6 15 ♗f4 ♘b6 was D.Langner-B.Rasmussen, Manitoba 1996, and now after 16 ♘d2 White's doubled pawns are less significant than his bishop pair and Black's weakened kingside.

c22) 11...a6 12 ♖e1 ♘b6 13 ♗e3 ♕c7 14 ♕d2 ♗g4 15 ♗f4 ♕c8 16 b3 ♖e8 17 h3 ♗f5 was tried in D.Navara-E.Siebenhaar, Mainz (rapid) 2009. So far White has built up a commanding position with simple developing moves and at this point the simplest way of increasing his advantage would have been 18 ♖ad1, developing the last piece while avoiding any trickery along the a1-h8 diagonal.

7 c4 ♘5f6

The bishop exchange does not alter the evaluation: 7...♗b4+ 8 ♗d2 ♗xd2+ 9 ♕xd2 ♘5f6 10 ♘c3 and White keeps a slight but definite plus.

8 ♘c3 c5 9 ♗e2

9 d5 also gives decent chances for an edge, in a different type of position. **9...cxd4 10 ♘xd4**

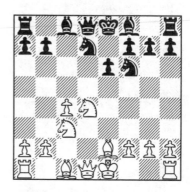

10...♗e7

This looks better than 10...♗b4 11 0-0 0-0 (11...♗xc3 12 bxc3 would leave Black too vulnerable on the dark squares) 12 ♕c2 when the following two games illustrate Black's difficulties:

a) 12...a6 13 a3 ♗c5 14 ♖d1 ♕c7 15 b4 ♗d6 16 h3 (16 g3 would have been my choice, but the text move had the merit of enticing Black into the following unsound sequence...) 16...a5? 17 ♘cb5 ♗h2+ 18 ♔h1 ♕b8 19 g3 ♗xg3 20 fxg3 ♕xg3 21 ♕d3 ♕h4 22 ♖g1 ♘e4 23 ♔h2 and Black had nowhere near enough for the sacrificed piece in E.Najer-D.Fridman, Internet (blitz) 2004.

b) 12...e5 13 ♘f5 ♘c5 14 ♖d1 ♗xf5 15 ♕xf5 ♕c8 16 ♕xc8 ♖axc8 17 ♘d5 ♘xd5 18 ♖xd5 e4 19 ♗e3 ♘d3 20 ♗xd3 exd3 21 ♖xd3 ♖xc4 22 ♗xa7 and White eventually converted his extra pawn in

J.Klovans-W.Pajeken, Pardubice 1995.
11 0-0 0-0

This seems like a good moment to assess the outcome of the opening. White's pieces are a little more actively placed, but the defining feature of the position is the presence of mutual pawn majorities. If everything else was equal, the structure would be slightly favourable to Black, as his extra central pawn has the potential to exert a greater influence on the game than White's c-pawn. For this reason, it would be unhelpful to make a comment along the lines of 'White stands better thanks to his queenside majority'. As a matter of fact I believe White does stand better, but only because his superior pieces allow him to make better use of his majority than Black.

12 ♗e3 a6

The black queen belongs on c7, but she does not want to be harassed by an enemy knight.

13 ♕a4!?

This seems like a rather odd choice. It works well in the game, but I have my doubts as to whether it is really the strongest move.

If I reached this position over the board, I would be more inclined to choose the natural 13 ♕d2! when White should preserve a slight edge.

Here are a few possible continuations:

a) 13...♗b4 should be met by 14 ♕c2, preventing ...♘e4 and preparing to chase the bishop away with a3.

b) 13...♘e5 14 ♖fd1 ♗d7 (14...♘eg4 achieves nothing after 15 ♗g5) allows White to choose between 15 ♘f3 and 15 ♘b3!?, in both cases keeping the slightly freer game and a small but definite plus.

c) 13...♕c7 14 ♗f4!? (14 ♖fd1 is a good alternative) 14...♕b6 (14...e5 15 ♘f5) 15 a3 ♖e8 (defending the bishop and thus threatening ...e5) 16 ♘f3 when White intends to play ♖fd1 and perhaps later b4 when the time is right.

In all these examples, it is noticeable that Black is unable to utilize his extra central pawn in a constructive way.

13...♞e5

13...♞c5 would have been met by 14 ♕c2 when the knight is misplaced and will have to worry about being driven away by b4.

14 h3 ♕c7 15 ♖ac1 ♗d7 16 ♕b3

16...♞c6?!

This passive move hands White the initiative.

The natural 16...♖ac8 would have been stronger, developing another piece and making use of the knight on e5. Black may have been concerned about 17 ♞a4, but after 17...♞e4!? 18 ♞b6 ♖cd8 19 ♞xd7 ♖xd7 20 ♕c2 ♞f6 his pieces are harmoniously placed and White's bishop pair is not really making its presence felt. Black should be close to equal here.

17 ♞f3!

The knight exchange would have freed Black's position to some extent. After the move played, the d7-bishop remains a problem.

17...♖ac8 18 ♖fd1!

With this move, Lutz anticipates Black's next and sets up an indirect defence of the c4-pawn.

18...♞a5

Black would love to play 18...♖fd8, but obviously 19 ♗b6 is a problem.

Perhaps he should have considered 18...♗e8 or 18...♕b8, although in both cases his position remains uninspiring.

19 ♕b6!

19...♕xb6

19...♞xc4 20 ♕xc7 ♖xc7 21 ♗xc4 ♖xc4 22 ♞e5 wins material.

20 ♗xb6 ♞c6

20...♞xc4 21 ♗xc4 ♖xc4 22 ♞e5 is similar to the previous note; in both cases Black must lose an exchange for insufficient compensation.

21 a3

In some ways this queenless position is pretty typical for this whole line. White has retained some initiative and I would advise the reader to pay close attention to the way Lutz improves his position.

21...♗d8 22 ♗c5!

Exchanging bishops would assist in the activation of the f8-rook, so White does better to retreat.

22...⊞e8

22...♝e7 was also possible, although 23 ♝xe7 (23 ♝e3!?) 23...♞xe7 24 ⊞d2 keeps a pleasant edge for White.

23 b4 ♝c7 24 ♞d2

24 ♝d6 was also good for White, but Lutz prefers to avoid simplification for the time being in favour of transferring the knight to the queenside, while also clearing the f3-square for the bishop.

24...♞e7 25 ♞b3 ⊞cd8 26 ♝f3

26...♝c6?!

This allows a fracturing of Black's queenside structure. The lesser evil was 26...♝c8 27 ⊞xd8 ♝xd8 when Black has an inferior but probably still defensible position.

27 ⊞xd8 ♝xd8 28 ♝xe7 ♝xe7 29 ♝xc6 bxc6 30 ♞a4

White has a choice of good lines here, with 30 ♞a5 ⊞c8 31 ⊞d1 also being tempting.

30...⊞a8 31 ♞b6 ⊞b8 32 c5 ♝d8

A better chance may have been 32...♞d5!? 33 ♞a5 (33 ♞xd5 exd5 looks a bit unpleasant, but is probably ten-

able for Black) 33...♝g5! 34 ⊞c2 ♞e7!. Black's position is grim, but there is no clear win for the time being. (But note that 34...⊞xb6?! 35 cxb6 ⊞xb6 36 ⊞xc6 ⊞xc6 37 ♞xc6 should win for White.)

33 ♞a5

The clearest route to victory would have been 33 ♞c4! ⊞c8 34 ♞d4 ♞d5 35 ♞e5 ♝g5 (35...♞e7 36 ⊞d1 intending ♞dxc6 wins a pawn) 36 ⊞d1 and Black has no good way to save the c6-pawn, as 36...♞e7 37 ♞df3 ♝f6 38 ⊞d7 intending ⊞a7 is winning for White.

33...♝xb6 34 cxb6

It seems that White must choose between two tempting continuations on every turn. On this occasion the alternative was 34 ♞xc6 ⊞b7 (34...♝c7 35 ♞xb8 ♝xb8 36 a4 gives White excellent winning chances) 35 cxb6 ⊞xb6 36 ♞e5 ♦f8 37 ⊞c7, winning a pawn.

34...⊞xb6 35 ⊞xc6 ⊞xc6 36 ♞xc6

39...♞d5

Knights are notoriously bad at dealing with outside passed pawns, so this ending must be considered highly unpleasant for Black. It is hard to give a definite verdict as to whether he can hold the position with perfect defence, and not especially relevant to our study of the opening. Therefore I will present the rest of the game with just a few light annotations.

37 ♔f1 ♔f8 38 ♔e2 ♔e8 39 ♘b8 ♘c7 40 ♔d3 ♔d8 41 ♔c4 ♔c8 42 ♘c6 ♘d5

The alternative was 42...♘b5 when 43 a4 ♘d6+ 44 ♔c5 ♔c7 45 ♘e5 maintains the pressure.

43 g3

Another idea was 43 ♘e5!? ♘f4 (43...f6 44 ♘d3) 44 ♘xf7 ♘xg2. Although White keeps some advantage here, it should be remembered that every pawn exchange on the kingside will bring Black closer to a draw.

43...♔c7 44 ♘e5 ♘b6+ 45 ♔c3 f6 46 ♘d3 ♘d5+

The best defensive chance looks to be 46...♘d7! guarding the sensitive c5-square. In that case it is not clear if White has more than a draw.

47 ♔b3 ♔d6?

Having suffered for a long time, Black finally collapses. 47...♔b6 or 47...♔c6 would have kept the game alive.

48 ♘c5 ♘c7

48...a5 49 ♘b7+ wins.

49 ♔a4 1-0

Black resigned, as he must lose the a6-pawn.

That concludes our coverage of 4...dxe5, and I like White's chances in every variation. Let's see if things are any different in the traditional main line.

Part 2 – 4...♗g4

Game 44
I.Glek-A.Kertesz
Bonn 1995

1 e4 ♘f6 2 e5 ♘d5 3 d4 d6 4 ♘f3 ♗g4

The old main line has become a bit less fashionable nowadays, but it is still a serious branch of theory which should be studied carefully.

5 ♗e2

White's first job is to break the pin.

5...e6

5...c6 will be considered in Game 46, 5...♘c6 in Game 47, and some unusual fifth moves will form the subject of Game 48.

6 0-0

Quite often White flicks in the move h2-h3 either here or over the next few moves. There are arguments for and against doing this, but I have chosen to refrain from it for reasons that will become apparent later in the present game.

6...♗e7

This is the usual choice. Alternatives will we covered in the notes to the next game.

7 c4 ♘b6 8 ♘c3 0-0 9 ♗e3 d5?!

This thematic move has been the most popular choice for Black, but it is in fact a significant error. We will examine the alternatives in the following game.

10 c5 ♗xf3

This capture provides the main justification for Black's previous move. White must either compromise his pawn structure or allow the knight in to c4.

11 gxf3!

11 ♗xf3 ♘c4 12 b3 ♘xe3 13 fxe3 may give White chances for a modest edge, but the text move is much more ambitious and forces the knight to retreat to a passive square.

11...♘c8

Alternatively:

a) 11...♘c4? 12 ♗xc4 dxc4 13 ♕a4 just wins a pawn.

b) 11...♘6d7 has been tried in a few games, but is generally considered less attractive as the knight will have a harder time finding a meaningful role in the game. White should respond with 12 f4 and continue in a similar fashion to the main game and subsequent notes.

12 f4

This seems like a good moment to take stock of the position. White has two major trumps in his serious space advantage and the bishop pair. True, the e3-bishop may not be contributing much at present, but you never know when the position might suddenly open up; besides, there is clearly no denying the potential of the light-squared bishop. Generally White will look to combine play on both flanks. He can gain some space on the queenside with b4-b5 to restrict the enemy pieces, although his long-term focus is likely to be on the kingside where he has good chances to develop an attack.

Black, on the other hand, can point to the doubling of White's f-pawns as a significant achievement. (Just as well really, as if the f2-pawn stood instead on g2 then Black's position would be strategically dire.) The second player will aim to fix the front f-pawn on f4, usually with ...f7-f5, although occasionally he might forsake this move in favour of ...g7-g6 and a possible knight transfer to f5. Black will aim to keep the position closed for the time being, which should favour his knights over the enemy bishops. Eventually, after suitable preparation, he may attempt a kingside break with ...f6, or if this pawn is already on f5, then ...g5.

The present position (or something very close to it) has occurred in several hundred games, sometimes with the white h-pawn on h3 instead of h2 (due to the insertion of the moves h2-h3 and ...♗g4-h5 somewhere between moves 6-9). Overall White has scored quite highly and this is especially true with the pawn on h2, as is the case here. As a matter of fact, nowadays most Alekhine experts will avoid this particular position like the plague. The main problem for Black is that with the pawn on h2, the white pieces will be able to make use of the h3-square for attacking purposes. This may not seem like a huge difference, but practice has demonstrated that it matters a great deal.

12...f5

Strictly speaking Black is not forced to play this move just yet, although in the majority of games he will play it sooner or later in order to prevent the white f-pawn from advancing any further.

Here are a few examples to show how the game might develop after other moves:

a) 12...♗h4 13 ♗d3 g6 14 ♕g4 ♔h8 15 b4 and White is in control on both sides of the board, R.Kapferer-R.Babinetz, Seefeld 1997. From a position like this his next few moves are likely to be ♔h1 and ♖g1, perhaps followed by ♖g2 and ♘e2-g1-f3 to improve the knight and drive the enemy bishop away from h4.

b) 12...♘c6 13 b4!. This move should almost always figure in White's plans at some point. Apart from the fact that it is generally useful to gain space on the queenside, White must also be mindful of the pseudo-sacrifice ...♗xc5, intending to meet dxc5 with ...d4, regaining the piece and creating some breathing room for the black pieces.

From here we will consider three continuations:

b1) After 13...♘xb4?! 14 ♖b1 White will regain the pawn and Black will suffer from weak light squares on the queenside. It should be noted that after 14...♘c6 15 ♖xb7, 15...♗xc5? does not work due to 16 dxc5 (16 ♕a4 is also good, but the text is even better) 16...d4 17 ♗f3 ♘8e7 18 ♕a4 when White remains a piece up.

b2) 13...a6 is better, but after 14 ♖b1 ♗h4 15 ♗d3 followed by ♔h1, ♖g1, and so on, White remains in control.

b3) 13...♗h4 14 ♖b1 ♘8e7 (by contrast with the main game, Black is trying to do without ...f5 and instead hopes to reserve that square for the use of his pieces) 15 ♗d3.

From this position I found a couple of practical examples:

b31) 15...g6 16 ♕g4 ♘f5 17 ♗xf5 exf5 18 ♕f3 ♘e7 19 b5 when Black's pieces are tied up and ♔g2-h3 is a serious threat. Still, there was no reason to self-destruct with 19...f6?, after which 20 ♕h3 led to the win of material and soon after the game in D.Wagner-T.Struening, Korbach 2007.

b32) 15...♘g6 was played in A.Groszpeter-P.Wells, Harkany 1993, and now White could have obtained a clear advantage with 16 f5!? (16 ♔h1 ♘ce7 17 ♕f3 is a decent alternative, while the game continuation of 16 ♕g4 is also not bad) 16...exf5 (after 16...♘gxe5 17 b5! ♘xd3 18 bxc6 Black loses a piece for insufficient compensation) 17 ♗xf5 ♘gxe5 (I assume this was the reason why White rejected the advance of the f-pawn, but his fears turn out to be unjustified) 18 dxe5 d4 19 b5! ♘e7 (Black is not helped by 19...♘xe5 20 ♗f4 or 19...dxe3 20 bxc6 ♗xf2+ 21 ♔g2) 20 ♗xh7+! ♔xh7 21 ♖b4!? (21 ♕h5+ ♔g8 22 ♖bd1 is also good) 21...♘f5 22 ♕h5+ ♔g8 23 ♕xf5 dxe3 24 fxe3 ♕g5+ 25 ♖g4 ♕xf5 26 ♖xf5 when Black faces a difficult defence in the endgame.

Returning to 12...f5:

13 ♔h1

White could also have flicked in 13 b4 first – the exact move order does not matter too much.

13...♗h4

The black bishop often comes here in order to make way for the knight to re-enter the game via e7. Unfortunately for Black, the bishop would be much happier in the position with a white pawn on h3, as in the present position a queen transfer to h3 could prove troublesome.

The following game also featured some instructive moments: 13...♞c6 14 b4 a6 (once again 14...♞xb4 15 ♖b1 does not help Black) 15 ♖b1 ♚h8 16 a4 (my personal choice would have been 16 ♖g1 followed by ♕h5 or ♕f3-h3, but in this game White has decided to expand on the queenside first) 16...a5 17 b5 ♞b4 18 ♖g1 ♖f7 19 ♗h5!? (White could also have opted for a more patient build-up with 19 ♖g3) 19...g6 20 ♖xg6!? (objectively this sacrifice should not be sufficient to win the game, but it is not unsound and it creates serious practical problems for the defence) 20...hxg6 21 ♗xg6

21...♕g8! (Black begins by finding the only correct defence) 22 ♕h5+ ♖h7 23 ♗xh7 ♕xh7 24 ♕e8+ ♕g8 25 ♕d7

♗f8? (under pressure, Black falters; it was essential to play 25...♗h4! 26 ♖g1 ♕f8 when White lacks a knockout blow and must settle for either 27 ♕xe6 ♞e7 with unclear play or 27 ♕xc7 ♕e7 28 b6 ♞a6 29 ♕xe7 ♞xe7 30 ♞b5 when I would take White's position if given the choice, but I suspect Black should be able to hold) 26 ♖g1 ♗g7 27 ♖g5 (the calm 27 ♕xc7 would also have put Black in a hopeless situation) 27...♚h7 28 ♞e2 ♕f8 29 ♕xe6 ♞e7 30 ♖h5+ ♗h6 31 ♞g3 (31 ♞g1! would have been the quickest route to victory) 31...♖e8 32 ♕d7 ♚g6 33 ♕e6+ ♚h7 34 ♖xh6+ ♕xh6 35 ♕f7+ ♕g7 36 ♕h5+ ♕h6 37 ♕xe8 ♕g7 38 ♕d7 (38 ♞h5) 38...♞d3 39 ♞xf5 ♞xf5 40 ♕xf5+ ♕g6 41 ♕h3+ 1-0 M.Bjelajac-L.Popov, Novi Sad 1981.

14 ♖g1 g6 15 b4 ♖f7

16 b5!?

White decides on a policy of aggressive queenside expansion, which works to perfection in the game.

A more patient alternative was 16 ♗d3 intending ♕f3. Once those pieces are in position, White can choose between further queenside expansion and a direct kingside attack. If he decides on the latter, then the typical plan of action will involve the moves ♕h3, ♖g2, ♘e2-g1-f3, and finally ♖ag1, by which time the black king is likely to be feeling distinctly uncomfortable.

16...♘d7

16...a6 17 a4 does not help Black.

17 a4 ♘f8 18 ♕f1

Here we see another route by which the queen can switch to the key h3-square.

18...b6?!

This only presents White with a target, although it was difficult to suggest a constructive plan for Black.

19 a5 ♖b8

After 19...bxc5 20 dxc5 White could add the use of the d4-square to his growing list of positional trumps.

20 axb6 axb6 21 c6

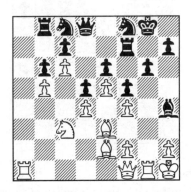

White seizes even more space, leaving his opponent with almost no room to manoeuvre.

21...♔h8

Black would like to contest the a-file, but 21...♘e7 22 ♕h3 forces the knight to take the rather humiliating step back to c8.

22 ♕h3 ♖g7 23 ♖a4

23 ♘b1 was a good alternative, intending ♘d2-f3.

23...♖g8

White has an absolutely dominant position, but there still remains a question mark as to how he can execute the final breakthrough. Fortunately his advantage is based on static features of the position, so he can take his time to manoeuvre, whereas the opponent faces the thankless task of shuffling around on the back few ranks while attempting to anticipate where the next threat might be coming from.

24 ♘d1 ♗e7 25 ♘b2 ♕e8 26 ♖ga1 ♔g7

Black could have attempted a break for freedom with 26...g5, but after 27 fxg5 ♗xg5 28 f4 (28 ♗xg5 ♖xg5 29 ♘d3 is also good, but in principle I would prefer to avoid exchanges) 28...♗e7 29 ♘d3 White remains in control and with the g-file open he may decide to switch his attention back to the kingside.

27 ♘d3 h6

With hindsight Black should probably have avoided weakening the g6-pawn, although it must be said that his position was downright depressing and it would have been practically impossible to avoid making a mistake at some point.

28 ♖g1 ♔h7 29 ♖g3 ♕f7 30 ♘e1 ♔g7 31 ♖a1 ♗b4 32 ♘f3 ♘e7 33 ♖b1 ♗c3

34 ♖b3 ♗a5 35 ♗c1!

After a period of manoeuvring White finds a way to improve another piece.

35...♖a8 36 ♗a3

Not only is the bishop generally active here, it is also perfectly placed to carry out the specific duty of eliminating the knight on e7, one of the key defenders of the vulnerable g6-pawn, at a moment's notice.

36...♕e8?

This loses immediately, although Black can barely move a piece and it is doubtful that he could have survived for much longer in any case. One of the many attacking plans at White's disposal was ♖g1 followed by ♘h4, ♖bg3, and perhaps even ♗h5, after which the g6-pawn would surely have met its maker.

37 ♕h4 ♘c8 38 ♕f6+ ♔h7 39 ♘g5+ 1-0

Black resigned as it is mate next move.

This game, along with those featured in the notes, provides a convinc-ing demonstration of why, in the line where White refrains from playing h2-h3, Black should avoid the blocked positions which arise after 9...d5. In the next game we will examine his various alternatives between moves 6 and 9.

Game 45
T.Oral-S.Cicak
Czech League 2004

1 e4 ♘f6 2 e5 ♘d5 3 d4 d6 4 ♘f3 ♗g4 5 ♗e2 e6 6 0-0 ♗e7

The only significant alternative is 6...♘c6, which is rarely seen but should not be underestimated. White should play 7 c4 when there are two moves worth considering:

a) 7...♘de7 8 exd6 ♕xd6 (8...cxd6 should be met by 9 d5) 9 ♘c3 and Black has tried three moves here:

a1) 9...0-0-0? 10 ♘g5 ♗xe2 11 ♘xe2 ♘xd4 12 ♘c3! and the impending fork on f7 proved decisive in D.Djaja-D.Janosevic, Belgrade 1948.

a2) 9...♘f5?! 10 d5 ♘ce7? was seen

in W.Schoenmann-I.Engert, Altona 1932, and now 11 ♘b5 wins easily: for instance, 11...♕d8 12 ♗f4 ♘d6 13 dxe6 or 11...♕b6 12 dxe6 fxe6 13 ♘e5 ♖d8 14 ♕a4.

a3) 9...♗xf3 10 ♗xf3 ♘xd4 (10...♕xd4 11 ♘b5 and 10...0-0-0 11 ♘b5 both give White a promising initiative as well) 11 ♗xb7 ♖d8 (or 11...♖b8, as in V.Ciocaltea-M.Knezevic, Vrnjacka Banja 1975, and now 12 ♕a4+ c6 13 ♕xa7 gives White a safe extra pawn, since 13...♕c7?? is refuted by 14 ♗xc6+) 12 ♕a4+ c6 13 ♗e3 ♕c7 14 ♕xa7 e5.

This position was reached in N.De Firmian-L.Shamkovich, USA 1994, and now after 15 ♗xd4 exd4 16 ♘e4 ♘g6 17 ♕a6 ♘e5 18 f4 ♖b8 19 fxe5 ♕xb7 20 ♕xb7 (20 ♕a4!?) 20...♖xb7 21 b3 White should win the ending.

b) 7...♘b6 should be met by 8 exd6 cxd6 9 d5 when Black can try two moves:

b1) 9...♗xf3 10 ♗xf3 exd5 11 ♗xd5 ♗e7 12 ♗f4 0-0 13 ♘c3 and White had a slight but clear advantage in

I.Svensson-N.Tagnon, Haifa 1976.

b2) 9...exd5 10 cxd5 ♗xf3 11 gxf3! ♘e5 12 ♗b5+ and now:

b21) 12...♘ed7 13 ♕d4 ♕f6 14 ♖e1+ ♔d8 (14...♗e7 15 ♕xf6 gxf6 16 ♘c3 left Black facing a difficult defence in the queenless middlegame in L.Vogt-D.Uddenfeldt, Skopje 1972) 15 ♕d1! when the unfortunate position of Black's king is more significant than the doubled f-pawns, T.Kroeger-K.Junge, German League 1995.

b22) 12...♘bd7 13 f4 ♘g6 (or 13...a6 14 fxe5 axb5 15 e6 ♘c5 16 ♕e2 b4? – Black cannot afford this loss of time, although his position was obviously difficult in any case – 17 ♕b5+ ♔e7 18 ♗g5+ f6 19 ♗e3 ♕a5 20 ♕c4 with an overwhelming positional advantage for White, M.Womacka-M.Kopylov, Internet (blitz) 2006) 14 f5 ♘ge5?! (14...♘e7 was the lesser evil, although 15 ♖e1 is still unpleasant for Black) 15 ♕e2 a6? (the only way to avoid the loss of a piece was 15...g5, although White still keeps a big advantage after 16 fxg6 ♕e7 17 gxf7+ ♘xf7 18 ♘c3) 16 ♗xd7+

1-0 M.Wahls-A.Ostl, German League 1989.

Returning to 6...♗e7:

7 c4 ♘b6 8 ♘c3 0-0 9 ♗e3

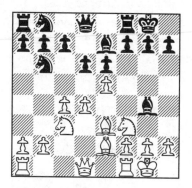

In the previous game we saw that forcing the issue in the centre with 9...d5 was a bad idea with the white h-pawn on h2 instead of h3. Now it is time to turn our attention to Black's other options.

9...♘8d7

A quick check of the database reveals that Black has tried a plethora of alternatives here. There is little point in attempting to cover everything, so I focused on a few of the more significant options.

a) 9...dxe5?! 10 ♘xe5 ♗xe2 11 ♕xe2 gives White an easy game: for instance, 11...♘8d7 12 ♖ad1 c6 13 ♗f4 ♘f6 14 ♖d3 when Black has a passive position with no counterplay and will soon have to worry about a kingside attack, V.Anand-E.Ubilava, Villarrobledo (rapid) 2001.

b) 9...a6 is partially a waiting move, although it should be noted that Black is also creating a positional threat of ...♗xf3, since the reply ♗xf3 can safely be met by ...♘xc4 as the rook will no longer be trapped on a8. Therefore I suggest: 10 exd6 cxd6 11 ♕b3!? (11 b3 should also suffice for a slight plus; the text move is an interesting attempt to trouble the opponent by creating concrete threats) 11...♘8d7 12 a4!? ♗xf3 13 ♗xf3 ♕c7 14 ♖fc1 ♘xc4 (14...♕xc4 15 ♕a3! would be too risky for Black) 15 ♘d5 exd5 16 ♗xd5 ♘db6 17 ♗xc4 ♘xc4 18 ♖xc4 ♕d7 19 ♖ac1 ♖ac8 20 d5 and White's control over the c-file gave him a slight but stable advantage, which he eventually converted to the full point in P.Blatny-K.Bischoff, Brno 1994.

c) 9...♘c6 is arguably the most critical way for Black to try and exploit White's refusal to play h3. The critical continuation is 10 exd6 cxd6 11 d5 with two possibilities:

c1) 11...♗xf3?! 12 ♗xf3 ♘e5 13 dxe6 leads to a situation where Black will have no real compensation for the vulnerability of the d6-e6 pawn duo: for instance, 13...fxe6 (13...♘xf3+ 14 ♕xf3 fxe6 15 ♕e4 ♖f6 16 b3 was a similar story in M.Abarca Aguirre-R.Vidal, Santiago de Chile 1980) 14 ♗g4 ♘xg4 15 ♕xg4 ♖f6 16 ♖ad1 ♕c7 17 b3 and White enjoyed a stable advantage in M.Schlosser-Y.Schlueter, Muerren 1987.

c2) Much better is 11...exd5 12 ♘xd5 ♘xd5 13 ♕xd5.

In the analogous position which could have been reached with the moves h2-h3 and ...♗g4-h5 inserted, Black would stand significantly worse, mainly because he would have to spend an important tempo dealing with the attack on the h5-bishop. In the present position there is no such threat and in certain lines Black may also benefit from the option of dropping his bishop back to e6 to assist in the fight for the central squares. Despite these factors, I am still not convinced that Black can achieve full equality. At the very least, his margin for error will be somewhat smaller than White's.

The present variation is one of the most theoretically critical of the pre-

sent chapter and White will have to play with great precision to secure an advantage. Therefore I would advise the reader to pay close attention to what follows. After 13...♗f6 I spent quite some time analysing the different possibilities and eventually concluded that 14 ♖ad1!? was the most promising option.

Black has tried two moves from here:

c21) 14...♕c8 does not really challenge the white position: 15 b3 ♖d8 16 h3 ♗e6 17 ♕h5 ♗f5 18 ♗d3 ♗g6 19 ♗xg6 hxg6 20 ♕d5 ♘e7 was R.Winsnes-L.Liljedahl, Stockholm 1987, and now after 21 ♕e4 White keeps an edge thanks to the isolated d-pawn.

c22) 14...♗xb2 is the critical continuation: 15 ♕b5 ♗f6 16 c5 d5 17 ♕xb7 ♖c8. This position was reached in E.Liss-M.Shrentzel, Israeli League 1999. Material is equal, but it seems to me that White's chances should be somewhat higher, as the d5-pawn is slightly vulnerable and White's queen has a certain nuisance value on b7. At this point I think White's most promising course of action would have been 18 h3!, forcing the bishop to make a decision.

I checked the following replies:

c221) 18...♗f5 19 ♗d3 maintains an edge after 19...♗xd3 20 ♖xd3 or 19...♗e6 20 ♗f4.

c222) 18...♗e6 19 ♗f4 (19 ♗b5 would be quite tempting, were it not for 19...♕a5! intending to meet 20 ♗xc6 with 20...♖b8 when the queen is trapped) 19...♗e7 20 ♖c1 and White keeps an edge, with ♖fd1 and ♗b5 being two of the main ideas.

c223) 18...♗h5 maintains the pressure along the d1-h5 diagonal, but the drawback is that the bishop can no longer be called upon to protect the d-pawn via the e6-square: 19 ♗f4 ♗e7 (or 19...♖e8 20 ♗a6) 20 ♕b3!? ♗xf3 21 ♗xf3 ♗xc5 22 ♖xd5 ♕b6 23 ♕xb6 axb6 24 ♖fd1 and White's bishop pair gives him an ongoing advantage despite the reduced material.

After that long but important analysis, we can return to 9...♘8d7:

10 exd6 cxd6 11 b3

White's extra space and harmonious development give him a slight but pleasant edge. It is not easy for Black to generate counterplay, especially with his knight misplaced on b6.

11...♘f6 12 a4!? a5

Evidently Black found the prospect of a5-a6 unappealing, but the text move is far from ideal, especially as Black's knights are in no position to take advantage of the hole on b4.

13 ♖c1 d5 14 ♘b5 ♘e8

I also checked 14...♖c8 15 ♘e5 (15 c5 ♘bd7 doesn't look so bad for Black) 15...♗xe2 16 ♕xe2 dxc4 17 bxc4 ♘xa4 18 ♕a2 (18 c5!?) 18...♘b6 19 ♕xa5 when White keeps an edge.

15 ♕d2 dxc4 16 bxc4 ♗b4 17 ♕a2 ♘c7 18 ♖fd1 ♘xb5

Black eliminates the annoying knight, but in doing so he allows White to improve his pawn structure.

19 axb5 ♘c8?!

Black should have preferred something like 19...♕c7, although there is no doubting White's advantage.

20 h3 ♗f5 21 d5!

Unleashing the potential of White's centralized pieces.

21...♕e7

21...exd5 also fails to solve Black's problems: 22 ♖xd5 ♕f6 23 g4! ♗e4 (23...♗e6? 24 ♗g5 ♕g6 25 ♘h4 ♕e4 26 f3 wins the queen) 24 g5 ♕g6 25 ♖e5 ♗xf3 (the threat was ♘h4) 26 ♗xf3 ♘d6 27 c5 ♘xb5 28 ♗xb7 and the passed c-pawn will be hard to stop.

22 ♘d4

22 c5 exd5 23 ♕xd5 ♗e4 24 ♕d7 also looks strong.

22...♗c5 23 ♗f3 ♗xd4 24 ♗xd4 exd5

24...e5 is refuted by 25 d6! ♘xd6 (25...♕xd6 26 ♗xb7) 26 ♗c5 ♖fd8 27 ♕a3, winning.

25 ♗xd5

The computer points out that 25 ♕b2! would have been even more accurate, but the game continuation also leads to a huge advantage.

25...♔h8 26 c5

There was also a tactical solution in 26 ♕b2 f6 27 ♖e1 ♕d7 28 ♕a3! ♖d8 29 ♕f3! ♖b8 30 g4! winning, but the text

move spoils nothing, as White's pieces are dominant while Black remains almost paralysed.

26...♗e6 27 ♗xe6 ♕xe6 28 ♕xe6 fxe6 29 ♗e5

White has an overwhelming positional advantage and the endgame is an easy win.

29...♔g8 30 ♖d7 ♖f7 31 ♖cd1 b6 32 ♖d8+ ♖f8 33 ♖8d7 ♖f7

Perhaps White was short of time and decided to repeat the position once in order to get closer to move 40.

34 ♖d8+ ♖f8 35 ♖xf8+ ♔xf8 36 ♖d8+ ♔e7 37 ♖xc8! ♖xc8 38 cxb6 1-0

That concludes our coverage of 5...e6. We will now move on to Black's 5th-move alternatives, beginning with a different pawn move.

> *Game 46*
> **J.Emms-G.Burgess**
> British League (4NCL) 1999

My thanks go to John Emms for

sharing his thoughts on this game.

1 e4 ♘f6 2 e5 ♘d5 3 d4 d6 4 ♘f3 ♗g4 5 ♗e2 c6

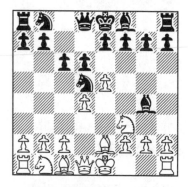

The main purpose of this move is to fortify the h1-a8 diagonal in order to prepare an exchange on f3.

6 c4

This is the move I like best, although there are a few other possibilities:

a) Black's main idea is revealed after 6 0-0 ♗xf3 7 ♗xf3 dxe5 8 dxe5 e6 intending ...♘d7, ...♕c7, and later ...♘e7-g6 with an all-out assault on the g5-pawn. Actually White should be able to fight for an advantage here as well, but I think it makes sense to avoid giving the opponent an easy plan involving a sequence of natural moves.

b) The other main line is 6 ♘g5!? ♗f5 (6...♗xe2 7 ♕xe2 would leave the queen ideally placed) when White's options include:

b1) Firstly, it should briefly be noted that 7 c4?! would be a mistake here due to 7...♘b4!.

b2) With the quiet 7 ♗d3 White insists on the exchange of bishops, al-

though after 7...♗xd3 8 ♕xd3 the queen is slightly worse on d3 than e2 where Emms places it.

b3) Finally, the aggressive 7 e6!? fxe6 leads to a double-edged position where White has some chances for an edge, but ultimately I believe that the text move should lead to greater rewards while requiring less effort.

6...♘b6

This is generally regarded as the most challenging move. The main idea is that, by eyeing the c4-pawn, Black creates a significant positional threat in ...♗xf3.

6...♘c7 is a playable though somewhat passive alternative.

White has a few different routes to a slight plus. Perhaps the most straightforward is 7 exd6 when Black can try either recapture:

a) 7...♕xd6 8 ♘c3 g6 (it is hard to believe that 8...♗xf3?! can be a good idea and after 9 ♗xf3 e5 in A.Jackson-C.Crouch, British League 2003, White could have secured an edge with 10 d5 cxd5 11 ♘xd5 when his light-squared bishop will be strong) 9 0-0 ♗g7 10 ♗e3 0-0 11 ♕d2 ♘ba6 12 ♖ad1 and White kept a slight plus in S.Dolmatov-T.Petrosian, Moscow 1981.

b) 7...exd6 8 ♕b3!? is an interesting attempt to inconvenience the second player. Note that the same idea would not have been available had the knight retreated to b6 instead of c7. Black can try:

b1) 8...b6 seems like a questionable choice and after the further 9 ♘c3 ♗e7 10 h3 ♗h5 11 ♗e3 ♕c8 12 0-0 0-0 13 ♖fe1 ♖e8 14 ♖ac1 ♘d7 15 ♕a4 Black's light-squared weaknesses meant he had failed to equalize in S.B.Hansen-T.Hillarp Persson, Gentofte 1999.

b2) 8...♕c8 9 ♘c3 ♗e7 10 h3 ♗h5 11 0-0 0-0 12 d5! cxd5 (12...♘ba6 13 ♗e3 and 12...c5 13 ♗f4 are both clearly better for White according to Khalifman) 13 cxd5 ♘d7 was reached in K.Pytel-R.Tomaszewski, Lubniewice 1981, and here I think the best way for White to complete his development would have been 14 ♗e3: for instance, 14...♘c5 (14...♖e8 15 ♖ac1 keeps an edge, while 14...♘e5 15 ♘xe5 ♗xe2 can be met by 16 ♘xe2 dxe5 17 ♖ac1 or even 16 ♘g6!? hxg6 17 ♘xe2 when White remains on top) 15 ♕c4 a5 and now both 16 ♖fe1 and 16 ♗xc5 dxc5 17 ♘e5 give White a pleasant edge.

7 ♘g5!?

The point of this move is to aim for an improved version of the 6 ♘g5 variation noted earlier. The fact that the black knight has already been driven

away from the centre makes a real difference in many lines.

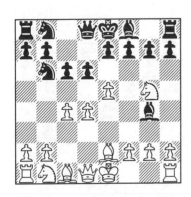

I first became aware of this idea when researching the present chapter and initially viewed it with some scepticism. If it really did lead to an improved version of a main line, then why had it not usurped the main line in question? And why did it not feature in any of the Alekhine books I had checked? I do not know the answers to these questions, but what I do know is that, having analysed it in some detail, I have not found any reason not to play it. I even contacted the winner of the present game to ask if he had since become aware of any problems, but he also seemed happy enough with White's chances. In short, the system featured here really does seem like an excellent try for an advantage.

7...♗xe2

7...♗f5 looks dubious here due to 8 e6! (8 g4 should also give White the better chances, but I think the text is even better) when Black faces a difficult choice:

a) 8...♗xe6 9 ♘xe6 fxe6 was played in J.Morin-S.Schneider, Haninge 1997, and now after the simple 10 ♘d2 intending ♘e4-g5 and perhaps ♗g4, Black faces serious problems on the light squares.

b) The position after 8...fxe6 should be compared with the variation 6 ♘g5 ♗f5 7 e6!? fxe6, as referenced in note 'b3' to White's sixth move in the present game.

In that particular line, the black knight would commonly retreat to f6 to defend the kingside or perhaps even c7 to defend the e6-pawn. In the present position it is clearly misplaced on b6, where it contributes nothing to the defence and White can obtain an excellent position as follows: 9 g4! ♗g6 (9...♗xb1 10 ♖xb1 looks horrible for Black) 10 ♗d3 ♗xd3 11 ♕xd3 ♘a6 (in the event of 11...♘6d7, as in T.Barendse-M. De Waal, Enschede 1992, both 12 ♘xh7 and 12 ♕e4!? look strong) 12 ♕f3! (White is not concerned about regaining the e6-pawn just yet and instead threatens a deadly

invasion on f7) 12...♕c8 13 c5! (White is playing with great energy to carve open the opponent's defences) 13...♘d5 (after 13...dxc5 14 dxc5 ♘xc5 15 b4! the opening of the d-file is too dangerous for Black) 14 ♕f7+ ♔d8 15 cxd6 h6 16 ♘xe6+ ♔d7. This position was reached in R.Weis-U.Floegel, German League 1989, and now after the straightforward 17 0-0 ♔xd6 18 ♖e1 the black king's days are surely numbered.

8 ♕xe2

8...h6

8...dxe5 9 dxe5 is unlikely to alter the position in any fundamental way, unless Black tries something rash like 9...♕d4?!, as occurred in the game E.Weinzettl-J.Lundin, Belgrade 2002. Here the strongest continuation looks to be: 10 e6! (the game continuation of 10 ♘d2 also sufficed for a pleasant advantage; the black queen has no business lunging into the centre at such an early stage of the game) 10...f6 11 ♘f7 ♖g8 12 ♘a3 when Black will have a hard time completing development.

Instead 9...h6 10 ♘f3 transposes to the main game, while 9...e6 10 0-0 ♗e7 11 ♘f3 leads to a similar position. It is not clear whether the developing move ...♗e7 is really more useful than ...h6, as the bishop might have better squares available to it. In any case, White keeps a pleasant advantage and can develop in a similar fashion to the main game and accompanying notes.

9 ♘f3 dxe5

Black should not forget to include this exchange. After the careless 9...e6?? 10 exd6 ♗xd6 11 c5 he lost a piece in E.Carl-W.Schley, German League 2000.

10 dxe5 e6 11 0-0 ♘8d7 12 ♘c3 ♕c7 13 ♗f4

White has almost completed development and now intends ♘e4 and perhaps a rook to the d-file, followed by a timely knight jump to the inviting hole on d6.

13...g5!?

Burgess, an Alekhine specialist, recognizes that he is quickly drifting into a difficult situation and attempts to create some counterplay. Here are a few other examples which illustrate White's chances:

a) 13...0-0-0 14 a4!? (the immediate 14 ♘e4 is also promising, but White decides to begin by provoking a potential queenside weakness) 14...a5 15 ♘e4 f5? (Black had to try 15...♔b8 16 ♘d6 ♘c5, although after 17 ♕e3 White has an obvious advantage) 16 ♘d6+ ♔b8 17 ♘f7 and White won the exchange and later the game in Y.Dembo-H.Faber, Kavala 2004.

b) 13...♘c5 14 ♖ad1 a5 15 b3 (White could even have been a little more precise with the immediate 15 ♘d2!) 15...♗e7 16 ♘d2! 0-0-0 17 ♘de4 (we can see a pattern emerging: once a white knight establishes itself on e4, the threat of invading on d6 becomes highly unpleasant for Black) 17...♔b8 18 ♘d6 and White was clearly better in R.Lau-G.Schroll, Vienna 1998.

14 ♗g3 ♗g7

Here is one more example to illustrate the difficulties faced by Black in this variation: 14...0-0-0 15 ♘e4 (White could also play 15 a4, à la Dembo) 15...♔b8 16 ♖ad1 ♗e7 17 ♘d6 ♖h7 18 ♘d4 ♘f8 19 b4 (19 ♘b3!?) 19...h5 20 h3 ♘g6 21 ♕e4 ♖g8 22 ♖d3 h4 23 ♗h2 f5? (better was 23...♖hg7, although Black is still in deep trouble after 24 ♖b3 ♘f4 25 c5 ♘d7 26 ♖c1 intending b5 with a huge attack) 24 exf6 ♗xd6 25 ♘xc6+ ♔a8 (25...♕xc6 26 ♖xd6!) 26 ♖xd6 bxc6 27 ♖xc6 ♕b7. This was D.Vasiesiu-M.Grunberg, Targoviste 2001, and here the most straightforward continuation would have been 28 ♕xe6 when Black is unlikely to survive for much longer.

15 ♘e4

15...♘c8?!

The computer prefers 15...0-0, but it goes without saying that this was not what Black had in mind when playing 13...g5.

16 ♖ad1

Calmly bringing another piece into action. Black's position is already close to lost.

16...♕a5

It is amusing to see the consequences of 16...g4 intending to snatch the e5-pawn: 17 ♘d4 ♗xe5 (if 17...h5 18 ♘f6+ or 17...♘xe5 18 ♘c5 when the knight is trapped in a fatal pin, and Black has no good defence against ♖fe1 or ♘d3) 18 ♘f6+! ♘xf6 19 ♗xe5 ♕e7 (now White strikes the death blow with a simple but attractive combination) 20 ♘f5! exf5 21 ♗xf6! ♕xe2 22 ♖d8 mate.

17 ♕d3 ♘cb6

This drops the b7-pawn, but it was

hard to suggest anything else.

18 ♘d6+ ♔f8 19 ♘xb7 ♕xa2 20 ♘d6 ♕a5 21 ♕e4

Defending e5 and attacking c6. White's play is absolutely logical and easy to understand.

21...♕c5 22 ♖d2

Technically speaking White could have ended the game more quickly with 22 ♘d4!, although from a practical perspective it is almost always better to take the slow but certain win instead of the quick, flashy one. Here are the highlights anyway: 22...♘xc4 (alternatively, 22...♗xe5 23 ♘xe6+! fxe6 24 ♕g6 or 22...♘xe5 23 ♘xe6+! fxe6 24 b4! ♕xb4 25 ♗xe5) 23 ♘xf7! (even better than 23 ♘xe6+ fxe6 24 ♘xc4) 23...♔xf7 24 ♘xe6 ♔xe6 25 ♕g4+ and the attack crashes through.

22...♖b8 23 ♖fd1 ♔g8 24 h4!

Having improved his pieces to the greatest extent possible, Emms now turns his attention to carving open Black's fragile kingside.

24...gxh4 25 ♕xh4 ♘xe5?

Losing immediately, although

Black's position was hopeless in any case.

26 ♗xe5 ♗xe5 27 b4! 1-0

Our next game features the black knight moving to c6 instead of the pawn.

Game 47
A.Gabrielian-K.Sek
Ulan Ude 2009

1 e4 ♘f6 2 e5 ♘d5 3 d4 d6 4 ♘f3 ♗g4 5 ♗e2 ♘c6

This is not such a well-known move, but it features in over 800 games on the database and has been tested by some high-ranking grandmasters including Avrukh and Zvjaginsev.

6 0-0

6...dxe5

This is the consistent move, but it runs into a convincing reply. Alternatives include:

a) 6...e6 transposes to the note to Black's sixth move in Game 45.

b) 6...♘b6 7 h3 ♗xf3 8 ♗xf3 dxe5 9 ♗xc6+ bxc6 10 dxe5 and Black has no compensation for his shattered queenside structure.

c) 6...g6 tends not to combine well with an early ...♗g4. Amongst several promising continuations, perhaps the most ambitious is 7 e6! fxe6 (after 7...♗xe6? 8 c4 Black loses a piece) 8 ♘g5 ♗xe2 9 ♕xe2 ♘xd4 (or 9...♕d7 10 ♘xe6 ♘d8 11 ♘xf8 ♖xf8 12 c4 ♘f4 13 ♗xf4 ♖xf4 14 ♕e3 ♖f5 15 ♘c3 and White had an obvious advantage in Dang Vu Quang-Nguyen Duc Hoa, Hanoi 2002).

This position was reached in F.Zita-M.Vidmar, Karlovy Vary 1948, and here White should have played 10 ♕d3! (10 ♕e4 has been played in a few games, but 10...c5 11 c3 ♘f6 is not altogether clear; the text move is a definite improvement) 10...♘c6 (10...c5 11 c3) 11 ♘xe6 ♘db4 12 ♕c3 ♕d7 13 ♖e1 ♖g8 14 ♕b3 when Black faces serious problems.

7 ♘xe5!

Earlier in the chapter we saw some

examples where White went out of his way to avoid a knight exchange on this square, whereas now he is happy to encourage it. The apparent inconsistency is justified by the specific features of the position. Indeed, both practice and analysis have confirmed that White is doing well here.

7...♗xe2

There is also 7...♘xe5 8 dxe5 with two possibilities:

a) 8...♗xe2 9 ♕xe2 ♕d7 (or 9...e6 10 ♕b5+) 10 c4 ♘b6 11 ♖d1 with an obvious initiative for White.

b) 8...♗f5 9 c4 ♘b6 10 ♕b3! e6 11 ♖d1 ♕c8 (Black was quickly crushed after 11...♕e7 12 ♘c3 g5 13 ♗f3 c6 14 ♘b5! in E.Alekseev-V.Kupreichik, Ekaterinburg 2002) 12 ♕g3 ♗c2 13 ♖d4 ♗g6 14 h4 c5 15 ♖d1 with a clear plus, O.Korneev-A.Panchenko, Berga 1996.

8 ♕xe2 ♘xd4

Accepting the sacrificed is a principled but extremely risky endeavour.

Instead 8...♘xe5 9 dxe5 transposes to variation 'a' in the previous note.

9 ♕c4

Attacking the knight on d4, while also eyeing f7 and preparing an awkward pin on the d-file.

9...f6

This leaves Black clearly worse, but he must already resort to drastic measures in order to survive the opening. He has tried two other continuations, neither of which come close to equalizing:

a) 9...♘e6 10 ♖d1 c6 was seen in K.Ragsch-H.Liesenfeld, Goch 2004. At this point the strongest continuation would have been 11 ♘c3! (the game continuation of 11 ♘xc6!? was enough to regain the pawn while keeping some initiative, but it turns out that White does not need to rush with this idea) when Black faces difficult problems, with one possible continuation being 11...♘ec7 (or 11...♕a5 12 ♘xc6 ♕c7 13 ♘xd5 ♕xc6 14 ♕e4) 12 ♘xc6! bxc6 13 ♕xc6+ ♕d7 14 ♕xd7+ ♔xd7 15 ♘xd5 and White should have no problem winning the ending a pawn up.

b) 9...c5 10 ♗e3 leads to a virtually forced sequence resulting in a hopeless position for Black: 10...a6 11 ♘c3 e6 12 ♗xd4 ♘b6 13 ♕b3! cxd4 14 ♘a4! ♘xa4 15 ♕xb7 ♕d5 16 ♕xf7+ ♔d8 17 ♖fe1 (Black's extra piece is nowhere near enough to make up for his dreadful king position) 17...♘c5 (17...♗c5? led to an even quicker defeat after 18 c4! ♕d6 19 ♕b7 1-0, O.Korneev-G.Rojo Huerta, Corunha 2000) 18 ♖ad1 ♔c8 19 c3 d3 20 b4 d2 21 ♖e2 ♘d7 22 ♘f3 1-0 K.Thorsteins-Cu.Hansen, Reykjavik 1985.

10 ♕xd4 fxe5 11 ♕xe5

White has regained his pawn to reach a position with a better structure and safer king – a pleasing outcome after just eleven moves.

11...♕d6 12 ♕e2 0-0-0 13 ♘a3!

This excellent move forces Black to worry about possible knight developments to c4 and b5. White also strengthens the potential threat of ♖d1, which can no longer be met by any ...♘f4 trickery.

13...♕c6 14 ♘b5 ♕b6 15 ♖d1 a6 16 c4!

White continues to play energetically, creating plenty of problems before his opponent manages to catch up on development.

16...axb5

16...♘f6 is met by the simple 17 ♖xd8+ ♔xd8 18 ♗e3.

17 cxd5

17 ♖xd5 bxc4 18 ♖xd8+ ♔xd8 19 ♕xc4 also looks strong.

17...e6?!

This allows White to obtain a powerful passed pawn.

The only chance to prolong the game was 17...e5! 18 a4! (after 18 ♕xe5 ♗c5 Black is a pawn down, but he can complete his development and create some counterplay against f2) 18...b4 19 a5 ♕a6 (Black needs to block the a-pawn) 20 ♕xe5 when White's extra pawn makes him the strong favourite to win the game, but Black can still resist for a while.

18 ♗e3 ♕a6 19 dxe6 ♖e8

No better is 19...♗d6 20 ♕g4.

20 ♖ac1! ♖xe6 21 ♕g4!

White has returned the extra pawn in order to complete development and secure a deadly pin along the h3-c8 diagonal.

21...h5 22 ♕f5 ♗e7

22...g6 loses to 23 ♕d5 (23 ♕f7 is also good enough) 23...♕d6 (or 23...♖d6 24 ♕e5) 24 ♕xb5, winning easily in a few more moves.

23 ♗f4 ♔b8 24 ♖xc7 ♔a8 25 ♖dc1 ♔a7?

Losing instantly, although the position was hopeless in any case.

26 ♖xe7 1-0

In view of 26...♖xe7 27 ♕c5+.

In the next game, the last of this section, we will consider Black's 5th-move alternatives after 4...♗g4 5 ♗e2. The following encounter should not be taken too seriously, as the winner was rated 1922 and the loser just 1566 at the time. However, it still provides a spectacular example of how quickly things can go wrong for Black after just a small slip-up in the opening.

Game 48
M.Brenco-M.Menichini
Genoa 2007

1 e4 ♞f6 2 e5 ♞d5 3 d4 d6 4 ♞f3 ♝g4 5 ♝e2

5...dxe5?!

As we will see, there are good reasons why this exchange usually takes place one move earlier, if Black plays it at all. Here are a few other minor options:

a) 5...♞b6 6 h3 (6 0-0 is also fine) 6...♝xf3 7 ♝xf3 ♞c6 was seen in J.Olsar-V.Pacl, Czech League 1995, and here the simplest route to a white advantage looks to be 8 ♝xc6+ bxc6 9 ♞d2 when Black's weak queenside structure will be a long-term problem.

b) 5...g6 allows White to choose between a few attractive continuations: 6 ♞g5!? (6 h3 ♝xf3 7 ♝xf3 should also suffice for an edge) 6...♝xe2 7 ♛xe2 dxe5?! (safer is 7...e6, although after 8 c4 ♞b6 9 ♛f3! ♛d7 10 ♞e4 ♝e7 11 exd6 cxd6 12 ♞f6+ ♝xf6 13 ♛xf6

Black's dark squares were a source of concern in M.Mrdja-B.Joguet, Le Touquet 2001) 8 ♛f3! ♞f6 (8...f6? loses a piece after 9 ♞e6 ♛d6 10 ♛xd5, as in E.Varnusz-A.Ponyi, Salgotarjan 1978) 9 dxe5 h6 10 ♞xf7 ♚xf7 11 exf6 exf6 12 ♛xb7. White had an extra pawn and the better position in V.Jansa-A.Haik, Kladovo 1980.

6 ♞xe5 ♝xe2 7 ♛xe2

Compared with the quite respectable variation 4...dxe5 5 ♞xe5, Black's position is already precarious.

7...♞d7?

Losing immediately. Only the second of the following alternatives could have given Black the slightest chance of reaching an acceptable position:

a) 7...e6?! just loses a pawn after 8 ♛b5+ ♞d7 9 ♛xb7 ♞xe5 10 dxe5 ♝e7 11 ♛c6+ ♚f8 12 0-0, as seen in E.Koster-D.McFay, East Lansing 1982.

b) The best chance was 7...c6, although White can still create problems with 8 ♛f3! ♞f6 9 ♛b3 and now:

b1) 9...e6 10 ♛xb7 ♛xd4 was played in M.Grishin-M.Gush, Serpukhov 2001, and here the most accurate continuation would have been 11 ♕c8+ ♔e7 12 ♕b7!+ (repeating the position, but eliminating any possibility of Black castling) 12...♔e8 13 ♘d3 ♕e4+ 14 ♗e3 c5 15 ♕c8+ ♔e7 16 0-0 and White should win this position.

b2) 9...♕xd4 occurred in N.Dragun-K.Mickeleit, Weymouth 1968, and now the easiest route to victory would have been 10 ♘xf7! ♖g8 11 ♕xb7 ♕e4+ 12 ♗e3 c5 13 ♕xe4 ♘xe4 14 ♘e5, with an extra pawn plus a huge positional advantage for White in the endgame.

8 ♘xf7!

In the notes to Game 43, after 4...dxe5 5 ♘xe5 ♘d7, I cautioned the reader against the notorious 6 ♘xf7 sacrifice. The present version of the sacrifice leads to an identical position except for the removal of both light-squared bishops, which is enough to change the evaluation from 'somewhat promising, but unclear and generally impractical' to 'leads to a winning position by force'!

8...♔xf7 9 ♕h5+ ♔e6

9...g6 10 ♕xd5+ handed White a material advantage on top of his attack in J.Dos Santos-J.Rodrigues Neto, Idaial 2004.

10 c4

10...♘5f6

10...♘b4 led to another massacre in the following game: 11 d5+ ♔d6 12 0-0 (12 ♗f4+ e5 13 dxe6+ ♔xe6 14 0-0 g6 15 ♕h3+ ♔f7 16 ♖d1 is also good enough) 12...♘c5 (12...♘f6 13 ♕f5 ♕c8 14 ♗f4+ e5 15 dxe6+ ♔e7 16 ♘c3 is winning for White) 13 ♗e3 ♕e8 14 ♕f5 e5 (14...♘bd3 15 b4) 15 dxe6 ♔c6 16 ♗xc5 ♗xc5 17 a3 ♘a6 18 b4 1-0 W.Weiler-V.Markic, correspondence 2000.

11 d5+ ♔d6 12 ♕f5!

Here is where Black really misses his light-squared bishop. There is simply no satisfactory defence against the numerous threats.

12...♔c5?

Black tries a desperate and rather comical attempt to escape with his king.

According to the computer his only

chance to prolong the game was 12...c6 13 ♗f4+ e5 14 dxe6+ ♔e7 15 exd7 ♕xd7, with some vague hopes of scraping a draw in the endgame a pawn down.

13 ♗e3+ ♔b4

13...♔xc4 14 ♘a3+ ♔b4 15 ♕d3 also leads to imminent mate.

14 ♕d3 1-0

That concludes our coverage of 4...♗g4. The remainder of the chapter will mainly be devoted to Black's 4th-move alternatives, although the final game will cover a few rare options on move 2.

Part 3 – Other lines

Game 49
P.Schneider-T.Nonnenmacher
Correspondence 1996

1 e4 ♘f6 2 e5 ♘d5 3 d4 d6 4 ♘f3 g6

This is the last of Black's big three lines.

5 ♗c4

This is almost universally recognized as White's most promising reaction, although later on he will have to choose between a few contrasting ways of handling the position.

5...♘b6

The less common but still quite respectable 5...c6 will be considered in the next game.

6 ♗b3 ♗g7

This natural move is the main line, although a few other moves have been seen from time to time:

a) 6...♗g4?? 7 ♗xf7+ would be embarrassing.

b) 6...d5 leaves Black passively placed after 7 h3 ♗g7 8 0-0 0-0 9 ♖e1 intending c3, ♗f4, and so on, with a slight but stable advantage.

c) This leaves 6...♘c6 as the only serious alternative worth considering, but here Black faces problems after 7 exd6:

c1) 7...♕xd6 fails to equalize: for instance, 8 0-0 ♗g7 9 c3 0-0 10 ♘bd2 ♗f5 11 ♖e1 ♖ae8 12 ♘e4 ♗xe4 13 ♖xe4 e5 14 ♕e2 ♘d7 15 ♗f4 ♖e7 and now in

J.Pribyl-L.Neckar, Czech League 2001, White could have posed his opponent awkward problems by means of 16 ♗g3! with the troublesome threat of ♖d1.

c2) 7...cxd6 8 d5 when Black has two sensible options:

c21) 8...♘e5 9 ♘xe5 dxe5 10 0-0 ♗g7 11 c4! (11 a4 has been played more frequently, but the black knight is misplaced on b6 so I see no reason to drive it to a better square) 11...♘d7 12 ♘c3 0-0 13 ♗e3 b6 (13...f5 14 f3 prevents all counterplay) 14 ♗a4 ♗a6 was G.Feher-P.Kindl, Zalaegerszeg 1993. Here the simple 15 b3 would have given White a pleasant edge.

c22) 8...♘a5 9 ♕d4! (the subsequent disruption to Black's development is more relevant than the loss of White's bishop pair) 9...f6 (9...♖g8 10 0-0 ♗d7 11 ♖e1 ♕c7 was seen in M.Golubev-S.Vanderwaeren, Leuven 2003, and here White should have played 12 ♘c3 as 12...♗g7 13 ♕h4 is strong) 10 ♗d2! (forcing an immediate exchange on b3 and thus activating the rook on a1)

10...♘xb3 11 axb3 ♗g7 12 ♗a5! (White makes full use of the newly opened queenside) 12...♗f5 (12...♗d7 13 ♗xb6 axb6 14 ♖xa8 ♕xa8 15 ♕xb6 left Black without any real compensation for the missing pawn in A.Volzhin-N.Davies, Dhaka 2001) 13 c4 0-0 14 0-0 ♕c8 15 ♖e1 and White had an obvious positional advantage in R.Ponomariov-V.Pesotsky, Kiev 1997.

Returning to 6...♗g7:

7 exd6!?

In the majority of games White has maintained the pawn on e5 in order to preserve a space advantage and restrict the g7-bishop. The text move may appear timid, but in reality it is deceptively dangerous and has been favoured by Anand.

7...cxd6

Instead 7...exd6 8 ♗g5 is awkward.

7...♕xd6 is almost never played. One game continued 8 0-0 ♗e6 and now in S.Vajda-A.Sasu Ducsoara, Calarasi 1995, instead of taking on e6 I propose 9 ♘c3! or 9 ♘bd2!, encouraging Black to capture on b3, after which the open a-file will add to the defender's worries.

8 0-0 0-0 9 ♖e1

In principle, Black's extra central pawn gives him the makings of a good position and if he were able to play ...e5 without coming to any harm, he could easily aspire to an advantage. Fortunately for us, this is easier said than done.

9...♗g4

Black is aiming for active play in the centre and is willing to part with a bishop in order to make it happen.

The alternative is 9...♘c6 10 c3 with two main lines:

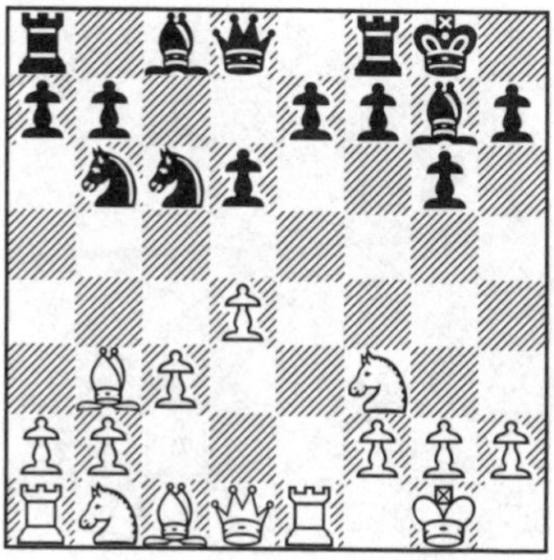

a) 10...♗g4 11 h3 ♗xf3 12 ♕xf3 transposes to the main game.

b) After 10...♗f5 11 ♗g5 White benefits from slightly the easier development and will gradually try to develop an initiative on the kingside. Here is one recent example showing how the game may develop: 11...d5 (this was not forced, but Black obviously wanted to restrict the bishop on b3 while also preventing any d4-d5 ideas) 12 ♘bd2 ♕d7 13 ♘f1 ♖fe8 14 ♘g3 ♗e6 15 ♕e2 ♘c4 16 ♖ad1 b5 17 ♗c1 ♗g4 (presumably Black was concerned about ♘g5 and preferred not to weaken her kingside with 17...h6) 18 h3 ♗xf3 19 ♕xf3 a5 20 ♘f1 e6 21 a3 ♘e7 22 ♘h2 ♘f5 23 ♘g4 f6 24 ♗c2 ♘cd6 25 ♗f4 ♘f7 26 ♕e2 ♘5d6 27 h4 ♖a7 28 h5 and after obtaining the advantage of the two bishops, White had managed to build up some kingside pressure in N.Kosintseva-Pham Le Thao, Ningbo 2009.

c) 10...e5 has seldom been played, but is possibly the most critical continuation. It is worth considering two replies for White:

c1) Khalifman recommends 11 ♗g5 ♕c7 12 ♘a3, but now after 12...a6!, as played in J.Remicio Duque-O.Villa, Cali 2007, I do not see anything special for White. Black's 12th move is a significant improvement over the previously played 12...♗g4 13 h3 (13 dxe5!? intending ♘b5 also looks interesting) 13...♗xf3 14 ♕xf3 exd4 15 ♘b5 ♕d7 16 ♘xd4 ♘xd4 17 cxd4 when White kept a slight plus in H.Vetter-Ziegler, German League 1984.

c2) In view of the above, I propose the following solution: 11 dxe5! dxe5 12 ♕xd8 ♖xd8 13 ♗g5 ♖e8 14 ♘bd2 ♗e6 15 ♘e4 ♗xb3 16 axb3 f5. This position was reached in L.Cesarini-N.Verrascina, Ostia 1996, and here White should have played 17 ♘d6 ♖eb8 18 ♖ed1 e4 19 ♘e1 when he keeps the better chances. Black has made some progress in the centre, but he is less than comfortable on the queenside.

10 h3

Another possible move order is 10 c3 ♘c6 11 h3 ♗xf3 12 ♕xf3, transposing to the game.

10...♗xf3 11 ♕xf3 ♘c6 12 c3

12...e5

In one game Black switched plans with 12...d5, but must soon have been regretting his decision: 13 ♗f4 f6?! (the start of a dubious plan; Black is playing far too optimistically, thinking he can seize the initiative in the centre having just relinquished the bishop pair) 14 ♗g3 e5 15 dxe5 fxe5 16 ♕g4 ♔h8 17 ♘a3 and with ♖ad1 on the way, Black was under heavy pressure and he soon collapsed in G.Kuzmin-E.Solozhenkin, St Petersburg 1997.

13 dxe5 dxe5 14 ♗e3 ♕c7

Alternatives also fail to equalize:

a) 14...♘a5? occurred in D.Marholev-P.Legrand, Le Touquet 2003, and now White could have won material immediately: 15 ♗c5! when the pressure against f7 forces Black to play 15...♘xb3 16 axb3 ♖e8, but now 17 ♕xb7 simply wins a pawn for no compensation whatsoever.

b) 14...♕e7 15 ♘d2 (15 ♗xb6!? axb6 16 ♘a3 was possible, with a slight but definite edge) 15...♘a5 16 ♗c2 ♘bc4 17 ♘xc4 ♘xc4 18 ♗c1. This retreat was only temporary and White retained a classical advantage with the bishop pair in an open position, A.Smith-S.Nilsson, Ballerup 2008.

15 ♘a3!

15 ♘d2 should also suffice for an edge, but the text move poses Black more concrete problems.

15...a6

This seems bit slow.

More challenging was 15...♘a5, although White still keeps an edge as follows: 16 ♘b5! (White can also base his strategy on the bishop pair with 16 ♗c2 ♘ac4 17 ♘xc4 ♘xc4 18 ♗c1, with a slight edge, but I prefer the more dynamic approach) 16...♕d7 17 ♕e2 a6 (this looks more or less forced, with ♖ad1 on the way and ♘xa7 tricks also in the air) 18 ♖ad1! (leading by force to a superior endgame) 18...♕xb5 19 ♕xb5 axb5 20 ♗xb6. Now Black must make a difficult choice between 20...♘xb3 21 axb3 ♖a2 22 ♖e2 and 20...♘c4 21 ♗xc4 bxc4 22 a3, both of which result in an unpleasant defensive struggle for him.

16 ♗c5!

Exploiting Black's temporary lack of coordination.

16...♘e7

Black cannot move the rook, as the reply 17 ♗xb6 would draw the queen away from the defence of f7.

17 ♗b4!

The configuration of White's queenside pieces is as effective as it is unorthodox.

17...♔h8?!

This looks too slow, although the position was probably already untenable. For instance, the more resilient 17...♘bc8 could be met by 18 ♘c4 a5 19 ♗xa5! ♖xa5 20 ♘xa5 ♕xa5 21 ♕xb7 when the three queenside pawns should ensure White of victory.

18 ♖ad1 ♘bc8

Not a nice move to make, but Black had to do something about the threat of ♗d6.

19 ♗a4!

Just a few moves out of the opening, the game is already over as Black has no good defence against ♖d7.

19...♖b8

The queen sacrifice 19...a5 20 ♖d7 ♕xd7 21 ♗xd7 axb4 22 cxb4 is also hopeless.

20 ♖d7

Winning a piece. The rest can pass without comment.

20...♕b6 21 ♗xe7 ♘xe7 22 ♖xe7 ♕xb2 23 ♘c4 ♕xa2 24 ♘b6 1-0

Game 50
S.Tiviakov-N.De Firmian
Gjovik 2009

1 e4 ♘f6 2 e5 ♘d5 3 d4 d6 4 ♘f3 g6 5 ♗c4 c6

This time Black does not wish to retreat the knight from the centre.

5...dxe5?! is not really a serious option, as after the natural sequence of 6 dxe5 c6 7 ♘c3 ♗e6 (not 7...♘xc3?? 8 ♗xf7+) 8 ♘g5 ♗g7 9 ♘xe6 fxe6 10 ♕g4 ♘xc3 11 bxc3 ♘d7 12 f4 White was clearly better in W.Browne-B.Sperling, Fairfax 1976.

6 0-0

6 exd6 ♕xd6 7 0-0 ♗g7 is an equally valid move order.

6...♗g7 7 exd6

Once again I have no qualms about

exchanging the advanced e-pawn, as White enjoys a pleasant edge in the resulting position.

7...♕xd6

7...exd6?! is never played, as after 8 ♗xd5 cxd5 Black's d-pawns are too weak.

8 h3

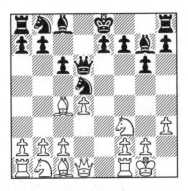

Tiviakov immediately prevents his opponent from exchanging the c8-bishop, which can become something of a problem piece for Black.

8...0-0 9 ♘bd2 ♘d7 10 ♗b3 ♘7f6

Not long after this encounter, Tiviakov won another nice game against a high-ranking opponent. On that occasion Black varied with 10...b6, but once again failed to equalize: 11 ♘e4 ♕c7 12 ♗g5 ♘7f6 13 ♖e1 ♗a6 14 ♕d2 ♖ad8 15 ♘xf6+ exf6!? (other recaptures would leave White with a slight but persistent edge, so Black puts his faith in the dynamic approach) 16 ♗h4 ♘e7 17 ♗g3 ♕b7 18 c3 ♘f5 19 ♗f4 c5 20 ♗c2! ♘d6 21 dxc5 ♘c4 22 ♕c1 bxc5 23 b3 ♘d6 24 c4 and White had skilfully defused his opponent's counterplay to reach a stra-

tegically winning position, S.Tiviakov-R.Vaganian, Moscow 2009.

11 ♘c4 ♕c7 12 ♘ce5 ♗f5

In his annotations Tiviakov mentioned 12...b5!?, securing the future of the knight on d5 at the expense of some potential long-term weaknesses. In that case White should continue with something like 13 c3, intending ♖e1, ♗g5, and so on, keeping a slight advantage as is typical for such positions.

13 c4!

White takes the opportunity to gain some space and drive the knight to a passive square.

13...♘b6 14 ♗f4 ♕d8 15 ♕e2 ♘fd7 16 ♖ad1 ♘xe5 17 ♘xe5

17 dxe5 ♕c8 keeps White's advantage within manageable boundaries. Tiviakov considers it more important to keep a piece outpost on e5 and I think he is correct.

17...a5

Aiming for some queenside counterplay.

17...♘d7 is inadequate due to 18

g4!? (even if this forceful move did not work, White could still keep a pleasant edge with the quiet 18 ♘f3) 18...♘xe5 (or 18...♗e6 19 d5 ♘xe5 20 dxe6 ♕a5 21 ♖fe1) 19 dxe5 ♗d7 20 e6 fxe6 21 c5 ♖xf4 22 ♖xd7 when White keeps a clear advantage according to Tiviakov.

18 g4!

Tiviakov points out that 18 a3 could be met by 18...♘d7!. Compared with the previous note, the inclusion of the pawn moves ...a7-a5 and a2-a3 helps Black after 19 g4 ♘xe5 20 dxe5 ♕b6! when the defender is only marginally worse.

18...♗c8

Black decides to keep the bishop well out of harm's way.

18...♗e6 was possible, although White keeps a sizeable advantage after 19 a4, as pointed out by Tiviakov.

19 ♖fe1

White could have improved slightly with 19 a4! in order to keep his bishop on the a2-g8 diagonal.

19...a4 20 ♗c2 e6

Black should have taken the opportunity to play 20...♗e6! when White would at least have had to pay attention to the weak c4-pawn. After the passive game continuation he is able to build up the initiative at his leisure.

21 ♗g3 ♘d7 22 h4

By this stage White is not worried about his knight being exchanged, as the reply dxe5 will leave Black with a rotten light-squared bishop and a gaping hole on d6.

22...♕b6 23 ♗b1 ♘f6 24 h5 c5

Black has to do something before he gets smashed on the kingside.

25 dxc5 ♕xc5 26 ♕f3!

Apart from the minor inaccuracy on move 19, the present game is a model demonstration of how one may convert a normal-looking 'plus-equals' position into a serious advantage. With the text move White prepares ♗h4, driving another enemy piece to a passive position.

26...♖a6

The c8-bishop cannot move, so Black has to resort to a more exotic method of activating his rook.

27 ♗h4 ♘e8 28 ♘d7!

The bishop may have been passive on c8, but its exchange will open up the seventh rank to the eager white rook.

28...♗xd7 29 ♖xd7 ♕xc4

29...g5 30 ♗g3 ♗xb2 is refuted beautifully by means of 31 ♗xh7+! (even stronger than 31 ♖xb7 as mentioned by Tiviakov) 31...♔xh7 (31...♔g7 does not help due to 32 h6+!) 32 ♖xf7+

when Black has three different ways to lose:

a) 32...♔g8 is refuted by 33 ♖xf8+ ♕xf8 34 ♕xb7, forking the rook on a6 and bishop on b2.

b) 32...♖xf7 33 ♕xf7+ ♘g7 (33...♔g7 34 ♕xe8) 34 h6! wins, as 34...♔xh6 35 ♔g2 is the end.

c) 32...♔g7 33 ♖xf8 ♕xf8 (33...♔xf8 34 ♕xb7+) 34 ♕xb7 ♖a5.

In this position the computer's top choice is 35 ♖xe6, but I cannot resist mentioning the following alternative winning line: 35 h6 ♔xh6 36 ♕h1+! ♔g6 37 ♕e4+ ♔h6 (37...♔f7 38 ♕xe6 mate) 38 ♔g2 ♗b2 39 ♖h1+ ♔g7 40 ♕h7+ ♔f6 41 ♖h6+ and Black must give up the queen.

30 ♗e7

White 'cashes in' his initiative for an extra exchange, which should be enough to decide the game.

30...♕c6

Tiviakov points out that 30...♘f6 31 ♖xb7 ♕xg4+ 32 ♕xg4 ♘xg4 33 ♗xf8 is just another way for Black to reach a hopeless endgame.

31 ♕xc6 bxc6 32 g5!?

White could also have defended the b-pawn with 32 ♖b7, but Tiviakov instead aims to restrict Black's kingside pieces.

32...♗xb2 33 ♖e3 ♘g7?

Somewhat more challenging would have been 33...♖a5, although White still keeps a decisive advantage after 34 ♖f3 or 34 ♗e4!?, as pointed out by Tiviakov.

34 ♗xf8 ♔xf8 35 h6

The advanced h-pawn, combined with White's extra exchange and active rooks, makes the win a formality.

35...♘f5

35...♘e8 36 ♖f3 is the end.

36 ♗xf5 gxf5 37 ♖ed3 ♖a8 38 ♖b7 ♗c1 39 ♖dd7 ♗xg5 1-0

According to the game score, Black resigned here without waiting for 40 ♖xf7+.

Overall it seems to me that White has good chances for an edge against 4...g6. We will now turn our attention to something more combative.

Game 51
B.Macieja-I.Chigladze
Athens 2007

1 e4 ♘f6 2 e5 ♘d5 3 d4 d6 4 ♘f3 ♘c6!?

This provocative move remains somewhat controversial, a bit like the 4...dxe5 5 ♘xe5 ♘d7 line from Game 43. Once again White can choose between a critical attempt at refutation and a far less theoretically intensive line, aiming for a positional advantage.

5 ♗b5!?

Just as before, I have chosen to recommend what I consider the more pragmatic choice.

5 c4 ♘b6 6 e6 fxe6 is the sharp approach. The theory extends to some twenty-plus moves in several branches, and you can bet your bottom dollar that anyone playing this line with Black will have prepared for this in some detail. The text move has not been played anything like as often, but I consider it a legitimate try for an advantage.

5...a6

Black can avoid doubled pawns with 5...♗d7, but this fails to equalize after 6 c4 ♘b6 7 ♘c3, for instance:

a) 7...♘a5?! 8 ♗xd7+ ♕xd7 9 b3 0-0-0 10 0-0 f6 was F.Zimmermann-F.Eberhardt, St Ingbert 1987, and here White should have played 11 exd6 exd6 12 d5 with a huge advantage.

b) A better attempt is 7...a6 8 ♗xc6 bxc6 (after 8...♗xc6?! 9 d5 ♗d7 10 ♕d4 Black is already in danger of being smothered) 9 b3 when the position resembles the main game, except that Black's bishop has voluntarily moved to the passive d7-square.

6 ♗xc6+ bxc6 7 h3

I think it is worth investing a tempo to prevent ...♗g4. Now Black may have problems finding a useful role for his light-squared bishop.

7...g6

The fianchetto development looks sensible. Black hopes to exert pressure against the enemy centre and, in an ideal world, execute the undermining move ...c6-c5, solving the problem of his pawn weakness as well as liberating the light-squared bishop.

The alternative was 7...♗f5 8 0-0 (8 ♘h4!?) 8...e6, as played in P.German-C.Paglilla, Acasusso 1994, and now White could have kept a pleasant edge with 9 c4 ♘b6 10 b3 or 10 ♗g5!?.

8 0-0 ♗g7 9 c4 ♘b6 10 b3 a5

Alternatively 10...0-0 11 ♖e1 h6 occurred in D.Pribeanu-A.Smarandoiu, Eforie Nord 2009, and here the straightforward 12 ♘c3 gives White a fine position.

11 a4

This rather double-edged move fixes the a5-pawn as a weakness, but also leaves b3 as a target.

I would have been tempted to consider 11 ♘c3!? a4 12 ♗e3, allowing Black to exchange off one weakness, but still leaving the problem c-pawns on the board. Meanwhile White has accelerated his development and intends to exchange the dark-squared bishops with ♕d2 and ♗h6, which will rob the black position of much of its dynamic potential. Overall I slightly prefer this over the game continuation, so 11 ♘c3 would be my recommendation in the event that you reach the same position over the board.

11...dxe5!?

Black could have developed patiently, but instead decides to force an immediate change in the position.

In the event of 11...0-0 White should strengthen his position with 12 ♖e1.

12 dxe5

12 ♘xe5 c5! was Black's idea.

12...♕xd1 13 ♖xd1 ♘d7!

Black wastes no time improving his worst piece.

14 ♗f4 ♘c5 15 ♘d4 ♘e6

15...♖a6!? was worth considering.

16 ♘xe6 ♗xe6 17 ♘d2 ♖b8 18 ♘f3 0-0

After 18...♖xb3 19 ♘d4 ♖b6 20 c5 ♖b4? 21 ♘xc6 the bishop is untouchable due to mate on d8.

19 ♘d4

I also analysed 19 ♗d2!? ♖xb3 20 ♘d4 ♖d3 21 ♘xc6 ♖a8 (21...♗xc4 22 ♗xa5) 22 ♘xe7+ ♔f8 23 ♘d5 ♗xd5 (if 23...♗xe5 24 ♗h6+ ♔g8 25 ♖xd3 ♗xa1 26 ♗f4) 24 cxd5 ♗xe5 25 ♗h6+ ♔e7 26 ♖xd3 ♗xa1 when White is marginally better, but Black should hold without too many problems.

19...c5 20 ♘xe6 fxe6 21 ♗h2 ♖xb3 22 ♖d7

Despite his nominal material advantage, Black is under some pressure as his pawns are weak and his bishop is restricted.

22...♖fb8 23 ♖e1

After 23 ♔f1 ♖b1+ 24 ♖xb1 ♖xb1+ 25 ♔e2 ♖b2+ Black should be okay.

23...✿f7 24 ♖xc7 ♖8b4 25 ♖xc5 ♖xa4 26 ♗f4 ♖c3

26...♖a2! looks more accurate. In any case, I suspect that Black should hold the endgame, but I do not want to get too side-tracked so I will keep the analysis to a minimum from here.

27 ♖e4 ♖a1+ 28 ✿h2 a4 29 ♗e3 ♖d3 30 ♖c8 g5

Forced, as otherwise ♖f4+ would be devastating.

31 ♗xg5 a3 32 ♖a8

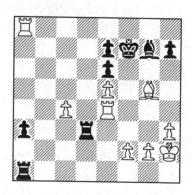

32...♖c3

32...h6! 33 ♗e3 ✿g6 would have prevented the idea in the next note.

33 ♖a7

Best was 33 ♖f4+! ✿g6 34 ♗xe7 h5 (Black has to prevent ♖g4+) 35 ♗d6 a2 36 ♖a7 ♖c2 37 ♖ff7 ♗h8 38 ♖f8 ♖e1 39 ♖g8+ ✿f5 40 ♖xh8 a1♕ 41 ♖xa1 ♖xa1 42 ✿g3 ♖xc4 43 ♖xh5+ ✿g6 44 ♖h8 with excellent winning chances.

33...✿g6 34 ♗f4 ♖c2 35 ♗e3 a2 36 ♖g4+ ✿f7 37 ♖f4+ ✿e8?!

Black could have secured a draw with 37...✿g6. He may have been afraid of 38 ♖a6 (38 ♖g4+ repeats the posi-

tion), but after 38...♗xe5 39 ♖xe6+ ♗f6 40 ♗d4 ♖d1 41 ♗xf6 exf6 42 ♖exf6+ ✿g7 43 ♖f7+ ✿g8! 44 ♖f8+ ✿g7 White must take a perpetual.

38 ♖a8+ ✿d7 39 ♖d4+ ✿c6 40 ♖a6+ ✿c7

40...✿b7 41 ♖d7+! wins nicely.

41 ♖a7+ ✿c8 42 ♖g4 ♗xe5+ 43 g3 ♗c7 44 ♖g8+ ✿d7 45 ♖ga8 e5 46 c5 h5 47 ✿g2 e4 48 ♗f4 ♖xc5 49 ♗xc7 ♖xc7 50 ♖xa2

I am not sure if this endgame is technically a win for White or a draw, but in the game the problems were too much for the defender.

50...♖d1

50...♖xa2 51 ♖xa2 ✿e6 may have been a better chance to hold.

51 ♖e2 ♖c4 52 ♖a5 h4 53 g4 ♖cc1 54 ♖xe4 ♖g1+ 55 ✿f3 ♖c3+ 56 ✿f4 ♖f1 57 ♖e2 ✿d6?

57...♖xh3 was the last chance.

58 ♖a6+ ✿d5 59 ♖e5+ ✿c4

59...✿d4 60 ♖a4+ ✿d3 61 ♖e3+ ✿d2 62 ♖a2+ ♖c2 63 ♖xc2+ ✿xc2 64 ✿f3 is also hopeless for Black.

60 ♖c6+ ✿b4 61 ♖xc3 ✿xc3 62 ✿f3 1-0

In the final two games of the chapter we will consider some rare sidelines. The following game will deal with some of the deviations which may occur on the fourth move.

Game 52
A.Heinz-N.To
Budapest 2009

1 e4 ♘f6 2 e5 ♘d5 3 d4 d6

Black almost never plays anything else here, and I do consider it worthwhile to delve into any exotic alternatives as in most cases White can just develop normally to obtain a safe advantage.

4 ♘f3

4...♘b6

This is a semi-respectable deviation. Black pre-empts any potential attacks on the knight and prepares to meet a quiet response such as 5 ♗e2 with 5...g6, angling for a fianchetto variation having avoided White's most dangerous systems involving ♗c4.

Here are a few other rare continuations:

a) 4...c6 isn't such a bad move. After 5 ♗e2 play usually continues with either 5...dxe5 6 ♘xe5, taking us back into the realm of Games 38-41, or 5...♗g4, transposing to Game 46. Instead 5...g6 6 c4 ♘c7 (if 6...♘b6 then 7 exd6 exd6 8 ♗g5! ♗e7 9 ♗h6) 7 exd6 ♕xd6 (7...exd6 is met by 8 ♗g5!) 8 ♘c3 ♗g7 9 0-0 0-0 10 ♗e3 ♗g4 11 ♕d2 ♘e6 12 ♖ad1 left White with a typical space advantage and with possibilities for d4-d5 in J.Polasek-R.Antoniewski, Czech League 2006.

b) 4...e6 is solid but passive, and after any sensible reply such as 5 ♗e2 or 5 c4 ♘b6 6 ♘c3, Black will have a hard time finding a useful role for the c8-bishop.

c) 4...♗f5 is not bad, but is less active than the normal 4...♗g4. White should be able to obtain a pleasant edge with 5 ♗d3 (5 ♗e2 is also not bad) 5...♗xd3 6 ♕xd3 ♘c6 (for 6...e6 7 0-0 ♘c6 – see variation 'b1' below) 7 0-0 with two main possibilities for Black:

c1) 7...e6 8 c4 ♘b6 9 exd6 cxd6 10 d5 (White can also play more patiently with 10 ♘c3, but the text is direct and strong) 10...♘e5 (if 10...exd5 11 cxd5 ♘e5 12 ♖e1) 11 ♘xe5 dxe5 12 ♕e4 ♕f6 13 ♘c3 ♖c8 was F.Guido-R.Gervasio, St Lorrain 1999, and here it looks good to play 14 dxe6 ♕xe6 15 ♕xb7 (15 b3!?) 15...♕xc4 16 ♗e3 ♕c6 17 ♕xc6+ ♖xc6 18 ♖ac1 when Black faces a tough endgame.

c2) 7...dxe5 8 ♘xe5 ♘xe5 9 dxe5 ♕d7 (after 9...e6? 10 ♕b5+ Black was dropping a pawn in H.Momeni-M.Yousefzadeh, Iran 1993) occurred in C.Kedziora-A.Panchenko, Essen 2000, and here I propose 10 ♖d1 e6 11 c4 ♘b6 12 ♕e2 ♕c6 13 b3 with a modest but pleasant edge for White.

5 a4!

White immediately targets the well-travelled knight.

5...a5

Practice has shown that the inclusion of the mutual a-pawn advances is more likely to benefit White, although there are a few different ways in which he can attempt to show it.

6 ♘c3!?

Usually the knight only comes to this square in the Alekhine after a preliminary c2-c4, but now that the black knight has retreated from the centre voluntarily, it looks like quite an attractive option. In certain positions the knight may even threaten to occupy the b5-square, which was slightly weakened by Black's last move.

Before moving on, I will briefly note that 6 ♗b5+ has been the most popular continuation, followed by 6...c6 7 ♗d3 or 7 ♗e2 with a slight plus to White.

Also not bad is 6 exd6!? aiming for a modest edge. The move I am recommending is more ambitious.

6...dxe5?!

This is rather risky and Black should probably prefer one of the following alternatives:

a) 6...♗g4 7 h3 ♗h5 8 e6!? fxe6 9 ♗e2 ♗xf3 10 ♗xf3 c6 11 ♕e2 and White had more than enough compensation for the pawn in L.Christiansen-L.Alburt, South Bend 1981.

b) 6...g6 has been Black's most popular choice and looks to be his safest continuation. Nevertheless, White still keeps an edge with 7 exd6 cxd6 8 ♗b5+ ♗d7 9 0-0 ♗g7 10 ♖e1 0-0 11 ♗g5, A.Sokolov-L.Krizsany, Lenk 2003.

7 ♘xe5 ♘8d7 8 ♗f4!

Not only preparing to recapture on e5 with a piece, but also hinting at a possible ♘b5.

8...c6

Preventing the aforementioned idea at the cost of an important tempo. Here are a few other possibilities:

a) 8...♘xe5 9 ♗xe5 c6 10 ♗e2 ♗f5 11 g4!? ♗g6 12 h4 h5 (perhaps Black should have considered the more solid 12...h6, although the initiative is clearly with White in any case) 13 gxh5 ♗f5 14 ♕d2 was M.Adams-S.Drazic, Koge 1997. White stands clearly better: his pieces are more active, the doubled h-pawns are not weak, and the open g-file is an important asset.

b) 8...e6 9 ♕h5! ♘xe5 (9...g6 10 ♕f3 ♗g7 11 0-0-0 0-0 12 h4! also looks troublesome for Black) 10 ♗xe5 ♗d7 11 0-0-0! ♗b4 (there is no time for 11...♘xa4? 12 ♘xa4 ♗xa4 on account of 13 d5! exd5 14 ♖e1 with a crushing initiative) 12 d5!. This powerful breakthrough gave White a serious initiative in G.Guseinov-E.Janev, Istanbul 2007.

9 ♗d3 ♘f6 10 ♕f3!

10 0-0 would have given a slight plus, but White has something altogether more aggressive in mind.

10...g6?!

The greedy 10...♕xd4? is punished by 11 0-0-0 ♕b4 12 ♘b5! ♘bd5 13 ♗c4 with a crushing attack: for instance, 13...♗e6 14 ♖xd5! ♘xd5 15 ♗xd5 and White wins.

However, Black should have played 10...♗e6 or 10...e6 to prevent the devastating blow that occurs in the game. In both cases White keeps an ominous lead in development, but there is no clear breakthrough.

11 d5!!

In one fell swoop, this lowly pawn morphs into a wrecking ball which destroys the opponent's flimsy barricades.

11...cxd5?

Still reeling from the impact of the last move, Black immediately collapses. To be fair, the alternatives were less than appealing as well:

a) 11...♘fxd5 runs into 12 ♘xf7! when Black's only defence is 12...♗g4!, but even here after 13 ♕xg4 ♔xf7 14 ♘xd5 ♘xd5 (14...♕xd5? 15 ♗e3!) 15 0-0-0 ♗g7 16 ♖he1 White has a huge initiative.

b) The best chance was 11...♘bxd5 12 ♘xd5 ♕xd5 (12...♘xd5 13 ♘xf7 ♗g4 will transpose to variation 'a' above) 13 ♗c4 ♕xf3 14 ♗xf7+ ♔d8. White has regained the sacrificed pawn and can now choose between 15 ♘xf3, with an obvious advantage in the queenless middlegame, and the even stronger 15 gxf3!, compromising the pawn structure in order to maintain the powerful position of the knight.

12 &b5+

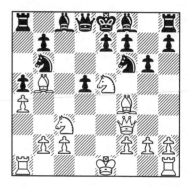

12...&bd7

12...&d7 is refuted by 13 &xd7 &bxd7 (13...&fxd7 14 &xd5 is the same) 14 &xd5 &xd5 15 ₩xd5 when the pin on the d7-knight will prove fatal.

13 &xd5 &xd5 14 ₩xd5 e6 15 ₩f3 1-0

Black resigned as he will soon lose a piece: for instance, 15...&d6 16 &xd7 &xd7 17 0-0-0 &xf4+ (or 17...&xb5 18 &xd6) 18 ₩xf4 etc.

Game 53
J.Shaw-C.Rossi
British League (4NCL) 2000

---

1 e4 &f6 2 e5

In this, the final game of the chapter, we will consider Black's unusual second moves.

2...&g8

2...&e4?! is not really a serious option and White obtains a clear advantage after 3 d3 (3 d4 is also good) 3...&c5 4 d4 &e6 5 &f3 d5 and here in

J.Fuksik-M.Manik, Prague 1995, 6 c4! looks like the strongest idea.

3 d4

3...d5

The main alternative is 3...d6 when play usually continues 4 &f3 &g4 5 h3 &h5. At this point White can put his opponent under unpleasant pressure with the thematic sacrifice 6 g4 &g6 7 e6!?, with two choices for Black:

a) 7...₩c8 8 &c4 fxe6 9 &g5 d5 10 &d3 &xd3 11 ₩xd3 gave White promising compensation in J.Klinger-S.Bücker, Buende 1985. Black will have a hard time developing his kingside pieces and White is risking very little as he should at the very least be able to regain the e6-pawn at some point.

b) 7...fxe6 was played in L.Coelho-E.Limp, Santos 2000. Here the most promising continuation looks to be 8 &c4! ₩d7 (8...d5 9 &d3 is similar to the Klinger-Bücker game mentioned above) 9 ₩e2 e5!? (if 9...d5 10 &e5 or 9...&f7 10 &g5) 10 dxe5 d5 11 e6! (11 &b5!? followed by e6 also looks interesting) 11...₩d6 12 &b3 when White keeps some initiative in this somewhat irregular position.

4 c4!?

Black's opening is not particularly impressive; think of a Caro-Kann in which he has chosen to answer the well-respected 3 e5 with the illegal but in any case far from desirable retreat of the pawn from c6 to c7. It goes without saying that White could play just about any sensible move and reach an improved version of that opening, and the text seems like one of the most energetic and principled ways of doing so.

4...♞c6

Black has tried a few other moves, but White keeps an advantage by simple means in all cases. If we come back to the Caro-Kann analogy, at least the text move makes some sense in that Black is attempting to derive some benefit from the absence of the move ...c7-c6.

5 ♗e3 ♗f5

White is also comfortably better after the more passive 5...e6 6 ♘c3 ♘ge7 7 ♘f3 as occurred in C.Goralski-K.Naumann, German League 1995.

6 cxd5

White could also have played more aggressively with 6 ♘c3 e6 7 g4!? ♗g6 8 cxd5 exd5 9 ♘h3!. The plan is ♘f4 followed by either h4, to target the bishop on g6, or ♗g2, ramping up the pressure against d5.

6...♛xd5 7 ♘c3 ♛d7 8 ♘f3 e6 9 ♗e2

Once again White could have considered playing more actively with 9 ♗b5 or 9 ♗c4, but Shaw's more modest choice also keeps an edge.

9...♘ge7 10 0-0

10...♘d5?!

This natural move is an error.

10...h6 would have better, in order to give the light-squared bishop an escape square.

Another idea was 10...0-0-0!?, although after 11 ♛a4 Black risks falling under a dangerous attack.

11 ♘h4!

The loss of the light-squared bishop will be painful for Black, as its counterpart on e2 has enormous potential.

11...♘xc3

11...♗g6 is strongly met by 12 ♘xd5, when both 12...exd5 13 ♘xg6 hxg6 14 ♗g4 and 12...♕xd5 13 ♘xg6 hxg6 14 ♗f3 look highly unpleasant for Black.

12 bxc3 ♗e4 13 f3 ♗g6 14 ♘xg6 fxg6?!

I am not sure why Black felt the need to compromise his pawn structure like this, as it is hard to imagine him utilizing the open f-file in any meaningful way.

14...hxg6 was better, although White still keeps a clear advantage in much the same way.

15 ♖b1 ♖b8 16 ♖b3

White is spoilt for choice, as 16 ♕a4 and 16 f4!? are both strong as well.

16...♘e7 17 ♕b1 b6 18 ♕e4 ♕d5 19 c4 ♕b7

Black prefers to keep the f-file closed and 19...♕xe4 20 fxe4 ♘c6 21 ♗g4 would indeed have been depressing for him.

20 ♗d3 ♘f5 21 ♗f2 ♗e7 22 ♕xb7 ♖xb7 23 g4

23...♘h4?

23...♘h6 was necessary, although Black is strategically lost in any case. The problem with the text move is that, on top of his other problems, Black's knight becomes stranded.

24 ♗e4 ♖b8 25 ♗c6+ ♔f7 26 f4! h5

Losing quickly, although Black's situation was already hopeless with d5 on the way.

27 ♗xh4 ♗xh4 28 g5

Having enticed the bishop into the jar, White closes the lid.

28...♖bd8 29 d5 ♔e7 30 ♖h3 1-0

Conclusion

Phew! We have covered a lot of material in this chapter. I was slightly taken aback when I counted the number of illustrative games I had assembled, but now that the work is over I feel happy with the results. Black has a plethora of options at his disposal in the Alekhine and it is worth playing through the games and notes carefully in order to understand the pros and cons of each one, and how White should alter his approach depending on the situation. Throughout the chapter (and the book in general) I have strived to recommend strong moves which meet the demands of the position, whether that means embarking on a sacrificial attack or attempting to squeeze the opponent in the endgame.

Chapter Six
Other Defences

This chapter is divided into two main sections.

Part 1 – Nimzowitsch Defence
1 e4 ♘c6

This is the most significant of Black's irregular defences.

2 ♘f3

Overall I find this more convenient than 2 d4, although the choice may come down to one's repertoire choices in other openings such as the French and 1 e4 e5.

2...d6

Game 58 will deal with 2...♘f6,

along with Black's other unusual second moves.

3 d4 ♘f6

The dubious 3...♗g4?! is considered in Game 57.

4 ♘c3 ♗g4

Occasionally Black steers the game towards an unusual kind of Pirc with 4...g6, for which see Game 56.

5 ♗e3

From here the main line arising after 5...e6 is the subject of Game 54, while 5...e5 will be covered in Game 55, along with Black's other 5th-move alternatives.

Part 2 – Miscellaneous Defences

1 e4 b6

Owen's Defence is the most significant of the lines considered in this section.

Instead 1...a6 2 d4 b5 is the St George, for which see Game 61.

In Game 62 we turn our attention to the g-pawn with 1...g6 (1...g5 also gets a brief mention) 2 d4 ♘f6!?.

2 d4 ♗b7 3 ♗d3 e6 4 ♘c3

I like this aggressive development, which tends to offer good attacking chances for White.

4...♘f6

The important alternative of 4...♗b4 is mentioned in the notes to Game 60.

5 ♘ge2!

From here 5...c5 6 d5! is a promising pawn sacrifice examined in Game 59, while 5...d5 6 e5 gives White a promising version of a French, as shown in Game 60.

Let us now begin with the most significant of the openings covered in the present chapter.

Part 1 – Nimzowitsch Defence

Game 54
M.Golubev-T.Markowski
Biel 1995

1 e4 ♘c6

The game actually started with the sequence 1...d6 2 d4 ♘f6 3 ♘c3 ♘c6 4 ♘f3, but I have substituted the characteristic move order for the Nimzowitsch Defence in order to lay out the various alternatives that will be covered over the course of the next few games.

2 ♘f3

The main alternative is 2 d4 when Black's main replies are 2...d5 and 2...e5. There are arguments in favour of either sequence, but the text move is the one I prefer.

2...d6

According to the database, Black plays 2...e5 in just under 30% of all games. Most 1 e4 players will feel quite at home in the resulting position and can happily proceed with their favourite Ruy Lopez, Scotch, or 3 ♗c4 system. On the other hand, fans of the King's Gambit, Vienna, and other openings after 1 e4 e5 that do not involve 2 ♘f3 will have a problem. While I would love to be able to offer an anti-Nimzowitsch repertoire that caters for everyone, unfortunately I do not see how it can be done without using an inordinate amount of space, which would hardly be appropriate for a minority opening such as this. The proposed solution is one of the strongest available and it provides excellent chances to fight for an advantage against all of Black's alternatives to 2...e5, while remaining compatible with the repertoires of the majority of 1 e4 players, who answer 1...e5 with 2 ♘f3.

If your own pet system against 1 e4 e5 does not involve the move 2 ♘f3, then I'm afraid you will just have to find your own solution. Either learn a back-up line after 1 e4 ♘c6 2 ♘f3 e5, or investigate a different option after 1 e4 ♘c6, such as 2 d4 or perhaps 2 ♘c3.

Before we move on, let me add that 2...d5 3 exd5 ♛xd5 transposes to Game 7 in Chapter One, while Black's less common second moves will be covered in Game 58.

3 d4 ♘f6

This is the most natural follow-up, developing a piece and attacking White's centre.

4 ♘c3

We have now transposed back to

Golubev-Markowski.

4...♗g4

Once again this is Black's most consistent continuation. His alternatives on both this and the previous move will form the subject of Games 56 and 57.

5 ♗e3 e6

Black has tried a number of alternatives here, which will be considered in Game 55.

6 h3

It is useful for White to force the bishop to declare its intentions immediately. The present position can be considered the main tabiya for the present game, as well as arguably the main line of the entire Nimzowitsch Defence.

6...♗h5

6...♗xf3 is less common – hardly a surprising revelation, as Black relinquishes the bishop pair while helping White's development: 7 ♕xf3 d5 (7...♗e7 8 0-0-0 0-0 was E.Vasta-L.Scalise, Mar del Plata 2002, and now after a simple move like 9 ♔b1 White clearly has the brighter prospects) 8 e5 ♘d7. We have reached an odd version of a French Defence, in which White's chances should be somewhat higher. The following game saw both sides play in a logical and consistent manner: 9 ♕g3 (9 0-0-0 is also promising) 9...g6 10 h4 ♘b4 11 0-0-0 c5 12 h5 cxd4 13 ♗xd4 ♖g8 14 hxg6 hxg6 15 ♖h7 ♕a5.

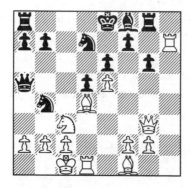

At this point in B.Socko-J.Przewoznik, Lubniewice 2005, White could have obtained a strong initiative as follows: 16 ♕f4! ♖g7 17 ♖xg7 ♗xg7 18 ♘b5! ♘xa2+ (18...♗f8 may be objectively better, although after 19 a3 ♘c6 20 ♗c3 intending ♘d6+ White keeps a

clear advantage at no material cost) 19 ♔b1 ♗f8 20 ♘d6+ ♗xd6 21 exd6 ♘b4 22 ♗c3! ♕a2+ 23 ♔c1 ♘c6 24 ♗b5 when it is doubtful that Black can withstand the attack.

7 d5!

7...exd5

Black is unlikely to benefit from omitting this move, although he does occasionally try one of the following options:

a) 7...♘e5 8 g4 can be compared with the note to Black's 8th move in our main game. Here 8...♗g6, attacking the e4-pawn, is the only serious reason Black might have to refrain from exchanging on d5 on the previous move. G.Ottolini-J.Cobb, correspondence 1997, continued 9 ♘xe5 dxe5 10 ♗b5+! (initiating a forcing sequence which highlights the drawbacks of Black's decision not to exchange on d5) 10...♘d7 11 dxe6 fxe6 12 ♗g5! ♗e7 13 ♗xe7 ♕xe7 14 ♕xd7+ ♕xd7 15 ♗xd7+ ♔xd7 and now after 16 ♔e2 White has a slight but permanent endgame advantage and can press for a win with no risk. Note that Black's bishop is severely restricted by the white pawns. The first player will solidify his pawn chain with f3 and can later manoeuvre his knight to an ideal outpost on d3, or possibly c4. Later too he can slowly look to advance his pawns on both sides of the board in order to create further weaknesses in his opponent's position.

b) 7...♘e7 should be met by 8 ♗b5+ c6 9 dxc6 when Black has two moves:

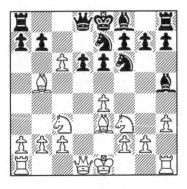

b1) 9...bxc6 10 ♗a4 ♕c7 11 ♕e2 is pleasant for White, who has scored 100% in five games from this position according to the database. Black's bishop is misplaced on h5 and would be much happier on d7 or b7.

b2) 9...♘xc6 10 e5 dxe5 11 ♕xd8+ when Black has two options, neither of which is particularly appealing:

b21) 11...♖xd8 12 ♘xe5 ♗b4!? was played in R.Felber-L.Noronha, correspondence 2001, and here the simplest route to an advantage looks to be 13 0-0 ♗xc3 (or 13...0-0 14 ♗xc6 ♗xc3 15 bxc3) 14 bxc3 0-0 15 ♗xc6 bxc6 16 c4! when the weakness of White's doubled

c-pawns is offset by his excellent control over the important queenside squares.

b22) 11...♔xd8 12 g4 ♗g6 was seen in H.Rittner-M.Zavanelli, correspondence 2004, and here White should have continued with 13 0-0-0+ ♔c7 14 ♗xc6 bxc6 15 ♘xe5. At this point Khalifman mentions the possibilities of 15...♗d6 16 ♘c4 and 15...♘d5 16 ♘xd5+ cxd5 17 c4!, both of which lead to a pleasant edge for White.

8 exd5

Now Black must decide what to do about his light-squared bishop. Usually he would prefer not to exchange it for a knight, but in the present position his bishop is liable to become a target for White's mobile kingside pawns.

8...♗xf3

This seems safest.

8...♘e5 should be met by 9 g4! when Black has two options:

a) After 9...♘xf3+ 10 ♕xf3 ♗g6 11 0-0-0 ♗e7 12 ♕g2! White's strategy is simple: advance the kingside pawns and bulldoze his opponent.

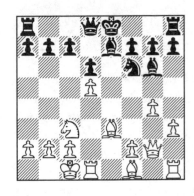

Here are a couple of practical examples:

a1) 12...h5 13 f4 ♘d7 was played in A.Dgebuadze-T.Slisser, Dieren 2002. At this point, out of several strong ideas, my preference would be for 14 ♖e1 with a big advantage.

a2) 12...♘d7 13 f4 f5 was reached in P.Kovacevic-N.Kostic, Bela Crkva 1990. Black has resorted to desperate measures to prevent the further advance of the f-pawn and in doing so he has created a huge weakness on e6. Therefore the strongest response should be 14 ♘b5! 0-0 (alternatively, 14...♗f6 15 g5 or 14...fxg4 15 ♘d4!) 15 ♘d4 ♘c5 16 ♗c4 when White is in full control and need not fear 16...fxg4 17 hxg4 ♗e4, as after 18 ♕h2! ♗xh1 19 ♖xh1 h6 20 g5 his attack should be enough to decide the game.

b) 9...♗g6 10 ♘d2! and once again White threatens to roll the f-pawn down the board.

Here are a few illustrative examples:

b1) 10...♘ed7 11 f4 ♕e7 12 ♖h2!

0-0-0 13 ♖e2 leaves Black already in serious trouble and in the following game he resorted to a desperate piece sacrifice: 13...♘xg4 14 hxg4 ♕h4+ 15 ♖f2 ♖e8 was J.Van der Veen-T.Slisser, Hoogeveen 2003, and now after 16 ♕e2 ♘f6 17 ♘f3 ♕xg4 18 0-0-0 Black has no compensation whatsoever.

b2) 10...♕e7 11 ♗g2 h5 12 g5

12...♘h7 (12...♘fd7 13 0-0 ♗f5? 14 ♘b5 ♘b6 15 ♗xb6 axb6 16 f4 was a disaster for Black in S.Kaphle-M.Gadschisade, Willingen 2007) 13 0-0 ♗f5 (13...♘d7 14 ♖e1 was nasty for Black in J.Magem Badals-A.Jerez Perez, Vendrell 1993). This position was reached in O.De la Riva Aguado-K.Spraggett, Santiago 1995, one of the few examples in which a grandmaster dared to test the black side of this variation. Spraggett eventually prevailed, but White's play can easily be improved. In the present position the simplest way of doing so is 14 ♕e2! (White can also obtain a big advantage with the computer's outlandish suggestion of 14 f4!? ♘g4 15 ♗xa7! ♖xa7 16 ♖e1) 14...0-0-0

(White was threatening to win a pawn with ♕b5+) 15 ♘b5 a6 16 ♘d4 when White has more or less completed his development and will soon play f4 with a dominant position.

Returning to the exchange on f3:

9 ♕xf3 ♘e5 10 ♕e2

10...a6

This has been the usual choice, although it is not strictly necessary to prevent ♕b5+.

10...♗e7 sees Black developing a little more quickly, although the fundamental character of the game remains more or less the same. White has the makings of a large advantage thanks to his bishop pair, extra space and the automatic plan of pushing the kingside pawns. The following is a good example of how he can increase his advantage: 11 0-0-0 0-0 12 f4 ♘ed7 13 g4 ♘c5 14 ♗d4 ♖e8 15 g5 ♗f8 16 ♕f3 ♘fe4? (this tempting move is a mistake; 16...♘fd7 was necessary, although after 17 h4 White remains firmly in control) 17 ♘xe4 ♘xe4 18 ♗b5! ♖e7 19 ♖hg1 a6 20 ♗d3 ♕e8. At

this point in M.Apicella-T.Porrasmaa, Chalkidiki 2002, the quickest route to victory would have been 21 ♗f6! ♘xf6 22 gxf6 ♖e3 23 fxg7 ♗xg7 (or 23...♖xf3 24 ♗xh7+ and mate in two) 24 ♕g4 ♕f8 25 ♕f5 ♖xd3 26 ♖xd3 when White wins, as pointed out by Mueller.

11 0-0-0 ♗e7 12 f4 ♘g6

Here is another game in which Black was swiftly annihilated: 12...♘ed7 13 g4 g6 14 h4 b5 15 ♗d4 0-0 16 h5 b4 17 hxg6! bxc3? (17...fxg6 was mandatory although White keeps a big plus after 18 ♘a4) 18 gxh7+ ♔h8 19 g5 cxb2+ 20 ♔b1 ♖e8 21 ♗h3 ♗f8 22 ♕g2 1-0 A.Hoffman-F.Fiorito, Villa Martelli 1996.

13 g4 ♘d7

It is unfortunate for Black that his knights find themselves in the path of the advancing kingside pawns, forcing him to lose additional time.

14 g5 0-0 15 h4 ♖e8 16 h5 ♘gf8

There is no time to exploit the alignment of rook and queen on the e-file: 16...♘xf4 17 ♗xf4 ♗xg5 18 ♕d2 and White is just a piece up for nothing.

17 ♕d2!

Not only sidestepping the gaze of the rook on e8, but also setting up the deadly threat of ♕d4 followed by h6.

17...c5 18 dxc6

18 h6 g6 19 ♘e4 was also extremely strong, but the text move was probably the best choice in a practical sense, as Black will be left with additional pawn weaknesses.

18...bxc6 19 h6 g6 20 ♘e4 d5 21 ♕c3 f6?

This leads to a fatal weakening of Black's kingside.

21...♘e6 was essential, although after 22 ♕xc6 White wins material while retaining his huge positional advantage.

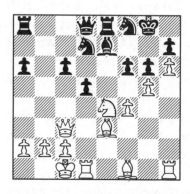

22 ♕xc6!

Golubev finishes the game with a stylish piece sacrifice.

22...dxe4 23 ♕c4+ ♔h8 24 ♕f7 ♘e6 25 ♗c4

Black is completely tied up, so there is no need to take the knight immediately.

25...♗d6!?

Black plans to trap the enemy queen, but White does not even have to prevent it.

26 ♖xd6! ♖e7 27 ♖xd7

Golubev chooses the simplest of many possible wins; one which leads to a trivial endgame.

27...♖xf7 28 ♖xd8+ ♘xd8 29 ♗xf7 ♘xf7 30 ♗d4 ♔g8 31 ♗xf6 ♘d6 32 ♖e1 1-0

Golubev's play certainly made for a powerful argument against Black's set-up. Let us see if the second player might fare any better with a different approach on move 5.

Game 55
N.Firman-A.Prihotko
Rodatychi 2006

1 e4 ♘c6 2 ♘f3 d6 3 d4 ♘f6

Once again I have taken a slight liberty with the move order, in order to emphasize what I consider to be the most accurate sequence for Black. The game continuation was 3...♗g4 4 ♗e3 ♘f6 5 ♘c3, but I believe White's most accurate response against this move order to be 4 d5!. Further details on this can be found in Game 57.

4 ♘c3 ♗g4

4...g6 is the subject of the next game.

5 ♗e3

So far the opening moves have been the same as in Golubev-Markowski. The present game will focus on Black's alternatives to 5...e6.

5...e5

This is by far the most popular of the said alternatives, although plenty of other options have been tried. Here is a summary of the most important ones:

a) It seems unnecessary to spend a whole tempo just to prevent ♗b5. After 5...a6 White should play 6 h3 with two branches:

a1) 6...♗xf3 7 ♕xf3 e5 8 d5 (8 dxe5!?) 8...♘b8 (if 8...♘d4 White replies 9 ♕d1) 9 g4 with an obvious initiative for White, A.Vajda-A.Zajarnyi, Bucharest 1996.

a2) 6...♗h5 7 d5 ♗xf3 (or 7...♘e5 8 g4 ♗g6 9 ♘d2 and with f4 coming next, Black's position was already unpleasant, S.Erendzhenov-M.Azahari, Elista Olympiad 1998) 8 ♕xf3 ♘e5. This was G.Garcia-A.Miles, Wijk aan Zee 1996, and now 9 ♕g3 intending f4 and long castling looks best.

b) 5...g6 6 h3 ♗xf3 7 ♕xf3 ♗g7 8 0-0-0 0-0

9 g4! (with two bishops and a useful space advantage, White is ideally placed to start an attack) 9...e5 10 dxe5 ♘xe5 11 ♕g2 a6 12 g5 ♘h5 13 ♗e2 f5? (this creates additional weaknesses, but Black's position was already unpleasant) 14 f4 ♘c6 15 exf5 ♖xf5 (15...♗xc3 16 ♗xh5 gxh5 17 ♕d5+ wins) 16 ♘d5 and White has a huge advantage, R.Hübner-K.Wockenfuss, German League 1986.

c) 5...d5 6 h3 ♗h5 (6...♗xf3 7 ♕xf3 e6 8 e5 transposes to the note to Black's sixth move in the previous game) 7 e5 ♘e4 was reached in Z.Hagarova-E.Danielian, Batumi 1999, and a few subsequent games. Here the most convincing route to an advantage looks to be 8 ♘xe4! (in the aforementioned game White was successful with 8 ♘e2, but the text move seems even stronger) 8...dxe4 9 g4. Now Black is clearly worse after 9...exf3 10 gxh5 ♕d5 11 c3 and 9...♗g6 10 ♘h4 e6 11 ♘xg6 hxg6 12 ♗g2 ♕d5 13 c3. In both cases White has a powerful pawn centre and a tremendous light-squared bishop, while Black must worry about defending a weak pawn in enemy territory.

Returning to 5...e5:

6 d5 ♘b8

Black hopes to achieve a harmonious set-up with the knight on d7 and bishop on e7.

6...♘e7 is possible, but Black runs the risk of his pieces becoming congested on the kingside. After 7 h3 ♗d7 (or 7...♗xf3 8 ♕xf3 when White will obtain a strong initiative with the easy plan of long castling followed by advancing the kingside pawns) 8 g4!? h6 9 ♕d2 I found three examples:

a) 9...g5?! is too committal: 10 0-0-0 ♘g6 was L.Perez Rodriguez-J.Salgado Gonzalez, Vila de Padron 2000, and here I would suggest 11 ♘e1! intending to regroup with f3 and ♘e2-g3, targeting the weak light squares.

b) 9...c6 was played in R.Jones-F.Eid, Dresden Olympiad 2008. It seems a bit too early for Black to open up the centre and this could have been highlighted by means of 10 g5! hxg5 11 dxc6! ♘xc6 12 ♘xg5 when White has

plenty of open lines along which to attack.

c) 9...♘g6 10 0-0-0 ♗e7 seems to be Black's most solid course of action and was played in M.Casella-T.Taylor, Los Angeles 2007. In this position I rather like the quiet 11 ♔b1, patiently improving the king's position and emphasizing the fact that the black king lacks a safe destination.

7 h3

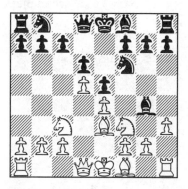

I would advise the reader to remember the following rule of thumb, which seems to be almost universally true in Nimzowitsch lines in which the black bishop comes to g4. The rule is: as soon as the centre has been stabilized, White should play h2-h3 at the first opportunity in order to force the enemy bishop to declare its intentions.

7...♗c8!?

Having induced an earlier blocking of the centre, Black decides it is worth losing time in order to keep his bishop. This idea does not equalize, but the same can be said of Black's alternatives:

a) 7...♗xf3 8 ♕xf3 ♗e7 was seen in P.Bank-S.Nielsen, Aarhus 1993, and here I think 9 0-0-0! is the most accurate move when White has an obvious initiative. (In all three of the games which I found on the database White preferred 9 g4, but this allows Black to make a favourable bishop exchange with 9...♘fd7! followed by ...♗g5 when his position is not so bad.)

b) 7...♗h5 should be met by the thematic 8 g4! ♗g6 9 ♘d2 when Black has tried two moves:

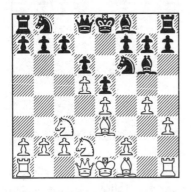

b1) 9...c6 was played in V.Nevednichy-D.Nicolescu, Romanian Team Championship 1992, and here White could have obtained a serious advantage with 10 g5!, as recommended by Khalifman. I have nothing to add to his analysis, so I will reproduce it here:

b11) 10...♘g8 11 h4 h6 12 ♕f3 hxg5 13 hxg5 ♖xh1 14 ♕xh1 ♘e7 15 dxc6 b6 16 0-0-0.

b12) 10...♗h5 11 ♗e2 ♗xe2 12 ♕xe2 ♘fd7 13 0-0-0.

b13) 10...♘h5 11 h4 h6 (11...♗e7? 12 ♗e2) 12 ♕f3 hxg5 13 hxg5 ♗e7 14 dxc6 bxc6 15 0-0-0 ♗xg5 16 ♘c4.

b14) 10...♘fd7 11 h4 h6 12 gxh6 gxh6 13 h5 ♗h7 14 ♖g1. White has a large advantage in all these variations.

b2) 9...♗e7 10 g5 ♘fd7 (the bizarre 10...♘xe4?? 11 ♘dxe4 just left Black a piece down in A.Parry-E.Van Dijk, correspondence 2003) 11 h4 f6 (White is also clearly better after 11...f5 12 h5 ♗f7 13 exf5 ♗xg5 14 ♘de4 ♗xe3 15 fxe3) 12 ♕g4 fxg5 13 hxg5 and Black was already under heavy pressure in L.Fressinet-G.Kovarcik, Montlucon 1997.

8 g4!

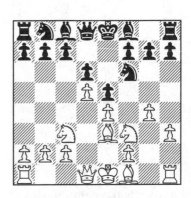

White has no reason to refrain from this thematic and energetic advance.

8...♗e7 9 g5 ♘fd7

9...♘h5? 10 ♘xe5 wins a pawn.

10 ♕d2 0-0 11 0-0-0 f5?!

Black tries to fight for space on the kingside, but only succeeds in weakening himself.

He should have preferred something like 11...a6, although White enjoys a clear head-start in the race between opposing attacks. Out of many possible moves, my personal favourite is 12 ♘h4!? when Black faces an unpleasant choice between allowing the knight into f5 and weakening his kingside with ...g6.

12 exf5

12 gxf6 would also have led to a clear advantage.

12...♖xf5 13 ♘h4!

Firman correctly decides to offer a pawn in order to maximize his initiative.

13...♖xg5

After 13...♖f8 14 ♗e2 White has a huge lead in development and will prepare to open the position with f4.

14 ♗e2

Threatening ♘e4.

14...e4

15 ♔b1?

Too slow. White could have fully justified his previous play with the energetic 15 f4! when I analysed the following lines: 15...exf3 (or 15...♖g3 16 ♘f5 ♖g6 17 ♗h5) 16 ♘xf3 ♖g2 (16...♖g6 17 ♗d3) 17 ♘e1 (17 ♖dg1

♖xg1+ 18 ♖xg1 also gives White excellent attacking chances in return for a mere pawn) 17...♖g6 (if 17...♖g5 18 ♔b1 ♖f5 19 ♗g4) 18 ♘d3 and White has a powerful initiative, with ♘f4 coming next.

15...♖e5?

15...♘b6! would have kept Black in the game.

16 f4!

White immediately makes amends for his previous inaccuracy.

16...exf3 17 ♘xf3 ♖xe3

Also after 17...♖f5 18 ♘d4 ♖f6 19 ♘e6 ♖xe6 20 dxe6 Black loses material under unfavourable circumstances and in the long run it is unlikely that he will survive.

18 ♕xe3 ♘f8 19 ♗d3

19 ♖hg1 would have been slightly more accurate, but the route chosen by White in the game is more than good enough to secure victory.

19...♘bd7 20 ♖de1 ♗f6 21 ♘e4 ♘c5

Black gives up a pawn, although I am not sure exactly what he hoped to gain in return. His position would have remained depressing after other moves as well.

22 ♘xc5 dxc5 23 ♕xc5 b6 24 ♕c4 ♕d6

24...♔h8 25 ♘e5 is horrible.

25 ♘d4

25 ♘d2! was even stronger.

25...♗b7

25...a6 would have resisted a while longer, albeit without threatening to alter the final result.

26 ♘b5 ♕d7 27 ♕xc7 ♕xc7 28 ♘xc7

White has a huge material advantage, and the remaining moves can pass without comment.

28...♖c8 29 ♘e8 ♗h4 30 ♘d6 ♖c7 31 ♖e8 ♗xd5 32 ♖f1 ♗e7 33 ♘b5 ♖b7 34 ♘c3 ♗f7 35 ♗xh7+ 1-0

Game 56
M.Kozakov-A.Zajarnyi
Lvov 1998

1 e4 ♘c6 2 ♘f3 d6 3 d4 ♘f6

Here is a summary of Black's alternatives on the third move:

a) 3...♗g4 is considered in the next

game.

b) Occasionally Black tries 3...e5 when White's most ambitious response is 4 ♗b5!, transposing to the Steinitz variation of the Ruy Lopez, which favours White. Readers wishing to learn more about this variation are invited to check out a certain chunky orange book on the subject, written by an author whose name escapes me. Of course, if White does not wish to enter Ruy Lopez territory then he can always settle for 4 dxe5, angling for a queenless position with a slight initiative.

c) Black's other main option is 3...g6 4 d5 ♘b8 (4...♘e5 5 ♘xe5 dxe5 6 ♗b5+ ♗d7 7 ♗xd7+ ♕xd7 8 c4 gave White a pleasant version of a King's Indian in H.Lehmann-A.Pomar Salamanca, Spain 1968). In this position White has a pleasant choice between 5 c4 ♗g7 6 ♗e2 ♘f6 7 ♘c3, with a favourable form of King's Indian, and 5 ♘c3 ♗g7 6 h3 ♘f6 7 ♗c4, transposing to a line of the Pirc in which White stands slightly better: for instance, 7...0-0 (or 7...c6 8 a4) 8 0-0 c6 9 a4 a5 10 ♖e1 ♘fd7 11 ♗e3 ♘a6 12 ♗d4 with an edge to White, N.Praznik-A.Beliavsky, Bled 1999.

4 ♘c3 g6

With this move Black transposes to a sideline of the Pirc. At first glance this might be seen as a problem for our repertoire, as f2-f4 is no longer possible. On the other hand, Black has committed his knight to the c6-square much sooner than he would normally do in the Pirc, which gives us some additional options.

4...e5 5 ♗b5 once again reaches a Ruy Lopez.

5 ♗b5!

White immediately highlights the problem piece in Black's position.

5...a6

This is practically forced, as after 5...♗d7?! 6 e5 dxe5 7 dxe5 ♘g4 8 ♕e2 ♗g7 9 ♗f4 a6 10 ♗c4 Black was already in trouble in A.Wojtkiewicz-H.Stenzel, Nassau 1999.

6 ♗a4!?

6 ♗xc6+ bxc6 is a good alternative, but the Ruy Lopez approach is an intriguing alternative which has seldom been tried. My database only shows eleven games with this move, so there is little established theory.

6...b5 7 ♗b3 ♗g7

7...b4 does not win a pawn, as after 8 ♘e2 ♘xe4?? 9 ♗d5 Black loses a piece.

8 h3

This may not be strictly necessary at this stage, but it is always useful to guard the g4-square in such positions.

8...0-0

8...♗b7 was Black's choice in C.Jaulneau-J.Bellec, correspondence 2007. In this case White could have tried 9 0-0!? to tempt his opponent with a pawn sacrifice, as after 9...b4 10 ♘d5 ♘xe4 11 ♕d3 (or 11 ♖e1) 11...♘f6 12 ♘xf6+ ♗xf6 13 ♗h6 White has promising compensation with the enemy king stuck in the centre.

9 0-0

9...e6

In the event of 9...b4, as in A.Bivol-Y.Voronov, Kiev 2010, White should play energetically with 10 ♘d5! ♘xd5 (10...♘xe4 11 ♖e1 ♘f6 12 ♗a4! wins material) 11 ♗xd5 ♗b7 12 a3!, fighting for the initiative on the queenside.

10 a3

Safeguarding both the e4-pawn and the b3-bishop.

10...♗b7 11 ♖e1 ♘a5 12 ♗a2 c5 13 d5 e5?!

Black opts for a Ruy Lopez set-up, but neither of his queenside minor pieces will be very happy with that!

Presumably Black did not want to concede an outpost in the centre with 13...exd5 14 ♘xd5, but in fact his position should be fine here after 14...c4 or 14...♘xd5 15 ♗xd5 ♗xd5 16 ♕xd5 ♘c4.

Objectively speaking, White should look for an earlier improvement; perhaps 6 ♗xc6+ is the way to go after all. Still, after witnessing White's fine middlegame play and fabulous winning combination, I decided to include this game even if his opening set-up was not strictly the best available.

14 b4! cxb4 15 axb4 ♕c7

After 15...♘c4 16 ♗xc4 bxc4 17 ♗e3 Black's bishop pair is not doing much, but his weak pawns are certainly relevant.

16 bxa5 ♕xc3 17 ♗d2 ♕c7

18 c4! ♘d7

18...bxc4 19 ♖c1 is also pleasant for White.

19 ♖c1 ♘c5 20 ♕e2 ♖ab8 21 cxb5 axb5 22 ♗b4 ♗a6 23 ♕e3

Another idea was 23 ♘d2 intending ♘b3, but as things turn out White must have been glad he left his knight on the kingside...

23...♖fc8 24 ♖c2 ♕e7 25 ♖ec1 ♗f8 26 ♖c3 ♔h8?

An unfortunate oversight.

26...♖c7 intending ...♖bc8 would have kept Black's disadvantage to a minimum.

27 ♘xe5!

A lovely combination.

27...♕xe5 28 ♖xc5 ♖xc5 29 ♖xc5 ♕a1+

Obviously 29...dxc5?? 30 ♗c3 is no good. The queen check seems more troublesome, but Kozakov has it all worked out.

30 ♖c1 ♕xa2 31 ♕a7!

Forking two pieces and obtaining a winning advantage.

31...♖c8

31...♖e8? 32 ♕xf7 wins immediately.

31...♖d8 would have lasted longer, but after 32 ♕xa6 White is a pawn up with a dominant position and should win comfortably.

32 ♖xc8 ♕a1+

32...♗xc8 33 ♕xf7 ♕a1+ 34 ♔h2 ♕g7 35 ♗c3! is another nice touch.

33 ♔h2 ♕e5+ 34 f4!

This final accurate move seals Black's fate. I wonder if Kozakov calculated all the way to here when contemplating his 27th move.

34...♕xf4+ 35 g3

The queen on a7 was not only forking two enemy pieces, but also monitoring the f2-square to prevent perpetual.

35...♕f3 36 ♖xf8+ ♔g7 37 ♖e8 ♕e2+ 38 ♔g1 ♕b2 39 ♗e1 1-0

An excellent performance from White, although I will have to leave it to the reader to decide whether the ♗b5-a4 plan is something to copy.

The next game features a provocative and dubious set-up from Black, which gives White the chance to offer a queen sacrifice as early as move five!

Game 57
J.Palkovi-J.Brandics
Hungarian League 1992

---

1 e4 ♘c6 2 ♘f3 d6 3 d4 ♗g4

This is the last variation that we will consider after 2...d6 3 d4.

4 d5! ♘e5?!

This is the consistent follow-up to Black's last move, but we will see that it carries great risk and is objectively dubious.

4...♘b8 is sounder, but after 5 h3 White may well be heading for an even more favourable version of note 'c' to

Black's third move in the previous game.

5 ♘xe5!

This elegant queen sacrifice effectively refutes Black's opening play.

5...♗xd1 6 ♗b5+ c6 7 dxc6 ♕a5+

The only move.

After 7...a6? 8 c7+ axb5 9 cxd8♕+ ♖xd8 10 ♘xf7 ♔xf7 11 ♔xd1 Black was a pawn down with an inferior structure in A.Rosino-F.Amrehn, Hockenheim 2007.

8 ♘c3

White is temporarily a queen for a piece down, but he has numerous threats. The bishop on d1 will soon be

captured and Black's queen is also short of squares.

8...0-0-0

Black tried 8...a6 in M.Duppel-R.Schlindwein, German League 2000, but this move can be refuted by the following recommendation of Khalifman: 9 b4! axb5 (not 9...♕xb4?? 10 cxb7+, while 9...♕xb5? 10 ♘xb5 axb5 11 cxb7 ♖b8 12 ♘c6 ♖xb7 13 ♔xd1 is winning for White – Khalifman) 10 bxa5 bxc6 11 ♘xc6 ♗xc2 12 ♘b4! ♗a4 13 ♘cd5! ♖xa5 (13...♖c8 14 ♘b6 ♖b8 15 a6! wins) 14 ♘c6 ♖a8 15 ♘c7+ ♔d7 16 ♘xa8 ♔xc6 17 ♗e3 ♘f6 18 ♖c1+ ♔b7 19 ♘b6 ♘xe4 20 ♘xa4 bxa4 21 f3 and White is winning.

9 ♘c4!

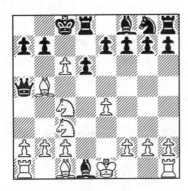

9...♕c7

There is nothing better:

a) 9...♕xc3+? 10 bxc3 ♗xc2 was played in M.Gaggiottini-S.Giurato, Gubbio 1999. At this point I would suggest 11 f3 bxc6 12 ♗xc6 ♔c7 13 ♔d2 ♔xc6 14 ♔xc2 intending ♖b1 and ♗e3, with serious threats against Black's vulnerable king.

b) 9...♕b4 was played in F.De Gleria-M.Molinaroli, German League 2000, and here White should have played 10 a3 ♕c5 11 ♗e3 ♕h5 12 ♖xd1 with a huge initiative.

10 ♘d5 ♗xc2

This is Black's best chance to reach an acceptable position, although he will still be in trouble if White plays accurately. The alternatives are considerably worse:

a) 10...♕b8? 11 c7 ♕a8 12 ♘cb6+ axb6 13 ♘xb6+ ♔xc7 14 ♘xa8+ ♖xa8 15 ♔xd1 when White has an extra pawn and a positional advantage to boot, J.Ramirez Gonzalez-M.Mingo Fernandez, Tarrega 1995.

b) 10...♗h5? 11 ♘xc7 ♔xc7 12 cxb7 ♔xb7 13 ♗e3 ♘f6 14 f3 d5 15 0-0-0 and White has a huge initiative to go with his extra pawn, Y.Boidman-F.Amrehn, Frankfurt 2008.

c) 10...bxc6? 11 ♗a6+ ♔b8 12 ♘xc7 ♗xc2 13 ♗d2! ♗xe4 was seen in J.Donaldson-F.South, Seattle 1988.

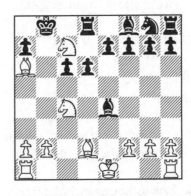

Here White could have refuted his opponent's play as follows: 14 f3! ♗f5

(if 14...♗d3 15 ♘a5) 15 ♖c1! ♔xc7
(15...♖d7 16 ♘b5! cxb5 17 ♘e3) 16
♗a5+ ♔d7 17 ♘e5+! ♔e6 18 ♗xd8
♔xe5 19 ♖xc6 and wins.

d) 10...♕xc6?! 11 ♗xc6 bxc6 12 ♘b4
c5 13 ♘c6 ♗xc2 14 ♘xd8 ♔xd8 15 f3
♗d3 16 b3 ♘f6 17 ♔d2 ♗xc4 18 bxc4
and White easily won the ending in
L.Bergez-P.Villalba, Creon 2000.

11 ♘xc7 ♔xc7 12 cxb7 ♗xe4 13 ♗e3

The material balance has more or
less been restored, but White still has
an overwhelming lead in development
and Black's king is gravely exposed.
Black may be able to grab a pawn or
two, but there is little chance that this
will save him.

13...♔xb7

Black should eliminate the dangerous pawn while he has the chance.

13...♗xg2 runs into 14 ♘a5! ♔b8
(14...♗xh1 15 ♗xa7 wins) 15 ♗c6!
when White has a huge initiative.

14 f3 ♗d5 15 ♘a5+ ♔b8

The inferior 15...♔a8? was played in
J.Friedel-M.Shibut, Philadelphia 2004.
White could have highlighted the

drawback of his opponent's last move
with 16 ♔f2, intending ♖hd1 and/or
♖ac1-c7 when Black has no good defence.

16 ♗c6?

This was White's only significant
inaccuracy of the game.

The best move was 16 ♖d1! when
Black faces an unenviable choice:

a) 16...♗a8 17 ♖d3 ♘f6 18 0-0! (intending ♖c1 and ♘c6+; 18 ♖b3 ♗d5
keeps Black alive for the moment)
18...♘d5 (or 18...♘d7 19 ♖c1 ♘b6 20
♘c6+) 19 ♖c1 ♘b6 (19...♘xe3 20 ♗c6!
wins) 20 ♘c6+ ♗xc6 21 ♗xc6 intending
a4-a5 with decisive threats.

b) 16...♘f6 17 ♗c6 e6 (17...♗e6 18
♖d4 transposes to the game having
avoided the improvement noted on
Black's 17th move) 18 ♗xd5 ♘xd5 19
♘c6+ (19 ♖xd5 is also reasonable, although after 19...exd5 20 ♘c6+ ♔c7 21
♘xd8 ♔xd8 22 ♗xa7 ♗e7 23 ♗d4 ♔d7
Black has chances to resist) 19...♔c7 20
♘xd8 ♘xe3 21 ♘xf7 ♘xd1 22 ♘xh8
♘xb2 23 ♔e2 and White should win
the endgame.

16...♗e6 17 ♖d1 ♘f6?

Black could have resisted more
stubbornly with 17...♖c8!, intending to
set up a defensive formation with the
rook on c7 and king on c8. White remains in the driving seat and is probably still winning with best play, but
considerable accuracy will be required.
After the move played, his path to victory is much more straightforward.

18 ♖d4 ♔c7 19 0-0 ♖b8

19...♗d7 allows White a choice of winning continuations, the most efficient being 20 ♗b7!.

20 ♖c1

20...♗d7

Unsurprisingly the desperate try 20...♖xb2 loses pretty quickly: 21 ♗a4+ ♔d8 (21...♔b8 fails to 22 ♗b3! with the terrible threat of ♖b4+) 22 ♖d2! ♗d7 (or 22...♖xd2 23 ♘b7 mate) 23 ♖xb2 ♗xa4 24 ♖b8+ ♔d7 25 ♖cc8 and White wins.

21 ♗b7+ ♔d8 22 ♖dc4

Black can do nothing about the threat of ♗xa7.

22...d5 23 ♖4c3 e5 24 ♗xa7 ♖xb7 25 ♘xb7+

White is a full exchange up and easily simplifies to a trivially won endgame.

25...♔e7 26 ♗c5+ ♔e6 27 ♗xf8 ♖xf8 28 ♘c5+ ♔f5 29 ♘xd7 ♘xd7 30 ♖c8 1-0

In the next game we will conclude our coverage of the Nimzowitsch Defence by examining Black's 2nd-move alternatives to 2...d6.

1 e4 ♘c6 2 ♘f3

2...♘f6

Black plays for a weird kind of Alekhine. Objectively it is dubious, but it has some interesting points and should be studied carefully.

Naturally there are a few other moves to consider as well:

a) 2...e6 3 d4 (creative players may wish to investigate the quirky 3 ♘c3 d5 4 ♗b5!?) 3...d5 and we have reached a French Defence with an early ...♘c6, which is a respectable sideline against most of White's main lines. Should the reader encounter this unusual move order, he can simply transpose back to his own favoured system against the French by means of 4 ♘c3, 4 ♘bd2, or 4 e5. Each of these has amassed its own considerable body of theory, so I hope the reader will forgive me for a rare moment of evasiveness on this occasion.

b) 2...g6 3 d4 ♗g7 4 d5 ♘e5 (4...♘b8 is likely to transpose to note 'c' to Black's third move in Game 56) 5 ♘xe5 ♗xe5 and White's chances are higher thanks to the misplaced bishop: for instance, 6 c4 d6 7 ♗d3 ♘f6 8 ♘c3 0-0 9 ♗h6 ♖e8 10 ♕d2 when White obviously had the more pleasant position in M.Matulovic-M.Stojanovic, Kladovo 1994.

c) 2...f5?! is too weakening, in view of 3 exf5 d5 4 ♗b5 ♗xf5 5 ♘e5.

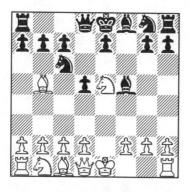

The outpost on e5 is more or less permanent. After completing his development White will usually aim to solidify his grip over the dark squares, although in some cases he may be able to open the position with moves like c2-c4. I do not see much value in covering every possible sub-variation, so will just mention a few relevant games that have taken place. After 5...♕d6 6 d4 ♘f6 7 0-0 ♘d7 (Black needs to challenge the powerful knight) 8 ♗xc6 bxc6 9 ♗f4 Black has problems, as illustrated in the following examples:

c1) 9...c5?! is too ambitious and in the following game Black soon fell into trouble: 10 ♘c3 c6 11 ♖e1 ♘xe5 12 ♗xe5 ♕g6 13 dxc5 ♗xc2 14 ♕d4 e6 15 ♖e3 ♕f7 16 ♖ae1 0-0-0 17 ♖c1 ♗f5 18 ♕a4 ♕b7 19 ♘e2 and Black was soon crushed in H.Jonkman-J.Lutton, Port Erin 2004.

c2) 9...♘xe5 10 ♗xe5 ♕g6 (10...♕d7 does not change much and White remains clearly better after 11 c4!? or 11 ♘d2) 11 c4 (11 ♘c3 is also good) 11...♗c2 (orr 11...♖b8 12 cxd5 e6, as in H.Schneider Zinner-C.Marzano, Vienna 2009, and then 13 ♕a4 exd5 14 ♘c3 with a clear plus for White) 12 ♕d2 e6 13 cxd5 ♗e4 14 f3 ♗xd5 15 ♗xc7 when White won a pawn and later the game in N.Sukhov-B.Hellbing, correspondence 2004.

Returning to 2...♘f6:

3 e5 ♘g4!?

This odd-looking move is what gives Black's pseudo-Alekhine Defence independent significance. Instead 3...♘d5 4 d4 d6 transposes back to the Alekhine – see Game 51 in the previous chapter.

4 d4 d6 5 h3 ♘h6 6 ♘c3!

White develops rapidly and flexibly. In certain lines he may wish to take on h6, but for the time being it is best to keep the opponent guessing.

6...a6

Controlling the b5-square is somewhat useful, but if this is the best Black can do...

The alternatives are uninspiring:

a) 6...dxe5?! 7 d5 and according to my database Black has scored a grand total of 0/13 from this position. Here are a few examples:

a1) 7...e4? 8 ♗xh6 ♘b4 9 ♘e5 when White is already winning, H.Krueger-F.Van Herreweghe, correspondence 2008.

a2) 7...♘d4? 8 ♘xe5 ♘hf5 9 ♗e3 c5 (or 9...♘xe3 10 fxe3) 10 dxc6 ♕d6 11 ♘c4! ♕e6 12 ♕d2 ♘xc6 13 ♘b5 ♕d7 14 0-0-0 ♘d6 15 ♘cxd6+ exd6 16 ♗f4 ♗e7 17 ♘xd6+ ♗xd6 18 ♗xd6 ♕f5 19 g4 ♕a5 20 ♕e3+ 1-0 A.Lautenbach-J.Yvinec, correspondence 2004.

a3) 7...♘b8 8 ♘xe5 ♘f5 9 ♕f3 (there are many routes to an advantage, but this is the most direct) 9...g6

10 ♘xf7! ♔xf7 11 g4 ♗g7 12 gxf5 ♗xf5 was A.Romero Holmes-M.Narciso Dublan, Terrassa 1994. Now the most flexible approach looks to be 13 ♗f4 when White will castle long and then decide whether to put his bishop on d3 or c4.

b) 6...g6 7 ♗f4 dxe5 (7...♗g7 was played in A.Areshchenko-S.Kristjansson, Reykjavik 2009, and now the simplest route to a comfortable edge would have been 8 ♕d2 ♘f5 9 0-0-0) 8 dxe5 ♘f5 9 ♘b5 a6? (9...♗e6 was better, although after 10 ♕xd8+ ♔xd8 11 0-0-0+ ♔c8 12 ♗e2 the initiative is clearly with White) 10 ♕xd8+ ♔xd8 11 0-0-0+ ♗d7 12 e6 fxe6 13 ♘xc7 ♖c8 14 ♘xe6+ ♔e8 15 ♗c4 1-0 D.Hughes-H.Renette, correspondence 1998.

7 ♗g5!

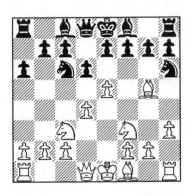

White continues to develop rapidly.

7...♗f5

Other moves also fail to solve Black's problems:

a) 7...g6 8 ♕d2 ♘f5 9 g4 ♘g7 10 exd6 ♕xd6 11 ♗f4 ♕d8 12 d5 ♘a7 13

0-0-0 and Black's position was already a disaster in R.Ferran Biosca-F.Zancas Vidal, St Cugat 1995.

b) 7...dxe5 8 d5 ♘b8 9 ♘xe5 g6 (9...♘f5 10 ♗d3 g6 11 ♗f4 ♗g7 12 0-0 0-0 13 ♖e1 was also tough for Black in G.Deschamp-G.Cesbron, correspondence 2002) 10 ♕d2 ♘f5 11 g4 ♘d6 12 ♗h6 ♘d7 13 ♘xd7 ♗xd7 14 0-0-0 and White was fully in control, T.Craig-I.Schrancz, correspondence 1999.

8 ♘h4! ♕d7

8...g6 9 e6! is unpleasant.

9 g4!

In a previous game White was successful with 9 exd6, but the text move is much more forceful.

9...♗g6 10 d5!

White cleverly exploits the fact that capturing the e5-pawn would cost Black a piece.

10...♘d8 11 f4

Already White has an overwhelming space advantage. Black's pieces are cramped and horribly uncoordinated.

11...e6 12 dxe6

Jones decides to force a weakening of the opponent's structure. Another promising continuation was 12 ♕e2 followed by long castling.

12...fxe6

12...♘xe6 13 ♗xh6 gxh6 14 f5 wins a piece, and 12...♕xe6? 13 ♘d5 is just awful for Black.

13 ♘xg6 hxg6 14 ♗d3 ♘df7

Giving up a pawn is hardly ideal, but Black was in trouble in all variations:

a) 14...♕f7 15 ♗e4! threatens ♕d3 and 15...d5 runs into 16 ♘xd5! exd5 17 ♗xd5 ♕d7 18 ♕d3 with a huge initiative for the sacrificed piece.

b) The best answer to 14...♔f7 looks to be 15 exd6, ensuring that the position will not become too closed after ...d5. Now both 15...♗xd6 and 15...cxd6 should be met by 16 ♕f3 when Black's position is a sorry sight.

15 ♗xg6 ♕c6 16 ♖f1 d5 17 f5

17...♗b4

17...♗a3!? is a cheeky attempt to confuse the issue. The strongest answer looks to be 18 ♘xd5 exd5 19 bxa3 ♕c3+ 20 ♔f2 ♕xh3 21 ♗xf7+! ♘xf7

(21...♔xf7 22 ♕xd5+) 22 ♖h1 when White is winning.

18 ♕d4 ♗xc3+ 19 bxc3 ♔d7?

This allows a quick tactical refutation, but Black's position was rotten anyway.

20 fxe6+ ♕xe6 21 ♖xf7+! ♘xf7 22 ♗f5

Winning the queen.

22...♘xg5 23 0-0-0 ♔e7 24 ♕c5+ ♔f7 25 ♗xe6+ ♘xe6 26 ♖f1+ 1-0

Part 2 – Miscellaneous Defences

We will begin this section with Owen's Defence, which does not have the best of reputations. Nevertheless, White should prepare carefully in order to maximize his chances of achieving an advantage should he encounter this system over the board.

Game 59
I.Smikovski-V.Osipov
Omsk 2001

1 e4 e6

Black feints at a French. The move order should not matter much, as after 1...b6 2 d4 ♗b7 3 ♘c3 Black usually plays ...e6 within the next move or two.

2 d4 b6 3 ♘c3

White often prefers 3 ♘f3 ♗b7 4 ♗d3, delaying the development of the queen's knight in order to meet ...c5 with c3. This should also suffice for an advantage, but I find the set-up with the knight on c3 to be objectively just as strong and arguably more danger-

ous. One advantage is that the move ...c5 can often be met by d5, as we will see in the present game.

3...♗b7 4 ♗d3 ♘f6 5 ♘ge2!

I find this move the most attractive. On a practical note, it is not really covered in Christian Bauer's *Play 1...b6*, which is likely to be a primary reference for many devotees of this opening.

A few brief comments about White's alternatives:

a) 5 ♘f3 ♗b4 is one of the main lines of Owen's Defence. This variation has built up a surprisingly substantial body of theory and I would rate Black's chances of equalizing as higher than after the continuation seen in the present game.

b) I briefly looked at 5 ♕e2 with the idea of playing flexibly and leaving the way clear for the f-pawn to advance, but in that case Black can consider 5...♘c6!? 6 ♘f3 ♘b4, which looks mildly annoying.

5...c5

Black's alternatives on both this and

the previous move will be dealt with in the next game.

6 d5!?

This pawn sacrifice is the most aggressive and ambitious approach, although it is worth mentioning two other ideas:

a) Fans of the Open Sicilian can consider 6 0-0 cxd4 7 ♘xd4, with a normal-looking position except that Black has committed his pawn to b6 instead of employing the more active set-up with ...a6 and ...b5.

b) Another promising though barely tested continuation is 6 e5!? ♘d5 7 ♘xd5 ♗xd5 8 ♘f4 ♗b7, as in A.Anderson-P.Blatny, Internet (blitz) 2004, and now 9 d5! exd5 10 0-0 gives White a strong initiative for the pawn.

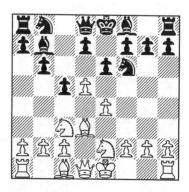

6...exd5

Accepting the challenge.

6...a6 looks rather slow: 7 0-0 (there is also 7 a4!? exd5 8 exd5 ♘xd5 9 ♘xd5 ♗xd5 10 ♘f4 ♗e6 11 ♗e4 ♖a7 12 0-0 ♗e7 13 ♖a3! when White had utilized the move a2-a4 to good effect and went on to win in nice style,

J.Speelman-M.Basman, Brighton 1984) 7...♕c7 (7...b5 should also be met by 8 ♘g3) was W.Kelleher-P.Oliveira, Philadelphia 1993, and here the most logical continuation looks to be 8 ♘g3 with some initiative for White.

7 exd5 ♘xd5 8 ♘xd5 ♗xd5 9 0-0!

9 ♘f4 is less accurate due to 9...♕e7+! (after 9...♗b7?! 10 0-0 White has tremendous compensation) 10 ♗e3 ♗b7 11 0-0 ♘c6 12 ♘d5 ♕e5 13 c4 0-0-0 when the position was rather unclear in S.Nordfjoerd-L.Perea Montero, correspondence 2000.

9...♘c6

9...♗e6 10 ♘f4 a6?! (10...♘c6 transposes to the main game) was played in H.Baldursson-I.Johannesson, Reykjavik 2004.

Here I would suggest 11 ♕f3 (11 ♗e4 ♖a7 12 ♕d3 also looks promising) 11...♖a7 12 ♕g3! ♘c6 (12...g6 13 ♘d5!) 13 ♖e1 when White has excellent compensation for the pawn and Black will have a hard time castling.

10 ♘f4 ♗e6 11 ♖e1

Natural and good, but 11 ♘xe6!?

deserves serious attention too: 11...dxe6 (11...fxe6?? loses to 12 ♕h5+) 12 ♗f4. Suddenly Black has real trouble on the light squares, for instance:

a) 12...♖c8 13 ♗a6 ♕xd1 14 ♖axd1 ♖d8 15 ♗b5 (or 15 ♖xd8+ ♔xd8 16 ♖d1+ ♔e7 17 ♗b7) 15...♖c8 16 ♖fe1 and Black will have a hard time completing his development.

b) 12...♗e7 13 ♗b5 ♖c8 14 ♗a6 ♕xd1 15 ♖axd1 ♖d8 16 ♖xd8+ ♘xd8 17 ♗b5+ ♔f8 18 ♖d1 when Black is in trouble.

c) 12...a6!? 13 ♕f3 ♕c8 (Black does not achieve much with 13...♘d4 14 ♕g3) 14 ♗e4 ♘d4 15 ♕e3 ♖a7 16 c3 ♘c6 17 ♕f3 and White's activity is worth more than a pawn.

11...g6

Black decides that a fianchetto development will help to fortify his kingside, but it costs an additional valuable tempo. The alternatives were:

a) 11...♗d6 12 ♘h5! is awkward for Black.

b) 11...♗e7 is possible, although White has a pleasant choice between

12 ♕h5 and 12 ♘xe6 dxe6 13 ♕g4 (13 ♗f4!?) when Black has to resort to 13...♔f8, as 13...0-0?? 14 ♕e4 wins a piece and 13...g6? 14 ♗b5 also wins at least an exchange.

12 ♕f3

White has a nice idea in mind, but it is not enough to prove a real advantage. Therefore I would recommend one of the following alternatives:

a) 12 ♗a6!? is one interesting idea, when White maintains a promising initiative.

b) A more forcing option is 12 ♘xe6!?, with two choices for Black:

b1) After 12...dxe6?! 13 ♕f3 ♖c8 (or 13...♘d4 14 ♗b5+!) 14 ♗b5 ♕d7 15 ♖d1 ♕b7 16 ♕c3 ♖g8 17 ♕d3 Black has serious problems.

b2) 12...fxe6 13 ♕g4! with a final division:

b21) 13...♕e7 14 ♗b5 ♖c8 15 ♗a6 ♖b8 16 ♗f4 e5 17 ♖ad1 ♗g7 18 c3 and White has more than enough for a pawn.

b22) 13...♗g7 14 ♖xe6+! dxe6 15 ♕xe6+ ♔f8 (after 15...♘e7? 16 ♗g5!

Black is busted) 16 ♕xc6 ♖c8 17 ♕f3+ ♕f6 18 ♕g3 when White has more than enough compensation for his modest material investment.

12...♗g7 13 ♘xe6! fxe6 14 ♖xe6+ dxe6 15 ♗b5

White's temporary rook sacrifice is dangerous, but Black should be able to survive if he defends accurately.

15...♖c8

The best defence looks to be 15...♖f8! 16 ♗xc6+ (not 16 ♕xc6+? ♔f7) 16...♔e7 17 ♗g5+ ♗f6 when I doubt that White has anything more than a draw, such as after 18 ♗h6 ♗g7 19 ♗g5+ ♗f6.

The remainder of the game is not especially important for our study of the opening, as promising alternatives and improvements have already been noted at moves 11 and 12.

16 ♗xc6+ ♖xc6 17 ♕xc6+ ♔f7

After 17...♕d7 18 ♕a8+ ♕d8 19 ♕xd8+ ♔xd8 20 c3 White has a tiny endgame advantage, although Black should hold.

18 ♕b7+ ♕e7 19 ♕f3+ ♕f6 20 ♕b7+

♕e7 21 ♕f3+ ♕f6 22 ♕a3 ♖d8

22...♖f8 23 ♕xa7+ ♔g8 24 ♗e3 ♕xb2 is similar.

23 ♕xa7+ ♔g8 24 ♗e3 ♕xb2 25 ♖f1 ♕xc2?

Better was 25...♕b5! 26 ♕c7 (26 a4 ♕c6) 26...♖d7 27 ♕c8+ ♔f7 28 h3 ♖d6 when the queen comes back to c6 or d7, and Black should be fine.

26 ♕xb6 ♗f6 27 ♕xe6+ ♔g7 28 g4!

Highlighting the weakness of Black's king. This factor, combined with White's extra pawn, is enough to win.

28...♖d1 29 ♖xd1 ♕xd1+ 30 ♔g2 ♗d4 31 ♕d7+ ♔g8 32 h4?

White misses an opportunity to end the game immediately with 32 ♗h6 ♕e2 33 ♕d5+.

32...h5 33 gxh5 gxh5 34 ♕d5+ ♔g7 35 ♕b7+ ♔g8 36 ♕b3+ ♕xb3 37 axb3

White has not converted his advantage in the most efficient way possible, but the bishop ending is still a fairly easy win.

37...♗f6 38 ♗g5 ♗d4 39 f4 ♔f7 40 f5 ♗c3 41 ♔f3 ♗e1 42 ♔e4 ♗f2 43 ♗d8 ♗g3 44 ♔d5 ♗f2 45 ♔d6 ♗g1 46 ♔e5

♝h2+ 47 ♔d5 ♝g1 48 ♔e4 ♝h2 49 ♔f3
♝e5 50 ♝g5 ♝c3 51 ♝e3 ♝e1 52 ♝xc5
♝xh4 53 b4 ♝d8 54 b5 ♔f6 55 ♔e4 h4
56 ♔f4 ♝c7+ 57 ♔g4 ♔e5 58 b6 1-0

Game 60
T.Oral-K.Gawehns
Hamburg 1999

1 e4 b6 2 d4 ♝b7 3 ♝d3

White can also play 3 ♘c3 followed by ♝d3; the move order is unlikely to make much difference.

3...e6

The actual sequence played in the game was 3...♘f6 4 ♘c3 e6 5 ♘ge2, but I have adjusted it in order to consider a few set-ups where Black delays or eschews altogether the development of the knight to f6.

4 ♘c3

4...♘f6

Here is a round-up of Black's 4th-move alternatives:

a) 4...c5 5 d5 leaves the bishop on b7 misplaced.

b) 4...f5?! is risky: 5 exf5 (a safe alternative is 5 ♕h5+ g6 6 ♕e2) 5...♝xg2 6 ♕h5+ g6 7 fxg6 ♝g7 8 gxh7+ ♔f8. This position was reached in W.Heimbrodt-S.Mueller, correspondence 1978, and several subsequent games. So far nobody seems to have played the strongest move: 9 ♘f3! ♘f6 (9...♝xh1 10 ♘e5 ♝xe5 11 ♕xe5 is winning for White) 10 ♕h4 ♝xh1 11 ♘e5 and Black is in trouble despite his extra rook.

c) 4...g6 5 f4 ♝g7 6 ♘f3 ♘e7 7 0-0 d6 is a dubious incarnation of a Hippo and 8 f5! gives White a promising attacking position.

d) The most important alternative is 4...♝b4. Again with 5 ♘ge2 we see the knight avoiding the f3-square.

Now Black has a couple of ways to strike at the enemy centre:

d1) 5...d5 6 exd5!? (6 e5 also gives White chances for an edge, but opening the centre seems more ambitious) 6...♕xd5 was K.Olsarova-V.Nedela, Ostrava 2010, and now after 7 ♘f4! followed by castling White has a nice lead in development.

d2) 5...c5 6 0-0 (this seems simplest, although White has a few other tempting options: 6 d5!? is a promising sacrifice which can be compared with the previous game; another possibility is 6 dxc5!? when after either recapture White will castle and look to exploit his lead in development, most probably by attacking on the kingside) 6...cxd4 7 ♘xd4 and White has a promising version of the Open Sicilian. Black's dark-squared bishop looks strange on b4 and if it exchanges on c3 then White's bishop could become powerful on a3.

Returning to 4...♘f6:

5 ♘ge2! d5

Black opts for a kind of French set-up, but this plan does not inspire confidence.

Instead 5...c5 was seen in the previous game, while after 5...♗b4 6 0-0 White enjoys easy and effective development.

6 e5

6...♘fd7

Two other moves have been tried:

a) 6...♘e4 7 ♗xe4 (7 ♘xe4!? may be even better, since 7...dxe4 8 ♗b5+ ♘d7 9 c3 leaves White obviously better) 7...dxe4 was seen in G.Rodriguez Rebull-A.Leiva Velasco, Barcelona 2004, and now after 8 ♗e3 White is ahead in development and the e4-pawn is weak.

b) 6...♘g8!? is not as ridiculous as it looks. Now in C.Plock-M.Rist, Seefeld 1996, White should have considered the unusual idea 7 ♘a4!?. White's main problem is that after ...c5 the bishop on d3 will be short of squares thanks to the knight on e2. Therefore he moves the other knight out of the way to prepare c3, which will bring some harmony to his position (7 ♘b1!? is another way of implementing the same idea and even 7 ♗b5+!? could be considered). After 7...♗a6 (or 7...c5 8 c3 when White is better and the knight on a4 will gradually make its way back into the game) 8 ♗xa6 ♘xa6 9 0-0 ♕d7 10 b3 White has a lead in development and can consider a timely opening of the queenside with c4.

7 ♘f4!

By threatening ♘xe6, White immediately puts his opponent on the defensive. He also frees a retreat square for his bishop, anticipating the threat of ...c5-c4.

7...g6

Black has not fared any better with the alternatives:

a) 7...♕h4?! 8 0-0 (8 ♘b5! looks even better) 8...♘c6 9 g3 ♕e7 10 ♘cxd5!? exd5 11 ♘xd5 ♕d8 12 e6 (12 ♗e4!?) 12...♘de5? (Black could have kept himself in the game with 12...♘xd4 13 exd7+ ♕xd7 14 c4 0-0-0) 13 ♗e4 (even stronger would have been 13 dxe5!) 13...♘g6? 14 exf7+ ♔xf7 15 ♕f3+ ♔e8 16 ♖e1 ♘ce7 17 ♘xe7 1-0 S.Satyapragyan-Z.Rahman, Kolkata 2000.

b) 7...♗e7?! 8 ♕g4 g6 9 ♘xe6! (White could have settled for a slight edge with 9 ♘ce2 c5 10 c3, but the sacrifice is much stronger) 9...fxe6 10 ♗xg6+ hxg6 11 ♕xg6+ ♔f8 12 ♗h6+ ♖xh6 13 ♕xh6+ ♔f7 (if 13...♔g8 14 ♕xe6+) 14 ♕h7+ ♔f8 (no better is 14...♔e8 15 ♕g6+ ♔f8 16 0-0-0).

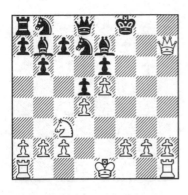

This position was reached in J.Solano Lasierra-A.Antonano Fernandez, Zaragoza 2001. So far White has played perfectly and had he continued 15 ♘e2! he would have obtained excellent chances to win the game, but instead he settled for a draw with 15 ♕h6+ ♔f7 16 ♕h7+.

8 ♕g4!

Threatening to take on e6 followed by g6, thereby forcing Black to make a difficult decision.

8...♕e7

Black fared no better in the following game: 8...♕c8 9 0-0 ♗a6 10 ♗xa6 (10 ♘xe6! and 10 ♘cxd5! were even stronger, but the text is good enough) 10...♘xa6 11 ♘xe6! ♘xe5 12 ♕e2 ♕xe6 13 ♕xa6 ♘g4 14 ♕b7 ♖d8 15 ♗g5 and Black's opening proved to be a disaster in D.Holemar-M.Zavadil, Brno 2008.

9 ♘b5!

Black's position is already a mess.

9...♘a6 10 b3

10 c3 is clearly better for White, but the text move creates a serious threat in ♗a3.

10...0-0-0

This loses a pawn, but it is hard to suggest anything else.

11 ♘xa7+ ♚b8 12 ♘b5 ♘b4 13 0-0 c5 14 c3 ♘c6

14...♘xd3 15 ♘xd3 leaves Black facing the threat of ♗g5.

15 ♕g3!

White is not only a pawn up, but he also enjoys a clear positional advantage. With his last move he sets up a trick on the h2-b8 diagonal.

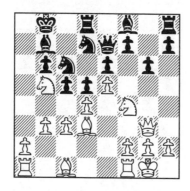

15...♕e8

15...♚a8 was worth considering, although White remains in complete control after 16 ♗e3 or 16 ♘e2.

16 ♘xd5! exd5 17 e6+ ♘de5 18 exf7 ♕xf7 19 dxe5

White emerges with a second extra pawn and is winning easily.

19...♕e6 20 f4 ♘e7 21 ♕g5 h6 22 ♕f6 ♕xf6 23 exf6 ♘f5 24 g4 ♘h4

Or 24...♘d6 25 ♘xd6 ♖xd6 26 g5 and White is winning comfortably.

25 ♚f2 h5 26 g5 ♗c8 27 f5!?

27 ♗d2 was fine, but Oral prefers to give back one pawn in order to activate

his bishop.

27...♗xf5 28 ♗xf5 ♘xf5 29 ♗f4+ ♚b7 30 a4 c4 31 b4 d4

32 ♘xd4?!

32 ♖ad1! would have won more easily, as Black is almost paralysed.

32...♘xd4 33 cxd4 ♗xb4?

33...♖xd4 would have offered much more resistance, although after 34 ♗e3 ♖h4 35 ♚g3 ♖g4+ 36 ♚f3 ♗xb4 37 ♖ab1 ♗a5 38 ♗f4 White should still win.

34 ♗e5 ♚c6 35 ♚e3 ♖hf8 36 ♖ab1 ♗d6 37 ♚e4 ♖f7 38 ♖fc1 1-0

In the last couple of games we will address the more unorthodox options at Black's disposal, beginning with the St George Defence.

Game 61
E.Gaisin-V.Serov
Correspondence 2002

1 e4 a6 2 d4 b5

Compared with Owen's Defence,

Black takes control of some extra space on the queenside at the cost of an additional tempo. White has a number of routes to an advantage, but I would generally recommend a policy of classical development combined with a timely a2-a4 to soften up Black's queenside.

3 ♗d3

White can also use the move order 3 ♘f3 ♗b7 4 ♗d3; it is unlikely to make a difference.

3...♗b7 4 ♘f3

Compared with Owen's Defence, it makes no sense to put the knight on c3, so White should settle for classical development.

4...e6

The usual continuation, although a few others deserve a mention:

a) With 4...g6? Black aims for a transposition to a Modern, having avoided the Austrian Attack. However, the problem is that his b5-pawn is an easy target, especially as the white knight has not yet gone to c3: 5 0-0 ♗g7 6 a4 (White has also done well

with 6 c3 intending a4 next) 6...b4 7 c3 bxc3 8 ♘xc3 d6 9 ♕b3 and White has a huge lead in development, N.Pogonina-V.Kirillova, Voronezh 2004.

b) 4...♘f6 is slightly risky and gives White a couple of tempting options:

b1) 5 ♘bd2 e6 6 0-0 c5 7 dxc5 ♗xc5 8 e5 ♘d5 9 ♘e4 ♗e7 10 a4 b4 and in this position White can obtain a promising initiative with Khalifman's recommendation of 11 c4! bxc3 12 bxc3.

b2) 5 e5!? ♘d5 6 ♘g5! forces Black to make a tough decision:

b21) 6...e6 7 ♕f3 f5 (7...♕e7 8 c3 leaves Black awkwardly placed) 8 exf6 ♕xf6 9 ♗xh7 ♕xf3 10 ♗g6+ ♔d8 11 ♘xf3 and White was a clear pawn up in E.Dearing-B.Tiller, British League 2010.

b22) 6...♘b4!? was played in V.Schulz-B.Schmitt, Baden 1997. Here White should settle for 7 ♗e4 ♗xe4 8 ♘xe4 with a pleasant positional edge, instead of the game continuation of 7 ♗xh7 ♖xh7 8 ♘xh7 which resulted in a quick win for White, but might have backfired had Black found 8...♗e4!.

5 a4!?

The main line is 5 0-0 c5 6 c3 ♘f6 7 ♕e2 when White's chances are somewhat higher. Still, I rather like the idea of targeting the b5-pawn. It has not been seen in many games, which makes it all the more dangerous as a practical weapon.

5...c5

This counterattacking move is the most principled reaction. For the time being the b5-pawn is indirectly defended, as taking it would cost White the e4-pawn. On the other hand, the opening of the queenside and centre should benefit White, who is the better developed.

The alternatives are:

a) 5...♘f6 was played in S.Movsesian-V.Popov, Panormo (blitz) 2002. White replied with 6 ♕e2 which was enough for a slight edge, but both 6 e5 and 6 axb5 look even more challenging.

b) 5...b4 6 0-0 (6 c4!? also looks promising) 6...c5 7 ♘bd2 cxd4 8 ♘xd4 ♘f6 9 e5 ♘d5 10 ♘c4 and White had

an improved version of an Open Sicilian in J.Polgar-G.Kamsky, Monte Carlo (rapid) 1994.

6 axb5 axb5 7 ♖xa8 ♗xa8 8 dxc5 ♗xc5 9 0-0

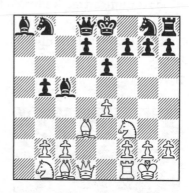

9...b4

A couple of other moves have been tried:

a) 9...♘e7 was played by a certain up-and-coming junior in V.McCambridge-N.Short, Hamburg 1981. White chose 10 ♕e2 and eventually won, but there were two even more tempting continuations available in 10 ♘bd2 and 10 ♘g5!?.

b) 9...♕b6 occurred in O.Mihok-J.Poecksteiner, Austrian League 2007, and here I would suggest 10 ♕e2 ♘f6 (or 10...b4 11 ♘bd2) 11 ♘c3 ♗c6 12 e5 ♘d5 13 ♘xd5 ♗xd5 14 ♗xb5 with an extra pawn for White. Black can damage White's structure by taking on f3, but this will not provide enough compensation.

10 ♘bd2 ♘c6?!

It looks somewhat safer to play 10...♘f6 as in J.Rios-D.Orrego, Antioquia 1995. Here the natural continuation looks to be 11 e5 (I would guess that this pawn advance is the reason Serov rejected 10...♘f6 in the main game) 11...♘d5 12 ♘e4 ♗e7 when 13 ♘fd2!? looks quite attractive for White. The knight prepares to come to c4 while making room for the queen to go to g4 or h5.

11 e5!

Even though this move does not attack a knight, it is even stronger here than after 10...♘f6.

11...d5?!

The further opening of the position carries great risk for Black. The best chance may have been 11...♕c7 when the pressure on e5 prevents the white knight from coming to e4. Play might continue 12 ♘c4 (or 12 ♕e2 ♘ge7 13 ♘b3 ♗b6 14 ♗e3 with an edge to White) 12...♘a5 (12...♘ge7?! 13 ♗e3!) 13 ♘xa5 ♕xa5 14 ♘g5!? (or 14 ♘d2) with some initiative for White.

12 exd6 ♗xd6 13 ♗b5!

This pin is highly unpleasant for Black and vindicates White's earlier decision to open the queenside.

13...♗c7 14 ♘e4 ♕xd1 15 ♖xd1

15...♘f6??

Simply blundering a piece.

15...♘ge7 was mandatory. Following 16 ♘d6+ ♗xd6 17 ♖xd6 0-0 White's bishop pair and active pieces give him a clear advantage in the ending, but the win is still a long way off.

16 ♘xf6+ gxf6 17 ♘d4 ♔d7 18 ♘xc6+ 1-0

In the next and final game of the chapter, we will take a look at a few of Black's unusual set-ups involving an early advance of his g-pawn.

> ## Game 62
> ## **J.Gdanski-L.Olsson**
> ## Swedish League 2006

1 e4 g6

1...g5 is the so-called 'Borg' Defence ('Grob' in reverse). I hardly need state that the early lunge with the g-pawn leaves Black with long-term kingside weaknesses, which White should look to exploit. With 2 d4 ♗g7!? (2...h6 3 ♘c3 ♗g7 4 ♗c4 transposes) 3 ♘c3 (after 3 ♗xg5 c5 Black intends ...♕b6 with counterattacking chances; White should be better here too, but it seems easier to avoid the whole issue) 3...h6 (3...c5!? 4 dxc5 ♕a5 was seen in M.Tscharotschkin-H.Mueck, Schwaebisch Gmuend 2008, and here the easiest route to a big advantage would have been 5 ♘ge2 ♕xc5 6 ♗e3 ♕a5 7 ♕d5! ♕xd5 8 exd5 h6 9 h4 g4 10 0-0-0 when White enjoys a huge lead in development) 4 ♗c4 White develops normally and should have no trouble developing a strong attack.

Here are a few practical examples:

a) 4...c5 5 ♘ge2 (5 ♗e3 is also good) 5...cxd4 6 ♘xd4 ♘c6 7 ♗e3 and Black had only succeeded in transposing to a highly dubious version of a Dragon in C.Carothers-A.Pfeiffer, correspondence 2001.

b) After 4...d6 5 ♘ge2 White will castle and play f4, with a ready-made kingside attack. Here is one example:

5...♘f6 6 0-0 (6 h4!?) 6...c6 7 f4 (I would have preferred 7 ♗b3 first, intending to meet ...d5 with e5) 7...g4? 8 e5 ♘h5 9 ♗e3 d5 10 ♗d3 f5 11 exf6 ♘xf6 12 ♗g6+ ♔d7 13 f5 ♕g8 14 ♗f4 ♘a6 15 ♘c1 ♘c7 16 ♘d3 ♔d8 17 ♘e5 ♗d7 18 ♘f7+ and White won easily in R.Alvarez-F.Theunisse, correspondence 1992.

2 d4 ♘f6!?

This is known as the North Sea Defence. It is rather obscure, but garnered some attention when Magnus Carlsen used it against Michael Adams at the 2010 Olympiad. He lost the game and has not tried it since.

3 ♘c3

This would be my recommendation in the unlikely event that you encounter the North Sea over the board. I find it the most pragmatic choice; Black must either transpose to a Pirc or accept an inferior position.

If White is determined to try and refute his opponent's opening, then 3 e5 is the move. After 3...♘h5 there are two options:

a) 4 ♘c3 d5 transposes to the main game and was actually the move order that occurred. However, Black has an independent option available in 4...d6!?, which is the is the reason why I consider it more practical to start with 3 ♘c3.

b) The really critical line is 4 ♗e2 when 4...d6! invites White to take on h5 in the hope of organizing a counterattack in the centre. I suspect that White can obtain some advantage here, but in practical terms Black is getting what he wanted from the opening: an unclear, murky position which he is likely to understand better than his opponent.

3...d5

This is the consistent move which keeps us in North Sea territory.

3...♗g7?! 4 e5 forces the knight to return to its original square, while 3...d6 transposes to the Pirc and is objectively Black's best option.

4 e5 ♘h5

The knight looks misplaced on h5 – and it is! – but White must exploit it in the correct way.

5 ♗e3!

White should resist the temptation to chase the knight. Compared with the Gurgenidze set-up examined in Chapter Two, the knight has spent two moves getting to h5, instead of one move to get to the superior h6-square. It will almost always retreat to g7 at some point, thereby costing another important tempo. It follows that if White simply 'pretends' he is facing a Gurgenidze system and plays in a similar way to how he does there, he will achieve a nice advantage almost without trying.

5 g4? is the last thing White wants to do and after 5...♘g7 Black is ready to hit back on the kingside with ...h5. Suddenly the knight on g7 is very well placed indeed!

5 ♗e2 is possible, but it is not clear how serious a threat ♗xh5 really is. After 5...♘c6 the position is starting to become rather murky.

5...♘g7

Other moves have been tried, but Black has to bring the knight back into the game at some point.

6 f4

White gains space while creating a retreat square for the bishop.

6...h5

After 6...♘f5 7 ♗f2 h5 8 ♘f3 Black has only succeeded in committing his knight prematurely.

7 ♕d2 ♗f5

Another game continued 7...c6 8 ♘f3 ♘d7 and here in T.Todorov-

M.Bonnafous, Toulon 1999, I like the look of 9 g3!?, setting the wheels in motion for h3 and a future kingside advance.

8 ♘f3 e6 9 g3!

White wastes no time in preparing a thematic kingside expansion.

9...c6

9...♗b4 is not a real solution. White should play 10 ♖g1! intending h3 and g4. If Black exchanges on c3 at any point, his dark squares will be chronically weak. In any case his light-squared bishop will not find peace on e4 with the move ♘f3-g5 available.

10 h3

It was well worth considering 10 a3!?, preventing ...♗b4 ideas altogether.

10...♕a5 11 ♖g1 b5?

Too slow.

11...♗b4 was the best chance, although 12 a3 still works out in White's favour, as sooner or later g4 will hurt.

12 g4 hxg4 13 hxg4 b4 14 ♘d1 ♗e4 15 ♘g5 ♘d7 16 ♘f2 f5

Otherwise Black simply loses a pawn.

17 exf6 ♘xf6 18 ♘fxe4 ♘xe4 19 ♘xe4 dxe4 20 ♗c4

The immediate 20 ♕g2 was also very strong.

20...0-0-0 21 ♕g2 b3+ 22 c3 ♗b4!?

In a desperate situation, Black comes up with a novel attempt to confuse his opponent.

23 ♕d2

23 ♔e2! was completely crushing and after 23...♗xc3 24 axb3 ♕b4 25 ♖a4 Black can resign.

23...♗e7 24 ♗xb3

It would have been vastly preferable if White could have captured here with his a-pawn instead of the bishop (see the last note). He is still completely winning though.

24...♖h3

24...♗h4+ 25 ♔d1 is nothing.

25 0-0-0 g5 26 ♔b1!

26 fxg5?? ♖xe3 would have been embarrassing.

26...♖f8 27 ♖h1 ♖g3 28 ♖h7 gxf4 29 ♗xf4 ♖xg4 30 ♗e5 ♗f6 31 ♕e2 ♖g5 32 ♖f1

Forcing the following desperate exchange sacrifice.

32...♖xe5 33 dxe5 ♛xe5 34 ♖e1 ♚c7 35 ♛xe4

White is the exchange up with a better pawn structure and the technical phase of the game is easy.

35...♛xe4+ 36 ♖xe4 ♚d6 37 ♖f4 ♚e5 38 ♖a4 ♖f7 39 ♖a6 ♖c7 40 ♚c2 ♚d6 41 ♚d3 ♗g5 42 ♗a4 ♗f6 43 b4 ♚d5 44 c4+ ♚d6 45 ♚e4 ♗c3 46 c5+ ♚d7 47 ♚d3 ♗f6 48 ♚c4 ♗e5 49 ♖h3 ♞f5 50 ♖d3+ 1-0

That brings us to the end of the game, the chapter, and the book! I hope you have enjoyed reading and I wish you all the best using the ideas presented in your own games.

Index of Variations

Note: Figures refer to page numbers of relevant games.

Scandinavian Defence

Modern Defence

3 ♘c3 d6
4 f4 c6
5 ♘f3

Pirc Defence

1 e4 d6 2 d4 ♘f6 3 ♘c3 g6 4 f4 ♗g7 5 ♘f3 0-0
6 ♗e3 b6
7 ♕d2 ♗b7
8 e5 ♘g4 9 0-0-0

Philidor and Czech Pirc

1 e4 d6 2 d4 ♘f6
3 ♘c3 e5
4 dxe5 dxe5 5 ♕xd8+ ♔xd8 6 ♗g5 ♗e6

Alekhine's Defence

Other Defences

Index of Complete Games